The Syntactic Process

Language, Speech, and Communication

Statistical Language Learning, Eugene Charniak, 1994

The Development of Speech Perception, edited by Judith Goodman and Howard C. Nusbaum, 1994

Construal, Lyn Frazier and Charles Clifton, Jr., 1995

The Generative Lexicon, James Pustejovsky, 1996

The Origins of Grammar: Evidence from Early Language Acquisition, Kathy Hirsh-Pasek and Roberta Michnick Golinkoff, 1996

Language and Space, edited by Paul Bloom, Mary A. Peterson, Lynn Nadel, and Merrill F. Garrett, 1996

Corpus Processing for Lexical Acquisition, edited by Branimir Boguraev and James Pustejovsky, 1996

Methods for Assessing Children's Syntax, edited by Dana McDaniel, Cecile McKee, and Helen Smith Cairns, 1996

The Balancing Act: Combining Symbolic and Statistical Approaches to Language, edited by Judith Klavans and Philip Resnik, 1996

The Discovery of Spoken Language, Peter W. Jusczyk, 1996

Lexical Competence, Diego Marconi, 1997

Finite-State Language Processing, edited by Emmanual Roche and Yves Schabes, 1997

Children with Specific Language Impairment, Laurence B. Leonard, 1997

Type-Logical Semantics, Bob Carpenter, 1997

Statistical Methods for Speech Recognition, Frederick Jelinek, 1997

WordNet: An Electronic Lexical Database, edited by Christiane Fellbaum, 1998

WordNet 1.6 CD-ROM, edited by Christiane Fellbaum, 1998

Investigations in Universal Grammar: A Guide to Experiments on the Acquisition of Syntax and Semantics, Stephen Crain and Rosalind Thornton, 1998

A Prosodic Model of Sign Language Phonology, Diane Brentari, 1998

Language Form and Language Function, Frederick J. Newmeyer, 1998

Semantics and Syntax in Lexical Functional Grammar: The Resource Logic Approach, edited by Mary Dalrymple, 1998

Understanding Language Understanding: Computational Models of Reading, edited by Ashwin Ram and Kenneth Moorman, 1999

The Syntactic Process, Mark Steedman, 2000

The Syntactic Process   Mark Steedman

A Bradford Book
The MIT Press
Cambridge, Massachusetts
London, England

First MIT Press paperback edition, 2001
©2000 Massachusetts Institute of Technology

This book was set in Times Roman by the author using LATEX 2ε, and was printed and bound in the United States of America.

Library of Congress Cataloging-in-Publication Data

Steedman, Mark.
  The Syntactic Process/Mark Steedman
    p. cm.—(Language, speech, and communication)
  "A Bradford Book."
  Includes bibliographical references (p.) and index.
  ISBN 0-262-19420-1 (hb), 0-262-69268-6 (pb)
  Grammar, Comparative and general—Syntax. I. Title. II. Series.
P291.S67 2000
415–dc21   99-27489
                                                          CIP

Contents

Preface   xi

Chapter 1

Introduction   1

PART I

Grammar and Information Structure

Chapter 2

Rules, Constituents, and Fragments   11

2.1 Constituents   12

2.2 Fragments   14

2.3 Issues of Power and Explanation   22

2.4 Grammar as an Applicative System   27

Chapter 3

Intuitive Basis of Combinatory Categorial Grammars   31

3.1 Pure Categorial Grammar   31

3.2 Interpretation and Predicate-Argument Structure   35

3.3 Coordination   39

3.4 The Bluebird   40

3.5 The Thrush   43

3.6 The Starling   49

Chapter 4
Explaining Constraints on Natural
Grammar   53

4.1 Intrinsic Constraints Limiting the
Set of Possible Rules   53

4.2 Linguistic Constraints on
Unbounded Dependencies   59

4.3 Linguistic Constraints on Bounded
Dependencies   64

4.4 Quantification in CCG   70

4.5 Summary: Surface Structure and
Interpretation   85

Chapter 5
Structure and Intonation   89

5.1 Surface Structure and Intonation
Structure   92

5.2 Two Intonation Contours and Their
Functions   95

5.3 Theme and Rheme   99

5.4 Focus and Background   106

5.5 Grammar and Information
Structure   109

5.6 Intonation and the Simplex
Clause   119

5.7 Intonation in Complex
Constructions   122

5.8 Conclusion   124

PART II
Coordination and Word Order

Chapter 6
Cross-Serial Dependencies in
Dutch   133

6.1 Word Order in Dutch   136

6.2 Verb Raising as Composition   138

6.3 Equi Verbs   144

6.4 Argument Cluster
Composition   146

6.5 Relative Clauses   155

6.6 Subject and Object Extraction from
Embedded Clauses   158

6.7 Dutch Main-clause Order   159

6.8 Interaction of Word order and
Quantifier Scope   164

6.9 On the Rarity of Crossing
Dependencies   166

Appendix: Summary of the Dutch
Fragment   167

Chapter 7
Gapping and the Order of
Constituents   171

7.1 Gapping and SOV Word
Order   172

7.2 Gapping and VSO Word
Order   176

7.3 Gapping and SVO Word
Order   179

7.4 Other Elliptical Phenomena   195

7.5 A Cautious Conclusion   197

PART III
Computation and Performance

Chapter 8
Combinators and Grammars   201

8.1 Why Categories and
Combinators?   201

8.2 Why Bluebirds, Thrushes, and
Starlings?   203

8.3 Expressive Power   207

8.4 Formalizing Directionality in
Categorial Grammars   213

Appendix: Directionality as a
Feature   216

Chapter 9

Processing in Context   225

9.1 Anatomy of a Processor   226

9.2 Toward Psychologically Realistic Parsers   246

9.3 CCG Parsing for Practical Applications   251

Chapter 10

The Syntactic Interface   255

10.1 Competence   255

10.2 Acquisition   258

10.3 Performance   259

Notes   263
References   283
Index   321

Preface

This book attempts to bring together in a single framework and a uniform notation a number of strands in a project that my colleagues and I have been pursuing over several years. The purpose of the research has been to develop a principled theory of natural grammar more directly compatible on the one hand with certain syntactic phenomena that flagrantly disrupt order and constituency, including coordination, extraction, and intonational phrasing, and on the other with psychological and computational mechanisms that can map such surface forms onto interpretable meaning representations. The book follows other computational approaches in claiming that syntactic structure is merely the characterization of the process of constructing a logical form, rather than a representational level of structure that actually needs to be built—hence its title. Syntactic structure so understood can depart quite radically from the standard notions of surface constituency, offering in return a simpler and more explanatory linguistic theory of these phenomena.

The work covers topics in formal linguistics, intonational phonology, computational linguistics, and experimental psycholinguistics, many of which have been presented previously in different frameworks and addressed to diverse specialized audiences. In every case the early results have been extended and reworked here for the present purpose, which is to present them as a whole in a form accessible to the general reader starting from any one of those fields.

This research has had the goal defined in Chomsky's earliest work, of formalizing an explanatory theory of linguistic form. Such a theory must do more than just capture the grammars of various languages, via a finite generative specification of all and only the sentence-meaning pairs that each allows. It must also explain why all such grammars appear to be drawn from a curiously restricted set subject to universal constraints.

The origin and even the precise nature of grammatical universals remains in many cases obscure. Potential sources are: the conceptual base (which means for example that it is hard for languages to do without verbs); the semantics (which means that it is hard for them to do without relative clauses); learnability by young children (which means that languages tend to have consistent head-complement linear order across related categories); and finally the inherent expressive power of the natural computational system itself, as reflected in the formal system of representation.

The influence of the last of these factors is much harder to illustrate with known universals of the kind that linguists usually find of interest. But since the expressive power of natural grammars (as distinct from the devices that process them) must be at least that of context-free grammars and the associated push-down automata, it is interesting to identify those phenomena that seem to require greater expressive power, and to ask how much greater power is needed to capture them. In this book, particular attention is paid to coordination, and to its interaction with other constructions, in a number of languages. In its explicit adherence to a formalization of low expressive power, the theory of Combinatory Categorial Grammar (CCG) that is presented here is most closely related to Generalized Phrase Structure Grammar (GPSG, Gazdar 1981), and to what Joshi, Vijay-Shanker and Weir (1991) have called "mildly" context-sensitive formalisms of Head Grammar (HG, Pollard 1984) and Tree-adjoining Grammar (TAG, Joshi, Levy and Takahashi 1975).

Because the emphasis has been on explanation and generalization across languages and constructions, CCG has like other explanatory frameworks been a prey to overgeneralization in the analyses that have been offered for particular constructions in particular languages. It is harder for the working descriptive linguist to control CCG than some other formalisms, because the emphasis in combinatory rules for combining types is towards generality. I have always been less worried by this tendency than my critics, because the overgeneralizations have usually seemed to be in the direction of phenomena that are attested in other languages, and hence which are allowed under universal principles. However, this attitude has understandably provoked a certain amount of irritation among my colleagues. In returning in the middle part of the book to purely linguistic concerns with the grammar of Dutch and English word order and coordination, I have tried to respond to their criticisms, and to bring the analysis under the same level of control as more orthodox grammars.

I have no doubt that both undergeneralizations and overgeneralizations remain. "All grammars leak," as Sapir (1921) says in a slightly different context, and this one is surely no exception. The test of a good theory of grammar is whether the specific places at which it leaks suggest ways forward to better theories. I hope that much at least will hold good.

At a number of points, the theory presented here offers dynamic and computational solutions, rather than the purely declarative ones that are more standard. (Examples are the analysis of scope ambiguity of natural language quantifiers in chapter 4, and the presuppositional analysis of theme and rheme in chapter 5.) This approach is common among computer scientists, because the objects that they formalize are inherently dynamic, and need to be thought of at the most basic level in those terms. The present claim is that human language users have the same characteristic.

Nevertheless, dynamic accounts always are declarativizable (for example using Dynamic Logic, (Harel 1984) or Temporal Logic (Gabbay, Hodkinson and Reynolds 1994). The dynamic aspects of the present proposals should not be taken as standing in opposition to declarative approaches to the theory of grammar, much less as calling into question the theoretical autonomy of grammar itself.

The work that is described here owes more than the standard form of acknowledgment can properly express to early collaborations with Tony Ades and Anna Szabolcsi. More recently Polly Jacobson and Mark Hepple, among many others listed below, have been very important influences. Polly, Bob Carpenter, and Mark Johnson read the manuscript for the MIT Press. They, Jason Baldridge and Gann Bierner gave extensive comments, keeping me from numerous errors. While this is not my first book, it is the one that I began first. This preface therefore seems a good place to record my debt to those who taught me the various cognitive sciences that I have tried to apply here: Stuart Sutherland, Rod Burstall, Christopher Longuet-Higgins, Stephen Isard, Jimmy Thorne, John Lyons, Keith Brown, Gillian Brown, and Phil Johnson-Laird.

Several early versions of this material circulated under various titles such as "Work in Progress," "Combinators and Grammars," and "The Syntactic Interface." Some were used as lecture notes for courses at the LSA Summer Institute at the University of Arizona, Tucson, June 1989; at the Third European Summer School in Language, Logic, and Information, Saarbrücken, August 1991; and at the University of Stuttgart, 1996. Thanks to the participants on those occasions; to Gerry Altmann, Emmon Bach, Jason Baldridge, Filippo Beghelli, Gann Bierner, Gosse Bouma, Cem Bozsahin, Mimo Caenepeel, Jo Calder, Michael Collins, Stephen Crain, David Dowty, Jason Eisner, Elisabet Engdahl, Tim Fernando, Janet Fodor, Bob Frank, Caroline Heycock, Julia Hockenmaier, Angeliek van Hout, Jack Hoeksema, Beryl Hoffman, Aravind

Joshi, Einar Jowsey, Lauri Karttunen, Ewan Klein, Martin Kay, Nobo Komagata, Susanne Kronenberg, Shalom Lappin, Anne Mark, Jim McCloskey, Marc Moens, Michael Moortgat, Glyn Morrill, Anneke Neijt, Michael Niv, Dick Oehrle, Jong Park, Martin Pickering, Scott Prevost, Ellen Prince, Steve Pulman, Mike Reape, Yael Sharvit, B. Srinivas, Susan Steel, Matthew Stone, K. Vijay-Shanker, John Trueswell, Shravan Vasishth, Bonnie Lynn Webber, David Weir, Mary McGee Wood, and Annie Zaenen (who introduced me to hippopotamus sentences); and to numerous other colleagues and students at the Universities of Warwick, Texas at Austin, Edinburgh and Pennsylvania, for comments and patient advice over the years.

    In the early stages of the research, I benefited on more than one occasion from the generous support for cognitive science provided by the Alfred P. Sloan Foundation in the early 1980s, under the good husbandry of Stanley Peters and Philip Gough at the University of Texas at Austin, Emmon Bach and Barbara Partee at the University of Massachusetts at Amherst, and Aravind Joshi at the University of Pennsylvania. More recent aspects of the research were partly supported under NSF grants IRI91-17110 and IRI95-04372, ARPA grant N66001-94-C6043, and ARO grant DAAH04-94-G0426 to the University of Pennsylvania, and under EEC ESPRIT grant: proj. 393 and ESRC Award Number M/423/28/4002 to the University of Edinburgh.

Chapter 1

Introduction

... to investigate speech as a natural phenomenon, much as a physiologist may study the beating of the heart, or an entomologist the tropisms of an insect, or an ornithologist the nesting habits of a bird.
George Kingsley Zipf, *The Psychobiology of Language*

This book argues that the Surface Syntax of natural language acts as a completely transparent interface between the spoken form of the language, including prosodic structure and intonational phrasing, and a compositional semantics. The latter subsumes quantified predicate-argument structure, or Logical Form, and discourse Information Structure.

That is to say that although surface forms of expression in all languages notoriously disorder elements that belong together at the level of meaning, and although information-structural distinctions like theme and rheme appear somewhat independent of traditional predicate-argument structure, there is a theory of grammatical operations that allows a unified semantic representation to be built directly from surface forms, without the intervention of any intermediate level of representation whatsoever. According to this theory, syntax subsumes Intonation Structure and semantics subsumes Information Structure, the two standing in what Bach (1976) has called a "rule-to-rule" relation. This means that each syntactic rule is paired with a rule of semantic interpretation, such rules being entirely compositional—that is, defined as a function of the interpretation of the constituents to which it applies. This position is closely related to the by now widely accepted requirement for "monotonicity" among modules of grammar—that is, the requirement that no component of grammar should have to modify a structure resulting from an earlier stage.

This is not a particularly startling claim, since some such direct relation between sound and meaning might be expected on evolutionary grounds, or from any other standpoint for which considerations of parsimony and economy are paramount. A similar assumption lies behind programs as apparently different as those of Montague (1970) and Chomsky (1995). However, the nature of the phenomena manifested by the languages of the world has made it extraordinarily difficult to deliver such theories, and in practice most theories of natural language grammar have drastically restricted their coverage of those phenomena, or have introduced additional levels of representation over and above the one directly related to meaning, or both. Such additional structural representations are often more than a dispensable notational convenience, for they tend to be accompanied by nonmonotonic structure-changing operations of movement, deletion, copying, reanalysis, restructuring, and the like. Insofar as such relations are predicated over structures at more than one level of representation, they compromise the assumption of transparency with which we began. They also tend to bring with them an increase in expressive power, jeopardizing the explanatory force of the theory.

This book argues that the problem with such theories stems from an understandable but mistaken desire to keep the rules of syntax and the Surface Structures that are implicit in syntactic derivation as close as possible to those that are manifested in the meaning representation. In the case of rigidly fixed word order languages like English, this temptation is particularly strong. An example that in fact provided the starting point for the present study is Transformational Grammar of the *Syntactic Structures/Aspects* vintage (Chomsky 1957, 1965). In such grammars, surface forms differ very little from underlying forms, and then only in very specific respects. For example, the dominance relations among the local complements of ditransitive verbs may be rearranged or "wrapped," a relativized *wh*-argument may "move" from the neighborhood of its verb in the underlying representation to the neighborhood of the root node in the Surface Structure of an arbitrarily complex relative clause, or constituents of one conjunct or the other that are represented in the underlying structure of a coordinate sentence may be deleted at Surface Structure. In most cases, however, the Surface Structure residue of wrapping, *wh*-movement, or deletion under coordination preserves as much as possible of the predicate-argument structure that provides its input.

Such analyses have captured profound insights into the nature of such phenomena and have provided the first systematization of the data on which all subsequent formal theories of syntax, including the present one, have built. However, there are two things wrong with this kind of account as a theory. First, as soon as we admit the possibility that the structure implicit in a derivation is not isomorphic to the structure implicit in interpretation, there is no reason why the derivation should bear any simple structural relation to the meaning representation. All that matters is that the derivation yield that interpretation. Indeed, in less rigidly ordered languages than English it is inevitable that the structures implicit in the derivation must be quite distant from those corresponding to canonical semantic representation.

The second error lies in viewing Surface Structure as a level of representation at all, rather than viewing it (as computational linguists tend to) as no more than a trace of the algorithm that delivers the representation that we are really interested in, namely the interpretation. Here an example may help. The Augmented Transition Network (ATN) of Woods (1970, 1973) was conceived in part as a direct implementation of Transformational Grammar, and the finite state transition networks that constitute the core of an ATN grammar correspond fairly closely to rules of a context-free surface grammar. However, one of the many interesting properties of the program was that it did the work of transformational rules like "passive," "dative movement," "*wh*-movement," and "deletion under coordination," without ever building any representation of surface structure. Instead, certain annotations or "augmentations" to those rules, specifying storage in, retrieval from, or testing of a fixed number of registers or storage locations, allowed the ATN to build the equivalent of Deep Structures incrementally, as a side effect of the analysis. For example, the analysis of a surface subject of a sentence would initially cause a pointer to a representation of that subject to be allocated to a SUBJ register. However, on encountering passive morphology later in the sentence, the program would transfer the pointer to the OBJ register. Even more interestingly, encountering a relative pronoun would cause a pointer to its head noun to be placed in a special relativization register called HOLD. At any point in the subsequent analysis of the relative clause, the contents of this register could be accessed in lieu of analyzing an NP or other argument in situ. The device thereby achieved the same effect as an unbounded movement.[1]

The interest of the ATN for present purposes lies not in providing a particularly constrained alternative to the transformational analysis—it is in fact too faithful a reconstruction of Transformational Grammar for that—but in showing that for both bounded and unbounded constructions, even in an *Aspects*-style theory, Surface Structure need not be viewed as a representational level. The interest of this observation lies in the fact that, if the statement of such analyses does not require transformations as such—that is, rules mapping entire trees onto other trees—then much of the motivation for keeping deep and surface analyses in line vanishes. (Such similarity simplifies transformational rules but is likely to be irrelevant to the more dynamic alternative.)

These two observations suggest that it might be possible to free derivation from predicate-argument structure in a much more radical way than either *Aspects*, the ATN, or most of their successors have done. Such a move has purely linguistic attractions, because once we move beyond the comparatively restricted bounded constructions like passive and the various sorts of raising, and beyond *wh*-movement among the unbounded constructions, there are in fact many constructions that appear to be much less dependent on the notion of structure that is relevant to predicate-argument structure. Coordination itself, though treated in illuminating ways in both *Aspects* and the ATN, is such a construction, because it can on occasion both delete and leave as residue objects that are not traditional constituents at all, as in the English "gapping" construction (Ross 1967):

(1) I *want to try to begin to write* a musical, and *you, a play.*

Other grammatical domains in which similarly free notions of structure seem to be needed are intonational phrasing and parentheticalization.

   On the basis of evidence from such phenomena, together with other constructions involving unbounded dependencies, a number of recent theories based on Categorial Grammar make the claim that substrings like *Anna married* are possible surface syntactic constituents of sentences, even in simple examples like the following:[2]

(2) Anna married Manny.

According to these theories, even such minimal sentences have two possible Surface Structures:

   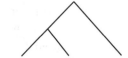

(3) a. Anna   married   Manny   b. Anna   married   Manny

More complex sentences like *Harry says that Anna married Manny* may have many Surface Structures for each reading.

   Such Surface Structures do not exhibit traditional notions of constituency, nor do they embody traditional notions of dominance and command. It follows that we must assume that all the grammatical phenomena that are typically explained in terms of such relations—notably, binding and control—are defined at the level of underlying or logical form, rather than at Surface Structure. (Such a proposal is foreshadowed by much work in Montague Grammar since Bach and Partee 1980, and in Government and Binding Theory (GB) since Lasnik and Saito 1984.) By not attempting to define such relations over Surface Structures, we continue to escape the need to represent Surface Structure explicitly, as a full representational level in addition to Logical Form, and thereby attain a more parsimonious theory, preserving desirable properties such as monotonicity and monostratality (see Steedman 1996b).

The above remarks concern the architecture of "competence" grammar, to use Chomsky's (1965) term, as distinct from the psychological "performance" mechanisms that actually deliver grammatical analyses (and may even on occasion systematically fail to deliver them). Although we will assume in what follows that syntax, semantics, and the workings of the processor are very tightly coupled, it does not follow that observations concerning any one of the members of this triad will necessarily be equally suggestive of insights into the nature of the system as a whole. Chomsky has repeatedly insisted that syntactic form, and syntactic form alone, provides an accessible and reliable source of information regarding the system as a whole. Although this is presented as a fact of research methodology, rather than as a necessary truth, the insight has been so productive of generalizations and lasting results that it is inconceivable that we should abandon it now. It is perhaps worth stating explicitly why this should be.

The methodological priority of competence over performance follows from the exceedingly fortunate fact that the computation involved in mapping natural language strings onto their interpretations appears to be one for which a "theory of the computation" can be specified independently of the particular algorithm that is actually used to perform the computation. That is, it is what Marr (1977) calls a "Type I" problem, or in Jerry Fodor's (1983) terms, a "modular" system.[3] We know that even for quite simple classes of language, there are infinitely many processing algorithms. Of course, relatively few of these are even remotely plausible in psychological terms. Nevertheless, in the absence of an adequate formulation of exactly what it is that the corresponding algorithms for natural language compute, we are unlikely to make progress in understanding the system as a whole on the basis of performance data.

Of course, technically speaking, there are also infinitely many grammars that will capture any given language, in the "weak" sense of defining the set of all and only the strings of the language. Here we are helped (up to a point at least) by the fact that very few of those grammars support a semantics that captures our fairly strong intuitions about meaning at the level of words and their predicate-argument relations, propositions, referring expressions, and relations among them, such as coreference and entailment. However, these aspects of meaning seem to capture only part of the semantics, and to arise at one remove from the level that shapes the superficial form of utterance. It has proved to be quite hard to explain the very diverse ways in which the same propositional meaning can be grammatically realized as an (active, passive, topicalized, cleft, elliptical, intonationally marked, etc.) sentence, in response to the demands of context. For that reason, standard notions of semantics do not seem to tell us enough for us to completely understand how utterances give rise to meanings. This process seems to be very opaque to introspection, and our most reliable source of information about it seems to be syntactic structure itself.

Indeed, one of the implications of the theory presented below is that contemporary theories of syntax have not been nearly ruthless enough in avoiding the temptation to draw strong conclusions from certain compelling but misleading intuitions about sentence meaning that confound two related but distinct components of meaning, only one of which is directly related to surface syntactic structure, properly understood.

Despite the methodological priority of competence grammar, it and the performance mechanism must have evolved as a package, and in the end theories of language must be evaluated as theories of both components. The significance of monotonicity in rules and monostratalism in representation partly lies in performance considerations. Such grammars make it easier to understand how a processor can make direct use of the competence grammar, a position related to the "Competence Hypothesis" widely endorsed within the generative tradition (see Chomsky 1965, 9; Chomsky 1975a, 7).

The book also investigates this relation. Since CCG integrates Intonation Structure and discourse Information Structure into the grammar itself, the claim is that it is directly compatible with parsing techniques that couple the resolution of local ambiguity and nondeterminism during processing to the semantic coherence and contextual appropriateness rival local analyses. There is considerable experimental evidence that this sort of mechanism is involved in human sentence processing. Although all grammatical theories are in principle compatible with such a mechanism, the one proposed here is more directly compatible. In particular, a processor for this kind of grammar does not need to build any structures other than those defined by the competence grammar itself in order to work in this way. The processor is therefore compatible with an extremely strict version of the principle that Bresnan and Kaplan (1982) endorse under the name of the *Strong Competence Hypothesis*. It will be convenient to refer to the present even stricter version as the *Strict Competence Hypothesis*.

The enduring methodological priority of the study of competence in this endeavor means that much of the material considered below must be presented in purely linguistic terms, to stand or fall on the usual criteria of that discipline.

Nevertheless, it will be clear throughout that the investigation is driven by questions about the language-processing system as a computational whole.

The main body of the book is therefore divided into three parts, the first two of which are entirely concerned with competence, and the last of which returns to questions of performance mechanisms and computational issues.

Part I, which can be read as a self-contained introduction to CCG, is entitled "Grammar and Information Structure." It argues that that surface syntactic derivation in CCG not only specifies Logical Form compositionally and monotonically, but also directly specifies the Intonation Structure of spoken English, and the partition of utterance content according to discourse-semantic relations that intonation conveys, and which is often referred to as Information Structure. The claim is that the traditional notion of Surface Structure can be entirely replaced by a freer notion of surface constituency corresponding to Information Structure, and that this is the only derivational notion of syntactic structure that is linguistically necessary. The argument in part I goes as follows: Chapter 2 provides some more detailed motivation for a radical rethinking of the nature of Surface Structure from coordination, parentheticalization, and intonation. Chapter 3 then outlines CCG in terms of simple examples that motivate the individual rule types. Chapter 4 defines the space of possible CCGs more exactly, and it briefly summarizes the ways in which some basic constraints on bounded and unbounded constructions, including some apparently "nonconstituent" coordinations, emerge as inevitable consequences of the theory. It also briefly considers the way in which scope ambiguities for natural language quantifiers can be handled within a strictly monotonic grammatical framework. Chapter 5 concludes part I by showing that the level of Intonation Structure identified by phonologists such as Selkirk (1984) can be directly subsumed under surface syntax as it is viewed here. It also shows that the level of Information Structure identified by discourse semanticists such as Halliday (1967b) and Prince (1986) is captured in the semantic interpretations that the grammar compositionally assigns to the nonstandard constituents of Surface Structure/Intonation Structure in this sense of the term. This chapter completely revises and extends my first attempt to solve this problem in Steedman 1991a to cover a wider variety of tunes and informational constituents including "discontinuous" themes and rhemes. It includes some discussion of the relation of the present proposals to other contemporary linguistic theories.

Part II continues the development of the grammatical theory in a more technical direction and consists of two connected case-studies. The first, in chapter 6, concerns the notorious cross-serial multiple dependencies characteristic of the "verb-raising" construction in Dutch (Huybregts 1984; Shieber 1985), a construction whose analysis is known to require an expressive power in the grammar greater than (but apparently not *much* greater than) context-free. This phenomenon is examined in interaction with the earlier account of extraction and coordination, revising Steedman 1985 (where I first looked at these questions in an earlier formalism) and taking account of more recent developments in the theory, extending the analysis to Germanic main-clause order, building on work by Hepple (1990). Chapter 7 looks at gapping in English and Dutch, revising and extending an account first sketched in Steedman 1990 via a new categorial theory of medial gapping and its relation to verb-initial coordination, to cover a wider range of constructions and the full range of language universals relating the direction of gapping to basic word order proposed by Ross (1970), including certain supposed counterexamples to Ross's generalization, Zapotec and Dutch itself among them. Taking the introductory chapters 3 and 4 as read, these chapters constitute a second self-contained (and more technical and purely linguistic) monograph, and they may well be skipped on a first reading. Nevertheless, I make no apology for their inclusion, for it is as a theory of multiple unbounded dependency and coordinate structure that I believe CCG has most to offer as a theory of grammar.

Part III turns to issues of computation and human grammatical performance. Chapter 8 examines questions of expressive and automata-theoretic power, the question of why natural grammars should take this combinatory form, and the general nature of the parsing problem for CCGs. Chapter 9 then discusses a specific architecture for a parser, including the role of semantic interpretation. It is at this point that the expectation of a direct relation between grammar and processor that was announced at the start of this introduction is shown to be well-founded. Chapter 10 summarizes the architecture of the theory as a whole, its role in acquisition and performance, and its relation to other theories of grammar.

PART I

Grammar and Information Structure

Chapter 2
Rules, Constituents, and Fragments

Only connect! That was the whole of her sermon. Only connect the prose and the passion . . . . Live in fragments no longer.
E. M. Forster, *Howards End*

The artificial languages that we design ourselves, such as logics or programming languages, exhibit a very strong form of the rule-to-rule relation between their semantics and the syntax as it is defined in the textbook or reference manual. This condition in its most general form means simply that there is a functional relation mapping semantic rules and interpretations to syntactic rules and constituents. We will return to the nature of the mapping and its consequences below, but the function of syntax as a vehicle to convey semantics makes the requirement of simplicity in the rule-to-rule mapping seem so reasonable and desirable that it might be expected to transcend all particulars of function and content.

When we finally come to understand the natural system, we must therefore expect to find a similarly direct relation between syntax and semantics, for it is hard to imagine any evolutionary pressure that would force it to be otherwise.

Indeed, there is at least one identifiable force that can be expected to work positively to keep them in line. It arises from the fact that children have to learn languages, apparently on the basis of rather unsystematic presentation of positive instances alone. Since under the simplest assumptions even such trivial classes of grammars as finite-state grammars are not learnable from mere exposure to positive instances of the strings of the language (Gold 1967), and since there appears to be little evidence that any more explicit guidance is provided by adults (Brown and Hanlon 1970 and much subsequent work), some other source of information, "innate" in the weak sense that it is available to children prelinguistically, must guide them. While statistical approximation and information-theoretic analysis using unsupervised machine learning techniques over large volumes of linguistic material remains a theoretically interesting alternative, the most psychologically plausible source for the information children actually use is semantic interpretation or the related conceptual representation.[1]

In the context of modern linguistics, the suggestion that children learn language by hanging language-specific rules and lexical categories on semantic or conceptual representations goes back at least to Chomsky (1965, 29, 59) and Miller (1967). Of course, the idea is much older. See Pinker 1979, 1994 and Fisher et al. 1994 for reviews of some proposed mechanisms, and see Gleitman 1990 for some cogent warnings against the assumption that such semantic representations have their origin solely in the results of direct perception of the material world in any simple sense of that term.

However inadequate our formal (and even informal) grasp on children's prelinguistic conceptualization of their situation, we can be in no doubt that they have one. If so, it is likely that this cognitive representation includes such grammatically relevant prelinguistic notions as actual and potential participants in, properties of, and causal relations among, events; probable attitudes and attentional focus of other conversational participants; and representations of more obviously material aspects of the instantaneously perceivable world.

2.1 Constituents

Three consequences follow from assuming a rule-to-rule relation between syntax and semantics. The first, which follows from the expectation of transparency between syntax and semantics, is so strong and so uncontentious that no theory of grammar has failed to observe it in spirit, though it is probably true to say that none has so far succeeded in following it to the letter. To say that syntax and semantics are related rule-to-rule is to say no more than that every syntactic rule has a semantic interpretation. However, it immediately follows that the syntactic entities that are combined by a syntactic rule must also be semantically interpretable. (Otherwise, they could not be combined by the semantic interpretation of the rule.) It follows that syntactic rules can only combine or yield *constituents*.

This condition, which has been called "The Constituent Condition on Rules," has been a central feature of Generative Grammar from its earliest moments. It frequently surfaces in that literature in the guise of "structure dependency" of grammatical rules. It is also the notion that is embodied in the "proper analysis" condition on transformations proposed in Chomsky 1975a (chapters written in 1955). Perhaps the most illuminating and ambitious early endorsement of this principle is to be found in Chomsky 1975a (210–211, chapters written in 1956), where the following four "criteria" (the scare quotes are Chomsky's) are offered as tests for grammatical constituents and constituent boundaries:

(1) a. The rule for conjunction
     b. Intrusion of parenthetical expressions
     c. Ability to enter into transformations
     d. Certain intonational features

These criteria are very cautiously advanced and carefully surrounded with qualifications, and the subsequent discussion is deliberately designed to demonstrate that some of them raise as many questions as they answer. Nevertheless, there is an implicit claim of great boldness, however programmatically stated. If these operations are tests for constituency, it can only be because they are rules of grammar, subject to the Constituent Condition on Rules. The bulk of Chomsky 1975a, and most work in Generative Grammar since, mainly bears on the claim relative to the third criterion, concerning transformational rules of movement (and their modern equivalents and alternatives), which it has overwhelmingly supported.

It has proved much more difficult to make good on the implicit claim with respect to the remaining three phenomena. Theories of coordination, intonation, and (insofar as there are any) parentheticalization have generally been forced at some point to compromise the Constituent Condition on Rules. The present work should be viewed as an attempt to bring Chomsky's original program nearer completion.

The second consequence of assuming a rule-to-rule relation between syntax and semantics is to imply that the *only* grammatical entities that have interpretations are constituents. This consequence is again entirely uncontentious, and virtually all theories of competence grammar have adhered to it (insofar as they have involved an explicit semantics at all). However, it will be relevant to the discussion of processing in part III.

Finally, the rule-to-rule hypothesis, and its justification in terms of its parsimony with respect to the theory of language learning and evolution, imply that syntactic and semantic rules should have the property of monotonicity. That is, there should be no rules like certain old-style transformations which convert structures that are ill formed (and hence uninterpretable) into structures which are well formed, and vice versa.

To claim that syntax is monotonic is not of course to deny that theories of language need different levels of rules, such as phonology, morphology, syntax, and semantics, or to deny the modular nature of the grammar. However,

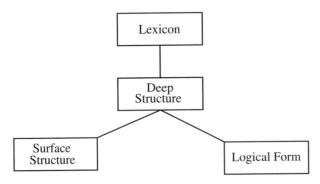

Figure 2.1
Architecture of a standard theory of grammar

It does imply that those levels too should be monotonically related, a point to which I return below.

2.2 Fragments

To what extent do the observed regularities of natural language syntax conform to the expectations set out above? As noted earlier, the generative theoretical tradition has had considerable success in accounting for many constructions involving discontiguities between elements that are semantically dependent upon one another. Many such constructions were originally brought within the fold of the Constituent Condition on Rules by the introduction of transformational rules of "movement" of constituents, relating an underlying level or levels of representation at which predicate-argument relations relevant to semantic interpretation were contiguously related, and from which a Logical Form representing further distinctions such as quantifier scope could be directly computed, to a surface structural level at which the discontiguities were manifest. The introduction of these rules gave rise to the familiar "Y-diagram" architecture of first-generation generative theories, shown in figure 2.1.[2] Theories within the generative tradition differ with respect to how many underlying levels they postulate (one in the case of *Aspects*-style Transformational Grammar "Deep Structures" and Lexical-Functional Grammar (LFG) "f-structure," two in the case of Government-Binding Theory (GB) "S-Structure" and "D-Structure," and even more in some cases). These theories also differ in how they interpret the notion of "movement." Nevertheless, they can all be seen as modifications of this architecture, and the metaphor of movement is so persuasive and revealing that I will use it freely to describe syntactic phenomena, even though the present theory eschews the notion of movement as a syntactic operation.

Movement transformations and the constructions that they capture fall naturally into two groups. The first group includes phenomena that can be accounted for entirely in terms of "bounded" dependencies—roughly, dependencies between items that occur within the same tensed clause, like those between *Dexter* and the verb *win* in the following examples:

(2) a. Dexter expects to win.
     b. Dexter is expected to win by Warren.

As Brame (1976, 1978) and Bresnan (1978) were among the first to point out, the clause-bounded nature of these dependencies means that they can be base-generated or (equivalently) specified in the lexicon, thus bringing them within the domain of the Constituent Condition on Rules without the use of movement as such, and explaining a number of "structure preserving" constraints upon such constructions (Emonds 1976).

This and much subsequent work has shown that the bounded constructions are subject to a number of apparently universal constraints upon such dependencies which reflect dominance and command and an "obliqueness" ordering of arguments of predicates, according to which subjects are ordered with respect to objects and other arguments. An important example for present purposes is afforded by asymmetries in binding possibilities for reflexives and reciprocals like the following, which Keenan (1988) shows to be independent of basic word order across languages:

(3) a. The dogs like each other./*Each other like the dogs.
     b. I showed the dogs to each other/*each other to the dogs.
     c. Sid wants Nancy to like herself/*himself.

I will return to the question of the source of such asymmetries.

The generative approach has also proved extremely successful in accounting for the phenomenon of unbounded dependency exhibited in relative clauses and topicalizations such as the following, again in terms of movement:

(4) a. a book which *I expect I will find*
     b. These articles, *I think that you must have read without understanding.*

In such constructions, elements that are related in the interpretation of the construction, such as the topicalized or relativized NPs and the verb(s) of which they are arguments, can be separated by arbitrarily long substrings and unbounded embedding. Although the residue of topicalization or relativization at first glance looks like a nonconstituent fragment of a sentence, it can be regarded as a constituent of type S, with a special kind of invisible coindexed or "moved" argument, and can thereby be brought under the Constituent Condition on Rules.

Examples like the following suggest that unbounded dependencies are also subject to constraints reflecting conditions of dominance and command involving obliqueness among arguments:

(5) a. *a man whom he thinks that Mary likes
     b. *a woman whom I persuaded to like

(The first cannot describe a man who thinks that Mary likes him, and the second cannot describe a woman whom I persuaded to like herself. Again, I will return to this question.)

It has proved much more difficult to account for coordination, parentheticalization, and phrasal intonation within the confines of the Constituent Condition on Rules. It is worth looking at some data in this connection.

2.2.1 Coordination and Parentheticals

At first glance, there is a striking overlap between the kinds of fragments that result from relativization and the related topicalizing construction, and those that can coordinate. In particular, practically everything that can occur as the residue of leftward movement can be coordinated, as in examples like the following:

(6) a. a book which *I expect I will find*, and *I think that you must have read without really understanding*
     b. *I expect I will find*, but *I think that you must have read without really understanding*, that novel about the secret life of legumes.

The second, (6b), involves rightward movement (again, the term is used descriptively).

There is a similar (though less complete) conspiracy between the residues of leftward and rightward movement. That is, most residues that arise from leftward movement can also arise from rightward movement. Moreover, both kinds of extraction are subject to very similar "island constraints:"[3]

(7) a. *a book which *I hope that I will meet the woman who wrote*
     b. *I hope that I will meet the woman who wrote*, and *you expect to inter-
         view the consortium that published*, that novel about the secret life of
         legumes.

However, the fragments that result from coordination are much more diverse
than those that result from (leftward and rightward) movement. For example:

(8) a. I *want to try to write*, and hope to see produced, a musical about the
         life of Sir Stafford Cripps.
     b. Give Deadeye Dick a sugar-stick, and *Mexican Pete, a bun*.
     c. I want to try to write a novel, and *you, a screenplay*.

The study of such constructions has revealed that they too are subject to some
very strong crosslinguistic constraints, many of which were first discussed by
Ross (1970), and which will be discussed at length in chapter 7. These can
be summarized as reflecting an "order-preserving" property of coordination,
whereby (in configurational languages, at least) if a leftmost constituent is
moved, is raised, or otherwise "goes missing" from one conjunct, then it shows
up to the left of the entire coordinate structure, whereas a missing rightmost
constituent turns up on the right. Thus, in a language like English whose basic
word order is Subject-Verb-Object, coordinate sentences like the following are
prohibited:[4]

(9) a. *A musical *want to try to write*, and hope to see produced, I.
     b. *Deadeye Dick a sugar-stick, and *Mexican Pete, a bun* give.
     c. *I a novel, and *you want to try to write a screenplay*

(I will show later in what sense example (9c) is an instance of the same universal.)

Although considerably less attention has been devoted to parenthetical utterances (but see Emonds 1976, II.9, and 1979, McCawley 1982, 1989, Levelt
1989, Espinal 1991, Croft 1995, Taglicht 1998 and Doran 1998), some similarly unconstrained fragments arise from their intrusion, as in (10):

(10) a. *Have you ever been*, they asked, a member of the Friends of the
         Ukraine Film Society?
     b. *You could give*, suggested Dexter, a policeman a flower.

The result has been that, although linguistic theories have had some success
in accounting for the relative-clause construction in terms of devices that reinstate the Constituent Condition on Rules by deriving such fragments from

traditional constituents such as S via devices like movement (Chomsky 1965), indexed "traces" (Chomsky 1975b), and feature passing (Gazdar 1981), they have been much less successful in showing that the same devices will account for coordination. Instead, coordination has led to the introduction of rules of deletion to supplement rules of movement. Such rules again attempt to reinstate the Constituent Condition over the rule of coordination, by deriving the fragments from underlying constituents of type *S*. However, the deletion rules themselves have generally failed to adhere strictly to that condition. For example, (8b) appears to require either the movement or the deletion of a non-constituent, and (8c) appears to offer no alternative to the deletion of the non-constituent *want to try to write*. More worrying still, this fragment looks suspiciously like the kind of fragment that is the surface-structural *result* of deletion or movement, as in (8a).

These complications are surprising, because intuitively all of these constructions appear to be related to the semantic notion of *abstraction*, or definition of a *property*. Most obviously, a restrictive relative clause like (11a) seems to correspond to a predicate or property of *being married by Anna*. Formally, such properties, concepts, or abstractions can be conveniently and transparently represented by terms in the λ-calculus like (11b):

(11) a. (the man that) Anna married

     b. $\lambda x.marry' x\ anna'$

Those who are unfamiliar with the λ-calculus are referred to Partee, ter Meulen and Wall 1990, chap. 13, for a full exposition. However, it will be sufficient for present purposes to note that the operator λ declares the symbol *x* to be a variable local to the expression that follows, distinct from any other variable elsewhere that happens to have the same name. The variable is thus in every way comparable to a parameter or formal variable of a subroutine or function in a computer programming language, which, when instantiated with a value, passes that value to the occurrences of the variable in the expression. The λ-term (11b) can therefore be thought of as defining a function in such a language that maps entities onto truth-values according to whether Anna married them or not. Here as elsewhere in the book, constants like *marry'*, distinguished from variables by primes, are used to identify semantic interpretations whose details are not of immediate interest. Application of a function *f* to an argument *a* is simply written *fa*, and a convention of "left associativity" of function application is observed, so that the above formula is equivalent to the following:

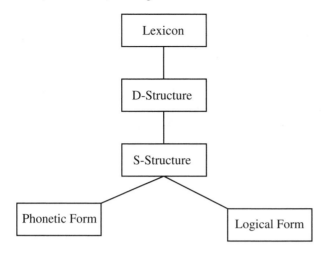

Figure 2.2
Architecture of a government-binding theory of grammar

(12) $\lambda x.(marry'x)anna'$

Most current theories of natural language grammar since "standard" Transformational Grammar (Chomsky 1965), including the present one, more or less explicitly embody the analogy between relativization and abstraction over a variable.

Nevertheless, in the case of coordination and these other unruly phenomena, their apparent freedom from the Constituent Condition on Rules has led to a situation in which, despite the apparently close relation between coordination and relativization, the responsibility for the former phenomenon, together with parentheticalization, and on occasion phenomena like "scrambling" in other languages, has been delegated to a separate, more surface-oriented domain of "stylistic" rules. This led directly to the distinction in GB between the level of S-Structure, at which relativization or *wh*-movement is defined in terms of traces closely resembling syntactic realizations of the bound variables of the λ-calculus, and the level of Phonetic or Phonological Form (PF), at which, contrary to what its name might suggest, significant syntactic work is done. (Chomsky 1986 refers to PF as "Surface Structure.") The result is the theoretical architecture shown in figure 2.2.

2.2.2 Intonation Structure

In a similar apparent contradiction to the Constituent Condition on Rules, some closely related fragments abound in spoken language, arising from phenomena associated with prosody and intonation, as well as less well behaved phenomena like restarts and the parentheticals discussed earlier. For example, one quite normal prosody for an answer to question (13a), involving stress on the word *Anna* and a rise in pitch at the end of the word *married*, imposes an Intonation Structure which is orthogonal to the traditional syntactic structure of the sentence, as informally indicated in (13b) by the parentheses (stress, marked in this case by pitch maxima, is indicated by capitals):

(13) a. I know that Alice married ALAN. But who did ANNA marry?
        b. (ANNA married)(MANNY).

We will of course need more empirical evidence and more formal notations to define this phenomenon more precisely in the chapters that follow. But the effect is very strong. (It is ironic that one of the difficulties in teaching introductory syntax is to persuade students that this is *not* the notion of structure that is relevant to the study of syntax. One conclusion that can be drawn from the argument in this book is that the students are, in an important sense, quite right.)

As is often the case with informally controlled contexts like this, other intonation contours are possible. In particular, because the context (13a) is compatible with an interpretation under which *Anna* is the topic or theme of the utterance, a contour with an intonational boundary separating the subject and predicate, *(ANNA)(married MANNY)*, is also possible. (For further discussion, see Jackendoff 1972; Steedman 1991a; and chapter 5 for further discussion.)

Intonation Structure nevertheless remains strongly constrained by meaning. For example, contours imposing bracketings like the following do not seem to be allowed, as Selkirk (1984) has pointed out:

(14) #(Three CATS)(in ten prefer CORDUROY).

Halliday (1967a) observes that this constraint, which Selkirk calls the "Sense Unit Condition," seems to follow from the *function* of phrasal intonation, which in English is in part to convey what Halliday called "Information Structure"—that is, distinctions of focus, presupposition, and propositional attitude toward entities in the discourse model. These discourse entities are more diverse than mere NP or propositional referents, but they do not seem to include such nonconcepts as "in ten prefer corduroy."

The question in (13), *Who did Anna marry?*, appears to introduce a new "theme" or topic of conversation, corresponding like the relative clause in (11a) to the concept of *someone such that Anna married them*. As Jackendoff (1972) points out, it is once again natural to think of this theme as a functional *abstraction* and to express it using exactly the same expression of the λ-calculus as was used in (11b) for the relative clause, repeated here:[5]

(15) λ*x.marry′x anna′*

When this function or concept is supplied with an argument *manny′*, it *reduces* to give a proposition, with the same function-argument relations as the canonical sentence (Again, function application associates to the left.)

(16) *marry′manny′anna′*

It is the presence of the abstraction (15) rather than some other that makes the intonation contour in (13b) felicitous. (That is not to say that its presence uniquely *determines* this response, or that its explicit mention is necessary for interpreting the response.)

These observations have led linguists such as Selkirk to postulate a level of Intonation Structure, independent of syntactic structure and related to an Information Structural component of LF, implying an architecture something like the one in figure 2.3 for the theory of grammar as a whole (see Selkirk 1984, 205, and cf. Chomsky 1971).[6]

The involvement of two apparently uncoupled levels of underlying structure on the way from sound to meaning in natural language grammar appears to complicate the path from speech to interpretation unreasonably, and to thereby threaten the entire theory of grammar (not to mention its worrying implications for the feasibility of a number of applications in computational speech recognition and speech synthesis).

In the light of the increasing complexity of the mainstream theories of grammar in the face of these less well behaved constructions, it is interesting to observe that the coordinate constructions considered in section 2.2.1, whose semantics also seems to be reminiscent of functional abstraction, are also subject to something like the Sense Unit Condition that limits intonational phrases. For example, strings like *in ten prefer corduroy* seem to be as reluctant to take part in coordination as they are to be treated as intonational phrases:

(17) *Three cats in twenty like velvet, and in ten prefer corduroy.

Parentheticalization is similarly bad at such junctures:

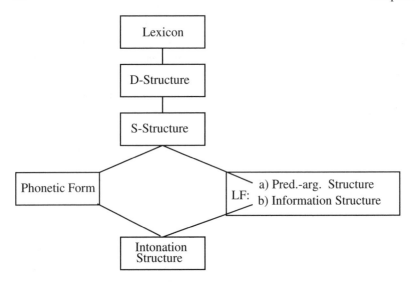

Figure 2.3
Architecture of a government-binding prosody

(18) *"Three cats," ejaculated Tom, prematurely, "in ten prefer corduroy."

Since coordinate constructions and parentheticals constitute major sources
of complexity for current theories of natural language grammar and also offer
serious obstacles to computational applications, it is tempting to suspect that
this conspiracy between syntax and prosody might point to a unified notion of
syntactic constituent structure that is somewhat different from the traditional
one, but that unifies the GB notions of S-Structure, PF and Intonation Structure
under a single notion that I shall call Information Structure, to avoid confusion
with other notions of Surface Structure that are in play.

2.3 Issues of Power and Explanation

To cut ourselves adrift from traditional linguistic notions of constituency is a
frightening prospect. Fortunately, there are other principles of linguistic investigation to guide the search for an alternative.

The first among these principles is Occam's razor, which says that we should
capture the phenomena of language in theories with as few degrees of freedom
as possible. The strength of a theory lies in the extent to which (a) it captures all
and only the phenomena that can occur, and (b) could not in principle capture

phenomena that we have good reason to believe could not occur, and therefore has no need to explicitly exclude them by stipulation.

It follows that a theory should involve as few levels of representation as possible, consistent with the main goal of capturing generalizations. Ideally, following the Montagovian tradition, we would like to assume no more than an interpretation related in a strictly monotonic fashion to syntactic derivation.

We should also try to minimize power in the modules of the theory, consistent with the primary goal of building interpretations that capture predicate-argument relations correctly. If we can do so with grammars that are provably low on the Chomsky hierarchy of formal languages and automata-theoretic power, then we are on stronger theoretical ground than if we adopted theories that achieve the same coverage at the expense of greater power, because greater automata-theoretic power increases the variety of alternative constructions and phenomena that we *could* capture beyond the point where there seems to be any motivation from empirical or imaginable semantic dependencies. Here I follow the tradition of Generalized Phrase Structure Grammar (GPSG; Gazdar 1982) and mildly context-sensitive theories of grammar such as Tree-Adjoining Grammar (TAG; Joshi, Levy and Takahashi 1975).

Of course, to achieve parsimony in automata-theoretic power is possible only to the extent that we have good information about the real space of possible natural languages and grammars. Fortunately there is a certain amount of information available on this question.

In asking what is the least powerful class of grammars on some scale such as the Chomsky hierarchy that includes all natural grammars, we must distinguish between "strong" and "weak" adequacy of grammars or sets of rules for capturing languages in the formal sense of sets of strings of words or other terminal vocabulary symbols. A grammar or set of rules that merely generatively specifies all and only the strings of a language may be only weakly adequate as a grammar for the language. To be strongly adequate, it must also assign a correct structural description to the string, where "correct" structural descriptions are the ones that support the semantics of the language. For example, a language whose semantics demands a context-free grammar whose rules happen to permit embedding only on rightmost elements has a weakly adequate finite-state grammar that generates all and only the same strings. However, the weakly adequate finite-state grammar does not directly express the embedding that supports the semantics. It is only the strongly adequate context-free grammar that does that.

However strong our intuitions may be concerning some aspects of meaning in natural language, we do not have access to natural semantics in the direct sense in which we have access to its strings. It follows that the only formal proofs that we can construct concerning lower bounds on the power implicit in natural languages involve weak adequacy. Of course, if we can show that some level of the automata-theoretic power hierarchy is not even weakly adequate to capture all natural languages, then it immediately follows that the level in question is not strongly adequate either. However, finding a lower bound on the power of strongly adequate grammars via a proof of weak adequacy depends on finding a construction in the language that not only has an intuitive semantics that demands that power to produce correct structural descriptions, but that also happens not to admit a weakly adequate grammar of lower power.

Partly because of the widespread presence of lexical ambiguity in natural languages, the search for a formal proof of a lower bound on weak adequacy was extremely protracted. Chomsky (1957) gave an early argument that nothing lower than context-free grammars—that is, grammars that can be written with production rules expanding a single nonterminal or phrasal type—could be weakly adequate. However, many of the earliest examples of constructions that were claimed to prove that the lower bound on power was strictly greater than context-free were flawed, either because they confounded extragrammatical factors with grammatical ones (like the argument from the English *respectively* construction) or because they depended on intuitive assumptions about strong adequacy and failed to exclude the possibility of a weakly equivalent grammar of lower power. These arguments are helpfully reviewed by Pullum and Gazdar (1982) and by Pullum (1987).

This curious delay in proving any lower bound on power greater than context-free should be kept in perspective. Since the late 1970s, there has been very little doubt that (a) the competence grammars implicated by the semantics or predicate-argument relations for natural languages were strictly greater than context-free in power, and (b) that power was not very much greater than context-free.

One reason for believing natural grammars not to greatly exceed context-free power, and in particular not to come anywhere near the power of context-sensitive grammars, is that most phenomena of natural languages, including those involving unbounded dependencies, can be captured by context-free rules. Although I will not at this point go into the way in which certain kinds of unbounded dependencies can be captured using context-free or near-context-free rules, the possibility is strongly suggested by the observation that the two dependencies in (19a) must nest, rather than intercalate, as they would have to for (19b) to have a meaning to do with playing sonatas on violins (the asterisk here means "not allowed with the intended reading.")

(19) a. a violin which$_i$ [this sonata]$_j$ is hard to play$_j$ upon$_i$
  b. *a sonata which$_i$ [this violin]$_j$ is hard to play$_i$ upon$_j$

To nest dependencies is of course the characteristic behavior of a pushdown automaton, which is the automaton for recognizing context-free languages, so it seems likely that there is a strongly adequate context-free grammar for this construction. GPSG (Gazdar 1981, 1982; Gazdar et al. 1985) extensively explored the extent to which all grammatical phenomena can be captured in context-free terms.

The reason for believing that natural grammars are of strictly greater than context-free power lies in the fact that, although nonnesting or intercalating dependencies are rare, strong adequacy will undoubtedly require them to be captured in some, and perhaps all, natural languages. The most convincing observation of this kind came from Dutch, in work by Huybregts (1976), although it was some time before a formal proof in the form of a proof of weak inadequacy of context-free grammars was forthcoming on the basis of a similar phenomenon in related Germanic dialects (Huybregts 1984; Shieber 1985).

In Dutch there is a strong tendency for all verbs in subordinate clauses to be clause-final and for matrix verbs to appear to the left of the verbs in their complements. This means that certain sentences with embedded infinitival complements that in English embed right-peripherally involve crossing or intercalating dependencies between predicates and arguments, as indicated by connecting lines in (20):[7]

(20) ... omdat   ik Cecilia Henk de nijlpaarden   zag helpen voeren.
  ... because I Cecilia Henk the hippopotamuses saw help   feed

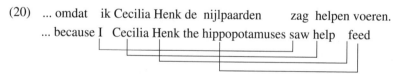

'... because I saw Cecilia help Henk feed the hippopotamuses.'

The important property of this construction is that the semantic dependencies between nouns and verbs do not nest in Dutch, as they do in English. They intercalate, or interleave. This means that any strongly adequate grammar for Dutch—that is, one that maintains a rule-to-rule relation between syntax and semantics and captures the dependencies correctly—is likely to be non-context-free (Wall 1972).

The challenge that is offered by the contrast between nesting examples like

(19) and intercalating examples like (20) is to find a strongly adequate class of grammars that is "mildly" context-sensitive, allowing these examples and the previous ones that are characteristic of coordination and prosody, without allowing all sorts of illicit phenomena.

There is a third source of information that we can draw upon in our search for such a class. There are a number of known crosslinguistic constraints on grammar that are so strong as to apparently constitute universal limitations on natural grammars. We will be concerned with many such universal constraints below, but two in particular will play a central role in the argument.

The first is due to Ross (1970), who pointed out that the construction that shows up in English as (medial) gapping, in sentences like (21), shows a strong crosslinguistic regularity concerning which of the two conjuncts undergoes "deletion" or otherwise has the verb go missing:

(21) Dexter likes cats, and Warren, dogs.

The pattern is that in languages whose basic clause constituent order subject-verb-object (SVO), the verb or verb group that goes missing is the one in the right conjunct, and not the one in the left conjunct. The same asymmetry holds for VSO languages like Irish. However, SOV languages like Japanese show the opposite asymmetry: the missing verb is in the *left* conjunct.[8] The pattern can be summarized as follows for the three dominant constituent orders (asterisks indicate the excluded cases):[9]

(22) SVO: *SO and SVO   SVO and SO
     VSO: *SO and VSO   VSO and SO
     SOV: SO and SOV *SOV and SO

This observation can be generalized to individual constructions within a language: just about any construction in which an element apparently goes missing preserves canonical word order in an analogous fashion. For example, English ditransitive verbs subcategorize for two complements on their right, like VSO verbs. In the following "argument cluster" coordination, it is indeed in the right conjunct that the verb goes missing:

(23) Give a policeman a flower, and a dog a bone.

The second phenomenon identified above, the crosslinguistic dependency of binding of reflexives and anaphors upon Jackendoff's Jackendoff (1972) obliqueness hierarchy is discussed by Keenan (1988) and Clark (1985, 1991), among others. Regardless of basic word order (here there are data from OS languages and constructions within languages), or indeed of configurationality itself, anaphoric pronouns like *themselves* and *each other* may corefer with another argument of the verb just in case that other argument is less oblique— that is, earlier in a series that places subject first, object next, and more oblique arguments later. In English this shows up in the fact that a subject may bind an object, but not vice versa:

(24) a. Dexter and Warren like each other.
     b. *Each other like Dexter and Warren.

In the case of the ditransitive verbs, it shows up in the fact that the first object can bind the second, but not vice versa (see Barss and Lasnik 1986 for discussion):

(25) a. I introduced Dexter and Warren to each other.
     b. *I introduced each other to Dexter and Warren.

This is not an idiosyncratic fact about English or SVO languages. Keenan shows that in VSO and even VOS and mixed VSO/VOS languages, less oblique arguments such as subjects bind more oblique arguments such as objects, and not vice versa.

2.4 Grammar as an Applicative System

The two universals singled out in the last section, both of which can conveniently be illustrated using the same English ditransitive construction, induce opposite tensions in the theory of grammar. For reasons that will be developed below, the dependency of gapping upon canonical word order suggests that directionality under concatenation is directly projected from the lexicon to the string by strictly concatenative rules. On the other hand, binding suggests the existence of a level of representation at which obliqueness is represented independently of surface order, or that projection is not strictly concatenative, or both.

It is interesting in this connection to note that there are alternative systems to the λ-calculus for capturing the notion of abstraction, and that these systems entirely avoid the use of bound variables. They are the combinatory systems invented by Schönfinkel (1924) and Curry and Feys (1958) as a formal foundation for the semantics of the λ-calculus. They are entertainingly discussed in Smullyan 1985, where the combinatory operators take the form of birds, and from which a number of the epigraphs to the present chapters are taken. In such systems, which I discuss in detail in chapter 8, terms equivalent to abstractions are built up using a few simple operations for combining functions, such as functional composition. Systems using quite small numbers of combinators can be shown to be equivalent in expressive power to the λ-calculi. The existence of these systems raises the possibility that alternative theories of grammar can be developed based as directly upon the combinatory applicative systems as the traditional ones implicitly are upon the λ-calculus. The significance of this possibility is that the different form that syntactic rules take in combinatory systems may lead us to look at the kinds of phenomena discussed above in a new way.

Because combinators are operations that map *functions* onto other functions, and because the categorial grammars that were originally developed in their "pure" context-free form by Ajdukiewicz (1935) and Bar-Hillel (1953) provide a notation in which functional type is made explicit, this insight has led in recent years to an explosion of research in frameworks that are collectively known as "flexible" categorial grammars (see, e.g., Lambek 1958; Montague 1970; Geach 1972; Cresswell 1973; Karlgren 1974; Bach 1976, 1979, 1980; Shaumyan 1977; Keenan and Faltz 1978; von von Stechow 1979; Levin 1982; Ades and Steedman 1982; Dowty 1982; Hausser 1984; van Benthem 1986; Flynn 1983; Huck 1985; Zwarts 1986; Uszkoreit 1986; Wittenburg 1986; Desclés, Guentchéva and Shaumyan 1986; Oehrle 1987, 1988; Zeevat, Klein and Calder 1987; Bouma 1987; Szabolcsi 1989; Moortgat 1988a; Hoeksema 1989; Carpenter 1989; Hepple 1990; Jacobson 1990; Segond 1990; Karttunen 1989; Hepple 1990; Jowsey 1989; Steele 1990; Reape 1996; Wood 1993; van der Linden 1993; Potts 1994; Houtman 1994; Ranta 1994; Morrill 1994; Hendriks 1995; and Aarts 1995.[10] One of the interesting properties of combinatory applicative systems is that in general they offer many equivalent combinatory expressions for a given normalized λ-term. This property is reflected in another distinguishing feature of certain of the above theories. The use of rules related to combinators encourages a property of "associativity" in linguistic derivations. That is, for any unambiguous sentence, there are typically several distinct categorial derivations, all of which are semantically equivalent in the sense that they deliver the same function-argument relations. The notion "constituent of a derivation" is correspondingly generalized to cover many of the puzzling fragments discussed above.

I will not attempt to review this very diverse literature here.[11] However, many of the ideas explored below draw upon these works, and I will try to make their parentage clear as we go. This book is most closely related to the subgroup of these theories developed by Ades, Oehrle, Jacobson, Szabolcsi, and Hepple, among other cited above, although they should not be assumed to endorse the present theory in all (or even many) respects. In these theories, syntactic rules corresponding to simple individual combinators such as functional composition are used to lend such fragments as *want to try to write* and even *a policeman a flower* the status of constituents, without the use of movement or deletion. Such grammars will be shown to provide a unified treatment of a wide variety of syntactic phenomena in natural language and to explain phenomena of long-distance dependency (including relativization), coordination, parentheticalization, and intonation, within the confines of the Constituent Condition on Rules and in terms of a single principle. That principle is that the predicate-argument relations that hold in sentences of natural languages are projected onto long-range syntactic dependencies from the relations defined locally in the lexicon by syntactic operations corresponding to combinators, rather than by syntactic operations involving empty categories or traces corresponding to syntactically realized bound variables.

In order to demonstrate that these novel grammars deliver the correct interpretations, we will need a semantic notation. Although we could use combinators for the purpose, λ-calculus is far more readable and in every way equivalent. The appearance of variables in the semantic notation might give the impression that traces have been reintroduced. However, these variables are no more than a readable notation for a uniform mechanism whereby *all* arguments, whether "extracted" or "in situ," get semantically bound to predicates.

Chapter 3

Intuitive Basis of Combinatory Categorial Grammars

Given any birds A, B, and C, the bird C is said to compose *A with B if for every bird x the following condition holds: Cx = A(Bx)*
Raymond Smullyan, *To Mock a Mockingbird*

Because combinators are operations on functions, we will need a notation for grammars that makes prominent the functional type or "category" of linguistic entities—that is, a notation that specifies the kinds of things that a linguistic entity combines with and the kind of thing that results. Categorial Grammar (CG), invented by Ajdukiewicz, Bar-Hillel, and others, which in its pure form is (weakly) equivalent to other context-free grammars, provides such a notation, and it is there that we will begin.[1]

3.1 Pure Categorial Grammar

Categorial grammars put into the lexicon most of the information that is standardly captured in context-free phrase structure (PS) rules. For example, consider the following PS rules, which capture some basic syntactic facts concerning English transitive sentences:

(1) $S \rightarrow NP\ VP$
   $VP \rightarrow TV\ NP$
   $TV \rightarrow \{married, finds, \ldots\}$

In a categorial grammar, all constituents—and in particular the lexical elements, such as verbs and nouns—are associated with a syntactic "category" that identifies them as either *functions* or *arguments*. In the case of functions, the category specifies the type and directionality of their argument(s) and the type of their result. The present work uses a notation in which the argument or domain category always appears to the right of the slash, and the result or range category to the left. A forward slash / means that an argument of the appropriate type must appear to the right of the functor; a backward slash \ means that the argument must appear to the left.[2] All functions are "Curried," so that a function of n arguments becomes a unary function onto a Curried function of $n - 1$ arguments. The category of a simple transitive tensed verb is therefore written as follows, capturing the same facts about English transitive sentences as the PS rules in (1):

(2) married $:= (S\backslash NP)/NP$

Curried functions, which are so-named after Haskell Curry, are equivalent to the corresponding "flat" functions of n arguments (Schönfinkel 1924), and it will be convenient to refer to S in the above function as its range, and the two NPs as its domain or arguments.

The class of all possible categories is recursively defined as an infinite set of terms including the basic categories S, NP, and so on, and all terms of the form α/β and $\alpha\backslash\beta$, where α and β are categories.

The lexicon of a given language is a finite subset of the set of all categories subject to quite narrow restriction that ultimately stem from limitations on the variety of semantic types with which the syntactic categories are paired in the lexicon. In particular, we can assume that lexical function categories are limited to finite—in fact, very small—numbers of arguments. (For English at least, the maximum appears to be four, required for a small number of verbs like *bet*, as in *I bet you five dollars he's a good dog.*)

The most basic assumption of the present approach is that the responsibility for specifying all dependencies, whether long-range or local, resides in the lexical specifications of syntactic categories for the "heads" of those dependencies—that is, the words corresponding to predicate-argument structural functors, such as verbs. This principle, which is related to the Projection Principle of GB, can be more formally stated as follows:[3]

(3) *The Principle of Lexical Head Government*
     Both bounded and unbounded syntactic dependencies are specified by the lexical syntactic type of their head.

This is simply to say that the present theory of grammar is "lexicalized," a property that makes it akin to LFG, TAG, Head-Driven Phrase Structure Grammar (HPSG; Pollard and Sag 1994), and certain recent versions of GB (see Hale and Keyser 1993; Brody 1995).

Lexicalized grammars make the lexical entries for words do most of the grammatical work of mapping the strings of the language to their interpretations. The size of the lexicon involved is therefore an important measure of a grammar's complexity. Other things being equal, one lexical grammar is simpler than another if it captures the same pairing of strings and interpretations using a smaller lexicon.

An important property of CCG, which it shares with LFG and GB, and which sets it apart from TAG, GPSG, and HPSG (which in other respects are more closely related), is that it attempts to minimize the size of the lexicon by adhering as closely as possible to the following stronger principle:

(4) *The Principle of Head Categorial Uniqueness*
A single nondisjunctive lexical category for the head of a given construction specifies both the bounded dependencies that arise when its complements are in canonical position and the unbounded dependencies that arise when those complements are displaced under relativization, coordination, and the like.

That is not to say that a given word may not be the head of more than one construction and hence be associated with more than one category. Nor does it exclude the possibility that a given word-sense pair may permit more than one canonical order, and hence have more than one category per sense. For example, in chapter 6 Dutch and German word order is captured by assuming that verbs in these languages systematically have two categories, one determining main-clause order and the other subordinate clause orders. Baldridge (1999) suggests that languages with freer word order such as Tagalog may have even more categories for verbs. The claim is simply that each of these categories specifies both canonical order and all varieties of extraction for the clause type in question. For example, a single lexical syntactic category (2) for the word *married*, which does not distinguish between "antecedent," "θ," or any other variety of government, is involved in all of the dependencies illustrated in (5):

(5) a. Anna *married Manny*.
   b. the man *that* I believe that Anna *married*
   c. I believe that Anna *married* and you believe that she dislikes, the man in the grey flannel suit.

In both TAG and GPSG these dependencies are mediated by different initial trees or categories, and in HPSG they are mediated by a disjunctive category.

We will on occasion be forced to allow exceptions to the Principle of Head Categorial Uniqueness. However, each such exception complicates the grammar and makes it compare less favorably with an otherwise equivalently valued grammar that requires no such exceptions.

Such functions can combine with arguments of the appropriate type and position by rules of functional application, written as follows:

(6) *The functional application rules*

    a. $X/Y \quad Y \quad \Rightarrow \quad X$ (>)

    b. $Y \quad X\backslash Y \quad \Rightarrow \quad X$ (<)

These rules have the form of very general binary PS rule schemata in which
X, Y, and the like, are variables ranging over categories. If the grammar is
limited to "pure" categorial grammar involving these schemata alone, then it
is nothing more than a context-free grammar that happens to be written in the
accepting, rather than the producing, direction, and in which the major burden
of specifying particular grammars has been transferred from the PS rules to the
lexicon. Although it is now convenient to write derivations as in (7a), below,
they are clearly equivalent to the familiar trees, (7b):

(7) a.   Anna   married   Manny   b.   Anna   married   Manny

           $\underline{NP}$ $\underline{(S\backslash NP)/NP}$ $\underline{NP}$ NP V NP

                    $\underline{\qquad\qquad}$>

                   $S\backslash NP$

        $\underline{\qquad\qquad\qquad}$<   VP

            S S

(Underlines in the categorial derivation indicate combination via the application rules, and the left/right arrows mnemonically indicate which rule has
applied.)[4]

    The basic categories like S and NP can, and in fact must, be regarded as
complex objects that include both major syntactic features, of the kind used
in $\bar{\text{X}}$-bar theory, and minor syntactic features like number, gender, and person
agreement. Such syntactic feature bundles will for present purposes be abbreviated as S, NP_{3s}, $S\backslash NP_{3s}$, and so on, since the particular feature set is not at
issue here, and the precise implementation of minor features or feature bundles
like agreement is of no immediate relevance. Thus, we will from time to time
want to write the category of *married* as follows:

(8) married $:= (S\backslash NP_{3s})/NP$

(9) Anna   married   Manny

    $\underline{NP_{3sf}}$ $\underline{(S\backslash NP_{3s})/NP}$ $\underline{NP}$

                  $\underline{\qquad\qquad}$>

              $S\backslash NP_{3s}$

    $\underline{\qquad\qquad\qquad}$<

          S

The derivation in (9) illustrates the way in which the syntactic features are used to capture agreement in categorial grammars, following Bach (1983).[5]

In such a framework, *3s*, *3sf*, and the like, can be regarded as abbreviations for particular, possibly underspecified values or sets of values for an attribute or set of attributes *AGR*. Variables such as *agr*, *agr₁*, and the like, can range over such values. Arguments that are unspecified for agreement (such as the object of *married*, (8)) by convention have such a variable as their value on this feature bundle or attribute, allowing them to "unify" with any more specified value in the sense of the term current in programming languages like Prolog. (See Sag et al. 1986 for the basic approach, and Bayer and Johnson 1995 for discussion of some complexities that we will also pass over here. Unification as a basis for combinatory rules is discussed in Steedman 1996b)

3.2 Interpretation and Predicate-Argument Structure

Although for many purposes we will continue to be able to ignore the details of semantics in derivations, it will from time to time be important to remember that categories also include semantic interpretations. Interpretations can be thought of either as purely model-theoretic objects or as predicate-argument structures (i.e., as Logical Forms in the logician's sense of the term). For present purposes, it will be helpful to think of them as predicate-argument structures.

One convenient way to capture the interpretation of a verb like (8) is to associate a λ-term with the syntactic category, via a colon operator, as follows:

(10) married := $(S\backslash NP_{3s})/NP : \lambda x.\lambda y.marry'xy$

Constants in such interpretations are again distinguished from variables by primes. The λ-operators define the way arguments are bound into lexical Logical Forms. This particular Logical Form could be further reduced by η reduction to the term *marry'*, and I will freely use such reduced forms where they save space.[6]

The syntactic and semantic components of such categories are related by the following principle, which is the categorial equivalent of a principle of "type driven translation" in rules (Klein and Sag 1985), and related to the $\bar{X}$ theory (Chomsky 1970; Jackendoff 1977).

(11) *The Principle of Categorial Type Transparency*
      For a given language, the semantic type of the interpretation together with
      a number of language-specific directional parameter settings uniquely de-
      termines the syntactic category of a category.

For example, a verbal function from subjects to propositions in English may
be of type $S \backslash NP$ whereas a function from objects to predicates must be S/NP.

The present use of the untyped λ-calculus as a simplified notation for Logical Forms does not help us to straightforwardly define this principle formally.
Even the typed version would require some extensions to distinguish nominal and verbal functions of type $e \rightarrow t$, and to distinguish subject arguments
from objects. Providing those extensions would in turn require considerable
argumentation, in view of the problematic status of notions like subject and
object across languages. Since this problem is essentially the same within all
grammatical frameworks, and the concerns of this book lie elsewhere, a formal definition will not be attempted here. However, the Principle has a number
of corollaries which limit the degrees of freedom that are available within the
CCG framework.

One such corollary of the Principle of Categorial Type Transparency is its
inverse: the semantic type of an interpretation is entirely determined by the
syntactic type on the left of the colon, under a function $\mathcal{T}$ (see Montague 1974,
who defines a similar mapping):

(12) *The Inverse of the Principle of Categorial Type Transparency*
      For any category $\Sigma : \Lambda$, Λ is of type $\mathcal{T}\Sigma$

$\mathcal{T}$ is recursively defined as follows:

(13) If Σ is a basic syntactic type *NP*, *S*, *N*, etc. then $\mathcal{T}\Sigma$ is a corresponding
      fixed semantic type such as e (entity), t (truth-value), $e \rightarrow t$ (property),
      etc. If Σ is a syntactic functor category α/β or $\alpha\backslash\beta$ then $\mathcal{T}\Sigma$ is a corre-
      sponding semantic functor of type $\mathcal{T}\beta \rightarrow \mathcal{T}\alpha$.

For example, the semantic type of a transitive verb like *married* (10) has
to be of type $e \rightarrow (e \rightarrow t)$ under this definition—a function from entities to
functions-from-entities-to-truth-values. We are not free to assume that it is
t, or $e \rightarrow t$ just because we feel like it. A fully explicit Logical Form for
the English SVO transitive verb in (10) would further specify that the first
argument is the object of the proposition and the second the subject, where
those roles are defined by a universal predicate-argument structure in which the
subject commands the object. This particular Logical Form could therefore be

simplified by "η-normalization" as *marry'*. However, the above definition of $\mathcal{T}$ would also permit an OVS language in which this category had the translation $\lambda y.\lambda x.marry'xy$, in which the subject combines first, followed by the object. Such a Logical Form cannot be simplified, and makes an essential, though entirely local, use of λ-abstraction. In Steedman 1996b, I argue that this degree of freedom in the lexical specification of Logical Forms is required to account for binding phenomena in English, as well as in VSO and OSV languages. In later sections we will see that it is also implicated by coordination phenomena in verb-initial constructions in English, and in other SVO and VSO languages.[7]

When interpretations are made explicit in this particular notation, the application rules must be similarly expanded to associate predicate-argument structures with (variables over) syntactic categories, as follows:

(14) *Functional application*

    a. $X/Y : f \quad Y : a \quad \Rightarrow \quad X : f\,a$ $(>)$

    b. $Y : a \quad X\backslash Y : f \quad \Rightarrow \quad X : f\,a$ $(<)$

It is important to notice that these two rules apply an identical compositional-semantic operation—functional application—in both syntax and semantics. This particular notation might make it appear that the theory allows the freedom to involve an arbitrary semantic operation associating some interpretation other than $f\,a$ with the result X of the rule—say, $f\,a\,a$ or $a\,f$. However, the Principle of Categorial Type Transparency means that such interpretations are incompatible with the semantic types that are involved. And in fact, the syntactic rule is simply the translation of a semantic rule of functional application. In general, all combinatory rules that are permitted in CCG are subject to the following principle, whose definition corrects an earlier version in Steedman 1996b:

(15) *The Principle of Combinatory Type Transparency*
    All syntactic combinatory rules are type-transparent versions of one of a
    small number of simple semantic operations over functions.

We have yet to see what is meant by "simple" and "small number" here, and we have already noted in the introduction that linguists have more secure access to the syntactic end of rules than to the semantic one. However, we may note that functional operations do not come much simpler than functional application, and that if the semantic types corresponding to X, Y, and X/Y, respectively, are x, y, and $y \to x$, then the term $f\,a$ is the *only* normalized λ-term of type x that can be formed from f and a. This is typical of all the combinatory rules we will consider.

The earlier derivation appears as follows in this notation:

(16)   Anna   married   Manny
$$\underline{NP_{3sf} : anna'}\quad \underline{(S\backslash NP_{3s})/NP : \lambda x.\lambda y.marry'xy}\quad \underline{NP : manny'}$$
$$\underline{\qquad\qquad\qquad S\backslash NP_{3s} : \lambda y.marry'manny'y \qquad\qquad}_{>}$$
$$\underline{\qquad\qquad\qquad\qquad S : marry'manny'anna' \qquad\qquad\qquad}_{<}$$

(The rules in (14) include higher-order variables like f ranging over functions like $\lambda x.\lambda y.marry'xy$.)

The example illustrates the way a derivation synchronously builds a predicate-argument structure for the sentence, via the interpretations of constituents. Interpretations obey a convention under which the application of a function (like *marry'*) to an argument (like *manny*) is represented by concatenation (as in *marry'manny'*), where such expressions "associate to the left." This means that the interpretation *marry'manny'anna'* of the S result in derivation (16) is equivalent to expression (17a), the brackets being suppressed by this convention:

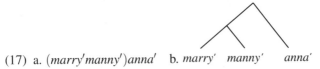

(17) a. $(marry'manny')anna'$ b. *marry'   manny'   anna'*

Predicate-argument structures like (17a) are therefore equivalent to binary trees, like (17b), which preserve traditional notions of dominance and command, but do not preserve the linear word order of the string. Word order is defined solely by the directional slashes in the syntactic category. CCG categories are therefore reminiscent of the lexical items of Zubizarreta (1987), Grimshaw (1990), or Williams (1994), and (less directly) those in HPSG (see Pollard and Sag 1987, 1994), or a restricted version of elementary trees in Lexicalized Tree-Adjoining Grammars (LTAG; see Joshi and Schabes 1992). CCG differs only in the way in which these predicate-argument relations are "projected" by the combinatory rules of syntax.

It is important to realize that the λ-notation is simply a convenient device for binding arguments into predicate-argument structures during a derivation like (10). The potentially powerful mechanism of λ-abstraction does no real work outside the domain of an individual lexical item, and its potential for application over unboundedly large structures is never invoked. It could therefore be replaced with less powerful finite-state devices or (at the cost of certain complications that we will come to) be eliminated entirely, as in the related Montagovian categorial tradition of Bach, Dowty and others.

3.3 Coordination

In earlier papers on the present theory, coordination was introduced via the following schema, which goes back at least as far as Chomsky 1957, 36, (26), and can be paraphrased as "Conjoin like categories":[8]

(18) *Simplified coordination rule* ($<\Phi>$)

$$X \quad CONJ \quad X' \Rightarrow X''$$

X, X', and X'' are categories of the same type but different interpretations. Using such a rule schema, transitive verbs (for example) can coordinate as follows:

(19)

$$
\begin{array}{cccccc}
\text{Anna} & \text{met} & \text{and} & \text{married} & \text{Manny} \\
\overline{NP} & \overline{(S\backslash NP)/NP} & \overline{CONJ} & \overline{(S\backslash NP)/NP} & \overline{NP} \\
& \multicolumn{3}{c}{\underline{\hspace{4cm}}_{<\Phi>}} & \\
& \multicolumn{3}{c}{(S\backslash NP)/NP} & \\
& & \multicolumn{3}{c}{\underline{\hspace{4cm}}_{>}} \\
& & & S\backslash NP & \\
\multicolumn{5}{c}{\underline{\hspace{6cm}}_{<}} \\
\multicolumn{5}{c}{S}
\end{array}
$$

Such a rule is an oversimplification, because it runs counter Ross 's (1967, 90; 1986, 99) observation that in English (as opposed to other languages—see Schachter 1985, 47), conjunctions are "prepositional"—that is, they associate structurally with the right conjunct, not the left.[9] I will return to the question later, continuing to use the simplified coordination rule (18) in derivations.

The rule (18) is a schema over types, and semantically its instances must be distinguished, to differentiate coordination of nonfunctions, unary functions, binary functions, and so on. We can represent this by the following schema (which we will later need to restrict further):

(20) *Coordination* ($<\Phi^n>$)

$$X:g \quad CONJ:b \quad X:f \Rightarrow_{\Phi^n} X:\lambda...b(f\,...)(g\,...)$$

Apart from the simplification already mentioned, this is everyone's coordination rule (see Gazdar 1981). It captures the ancient intuition that *coordination is an operation that maps two constituents of like type onto a constituent of the same type*. Because X may be a functor category of any valency or number of arguments, the rule is formulated as a schema over such types.[10]

Given such a rule or rule schema, derivations like the following are permitted, and yield semantically correct results (agreement is omitted, and functions like $\lambda x.\lambda y.marry'xy$ are abbreviated as *marry'*):

(21)

Anna	met	and	married	Manny
NP	$(S\backslash NP)/NP$	$CONJ$	$(S\backslash NP)/NP$	NP
$: anna'$	$: meet'$	$: and'$	$: marry'$	$: manny'$

$$\frac{(S\backslash NP)/NP}{: \lambda x.\lambda y.and'(meet'xy)(marry'xy)}{<\Phi>}$$

$$\frac{S\backslash NP : \lambda y.and'(meet'manny'y)(marry'manny'y)}{S \ : \ and'(meet'manny'anna')(marry'manny'anna')}$$

The interpretation may give the impression that we have introduced rules of copying or deletion into the grammar. Any Logical Form of this kind must of course express the fact that the arguments appear in two predications. However, this is not the same as introducing *surface syntactic* operations of this kind. By operating in syntax entirely on types, we automatically ensure the equivalent of an "across-the-board" or "parallelism" condition on such deletions, excluding examples like the following without stipulation (see Williams 1978; Goodall 1987; Moltmann 1992):

(22) *Anna [met Manny]$_{S\backslash NP}$ and [married.]$_{(S\backslash NP)/NP}$

3.4 The Bluebird

In order to allow coordination of contiguous strings that do not constitute traditional constituents, CCG generalizes pure Categorial Grammar, to include certain further operations on functions related to Curry's combinators (Curry and Feys 1958). For example, functions may *compose*, as well as apply, under the following rule:

(23) *Forward composition* (>**B**)
        $X/Y \quad Y/Z \quad \Rightarrow_{\mathbf{B}} \quad X/Z$

The most important single property of combinatory rules like this is that they have an invariant type-driven semantics, as required by the Principles of Categorial and Combinatory Type Transparency, (11) and (15). The semantics of this rule is almost as simple as functional application. It is in fact functional *composition*. The combinator that composes two functions f and g is called **B** by Curry, and is the Bluebird in Smullyan's (1985) combinatory fable.[11] It can be defined by the following equivalence:

(24) $\mathbf{B}fgx \equiv f(gx)$

A convention that application associates to the left is again followed, so that the left-hand side is equivalent to $((\mathbf{B}f)g)x$. It follows that we can consider the application of $\mathbf{B}$ to f and g as producing a new function equivalent to abstracting on x in the above expression, thus:[12]

(25) $\mathbf{B}fg \equiv \lambda x f(gx)$

The new rule (23) is semantically a typed version of this combinator. Hence, the arrow in the rule is subscripted $\Rightarrow_\mathbf{B}$, and the application of the rule in derivations is indexed $>\mathbf{B}$.

Using this rule, sentences like *Anna met, and might marry, Manny* can be accepted syntactically as follows:

(26)

Anna	met	and	might	marry	Manny
NP	$(S\backslash NP)/NP$	$CONJ$	$(S\backslash NP)/VP$	VP/NP	NP

$$\underline{\qquad\qquad}_{>\mathbf{B}}$$
$$(S\backslash NP)/NP$$
$$\underline{\qquad\qquad\qquad}_{<\Phi>}$$
$$(S\backslash NP)/NP$$
$$\underline{\qquad\qquad\qquad\qquad}_{>}$$
$$S\backslash NP$$
$$\underline{\qquad\qquad\qquad}_{<}$$
$$S$$

In semantic terms the rule can be written in full as follows:[13]

(27) *Forward composition* $(>\mathbf{B})$
   $X/Y : f \quad Y/Z : g \quad \Rightarrow_\mathbf{B} \quad X/Z : \lambda x.f(gx)$

Derivation (26) then appears as follows:[14]

(28)

Anna	met	and	might	marry	Manny
NP	$(S\backslash NP)/NP$	$CONJ$	$(S\backslash NP)/VP$	VP/NP	NP
$: anna'$	$: meet'$	$: and'$	$: might'$	$: marry'$	$: manny'$

$$\underline{\qquad\qquad}_{>\mathbf{B}}$$
$$(S\backslash NP)/NP$$
$$: \lambda x.\lambda y.might'(marry'x)y$$
$$\underline{\qquad\qquad\qquad}_{<\Phi>}$$
$$(S\backslash NP)/NP$$
$$: \lambda x.\lambda y.and'(might'(marry'x)y)(meet'xy)$$
$$\underline{\qquad\qquad\qquad\qquad}_{>}$$
$$S\backslash NP$$
$$: \lambda y.and'(might'(marry'manny')y)(meet'manny'y)$$
$$\underline{\qquad\qquad\qquad}_{<}$$
$$S : and'(might'(marry'manny')anna')(meet'manny'anna')$$

The formalism immediately guarantees without further stipulation that this operation will compose the interpretations, as well as the syntactic functional types.[15]

The result of the composition has the same syntactic type $(S \backslash NP)/NP$ as a transitive verb, and readers may easily satisfy themselves that its translation is such that, if applied to an object and a subject, it is guaranteed to yield exactly the same predicate-argument structure for the sentence *Anna might marry Manny* as would have been obtained without the introduction of this rule.

Of course, the grammar continues correctly to exclude examples like the following, because only *adjacent* like categories can coordinate:

(29) *Anna [met Manny]$_{S \backslash NP}$, and [might marry]$_{(S \backslash NP)/NP}$.

A generalization of composition is required for sentences like the following:[16]

(30)
I	offered,	and	may	give,	a flower	to a policeman
$\overline{NP}$	$\overline{((S \backslash NP)/PP)/NP}$	$\overline{CONJ}$	$\overline{(S \backslash NP)/VP}$	$\overline{(VP/PP)/NP}$	$\overline{NP}$	$\overline{PP}$

$$\frac{}{((S \backslash NP)/PP)/NP} {>} \mathbf{B}^2$$

The generalization simply allows composition into certain functions of more than one argument. The requisite composition rule is stated as a schema over functions of varying numbers of arguments, as follows:

(31) *Generalized forward composition ($>\mathbf{B}^n$)*
$$X/Y : f \quad (Y/Z)/\$_1 : \ldots \lambda z.gz\ldots \quad \Rightarrow_{\mathbf{B}^n} \quad (X/Z)/\$_1 : \ldots \lambda z.f(gz\ldots)$$

The rule uses a notation introduced in a more general form in Ades and Steedman 1982 to schematize over verbs with different numbers of arguments, which I will call the "\$ convention." It can be defined recursively as follows:

(32) *The \$ convention*
For a category α, $\{\alpha\$\}$, (respectively, $\{\alpha/\$\}$, $\{\alpha\backslash\$\}$) denotes the set containing α and all functions (respectively, leftward functions, rightward functions) into a category in $\{\alpha\$\}$ (respectively, $\{\alpha/\$\}$, $\{\alpha\backslash\$\}$).

I will use unbracketed $\alpha\$$, $\alpha/\$$, and $\alpha\backslash\$$ to schematize over the members of the sets $\{\alpha/\$\}$, $\{\alpha/\$\}$, and $\{\alpha\backslash\$\}$ respectively, using subscripts as necessary to distinguish distinct schematizations. For example, $\{S/\$\}$ is the set $\{S, S/NP, (S/NP)/NP, \ldots\}$ and $S/\$$, $S/\$_1$, and so on, are schemata over that set. The use of $\$_1$ in rule (31) indicates that these are occurrences of the *same* schema.

$(Y/Z)/\$$ is thereby defined as a schema over functions yielding Y combining with n arguments to the right, the last or "innermost" of which is of type Z, where we can assume for English that $n \leq 3$. In essence this makes the rule equivalent to a finite set of rules specified for all the verbal categories of the English lexicon.[17] The semantics of each instance depends on the value of n and is one of the series of combinators called **B**, $\mathbf{B}^2, \mathbf{B}^3$. It is represented by Curry's own schematization of these composition combinators as $\mathbf{B}^n$, as the annotation on the arrow indicates.[18]

3.5 The Thrush

Combinatory grammars also include type-raising rules, which turn arguments into functions over functions-over-such-arguments. Since these rules allow arguments to become functions, they may by that token compose with *other* functions, and thereby take part in coordinations like *Anna married, and I detest, Manny*. Like composition, the type-raising rules have a simple and invariant semantics, as required by the Principle of Combinatory Type Transparency. The semantics corresponds to another of Curry's basic combinators, which he called $\mathbf{C}_*$ but which I will here call **T** for type-raising, following Rosser (1935) and to Smullyan (1985), in whose book it appears in the guise of the Thrush.[19] It is defined by the following equivalence:

(33) $\mathbf{T}xf \equiv fx$

It follows that **T** applied to an argument creates the following abstraction over the function:

(34) $\mathbf{T}x \equiv \lambda f\, fx$

For example, the following syntactic rule, indexed $>\mathbf{T}$, is needed for coordinate sentences like *Anna married, and I detest, Manny*:

(35) *Subject type-raising* ($>\mathbf{T}$)
    $NP \quad \Rightarrow_\mathbf{T} \quad S/(S\backslash NP)$

Derivations like the following are therefore allowed, and deliver appropriate interpretations:

(36)

Anna	married	and	I	detest	Manny
NP	$(S\backslash NP)/NP$	$CONJ$	NP	$(S\backslash NP)/NP$	NP

$$\begin{array}{c}
\cfrac{\cfrac{NP}{S/(S\backslash NP)}\ ^{>\mathbf{T}} \quad (S\backslash NP)/NP}{S/NP}\ ^{>\mathbf{B}} \qquad \cfrac{\cfrac{NP}{S/(S\backslash NP)}\ ^{>\mathbf{T}} \quad (S\backslash NP)/NP}{S/NP}\ ^{>\mathbf{B}}
\end{array}$$

with derivation continuing:

$$\cfrac{\quad S/NP \qquad CONJ \qquad S/NP \quad}{\cfrac{S/NP}{S}\ ^{>}}\ ^{<\Phi>}$$

Of course, the following example is excluded, because, once again, only *adjacent* categories can coordinate:

(37) *[Anna married]$_{S/NP}$ [Manny]$_{NP}$ and [I detest.]$_{S/NP}$

This example illustrates an important general property of CCGs: even in coordinate constructions, directionality and word order are projected consistently from the lexicon by the combinatory rules.

The combinatory rules of which (35) is an example can be captured in the following two rule-schemata, complete with their interpretation:

(38) *Type-raising*

   a. $X : a \;\; \Rightarrow_{\mathsf{T}} \;\; T/(T\backslash X) : \lambda f.f\, a$ $(>\mathsf{T})$

   where $T\backslash X$ is a parametrically licensed category for the language

   b. $X : a \;\; \Rightarrow_{\mathsf{T}} \;\; T\backslash(T/X) : \lambda f.f\, a$ $(<\mathsf{T})$

   where T/X is a parametrically licensed category for the language

T is a variable over categories, ranging over the result types of functions over X. (It is distinguished by roman typeface, because strictly speaking it is a variable of the metalanguage. Each type-raised category has its own unique variable of this kind, and when the corresponding variables need to be distinguished at the object level we will distinguish them as T_i, T_j, and so on. Otherwise, the unadorned metavariable T is used whenever possible, to reduce notational clutter.)

The restriction limits $T\backslash X$ and T/X to types that are permitted under the (informally defined) Principle of Categorial Type Transparency. Among other things, I will assume it prevents infinite recursion of type-raising (because the parametric specification of legal categories must presumably make reference to a fixed set of basic types). The restriction, which is discussed further in chapters 4 (10) and 7 (64), also means that, for example, in English, as opposed to German, $T\backslash X$ cannot be instantiated as $(S\backslash NP)\backslash NP$. At least in English, and possibly in all languages, we can assume that this restriction limits $T\backslash X$ to a finite set of categories,

The rules as stated also only turn an argument category such as *NP* into either a rightward-looking functor over leftward-looking functors over *NP*, or a leftward-looking functor over rightward-looking functors over *NP*. They are therefore "order-preserving" with respect to the linear order of function and argument as defined in the lexicon. This restriction is discussed further in chapter 8.

Derivation (36) then appears as follows:

(39)

Anna	married	and	I	detest	Manny
$T/(T\backslash NP_{3sf})$	$(S\backslash NP_{3s})/NP$	CONJ	$T/(T\backslash NP_{3s})$	$(S\backslash NP_{3s})/NP$	$T\backslash(T/NP_{3p})$
$: \lambda f.f\ anna$	$: \lambda x.\lambda y.marry'xy$	$: and'$	$: \lambda f.f\ i'$	$: \lambda x.\lambda y.detest'xy$	$: \lambda f.f\ manny'$

$$\frac{}{S/NP : \lambda x.marry'x\ anna'}{>}\mathbf{B} \qquad \frac{}{S/NP : \lambda x.detest'x\ i'}{>}\mathbf{B}$$

$$\frac{}{S/NP : \lambda x.and'(detest'x\ i')(marry'x\ anna')}{<\Phi>}$$

$$\frac{}{S : and'(detest'manny'i')(marry'manny'anna')}{<}$$

The composition of substrings like *Anna married* yields semantically interpreted functions that, if reduced with an object *Manny*, yield the same result that we would have obtained from the traditional derivation shown in (16), namely, $S : marry'manny'anna'$, thus guaranteeing that the coordination will deliver the correct predicate-argument structure, preserving traditional relations of dominance and c-command. This is an important observation, since as far as Surface Structure goes, we have now compromised both those traditional relations.

Type-raising was first used by Lewis and Montague as a semantic device to capture the type of generalized quantifiers. However, the present syntactic use is distinct, and the intuition behind cases like rule (35) is more reminiscent of the linguists' ancient notion of "nominative case."[20] In a language like Latin, nominative case determines an NP argument like *Balbus* to be something that must combine with a predicate, like *ambulat* or *murum ædificat*, to yield a proposition such as $walk'balbus'$ or $build'wall'balbus'$. In categorial terms, nominative case turns *Balbus* into a function whose interpretation is precisely $\mathbf{T}balbus'$—that is, $\lambda p.p\ balbus'$, a function over functions-over-subjects, or predicates. Similarly, accusative case turns NPs into functions over a different type of functions, functions over objects, with a semantics that is again defined in terms of $\mathbf{T}$. The restriction of the general form (38) of type-raising to categories that are arguments of verbs is in fact a natural consequence of its relation to a notion of case generalized to non-nominal arguments.

Thus, the only cause for surprise at this ingredient of CCG is that English behaves like a cased language without in general marking even nominal case morphologically.

Evidence that type-raising is as generally applicable to arguments as case is in other languages is available from the following observation, which originates with Dowty (1988) and a related analysis of Dutch coordination in Steedman 1985.[21] On the assumption that all English NPs can freely type-raise, together with that of a further backward rule of function composition corresponding to the mirror image of rule (23), the existence of the following construction in English is immediately predicted. (The variable T in the raised categories is here instantiated by the actual categories involved. The symbol *DTV* abbreviates $(VP/NP)/NP$, the category of a ditransitive verb, and *TV* abbreviates VP/NP, that of a transitive verb.)

(40) give   a teacher   an apple   and   a policeman   a flower
$$\frac{\underbrace{\frac{}{DTV}}\ \underbrace{\frac{}{TV\backslash DTV}}_{<T}\ \underbrace{\frac{}{VP\backslash TV}}_{<T}\quad \frac{}{CONJ}\quad \underbrace{\frac{}{TV\backslash DTV}}_{<T}\ \underbrace{\frac{}{VP\backslash TV}}_{<T}}{}$$

$$\frac{\qquad\qquad VP\backslash DTV \qquad\qquad\qquad\qquad\qquad VP\backslash DTV \qquad\qquad}{VP\backslash DTV}{}_{<\Phi>}$$

$$\frac{\qquad\qquad\qquad\qquad VP\backslash DTV \qquad\qquad\qquad\qquad}{VP}{}_{<}$$

This construction is often referred to as "left-peripheral deletion" or "nonconstituent coordination." However, neither name sits well with the present theory, according to which there is no such thing as deletion, and no such thing as coordination of nonconstituents. I have on occasion followed Schachter and Mordechai (1983), in referring to such sentences as "left node raised," but I will here refer to these constructions as "argument cluster coordination."

The important fact to note about this derivation is that the type-raised categories of the indirect and direct objects are simply those that are allowed by the order-preserving backward type-raising rule (38b), given the category of the English verb. The *only* rule of composition that will permit these categories and adjuncts to combine is the following mirror image of the earlier composition rule (23):

(41) *Backward composition* ($<$ **B**)
$$Y\backslash Z \quad X\backslash Y \quad \Rightarrow_{\textbf{B}} \quad X\backslash Z$$

The restriction of type-raising to raising over categorially type-transparent function types means that compositions like the following are excluded in English:

(42) $\dfrac{S/(S\backslash NP)\ \ T/(T\backslash NP)}{S/((S\backslash NP)\backslash NP)}{}_{>\textbf{B}}$

The combination would require the second type-raised category to be instantiated as as function $(S\backslash NP)\backslash NP$, which is not a parametrically licensed category of English.

The possibility of argument cluster coordinations like (40) is therefore predicted by exactly the same ingredients of the theory that were introduced to explain right node raising—namely, order-preserving type-raising and composition. The existence of argument cluster coordination in SVO languages, together with the related dependency of so-called forward and backward gapping on VSO and SOV word order discussed in chapter 7, is in fact one of the strongest pieces of confirmatory evidence in favor of the grammars that admit these two combinatory operations. It is with respect to these constructions that the theory should be contrasted with other closely related function-oriented and unification-based theories, such as those advanced by Joshi, Levy and Takahashi (1975), Bresnan (1982), Karttunen (1989), Uszkoreit (1986), Wittenburg (1986), Zeevat, Klein and Calder (1987), Pickering and Barry (1993), and Pollard and Sag (1994).

The earlier analogy between type-raising and case also suggests an option in the theory. Should we consider type-raising to be an operation of active syntax, like composition, or to be a rule of the lexicon or of morphology? In the latter case, of course, not only nominative NPs like *I*, but also uninflected NPs like *Anna*, and even articles like *the* would have to bear a number of additional categories such as $S/(S\backslash NP)$ and $(S/(S\backslash NP))/N$, and so on, like *Balbus* and *ille* in Latin.

I will return to this point in chapter 4. But one (case-marked) category related to type-raising that certainly must be lexically assigned is the category of the relative pronoun, for the addition of type-raising and composition to the theory of grammar provides everything needed in order to account for leftward extractions in relative clauses. I will assume as in Steedman (1996b) and other earlier work that relative pronouns bear the categories in (43) (Many North American dialects do not allow extraction of "internal" arguments, as in *a policeman whom$_i$ I gave t$_i$ a flower*, and *a man whom I bet t$_i$ \$10 that Ipswich would win the Cup*, and therefore only require the first two of these.)[22]

(43) a. *who/that/which* := $(N\backslash N)/(S\backslash NP)$

    b. *who(m)/that/which* := $(N\backslash N)/(S/NP)$

    c. *who(m)/that/which* := $((N\backslash N)/X)/((S/X)/NP)$

    d. *who(m)/that/which* := $(((N\backslash N)/X)/Y)/(((S/X)/Y)/NP)$

The second of these is a function from fragments like *Anna married* to noun modifiers. The following relative clause is therefore accepted:

(44) (the man)

$$
\begin{array}{ccc}
\text{that} & \text{Anna} & \text{married} \\
\hline
(N\backslash N)/(S/NP) & S/(S\backslash NP) & (S\backslash NP)/NP \\
& \overset{>\text{T}}{} & \\
\end{array}
$$

$$
\cfrac{(N\backslash N)/(S/NP) \quad \cfrac{S/(S\backslash NP) \quad (S\backslash NP)/NP}{S/NP} \;{>}\text{B}}{N\backslash N} \;{>}
$$

It should be obvious that the theory immediately predicts that leftward and rightward extraction will be unbounded, since embedded subjects can have the raised category, and composition can apply several times, as in the following cases:

(45) a. Anna married, but I doubt whether she can afford, Manny.

b. the man who Anna married, but I doubt whether she can afford

In offering a common origin for phenomena of coordinate structure and relativization, the present theory has some affinity with GPSG (Gazdar 1981; cf. Gazdar et al. 1985). It differs from GPSG and its descendants in doing so entirely on the basis of projection from the lexical subcategorization implicit in the category, as is required by the Principle of Lexical Head Government, rather than via a SLASH mechanism distinct from subcategorization.

The advantage of this tactic is that the generalization (31) of composition to functions with more than one argument allows multiple extractions combining rightward and leftward extraction (see (30)), which Maling and Zaenen (1978) noted present problems for GPSG:[23]

(46) a. the policeman to whom I offered, and may give, a flower

b. the policeman to whom I offered, and you may give, a flower

As in GPSG, leftward and rightward extraction are forced without further stipulation to obey the "across-the-board" condition of Williams (1978) on extraction out of coordinates, including the "same case" exceptions, because the grammar does not yield categories of like type for the conjuncts in examples like the following:

(47) a. *(A man who) [Anna married]$_{S/NP}$ but [I dislike him]$_S$

b. *(A man who) [Anna married]$_{S/NP}$ and [irritates me]$_{S\backslash NP}$

We will see in chapter 4 that many more of the notorious constraints on extraction that have been identified by the transformationalists follow from the combinatory theory in a similarly elegant way, without stipulation. But it is appropriate to briefly consider island constraints here, since they constitute a notorious limitation on the unboundedness of rightward and leftward movement that we have just captured.

The fact that adjuncts are in general islands might seem to be a natural consequence of the assumption that they are backward modifiers, as can be seen from the categories in the following unacceptable example:

(48) * a book [which]$_{(N\backslash N)/(S/NP)}$ [I will]$_{S/VP}$ [walk]$_{VP}$ [without reading]$_{(VP\backslash VP)/NP}$

However, this leaves unexplained the fact that they are equally strong islands in languages that have preverbal modifiers, such as Dutch and German. Even in English, it follows only on the assumption that verbs like *walk* cannot in general be type-raised over adjuncts, to become $VP/(VP\backslash VP)$. Since at least some VPs are arguments, the definition (38) allows them to acquire this category and compose into the adjunct, allowing the extraction.

The possibility of exceptions to the island status of NPs and adjuncts, and their equally notorious dependence on lexical content and such semantically related properties as definiteness and quantification, can be explained on the assumption that the results of composition are subject to a performance-related pragmatic condition requiring their interpretation to be a "natural kind" giving rise to useful inference in the knowledge base. Concepts like *painting a picture of something* and even *dying without finishing something* can reasonably be supposed to be natural kinds in this sense, but the concept of *walking without reading something* presumably is not, except possibly among the more morbid variety of linguist.[24]

(49) a.   the man who Mary painted a picture of
      b.   a symphony which he died without finishing
      c.   #a book which he walked without reading

Since type-raised categories are a little unreadable, it will often be convenient to abbreviate them as $NP^{\uparrow}$, $PP^{\uparrow}$, and so on, where the context makes it obvious which specific instance is involved.

3.6 The Starling

The theory requires one further type of combinatory rule. Example (50), which is of a kind first noticed by Ross (1967), and discussed by Engdahl (1983) and Taraldsen (1979) under the name of the "parasitic gap" construction, is of interest both because it involves the extracted item in more than one dependency and because one of those dependencies is upon an item inside an island which is not normally accessible to extraction, as shown in (51).

(50) articles which$_i$ I will file$_i$ without reading$_i$

(51) a.   articles which$_i$ I will *file$_i$* before reading your instructions
      b.   #articles which$_i$ I will read your instructions *before filing$_i$*

Parasitic gaps are therefore unlike the multiple dependencies that are permitted "across the board" in the coordinate structures considered earlier, where neither extraction is possible alone:

(52) a. *(articles) which I will file them and you will *forget*
     b. *(articles) which I will *file* and you will forget them

They are extensively discussed in categorial terms in Steedman 1996b and can be briefly summarized for present purposes as follows.

The lexical categories for (50) are as follows:

(53) (articles)   which   I will   file   without   reading
                $\overline{(N\backslash N)/(S/NP)}$ $\overline{S/VP}$ $\overline{VP/NP}$ $\overline{(VP\backslash VP)/VPing}$ $\overline{VPing/NP}$
                                                     $\underline{}$ >**B**
                                                                $(VP\backslash VP)/NP$

The combinatory rules introduced so far allow us to compose *without* and *reading*, but there the analysis blocks. Composition will not help, nor will the coordination rule (since the categories of *file* and *without reading* are not the same). The introduction of some further operation or operations appears to be inevitable.

The intuition that sequences like *file without reading* constitute a semantically coherent entity of some kind in this construction is very strong. The fact that such sequences can occur in isolation in instructions like *shake before opening* and that they can coordinate with transitive verbs in phrases like *file without reading and forget* suggests that they are predicates of some kind— more specifically, that they bear the category of a transitive verb, VP/NP.[25] Szabolcsi (1983, 1989) proposed a combinatory rule to combine the VP/NP and the $(VP\backslash VP)/NP$ to yield this VP/NP. The rule was a special case of the following one:

(54) *Backward crossed substitution* ($<$**S**$_\times$)
     $Y/Z \quad (X\backslash Y)/Z \quad \Rightarrow_\mathbf{S} \quad X/Z$

This rule, which unlike composition and type-raising is not a theorem of the Lambek calculus, is the *only* further rule type that will be needed. Since it provides a strong clue to the nature of the entire space of rules from which we are choosing instances, it is worth examining at some length.

The rule (54) (whose index $<$**S**$_\times$ will be explained later) allows derivations like the following:

(55) (articles)   which   I will   file   without   reading

$$\underline{\quad} \quad \underline{(N\backslash N)/(S/NP)} \quad \underline{S/VP} \quad \underline{VP/NP} \quad \underline{(VP\backslash VP)/VPing} \quad \underline{VPing/NP}$$

$$\frac{\qquad\qquad\qquad\qquad\qquad}{(VP\backslash VP)/NP} >\mathbf{B}$$

$$\frac{\qquad\qquad\qquad\qquad\qquad\qquad}{VP/NP} <\mathbf{S}_\times$$

$$\frac{\qquad\qquad\qquad\qquad\qquad\qquad\qquad}{S/NP} >\mathbf{B}$$

$$\frac{\qquad\qquad\qquad\qquad\qquad\qquad\qquad\qquad}{N\backslash N} >$$

As usual, the parallel rightward extraction is correctly predicted to be possible:[26]

(56) Mary will [copy]$_{VP/NP}$, and [file without reading]$_{VP/NP}$, any article longer than ten thousand words.

As usual, the rule has a simple and invariant semantics. It is a close relative of functional composition and corresponds to a third very basic combinator in Curry's system, called **S**. It is called here "functional substitution" and is the Starling in Smullyan's (1985) fable. It is defined by the following equivalence:

(57) $\mathbf{S}fgx \equiv fx(gx)$

It follows that the application of the combinator to two functions is equivalent to the following abstraction:

(58) $\mathbf{S}fg \equiv \lambda x\ fx(gx)$

Again we must assume that the variable Y in the substitution rule (54) is restricted to predicate categories like VP, in a way I will spell out in detail later.[27] Note that the rule will not allow arbitrary double dependencies, preventing the following from meaning "a man such that I showed him himself" without further stipulation:

(59) *(a man)   who(m)   I showed

$$\underline{\quad} \quad \underline{(N\backslash N)/(S/NP)} \quad \underline{(S/NP)/NP}$$

$$\frac{\qquad\qquad\qquad\qquad\qquad\qquad}{} *<\mathbf{S}_\times$$

We will see in chapter 4 that extraction from the first site alone, as in (51a), is still allowed, and extraction from the second site alone, as in example (51b), is still excluded.

Rule (54) is therefore written in full as follows:

(60) *Backward crossed substitution* ($<\mathbf{S}_\times$)

$\qquad Y/Z : g \quad (X\backslash Y)/Z : f \quad \Rightarrow_\mathbf{S} \quad X/Z : \lambda x.fx(gx)$

$\qquad$ where $Y = S\backslash\$$

The rule permits the following derivation for sentences with the structure of (56):[28]

(61)

Mary will	copy	and	file	without	reading	these articles
S/VP	VP/NP	$CONJ$	VP/NP	$(VP\backslash VP)/VPing$	$VPing/NP$	$NP^{\uparrow}$
$: \lambda p.will'$	$: copy'$	$: and'$	$: file'$	$: \lambda p.\lambda q.$	$: read'$	$: articles'$
$p\ mary'$				$without'pq$		

$$\frac{}{\begin{array}{c}(VP\backslash VP)/NP \\ : \lambda x.\lambda q.without'(read'x)q\end{array}}{>}\mathbf{B}$$

$$\frac{}{\begin{array}{c}VP/NP \\ : \lambda x.without'(read'x)(file'x)\end{array}}{<}\mathbf{S}_{\times}$$

$$\frac{}{\begin{array}{c}VP/NP \\ : \lambda x.and'(without'(read'x)(file'x))(copy'x)\end{array}}{<\Phi>}$$

$$\frac{}{\begin{array}{c}VP \\ : and'(without'(read'articles')(file'articles')) \\ (copy'articles')\end{array}}{<}$$

$$\frac{}{\begin{array}{c}S \\ : will'(and'(without'(read'articles')(file'articles')) \\ (copy'articles'))mary'\end{array}}{>}$$

The restriction on rule (60) uses the $ convention (32) to permit only categories of the form (tensed, untensed, participial, etc.) S, $S\backslash NP$, and so on, to unify with the variable X. It excludes the analogous derivation for the following phrase:

(62) *a [picture of]$_{N/NP}$ [by]$_{(N\backslash N)/NP}$ [Rembrandt]$_{NP}$

Further cases of parasitic gapping are discussed in Steedman 1996b.

Chapter 4

Explaining Constraints on Natural Grammar

*"A Starling," said Bravura, "is a bird **S** satisfying the following condition:*
S*xyz = xz(yz)."*
"Why is that bird so important?" asked Craig.
"You will find that out when you reach the Master Forest," replied Bravura.
Raymond Smullyan, *To Mock a Mockingbird*

One might ask at this point what degrees of freedom are implicit in the choice of the rules proposed in chapter 3 in order to account for the facts of English, and from what space of possible alternatives we have been selecting the rules that happen to suit us. For in choosing those rules for English, we necessarily commit ourselves to the claim that other possible human languages might exercise the same degrees of freedom in other ways. If descriptive generalizations give reason to believe that human languages do not in fact vary in the predicted ways, then we have some further explaining to do.[1]

4.1 Intrinsic Constraints Limiting the Set of Possible Rules

It is interesting in this regard to examine the rule of functional substitution introduced in section 3.6, for it happens to conspicuously exploit one degree of freedom that we might not necessarily have expected to need, but that will be claimed here to be widespread in natural grammars. It equally conspicuously *fails* to exploit a number of further degrees of freedom that do not appear to be needed in natural grammars, and that, if exploited, would weaken the theory considerably. Here is the rule again:

(1) *Backward crossed substitution* $(<\mathbf{S}_\times)$
   $$Y/Z \quad (X\backslash Y)/Z \quad \Rightarrow_\mathbf{S} \quad X/Z$$
   where $X = S\backslash\$$

It will be useful in contemplating such rules to define the term "principal function" to refer to that function among the inputs to the rule which determines the range of the result—which in present notation is always X. The first thing to notice is that rule (1) combines a principal function that is looking *leftward* for an argument of type Y with a *rightward*-looking function into that category Y.

The effect of allowing such "slash-crossing" rules in the theory is likely to be far-reaching, because if they are allowed for substitution rules, then slash-crossing versions of composition rules are predicted as well. Since such rules are not theorems of the Lambek calculus, which is weakly context-free (Pentus 1993), it is likely that they will induce greater expressive power than context-free grammar. Nevertheless, derivation (55) in chapter 3 suggests rule (1) must be included, for as Szabolcsi (1983) points out, there does not seem to be any question about the choice of categories for the verb group and the adverbial modifier.

The second thing to notice about rule (1) is that it appears to conform in every other respect to the directionality that is implicit in the categories that it combines. The principal function over Y in the rule does indeed combine with something *to its left*. And the directionality of the Z argument in its result is the same as the directionality of the Z arguments in its inputs. In fact, *all* of the combinatory rules exemplified above conform to the directionality of their inputs in these respects, and we can characterize them all by the following three principles:[2]

(2) *The Principle of Adjacency:*
Combinatory rules may only apply to finitely many phonologically realized and string-adjacent entities.

(3) *The Principle of Consistency:*
All syntactic combinatory rules must be consistent with the directionality of the principal function.

(4) *The Principle of Inheritance:*
If the category that results from the application of a combinatory rule is a function category, then the slash defining directionality for a given argument in that category will be the same as the one(s) defining directionality for the corresponding argument(s) in the input function(s).

The first of these principles simply embodies the assumption that some set of combinatory rules will do the job. That is, it says that rules can only apply to finitely many contiguous elements.[3]

I have suggested in earlier papers that these principles are universal, and that they delimit the space of possible combinatory rules in all human languages. The Principle of Consistency excludes the following kind of rule:

(5) $X\backslash Y \quad Y \quad \not\Rightarrow \quad X$

The Principle of Inheritance excludes rules like the following instance of composition:

(6) $X/Y \quad Y/Z \quad \not\Rightarrow \quad X\backslash Z$

It also prohibits analogues of the coordination rule (18) of chapter 3 such as the following:

(7) $X/Y \quad CONJ \quad X\backslash Y \quad \not\Rightarrow \quad X/Y$

Together the principles amount to a simple statement that *combinatory rules may not contradict the directionality specified in the lexicon*. In Steedman 1987, 1991c, I argued that this in turn reflects the fact that directionality is a property of *arguments*—in other words, that these principles are corollaries of the Principles of Categorial and Combinatory Type Transparency, whose close relation to the Projection Principle of government-binding theory was noted in chapter 3.[4] The argument is somewhat technical and is deferred until chapter 8.

The principles permit the following instances of the two syntactic combinatory rule types, in which the $ generalization under the convention (32) of the last chapter can apply to both sets of rules, replacing Y/Z and $Y\backslash Z$ by $(Y/Z)/\$$, $(Y\backslash Z)\$$, etc. It is again assumed that such schemata are limited to a bounded number of arguments:[5]

(8) *Functional composition*

a. $X/Y \quad Y/Z \quad \Rightarrow_{\textbf{B}} \quad X/Z$ $(>\textbf{B})$
b. $X/Y \quad Y\backslash Z \quad \Rightarrow_{\textbf{B}} \quad X\backslash Z$ $(>\textbf{B}_{\times})$
c. $Y\backslash Z \quad X\backslash Y \quad \Rightarrow_{\textbf{B}} \quad X\backslash Z$ $(<\textbf{B})$
d. $Y/Z \quad X\backslash Y \quad \Rightarrow_{\textbf{B}} \quad X/Z$ $(<\textbf{B}_{\times})$

(9) *Functional substitution*

a. $(X/Y)/Z \quad Y/Z \quad \Rightarrow_{\textbf{S}} \quad X/Z$ $(>\textbf{S})$
b. $(X/Y)\backslash Z \quad Y\backslash Z \quad \Rightarrow_{\textbf{S}} \quad X\backslash Z$ $(>\textbf{S}_{\times})$
c. $Y\backslash Z \quad (X\backslash Y)\backslash Z \quad \Rightarrow_{\textbf{S}} \quad X\backslash Z$ $(<\textbf{S})$
d. $Y/Z \quad (X\backslash Y)/Z \quad \Rightarrow_{\textbf{S}} \quad X/Z$ $(<\textbf{S}_{\times})$

Any language is free to restrict these rules to certain categories, or to entirely exclude a given rule type. But the above is the entire catalogue of types.

Some of these rules—namely, $>\textbf{B}_{\times}$ and $<\textbf{B}_{\times}$, as well as all four rules related to the combinator $\textbf{S}$—are *not* theorems of the Lambek calculus. Their inclusion represents a point of divergence between the present theory and those derived from the Lambek calculus (see van Benthem 1986, chap. 7; Moortgat

1988a, 1997; Hepple 1990; Morrill 1994. The significance of this departure is as follows.

The composition rules $>\mathbf{B}$ and $<\mathbf{B}$ are order-preserving, in the restricted sense that their addition to a pure categorial grammar that does not include higher-order functor categories—that is, ones that take functions as arguments—introduces only new derivations, not new word orders.[6]

On the other hand, the rules $>\mathbf{B}_\times$, $<\mathbf{B}_\times$, $>\mathbf{S}_\times$, and $<\mathbf{S}_\times$ that combine functions of different directionality have a *permutation* property. That is, they have the effect of reordering arguments, even for first-order grammar fragments. Indeed, Moortgat (1988a), following van Benthem (1986), shows that merely adding non-order-preserving composition to the axioms of the Lambek calculus causes the system to collapse, generating the permutation closure on the context-free language defined by the lexicon.

It does not of course follow that adding such rules to other kinds of categorial grammar engenders the same collapse. We will see in part III some results due to Weir (1988) and Rambow (1994a,b), which show that a CCG of the present form is not permutation-complete and is in fact under certain assumptions weakly equivalent to TAG (Joshi, Levy and Takahashi 1975).[7]

However, any grammar for a configurational language that includes any of the non-order-preserving rules may have to restrict their application to certain types. (We have already seen one such restriction, in the case of the restriction of the variable X in the backward crossed substitution rule (1) to categories such as *VP*.) I will continue to defer discussion of how these type restrictions are imposed until a later chapter.

The existence of extremely nonconfigurational languages suggests that much of the freedom allowed by the three principles via the non-order-preserving rules may be exploited in other languages (see van der Zee 1982; Steedman 1985; Zwarts 1986; Bouma 1985). In particular, we will see that the combinatory grammars of English and Dutch between them require *all* of the above composition rules, both order-preserving and non-order-preserving.

The way in which the principles restrict the rules of type-raising (whether considered as lexical rules or rules of active syntax) is less obvious. This is dealt with in detail in chapter 8. For present purposes we can assume that type-raising is restricted to the following pair of rules:[8]

(10) *The Order-preserving type-raising rules*

    a. $X : a \quad \Rightarrow_T \quad T/(T\backslash X) : \lambda f. f\, a$ $(>T)$

        where $T\backslash X$ is a parametrically licensed category for the language

    b. $X : a \quad \Rightarrow_T \quad T\backslash(T/X) : \lambda f. f\, a$ $(<T)$

        where T/X is a parametrically licensed category for the language

The restriction, which was discussed in chapter 3, only allows type-raising over categories that are permitted for the language under the Principle of Categorial Type Transparency, defined informally in Chapter 3. It embodies the idea that raised categories are limited to a fixed set of functions sanctioned by the $\bar{X}$ theory and language-specific word order parameters. Without some such restriction, type-raising can be used to create types that will allow any two arbitrary adjacent categories to compose, causing overgeneralization, as Houtman points out (1994, 63-85).[9]

However, the way in which type-raising and composition interact to allow the equivalent of unbounded extraction still has the potential to create some non-nominal objects with the same parametrically licensed category as a type-raised subject, as in the following partial derivation:

(11) a man whom   I   think   that   Dexter   likes

               $\overline{S/(S\backslash NP)}$ $\overline{(S\backslash NP)/S'}$ $\overline{S'/S}$ $\overline{S/(S\backslash NP)}$ $\overline{(S\backslash NP)/NP}$

                        $\overline{ S/S' }$ >**B**

                      $\overline{ S/S }$ >**B**

                            $\overline{ S/(S\backslash NP) }$ >**B**

Whether the formation of such constituents should be welcomed depends upon whether right node raising of embedded tensed VPs is permitted, as in (12a), in a manner parallel to subject coordination apart from the details of agreement, as in (12b):

(12) a. ?[You   doubt   that   Dexter,]$_{S/(S\backslash NP)}$ but   [I   wonder   whether   Warren,]$_{S/(S\backslash NP)}$ is a genius.

      b.   [Dexter]$_{S/(S\backslash NP)}$ and [Warren]$_{S/(S\backslash NP)}$ are geniuses.

The fact that such nonstandard constituents would have the same syntactic type as a type-raised subject threatens to allow illegal coordinations like the following (discussed in Steedman 1987, Wood 1988, and Henderson 1992, among other papers), which are much worse:[10]

(13) *[Dexter,]$_{S/(S\backslash NP)}$ and [I wonder whether Warren,]$_{S/(S\backslash NP)}$ is a genius/are geniuses.

It is important to realize that this problem is not restricted to CCG. Any theory that treats sentences like (12a) as arising from the equivalent of right node raising the finite VP will overgeneralize in the same way. Elsewhere, (Steedman 1990, 222–223), I have proposed as a technical solution to exclude altogether the formation of "pseudosubjects" like *you doubt that Dexter*, via a restriction on forward composition, excluding composition with Z bound to the tensed predicate category. However, the marginal acceptability of (12a), coupled with the sensitivity of agreement to the distinction between (12a) and (12b), suggests that this proposal cannot be maintained—see Houtman (1994) for further discussion.[11]

The property of all nominal type-raised arguments including subjects that distinguishes them from propositional pseudosubjects is that semantically they are generalized quantifiers and/or referential expressions, headed by nouns. Such expressions have a number of distinctive semantic properties, such as "conservativity" (Keenan and Faltz 1985, 16-17) that are not shared by entities like *You think (that) Dexter*, which are headed by verbs. Conservativity is the property of a function f which makes the following equation true:

(14) f(students) are vegetarians $\iff$ f(students) are both students and vegetarians. (Keenan and Faltz 1985, 17)

Clearly, this is the defining property of determiners like *every*. Equally clearly, it does not even begin to apply to "pseudodeterminers" like *I think that*, which do not generate referential expressions at all.

Henderson (1992) shows how to use syntactic indices to distinguish the two types of category. However, it is also possible to argue that the anomaly in (13) is purely semantic, a variety of zeugma or equivalently syllepsis, arising from the incompatibility of their interpretations, comparable to that in the following real-life example, which I owe to Richard Shillcock:

(15) This flour is suitable for vegetarians, freezing, pizza dough, and home bread-making machines.

The increased anomaly of the pseudosubject example (13) could then be presumed to stem from the fact that pseudosubjects just don't make very good conjuncts in the first place—cf. (12a.).

4.2 Linguistic Constraints on Unbounded Dependencies

Chapter 3 showed that the involvement of combinatory rules offers a common mechanism for canonical word order, leftward extraction constructions, and right-node-raising constructions, based on a single lexical entry for the verb, in keeping with the Principle of Head Categorial Uniqueness. The combinatory theory accordingly makes a broad prediction that *any argument that can take part in a leftward extraction will also permit the corresponding rightward movement*. Adjunct island constraints and subjacency constraints, which follow from the categories of adjuncts themselves and the type-raised status of arguments, should apply similarly to either permit or prevent both varieties.

This prediction of the theory is broadly true. However, there are a number of exceptions which are considered in detail in Steedman 1996b. Here I briefly examine just two of them—namely, asymmetries associated with subject extraction and with heavy NP shift constructions.

4.2.1 Subject Extraction Asymmetries

A number of further constraints on long-range dependencies that are asymmetrical with respect to subjects and objects, and that have been argued to stem from Chomsky's (1981) Empty Category Principle (ECP), arise in present terms because the categories reflect the different directionality of the subject and object arguments of the SVO verb. This ingredient of the theory captures the concept of "canonical government configuration" or "direction of government" (see Kayne 1983, 167–169; Pesetsky 1982; and Koster 1986, 19) directly in the lexicon and its projections under the combinatory rules, as Bach (1988, 29), among others, has pointed out. In present terms, this principle is an inevitable consequence of the Principle of Inheritance.

For example, Szabolcsi (1989), Bach (1988), and I (Steedman 1987, 1996b) discuss the way that the theory predicts the following familiar asymmetry in extractability of English subjects and objects, which has been attributed in other frameworks to various constraints on subject positions, including the ECP:

(16) a. (a man who(m)) [I think that]$_{S/S}$ [Dexter likes]$_{S/NP}$

  b. *(a man who(m)) [I think that]$_{S/S}$ [likes Dexter]$_{S\backslash NP}$

According to the present theory, this asymmetry is possible in languages like English that have an SVO lexicon because the crucial composition that would potentially permit subject extraction by combining S/S and $S\backslash NP$ requires a distinct *slash-crossing* instance of composition, $>\mathbf{B}_\times$:

(17) $X/Y \quad Y\backslash Z \quad \Rightarrow \quad X\backslash Z$

Although such rules are permitted (and therefore predicted) by the theory, we cannot by adding such a rule specify a language that is exactly like English except for allowing general subject extraction. As I pointed out in the Steedman (1996b), if we did so, the grammar would lack another distinguishing property of English, namely, its configurationality. Word order would collapse entirely, allowing "scrambling" examples like the following:

(18) *I Dexter [think (that) likes Warren]$_{(S\backslash NP)\backslash NP}$

Thus, the theory predicts that asymmetries in extractability for categories that are arguments of the same verb depend upon asymmetries in the directionality of those arguments.[12] The fact that this particular asymmetry tends to be characteristic of configurational SVO languages and constructions therefore follows without the stipulation of any subject-specific condition or ECP.

A number of further phenomena including binding possibilities for certain negative polarity items such as *personne* in French and *nessuno* in Italian have been ascribed to the operation of the ECP at the level of LF (Kayne 1983; Jaeggli 1981; Rizzi 1982). These phenomena are shown in Steedman 1996b to also follow from the way in which directionality is projected in a combinatory grammar in Surface Structures, without the stipulation of subject-specific conditions or the equivalent of the ECP. Some related restrictions on quantifier scope alternation are discussed in section 4.4 below.

In Steedman (1996b) I also discuss some obvious exceptions to the general nonextractability of subjects, including the fact that English subjects can be extracted from bare complements:

(19) a. a man who(m) I think likes Dexter
     b. a man who(m) I think Dexter likes

We cannot include such sentences by allowing a rule of crossed forward composition, no matter how restricted. Such a mechanism would immediately cause overgenerations parallel to (18). The only degree of freedom that remains within the present theory is to assume that this phenomenon arises in the lexicon. We must assume that, in addition to obvious categories like VP/S' and VP/S, verbs like *think* bear a special subject-extracting category. I will assume that this category takes the form (20).

(20) think := $(VP/NP_{+ANT,agr})/(S\backslash NP_{agr})$

In essence, this category embodies the GPSG analysis of extractable subjects proposed by Gazdar (1981) and Gazdar et al. (1985), as modified by Hepple (1990, 58) within a different categorial framework. (The advantage of the present proposal lies in the way most subject extraction is *excluded*.)[13] The *NP* argument of this category bears a feature $+ANT$ (mnemonic for the GB concept of "antecedent government"), which, like Hepple's corresponding "modality" $\triangle$, prevents this argument from being saturated by a normal lexically realized argument of any kind. The feature is in every respect like the agreement features discussed earlier. Indeed, the argument in question includes a number agreement feature *agr*, which works in the usual way via the relative clause category $(N_{agr} \backslash N_{agr})/(S/NP_{agr})$ to exclude the following examples:

(21) a. *a man who(m) I think like marmalade
     b. *some men who(m) I think likes marmalade

Category (20) is clearly an exception to the Principle of Head Categorial Uniqueness, and as such counts against the theory as a stipulation. However, to the extent that it is a stipulation confined to the small number of subjects that *do* extract, rather than a negative constraint on the majority of subjects that do not, this lexicalist account may yet compare favorably with Chomsky and Lasnik (1977) *That*-Trace Filter–based and Chomsky's (1981) ECP-based accounts, especially in view of the evidence from Maling and Zaenen (1978; see also e.g. Chung 1983 and Engdahl 1985) that the general prohibition against subject extraction is not universal, and appears to correlate with canonical word order, as the present theory would predict.

On the assumptions (a) that arguments other than topicalized ones and relative pronouns are marked as $-ANT$, (b) that the restriction of X in the order-preserving type-raising rules to argument types includes this property by definition, (c) that all normal arguments of verbs are $?ANT$—that is, compatible with either $+$ or $-$ on this feature—and (d) that the argument of the relative-pronoun category is $S/NP_{?ANT,agr}$, we capture the following asymmetry:

(22) a man who(m)$_{(N \backslash N)/(S/NP_{?ANT,3sm})}$ [I think likes marmalade]$_{S/NP_{+ANT,3sm}}$

(23) *[I think likes marmalade]$_{S/NP_{+ANT,3sm}}$ [this very heavy man.]$_{NP^{\uparrow}_{-ANT,3sm}}$

Further details of the Fixed-Subject Condition and the bare-complement exception are explored in Steedman 1996b, where the feature $\pm ANT$ is called $\pm LEX$. Further support for the proposal that bare complement subject extraction is mediated by a special-case lexical category like the one proposed here is to be found in the careful corpus-based developmental work of Stromswold (1995), who shows that children acquire long-distance object questions before they acquire long-distance subject questions. In fact, embedded subject questions are extremely rare in young children's speech. Stromswold finds them in only 1 out of 11 children's data, and then only from age 5.0 (Stromswold 1995, sec. 8.2), suggesting that this construction is among the very last details of English grammar to be mastered, a point to which I will return in chapter 10.

4.2.2 Other Extraction Asymmetries

Although the restricted possibilities for subject extraction in English do not involve the forward crossed composition rule, the grammar of English does appear to require the other non-order-preserving composition rule permitted by the Principles of Consistency and Inheritance. In order to accommodate heavy NP shift and related coordinations like the following, Moortgat (1988a) and I (Steedman 1987) have proposed rules of backward crossed composition:

(24) *Backward crossed composition (preliminary version)* ($<\mathbf{B}_\times$)

$$Y/Z \quad X\backslash Y \quad \Rightarrow_\mathbf{B} \quad X/Z$$

where $X, Y = S\$$

Like the backward crossed substitution rule (1), this non-order-preserving rule must be restricted to combinations where Y is a verbal category $S\$$ such as VP or VP_{ing}.[14]

(25)

I	shall	buy	today	and	cook	tomorrow	the mushrooms ...
$S/(S\backslash NP)$	$(S\backslash NP)/VP$	VP/NP	$VP\backslash VP$	$CONJ$	VP/NP	$VP\backslash VP$	NP

$$\underbrace{VP/NP}_{<\mathbf{B}_\times} \qquad \underbrace{VP/NP}_{<\mathbf{B}_\times}$$

$$\underbrace{VP/NP}_{<\Phi>}$$

$$\underbrace{VP}_{>}$$

I will come back to the reason why the "shifted argument" must be "heavy" in chapter 5.

The same rule correctly applies to type-raised arguments:

(26)

I will	give	to my sister	an engraving by Rembrandt
S/VP	$(VP/PP)/NP$	$VP\backslash(VP/PP)$	NP

$$\underbrace{VP/NP}_{<\mathbf{B}_\times}$$

$$\underbrace{S/NP}_{>\mathbf{B}}$$

$$\underbrace{S}_{>}$$

The rule also allows leftward extraction of "nonperipheral" arguments, including examples like the following, relevant to the earlier discussion of parasitic gaps:

(27) (articles)

which	I will	file	tomorrow
$(N\backslash N)/(S/NP)$	S/VP	VP/NP	$VP\backslash VP$

$$\frac{\quad\quad\quad}{VP/NP}<\mathbf{B}_\times$$

$$\frac{\quad\quad\quad\quad\quad}{S/NP}>\mathbf{B}$$

$$\frac{\quad\quad\quad\quad\quad\quad\quad}{N\backslash N}>$$

Identical compositions are crucial in the derivation of other relativizations of nonperipheral elements including the following:

(28) a. an engraving which I will *buy today and sell tomorrow*
   b. an engraving which I will *show to him and give to you*
   c. a man who(m) I will *show a painting and give a flower*

However, the last of these shows that the general rule (24) must be replaced by a number of more specific instances, since examples like the following show that nominal ditransitives are an exception to the general rule that whatever can leftward extract can also rightward extract:

(29) *I will give a flower this very heavy policeman.

This asymmetry is related to the observation of Ross (1967) that Heavy NP shift, unlike relativization and right node raising, also cannot induce preposition stranding:

(30) a. the city which I will travel to today and return from tomorrow
   b. I will travel to and return from the beautiful city of Dublin.
   c. *I will travel to tomorrow the beautiful city of York.

As a technical device to capture these asymmetries, we can replace the backward crossed composition rule (24) by two more specific instantiations. The first allows both leftward extraction (28a,b) and heavy shift (25) and (26) of any argument not explicitly marked as forbidden to shift by a negative value of a feature *SHIFT*, with respect to which all normal arguments are assumed to be unspecified:[15]

(31) *Backward crossed composition I* ($<\mathbf{B}_\times$)
   $$Y/Z_{+SHIFT} \quad X\backslash Y \quad \Rightarrow_\mathbf{B} \quad X/Z_{+SHIFT}$$
   where $X, Y = S\$$

We may then assume that the dative NP argument of ditransitive verbs and the complement of prepositions are marked as $-SHIFT$:

(32) a. give := $(VP/NP)/NP_{-SHIFT}$

    b. to := PP/NP_{-SHIFT}

The second instance of the heavy-shifting backward crossed composition rule then allows such $-SHIFT$ nonperipheral arguments to leftward-extract, but not to rightward-extract, by marking them for antecedent government only:[16]

(33) *Backward crossed composition II* ($<\mathbf{B}_{\times}$)

    $Y/Z_{-SHIFT,+ANT}$ $X\backslash Y$ $\Rightarrow_{\mathbf{B}}$ $X/Z_{-SHIFT,+ANT}$

    where $X, Y = S\$$

The rule will therefore allow leftward-extraction in examples like (28c), while excluding (29). I will return to this restriction in chapter 6, where it will be apparent that a related restriction applies to Dutch (but not German) main-clause order.

As Ades and I note (Ades and Steedman 1982), the crossed composition mechanism automatically excludes extraction out of the shifted-over PP in examples like (26), even when the PP is subcategorized for, to exclude sentences like the following, which violate the Clause Non-Final Incomplete Constituent Constraint proposed by Kuno (1973):

(34) *a woman who(m) I will [give]$_{(VP/PP)/NP}$ [to]$_{PP/NP}$ [an engraving by Rembrandt]$_{NP}$

The crossed composition mechanism also automatically excludes heavy shift of subjects in (35a). However, it is only the stipulative restriction of the backward crossed rule to composition into verbs that prevents heavy shift out of subjects (35b):[17]

(35) a. *[Smiled]$_{S\backslash NP}$ [the man in the grey flannel suit.]$_{S/(S\backslash NP)}$

    b. *[Every friend of]$_{NP/NP}$ [smiled]$_{S\backslash NP}$ [the man in the grey flannel suit]$_{NP}$

4.3 Linguistic Constraints on Bounded Dependencies

It will be clear from the discussion in the previous sections that combinatory grammars embody an unusual view of Surface Structure, according to which strings like *Anna married* are, quite simply, surface constituents. We will see that this view directly generalizes to cover all of the "fragments" that arise under coordination and related constructions, including *a policeman a flower*, the serial verb clusters that are characteristic of Germanic "verb raising," and the strings that can be isolated as intonational phrases.

According to this view, Surface Structure is also more ambiguous than has previously been realized, for such strings must also be possible constituents of noncoordinate sentences like *Anna married Manny* and *Give a policeman a flower*, as well. It follows that such sentences must have several Surface Structures, corresponding to different sequences of composition, type-raising, and application.

For example, the derivation in (37) is allowed for the former sentence, in addition to the traditional derivation in (7) of chapter 3, and repeated here as (36).

(36)
$$
\frac{\begin{array}{ccc}
\underline{\text{Anna}} & \underline{\text{married}} & \underline{\text{Manny}} \\
NP & (S\backslash NP)/NP & NP \\
: anna' & : \lambda x.\lambda y.marry'xy & : manny' \\
\hline
\multicolumn{1}{c}{\dfrac{T/(T\backslash NP)}{: \lambda p.p\ anna'}} & & \dfrac{T\backslash(T/NP)}{: \lambda q.q\ manny'}
\end{array}}{}
$$

$$\frac{}{T/(T\backslash NP)}{}^{>T} \qquad \frac{}{T\backslash(T/NP)}{}^{<T}$$

$$\frac{S\backslash NP}{: \lambda y.marry'\ manny'\ y}{}^{<}$$

$$\frac{S : marry'\ manny'\ anna'}{}{}^{>}$$

(37)
$$
\begin{array}{ccc}
\underline{\text{Anna}} & \underline{\text{married}} & \underline{\text{Manny}} \\
NP & (S\backslash NP)/NP & NP \\
: anna' & : \lambda x.\lambda y.marry'xy & : manny' \\
\hline
\dfrac{T/(T\backslash NP)}{: \lambda p.p\ anna'}{}^{>T} & & \dfrac{T\backslash(T/NP)}{: \lambda q.q\ manny'}{}^{<T}
\end{array}
$$

$$\frac{S/NP}{: \lambda x.marry'x\ anna'}{}^{>B}$$

$$\frac{S : marry'\ manny'\ anna'}{}{}^{<}$$

The most important property of such families of alternative derivations is that they form semantic equivalence classes, for as the derivations show, the semantics of the combinatory rules guarantees that all such derivations will deliver an interpretation determining the same function-argument relations.[18] Indeed, there is a close relation between the canonical interpretation structures that they deliver according to the theory sketched above, and traditional notions of constituent structure.

One could in fact argue that the dominance of the traditional notion of Surface Structure is an instance of an error that Chomsky (1957, chap. 7) warned against, namely, that of depending upon ill-defined intuitions about meaning (with which most traditional tests for constituency other than susceptibility to coordination are confounded), rather than empirical data concerning syntactic form.

In CCG, the work that is done in GB by *wh*-trace, mediated or constrained by indexing, subject to structural relations such as c-command, is done without empty categories. CCG uses only the same lexical mechanism that binds arguments in situ to verbs, projected from lexical categories by the combinatory rules that mediate long-range dependencies.[19] This amounts to saying that the present theory eschews the distinction between "antecedent" government and "head" or "θ" government. There is only lexical head government, as the Principle of Head Categorial Uniqueness requires. All syntactic dependencies are projections of that, without mediation by empty categories or Ā structural positions. The consequences of this move for capturing *wh*-constructions and the constraints upon them is investigated in more detail in Steedman 1996b.

However, it follows that the entire range of grammatical phenomena that depend on structural relations like c-command, which have traditionally been dealt with in Surface Structure, must in a combinatory grammar be handled at the level of interpretation or predicate-argument structure.

4.3.1 Binding and Control

This important class of phenomena includes most of the class of constructions that were identified earlier as "bounded," importantly including the systems of (anaphor) binding and control. This proposal, including certain interactions of binding theory and *wh*-constructions, is also investigated in further detail in Steedman 1996b.

For example, the following category for "equi" verbs such as *tries* is proposed there:

(38) $(S \backslash NP_{3s})/(S_{to-inf} \backslash NP_{3s}) : \lambda p.\lambda y.try' \, (p \, (ana' \, y)) \, y$

This is essentially identical to the standard GB analysis, with two slight departures. First, the responsibility for determining dependencies that have sometimes been accounted for in terms of bounded movement has been relegated to the lexicon and to the relation between syntactic category and predicate-argument structure. Second, rather than merely using a constant such as *PRO* to represent the controlled argument at Surface Structure or S-Structure, leaving to the binding theory or an autonomous module of control theory the task of establishing the antecedent, the present theory makes the lexical entry for the control verb do part of that work, by making (the interpretation of) its complement's subject a "pro-term" ana' y resembling an anaphor bound to the (interpretation y of the) subject of the control verb.[20] On the assumption that the infinitival verb *like* has the obvious category (39a), and that the complementizer *to* has the trivial category (39b), which can compose with either infinitival, the category (38) will yield the results in (40):

(39) a. $like := (S_{inf}\backslash NP_{agr})/NP : \lambda x.\lambda y.like'xy$

    b. $to := (S_{to-inf}\backslash NP_{agr})/(S_{inf}\backslash NP_{agr}) : \lambda x.x$

(40)

Dexter	tries	to like	Warren
$\overline{NP_{3sm}}$	$\overline{(S\backslash NP_{3s})/(S_{to-inf}\backslash NP_{3s})}$	$\overline{(S_{to-inf}\backslash NP_{agr2})/NP}$	$\overline{NP}$
$: dexter'$	$: \lambda p.\lambda y.try'\,(p\,(ana'y))y$	$: \lambda x.\lambda y.like'xy$	$: warren'$

$$\frac{S_{to-inf}\backslash NP_{agr2} : \lambda y.like'warren'y}{} {}^{>}$$

$$\frac{S\backslash NP_{3s} : \lambda y.try'\,(like'warren'(ana'y))y}{} {}^{>}$$

$$\frac{S : try'\,(like'warren'(ana'dexter'))dexter'}{} {}^{<}$$

An appropriate binding theory can then be defined in terms of a relation of command over predicate-argument structures (say, as in Steedman 1996b).

A similar analysis can be applied to object control. The following is the full category of the verb *persuades* $((S\backslash NP)/(S\backslash NP))/NP$, reflecting the assumption that predicate-argument structures observe the obliqueness hierarchy:

(41) $persuades := ((S\backslash NP_{agr_2})/(S_{to-inf}\backslash NP_{agr_1}))/NP_{agr_1}$
        $: \lambda x.\lambda p.\lambda y.persuade'(p\,(ana'x))\,x\,y$

The category (41) again embodies a "wrap" analysis of object control verbs, akin to that proposed by Bach (1979, 1980), Dowty (1982), Szabolcsi (1989), Jacobson (1990), and Hepple (1990), again at the level of lexical predicate-argument structure or Logical Form rather than syntactic or phrasal derivation. That is, the command relation between the interpretation of the object NP and the predicate-argument is *reversed* with respect to the derivation. This represents a minor departure from the Montagovian mainstream, in which such use of Logical Form is frowned upon. However, the reason for embodying this widespread assumption in the lexicon rather than in active WRAP rules in syntax is implicit in the analysis of coordinations like (40) of chapter 3, and I will return to it frequently below.

When applied to an object like *Martha* and an infinitival like *to go*, the category (41) gives rise to derivations like the following:

(42)   George   persuades   Martha   to go

$\underline{NP_{3sm}}$ $\underline{((S\backslash NP_{3s})/(S_{to-inf}\backslash NP_{agr}))/NP_{agr}}$ $\underline{NP_{3sf}}$ $\underline{S_{to-inf}\backslash NP_{agr2}}$
$: george'$ $: \lambda x.\lambda p.\lambda y.persuade'(p\,(ana'x))xy$ $: martha'$ $: \lambda x.go'x$

$$\dfrac{(S\backslash NP_{3s})/(S_{to-inf}\backslash NP_{3sf})}{: \lambda p.\lambda y.persuade'(p\,(ana'martha'))martha'y} >$$

$$\dfrac{S\backslash NP_{3s}}{: \lambda y.persuade'(go'(ana'martha'))martha'y} >$$

$$\dfrac{}{S: persuade'(go'(ana'martha'))martha'george'} >$$

The predicate-argument structure of the category (41) embodies a very widespread generalization about categories (see the discussion of VSO and VOS languages in Keenan 1988, according to which rightward functor categories like VSO verbs, which obey the very strong tendency of the languages of the world to reflect obliqueness ordering in SO string order, must wrap—that is, reverse in the predicate-argument structure the command relations implicit in the syntactic category itself). This generalization can also be observed in the ditransitives discussed at the end of chapter 2, to which I will return in chapter 7:

(43) showed := $((S\backslash NP)/NP)/NP : \lambda x.\lambda y.\lambda z.show'yxz$

Following Clark (1997), auxiliaries can be handled as "raising" verbs with the following kind of category:[21]

(44) might := $(S\backslash NP)/VP : \lambda p.\lambda x.might'(p\,x)$

The following kind of derivation results:

(45)   Anna   might   marry   Manny

$\underline{S/(S\backslash NP)}$ $\underline{(S\backslash NP)/VP}$ $\underline{VP/NP}$ $\underline{S\backslash(S\backslash NP)}$
$: \lambda p.p\,anna'$ $: \lambda p.\lambda x.might'(p\,x)$ $: marry'$ $: \lambda p.p\,manny'$

$$\dfrac{S/VP : \lambda p.might'(p\,anna')}{}\quad >\mathbf{B}$$

$$\dfrac{S/NP : \lambda x.might'(marry'x\,anna')}{}\quad >\mathbf{B}$$

$$\dfrac{}{S : might'(marry'manny'anna')} >$$

To handle binding, raising, and control lexically via a level of interpretation or predicate-argument structure is not especially controversial. A similar move has been proposed within a Montague Grammar framework by Bach and Partee (1980), within LFG by Bresnan (1982), within GB by Lasnik and Saito (1984), and within HPSG by Pollard and Sag (1992). A similar position seems to be implicit in Hale and Keyser 1993 and Brody 1995, which suggest that much of the apparatus in GB and the Minimalist Program amounts to a theory of the

CCG lexicon—a component of the present theory that has been conspicuous by its absence in the presentation so far.

However, within this broad consensus concerning the domain of binding and/or control, two camps should be distinguished. In the first are the Montague Grammarians and the proponents of virtually all varieties of Flexible Categorial Grammar since Bach (1976), including Shaumyan (1977), Dowty (1979), Jacobson (1987), Szabolcsi (1989), Moortgat (1988b), Hepple (1990), Morrill (1994), and many others. These authors deny the existence of any autonomous level of semantic representation such as predicate-argument structure intervening between syntactic derivation and the model theory. That is to say, although they may use a Logical Form for notational transparency, they eschew the exploitation of any structural property of such notations, such as the analogue of GB c-command. There is a strong affinity between these researchers and the model-theoretic tradition in Mathematical Logic.

The members of the other camp, which includes most researchers in LFG, GB, G/HPSG, and the theory proposed here, as well as virtually all computational linguists, define an autonomous structural level of predicate-argument structure or Logical Form, and define the grammar of binding in terms of structural dominance and command, making an intrinsic use of predicate-argument structure. These researchers resemble in spirit the proof-theoretic tradition in Mathematical Logic.

The analogy with the proof-theory/model-theory duality in logic suggests that this difference may turn out not to be an empirically testable one. It is likely to be the case that anything that can be captured one way can be captured the other way, and vice versa. The question will probably be resolved on the basis of the simplicity of the rival theories. Since CCG is principally concerned with the unbounded constructions, it diverges from many of its categorial relatives in adopting an explicitly predicate-argument-structural account of binding, control, and the other bounded phenomena, simply because it seems to make life easier for the linguistically oriented reader.

This should not be taken as constituting a serious disagreement with these other categorial approaches. The very fact that these phenomena are all bounded by the local domain of the verb means that the mapping from linear order to obliqueness order is essentially trivial.

4.3.2 Adjunct-Argument Asymmetry

English prepositions heading adverbial PPs that one would normally think of as adjuncts rather than arguments can be "stranded" by relativization, as in the following example:

(46) the painting that I folded the rug over

One would not normally think of *fold* as subcategorizing for such a prepositional phrase. However, reflexive binding and the impossibility of parasitic
gapping makes it clear that the PP argument is more oblique than—that is, is
c-commanded at LF by—the object:[22]

(47) a.   I folded the rug over itself.
      b.   *the rug which I folded over

In categorial terms, there is really only one way to permit preposition stranding into such adjunct PPs while still accounting for the above facts. Any tactic
that makes the PP a rightmost argument—such as type-raising the VP over the
adjunct category, or assigning a particle-like higher-order category over VPs
to the preposition—will fail to yield the scope or c-command relations that
the binding phenomena require, unless it is accompanied by nontrivial manip-
ulations of Logical Form, in violation of the Principle of Combinatory Type
Transparency.

    Instead we must assume that the lexical categories for the relevant class of
verbs already allow for optional additional rightmost adverbial categories as
arguments, and that like all rightward arguments, they wrap at Logical Form,
so that their interpretations are more oblique than the obligatory arguments.
(Although I will not go into the question of exactly what Logical Form is involved, I assume that it amounts to a form of control—see (42). Hence, (47b)
is illicit for the same reason as *Who did you persuade to vote for?*.)

    I will largely ignore such optional adjunct-arguments in what follows, but
occasionally it will be necessary to recall that they and certain other adjuncts
often behave like arguments, rather than true adjuncts.

4.4 Quantification in CCG

Another phenomenon that is naturally analyzed in terms of relations of command at the level of Logical Form is quantifier scope.

    It is standard to assume that the ambiguity of sentences like (48) is to be
accounted for by assigning two Logical Forms which differ in the scopes assigned to these quantifiers, as in (49a,b):

(48) Every boy admires some saxophonist.

(49) a. $\forall x.boy'x \rightarrow \exists y.saxophonist'y \wedge admires'yx$

    b. $\exists y.saxophonist'y \wedge \forall x.boy'x \rightarrow admires'yx$

The question then arises of how the grammar can assign all and only the correct interpretations to sentences with multiple quantifiers.

This process has on occasion been explained in terms of "quantifier movement" or essentially equivalent computational operations of "quantifying in" or "storage" at the level of Logical Form. However, such accounts present a problem for monostratal and monotonic theories of grammar like CCG that try to do away with movement or the equivalent in syntax. Having eliminated nonmonotonic operations from the syntax, to have to restore them at the level of Logical Form would be dismaying, given the strong assumptions of transparency between syntax and semantics from which this and other monotonic theories begin. Given the assumptions of syntactic/semantic transparency and monotonicity that are usual in the Frege-Montague tradition, it is tempting to try to use nothing but the derivational combinatorics of surface grammar to deliver all the readings for ambiguous sentences like (48). Two ways to restore monotonicity have been proposed, namely: enriching the notion of derivation via type-changing operations; or enriching the lexicon and the semantic ontology.

It is standard in the Frege-Montague tradition to begin by translating expressions like *every boy* and *some saxophonist* into "generalized quantifiers"—in effect exchanging the roles of arguments like NPs and functors like verbs by type-raising the former (Lewis 1970; Montague 1973; Barwise and Cooper 1981; see Partee, ter Meulen and Wall 1990, 359 for a review):

In terms of the notation and assumptions of CCG, one way to incorporate generalized quantifiers into the semantics of CG determiners is to transfer type-raising to the lexicon, assigning the following categories to determiners like *every* and *some*, making them functions from nouns to type-raised NPs, where the latter are simply the syntactic types corresponding to a generalized quantifier:

(50) every := $(T/(T\backslash NP))/N : \lambda p.\lambda q.\forall x.px \rightarrow qx$

    every := $(T\backslash(T/NP))/N : \lambda p.\lambda q.\forall x.px \rightarrow qx$

(51) some := $(T/(T\backslash NP))/N : \lambda p.\lambda q.\exists x.px \wedge qx$

    some := $(T\backslash(T/NP))/N : \lambda p.\lambda q.\exists x.px \wedge qx$

Given the categories in (50) and (51), the alternative derivations that CCG permits will deliver the two distinct Logical Forms shown in (49), entirely monotonically and without involving structure-changing operations, as shown in (52) and (53).

(52)

Every	boy	admires	some	saxophonist
$(T/(T\backslash NP))/N$	N	$(S\backslash NP)/NP$	$(T'\backslash(T'/NP))/N$	N
$: \lambda p.\lambda q.\forall y.py \to qy$	$: \lambda x.boy'x$	$: \lambda x.\lambda y.admires'xy$	$\lambda p.\lambda q.\exists x.px \wedge qx$	$: \lambda x.saxophonist'x$

$$\frac{T/(T\backslash NP)}{: \lambda q.\forall y.boy'y \to qy} >$$

$$\frac{T'\backslash(T'/NP)}{: \lambda q.\exists x.saxophonist'x \wedge qx} >$$

$$\frac{S\backslash NP}{: \lambda y.\exists x.saxophonist'x \wedge admires'xy} <$$

$$\frac{S : \forall y.boy'y \to \exists x.saxophonist'x \wedge admires'xy}{} >$$

(53)

Every	boy	admires	some	saxophonist
$(T/(T\backslash NP))/N$	N	$(S\backslash NP)/NP$	$(T'\backslash(T'/NP))/N$	N
$: \lambda p.\lambda q.\forall y.py \to qy$	$: \lambda x.boy'x$	$: \lambda x.\lambda y.admires'xy$	$\lambda p.\lambda q.\exists x.px \wedge qx$	$: \lambda x.saxophonist'x$

$$\frac{T/(T\backslash NP)}{: \lambda q.\forall y.boy'y \to qy} >$$

$$\frac{T'\backslash(T'/NP)}{: \lambda q.\exists x.saxophonist'x \wedge qx} >$$

$$\frac{S/NP}{: \lambda x.\forall y.boy'y \to admires'xy} > B$$

$$\frac{S : \exists x.saxophonist'x \wedge \forall y.boy'y \to admires'xy}{} <$$

The idea that semantic quantifier scope is limited by syntactic derivational scope in this way has some very attractive features. For example, it immediately explains why scope alternation is both unbounded as in (54a) and sensitive to island constraints, as in (54b).

(54) a. At least one witness said that the accused knew every victim.

b. Some witness who saw every plaintiff denounced him.

However, linking derivation and scope as simply and directly as this makes the obviously false prediction that in sentences where there is no ambiguity of CCG derivation there should be no scope ambiguity. In particular, object topicalization and object right node raising are derivationally unambiguous in the relevant respects, and force the displaced object to command the rest of the sentence in derivational terms. So they should only have the wide scope reading of the object quantifier. This is not the case:

(55) a. Some saxophonist, every boy admires.

b. Every boy admires, and every girl detests, some saxophonist.

Both sentences have a narrow scope reading in which every individual has some attitude toward some saxophonist, but not necessarily the same saxophonist. This observation appears to imply that even the relatively free notion of derivation provided by CCG is still too restricted to explain all ambiguities arising from multiple quantifiers.

Nevertheless, (55b) has a further property, first observed by Geach (1972), that makes it seem as though scope phenomena are strongly restricted by surface grammar. Although the sentence has one reading where all of the boys and girls have strong feelings toward the same saxophonist—say, John Coltrane— and the reading already noted, according to which their feelings are all directed at possibly different saxophonists, it does not have a reading where the saxophonist has wide scope with respect to *every boy*, but narrow scope with respect to *every girl*—that is, where the boys all admire John Coltrane, but the girls all detest possibly different saxophonists. There does not even seem to be a reading involving separate wide scope saxophonists respectively taking scope over boys and girls—for example, where the boys all admire Coltrane and the girls all detest Lester Young.

These observations are very hard to reconcile with semantic theories that invoke powerful mechanisms like abstraction or Quantifying In and its relatives, (Montague 1973; Cooper 1983; Hobbs and Shieber 1987; Pereira 1990; Keller 1988), or quantifier movement. (Carden 1973; May 1985). For example, if quantifiers are mapped from syntactic levels to canonical subject, object (etc.) position at predicate-argument structure in both conjuncts in (55b) and then migrate up the Logical Form to take either wide or narrow scope, it is not clear why *some saxophonist* should have to take the *same* scope in both conjuncts. The same applies if quantifiers are generated in situ, then lowered to their surface position. Such observations might be countered by the invocation of a "parallelism condition" on coordinate sentences, of the general kind discussed by Fox (1995). But such rules are of very expressively powerful "transderivational" kind that one would otherwise wish to avoid. (See Jacobson (1998) for discussion and arguments against transderivational parallelism.)

Related observations led Keenan and Faltz (1978, 1985), Partee and Rooth (1983), Jacobson (1992a), Hendriks (1993), Oehrle (1994), and Winter (1995, to appear), among others, to propose considerably more general use of type-changing operations than are required in CCG, engendering considerably more flexibility in derivation than seems to be required by the purely syntactic phenomena that have motivated CCG up till now.[23]

Although the tactic of including such order-preserving type-changing operations in the grammar remains a valid alternative for a monotonic treatment of scope alternation in CCG and related forms of categorial grammar, there is no doubt that it complicates the theory considerably. The type-changing operations necessarily engender infinite sets of categories for each word, requiring heuristics based on (partial) orderings on the operations concerned, and raising questions about completeness and practical parsability. Some of these questions have been addressed by Hendriks and others, but the result has been to dramatically raise the ratio of mathematical proofs to sentences analyzed.

It seems worth exploring an alternative response to these observations concerning interactions of Surface Structure and scope-taking. The present section follows Woods (1975), VanLehn (1978), Webber (1978), Fodor (1982), Fodor and Sag (1982), and Park (1995, 1996) in explaining scope ambiguities in terms of a distinction between true generalized quantifiers and other purely referential categories. For example, in order to capture the narrow scope object reading for Geach's right-node-raised sentence (55b), in whose CCG derivation the object must command everything else, the present proposal follows Park in assuming that the narrow scope reading arises from a nonquantificational interpretation of *some saxophonist*, one that gives rise to a reading indistinguishable from a narrow scope reading when it ends up in the object position at the level of Logical Form. The obvious candidate for such a nonquantificational interpretation is some kind of referring expression.

The claim that many NPs that have been assumed to have a single generalized quantifier interpretation are in fact purely referential is not new. Recent literature on the semantics of natural quantifiers has departed considerably from the earlier tendency for semanticists to reduce all semantic distinctions of nominal meaning such as *de dicto/de re*, reference/attribution, etc. to distinctions in scope of traditional quantifiers. There is widespread recognition that many such distinctions arise instead from a rich ontology of different types of (collective, distributive, intensional, group-denoting, arbitrary, etc.) individual to which nominal expressions refer. (See for example Webber 1978, Barwise and Perry 1980, Fodor and Sag 1982, Fodor 1982, Hobbs 1983, 1985, Fine 1985, and papers in the recent collection edited by Szabolcsi 1997.)

One example of such nontraditional entity types (if an idea that apparently originates with Aristotle can be called nontraditional) is the notion of "arbitrary objects" (Fine 1985). An arbitrary object is an object with which properties can be associated but whose extensional identity in terms of actual objects is unspecified. In this respect, arbitrary objects resemble the Skolem terms that are generated by inference rules like Existential Elimination in proof theories of first-order predicate calculus.

I will argue that arbitrary objects so interpreted are a necessary element of the ontology for natural language semantics, and that their involvement in CCG explains not only scope alternation (including occasions on which scope alternation is *not* available), but also certain cases of anomalous scopal binding that are unexplained under any of the alternatives discussed so far.

4.4.1 Donkeys as Skolem Terms

One example of an indefinite that is probably better analyzed as an arbitrary object than as a quantified NP occurs in the following famous sentence, first brought to modern attention by Geach (1962):

(56) Every farmer who owns a donkey$_i$ beats it$_i$.

The pronoun looks as though it might be a variable bound by an existential quantifier associated with *a donkey*. However, no purely combinatoric analysis in terms of the generalized quantifier categories offered earlier allows this, since the existential cannot both remain within the scope of the universal, and come to *c*-command the pronoun, as is required for true bound pronominal anaphora, as in (57):

(57) Every farmer$_i$ in the room thinks that she$_i$ deserves a subsidy

One reaction to this observation has been to treat the existential as a universal in this case, as in Discourse Representation Theory (DRT, Kamp and Reyle 1993), or to generalize the notion of scope, as in Dynamic Predicate Logic (DPL, Groenendijk and Stokhof 1990). However, Webber (1978), Cooper (1979), Evans (1980), Hobbs (1983), and others have pointed out that donkey pronouns in many respects look more like *non*-bound-variable or discourse-bound pronouns, in examples like the following:

(58) Everybody who knows Dexter$_i$ likes him$_i$.

I will assume for the sake of argument that *a donkey* translates at predicate-argument structure as something we might write as *arb′donkey′*. I will assume that the function *arb′* yields a Skolem term—that is, a term applying a unique functor to all variables bound by universal quantifiers in whose extent *arb′donkey′* falls. Call it $sk_{donkey}x$ in this case, where sk_{donkey} maps individual instantiations of *x*—that is, the variable bound by the generalized quantifier *every farmer*—onto objects with the property *donkey′* in the database.

The mechanism by which *arb′* "knows" what scopes it is in is presumably the same mechanism whereby a bound variable pronoun "knows" about its binder. This mechanism might be formalized in terms of such "environment passing" devices as "storage" (Cooper 1983) or the related device proposed by Jacobson (1999). However, in the present theory, unlike those of Cooper, Keller (1988), Hobbs and Shieber (1987), Pereira (1990), and Shieber, Pereira and Dalrymple (1996), the mechanism in question offers no autonomous degrees of freedom to determine available readings. An arbitrary object is deterministically bound to *all* scoping universals at the time it is evaluated, and the available readings are thereby entirely determined by the combinatorics of syntactic derivation.

An ordinary discourse-bound pronoun may be bound to this arbitrary object, but unless the pronoun is in the scope of the quantifiers that bind any variables in the Skolem term, it will include a variable that is outside the scope of its binder, and fail to refer.

This analysis is similar to but distinct from the analyses of Cooper (1979) and Heim (1990), who assume that *a donkey* translates as a quantified expression and that the entire subject *every farmer who owns a donkey* establishes a contextually salient function mapping farmers to donkeys, with the pronoun specifically of the type of such functions. However, by making the pronoun refer instead to a Skolem term or arbitrary object, we free our hands to make the inferences we draw on the basis of such sentences sensitive to world knowledge. For example, if we hear the standard donkey sentence and know that farmers may own more than one donkey, we will probably infer on the basis of knowledge about what makes people beat an arbitrary donkey that the farmer beats all of them. On the other hand, we will not make a parallel inference on the basis of the following sentence (attributed to Jeff Pelletier), and the knowledge that some people have more than one dime in their pocket:

(59) Everyone who had a dime in their pocket put it in the parking meter.

The reason is that we know that the reason for putting a dime into a parking meter, unlike the reason for beating a donkey, is voided by the act itself.

The proposal to translate indefinites as Skolem termlike discourse entities is anticipated in much early work in Artificial Intelligence and Computational Linguistics, including Kay (1973), Woods (1975 76-77), VanLehn (1978), and Webber (1983, 353, cf. Webber 1978, 2.52), and also by Chierchia (1995), and Schlenker (to appear). Skolem functors are closely related to, but distinct from, "Choice Functions" (see Reinhart 1997, Winter 1997, Sauerland 1998, and Schlenker to appear for discussion. Webber's (1978) analysis is essentially a choice functional analysis, as is Fine's.)

4.4.2 Scope Alternation and Skolem Entities

If indefinites can be assumed to have a referential translation as an arbitrary object, rather than a meaning related to a traditional existential generalized quantifier, then other supposed quantifiers, such as *some/a few/two saxophonists*, may also be better analyzed as referential categories.

We will begin by assuming that *some* is not a quantifier, but rather a determiner of a (singular) arbitrary object. It therefore has the following pair of subject and complement categories, in place of those in (51):

(60) a. some $:= (T/(T\backslash NP))/N : \lambda p.\lambda q.q(arb'p)$
    b. some $:= (T\backslash(T/NP))/N : \lambda p.\lambda q.q(arb'p)$

In this pair of categories, the constant arb' is the function identified earlier from properties p to entities of type e with that property, such that those entities are functionally related to any universally quantified NPs that have scope over them at the level of Logical Form. If $arb'p$ is not in the extent of any universal quantifier, then it yields a unique arbitrary constant individual.

We will assume that *every* has at least the generalized quantifier determiner category given in (50), repeated here:

(61) a. every $:= (T/(T\backslash NP))/N : \lambda p.\lambda q.\forall x.px \to qx$
    b. every $:= (T\backslash(T/NP))/N : \lambda p.\lambda q.\forall x.px \to qx$

These assumptions, as in Park's related account, provide everything we need to account for all and only the readings that are actually available for Geach's sentence (55b), *Every boy admires and every girl detests some saxophonist.* Thus the narrow scope saxophonist reading of this sentence results from the (backward) referential category (60b) applying to the translation of *Every boy admires and every girl detests* of type S/NP (whose derivation is taken as read), as in (62).[24]

(62)

Every boy admires and every girl detests	some saxophonist
S/NP	$S\backslash(S/NP)$
$: \lambda x.and'(\forall y.boy'y \to admires'xy)(\forall z.girl'z \to detests'xz)$	$: \lambda q.q(arb'sax')$

$$S : and'(\forall y.boy'y \to admires'(arb'sax')y)(\forall z.girl'z \to detests'(arb'sax')z)$$
$$S : and'(\forall y.boy'y \to admires'(sk'_{sax_1}y)y)(\forall z.girl'z \to detests'(sk'_{sax_2}z)z)$$

Crucially, if we evaluate the latter Logical Form with respect to a database after this reduction, as indicated by the dotted underline, for each boy and girl that we examine and test for the property of admiring/detesting an arbitrary saxophonist, we will find (or in the sense of Lewis (1979) "accommodate" or add to our database) a potentially different individual, dependent via the Skolem functors sk'_{sax_1} and sk'_{sax_2} upon that boy or girl. Each conjunct thereby gives the appearance of including a variable bound by an existential within the scope of the universal.

The wide scope saxophonist reading arises from the same categories as follows. If Skolemization can act *after* reduction of the object, when the arbitrary object is within the scope of the universal, then it can also act *before*, when it is not in scope, to yield a Skolem constant, as in (63).

(63)

Every boy admires and every girl detests	some saxophonist

$$\frac{\begin{array}{cc} \underline{\hspace{4cm}S/NP\hspace{4cm}} & \underline{\hspace{1cm}S\backslash(S/NP)\hspace{1cm}} \\ : \lambda x.and'(\forall y.boy'y \to admires'xy)(\forall z.girl'z \to detests'xz) & : \lambda q.q(arb'\,sax') \\ & \overline{\hspace{1cm}: \lambda q.q(sk'_{sax})\hspace{1cm}} \end{array}}{S : and'(\forall y.boy'y \to admires'\,sk'_{sax}y)(\forall z.girl'z \to detests'\,sk'_{sax}z)}<$$

Since the resultant Logical Form is in all important respects model-theoretically equivalent to the one that would arise from a wide scope existential quantification, we can entirely eliminate the quantifier reading (51) for *some*, and regard it as bearing only the arbitrary object reading (60).[25]

Consistent with Geach's observation, these categories do not yield a reading in which the boys admire the same wide scope saxophonist but the girls detest possibly different ones. Nor do they yield one in which the girls also all detest the same saxophonist, but not necessarily the one the boys all admire. Both facts are necessary consequences of the monotonic nature of CCG as a theory of grammar, without any further assumptions of parallelism conditions.

In the case of the following scope-inverting relative of the Geach example, the outcome is subtly different.

(64) Some woman likes and some man detests every saxophonist.

The scope-inverting reading arises from the evaluation of the arbitrary woman and man *after* combination with *every saxophonist*, within the scope of the universal:

(65) $\forall x.saxophonist'x \to and'(like'x(sk'_{woman}x))(detest'x(sk'_{man}x))$

The reading where *some woman* and *some man* appear to have wider scope than *every saxophonist* arises from evaluation of (the interpretation of) the residue of right node raising, *some woman likes and some man detests*, before combination with the generalized quantifier *every saxophonist*. This results in two Skolem constants—here, sk'_{woman} and sk'_{man}—liking every saxophonist, again without the involvement of a true existential quantifier:

(66) $\forall x.saxophonist'x \to and'(like'x\,sk'_{woman})(detest'x\,sk'_{man})$

These readings are obviously correct. However, since Skolemization of the arbitrary man and woman has so far been assumed to be free to occur any time, it seems to be predicted that one arbitrary object might become a Skolem constant in advance of coordination and reduction with the object, while the other might do so after. This would give rise to further readings in which only one of *some man* or *some woman* takes wide scope—for example:

(67) $\forall x.saxophonist'x \rightarrow and'(like'x\ sk'_{woman})(detest'x(sk'_{man}x))$

The apparent nonavailability of such readings might again seem to call for transderivational parallelism constraints. Quite apart from the theoretically problematic nature of such constraints, they must be rather carefully formulated if they are not to exclude apparently legal conjunction of narrow scope existentials with explicitly referential NPs, as in the following:

(68)   Some woman likes, and Fred detests, every saxophonist.

We will assume instead that the non-parallel mixed-scope reading (67) is in fact available, but is pragmatically disfavoured, on the following argument.

On the analysis of intonation contour and its interaction with coordinate structures given in Steedman 1991a and chapter 5 below, the coordinate fragments that result from right node raising like *Some woman likes and some man detests* must coincide with information structural units of the utterance, such as the "theme." Such information structural units carry presuppositions about contextually available alternatives that must hold or be accommodated for the utterance to be felicitous, and are evaluated as a whole in the course of derivation. In the present framework, readings like (67) can therefore be eliminated without parallelism constraints, by the further assumption that Skolem binding of arbitrary objects can only be done over complete information structural units—that is, entire themes, rhemes, or utterances. When any such unit is resolved in this way, *all* arbitrary objects concerned are obligatorily bound.[26]

Although the present account of indefinites might appear to mix derivation and evaluation in a dangerous way, this is in fact what we would expect from a monotonic semantics that supports the use of incremental semantic interpretation to guide parsing, as humans appear to (see Crain and Steedman 1985 and below).

Further support for a nonquantificational analysis of indefinites can be obtained from the observation that certain nominals that have been talked of as quantifiers entirely fail to exhibit scope alternations of the kind just discussed. One important class is the nonspecific or non-group-denoting counting quantifiers, including the upward-monotone, downward-monotone, and nonmonotone quantifiers (Barwise and Cooper 1981) such as *at least three*, *few*, *exactly five*, and *at most two* in examples like the following, which are of a kind discussed by Liu (1990), Stabler (1997), and Beghelli and Stowell (1997):

(69) a. Some linguist can program in at most two programming languages.

    b. Most linguists speak at least three /few/exactly five languages.

In contrast to true quantifiers like *most* and *every*, these quantified NP objects appear not to be able to invert or take wide scope over their subjects. That is, unlike *Some linguist can program in every programming language*, which has a scope-inverting reading meaning that every programming language is known by some linguist, (69a) has no reading meaning that there are at most two programming languages that are known to any linguist, and (69b) cannot mean that there are at least three/few/exactly five languages for which there are distinct majority sets of linguist speakers, one set for each language.[27]

Beghelli and Stowell (1997) account for this behavior in terms of different landing sites (or in GB terms, functional projections) at the level of LF for the different types of quantifier. However, another alternative is to believe that in syntactic terms these NPs have the same category as any other but in semantic terms they are (plural) arbitrary objects rather than quantifiers, like *some*, *a few*, *six* and the like. This in turn means that they cannot engender dependency in the Skolem term subject arising from *some linguist* in (69a). As a result the sentence has a single meaning, to the effect that there is an arbitrary linguist who can program in at most two programming languages.

4.4.3 Binding Theory and Distributional Scope

The proposal that the nonspecific and counting so-called quantifiers aren't quantifiers at all does not explain how they induce the appearance of taking wide scope when they are subjects, in sentences like the following:

(70) a. Few/at most two/three boys ate a pizza.

    b. Few/at most two/three farmers who own a donkey beat it.

There is every reason to doubt that the distributive reading of this sentence, according to which the boys ate different pizzas, arises from a quantified subject. Unlike the behavior of true quantifiers, distributivity is strictly subject to the same *c*-command condition as the binding conditions as defined in CCG terms in Steedman 1996b, p19. That is, only those terms that *c*-command another term at Logical Form can take bind or take scope over it. Thus the unavailability of scope inversion in (71a) is paralleled by the unacceptability of the reflexive in (71b):

(71) a.   Some linguist knows at most two languages.

   b.   *Himself shaves Harry

Even more strikingly (since it is independent of derivational command, according to the treatment of binding in Steedman 1996b) the asymmetry in anaphor binding illustrated in (72) also shows up in scope alternation in (73). (That is, an indirect object can bind or take scope over a direct object a, but not vice versa b.)

(72) a.   I showed the dogs themselves/each other.

   b.   *I showed themselves/each other the dogs.

(73) a.   I showed three dogs some rabbit. *(ambiguous)*

   b.   I showed some dog three rabbits. *(unambiguous)*

It is therefore natural to follow Link (1983), van der Does (1992), and van den Berg (1996) in explaining the distributive behavior of plurals as arising from the Logical Form of verbs, in rather the same way as the behavior of reflexives. We will assume that, as well as having the normal translation (74a), and the "reflexivized" translation (74b) (adapted from Steedman (1996b), 21), all transitive verbs with plural agreement like *eat'* have a "distributivizing" category like (74c).

(74) a.   eat a pizza $:= S \backslash NP_{agr} : \lambda y.eat'(arb'pizza')y$

   b.   eat himself $:= S \backslash NP_{1sm} : \lambda y.self'(eat'(ana'y))y$

   c.   eat a pizza $:= S \backslash NP_{pl} : \lambda y.dist'(eat'(arb'pizza'))z$

Thus, subjects in examples like (70) can optionally distribute over the function that applies to them at the level of Logical Form, such as $eat'(arb'pizza)$, to yield not only standard forms like a, below, but also b:

(75) a. $eat'(arb'pizza')(arb'3boys')$

   b. $dist'(eat'(arb'pizza'))(arb'3boys')$

If *dist'* translates as (76), then an argument x can distribute over more oblique arguments.

(76) $\lambda f.\lambda x.\forall y \in x.fy$

For example:

(77)   Three boys   ate   a pizza

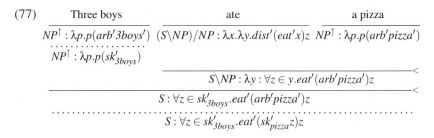

In invoking a "subordinated" use of universal quantification, this proposal resembles the treatment of distributive nonquantifiers in Kamp and Reyle 1993, 326-8. However, by tying it to the verb and its predicate-argument structure we explain the c-command condition on distribution, as evidenced by the fact that pizzas cannot distribute over boys in the following:

(78) A boy ate three pizzas.

4.4.4 Interaction of Word order and Quantifier Scope

We may assume (at least for English) that even the nonstandard constituents created by function composition in CCG cannot increase the number of quantifiable arguments for an operator beyond the limit of three or so imposed by the lexicon. It follows that the observation of Park (1995, 1996) that only quantified arguments of a single (possibly composed) function can freely alternate scope places an upper bound on the number of readings. The Logical Form of an n-quantifier sentence is a term with an operator of valency 1, 2 or 3, whose argument(s) must either be quantified expressions or terms with an operator of valency 1, 2 or 3, and so on. The number of readings for an n quantifier sentence is therefore bounded by the number of nodes in a single spanning tree with a branching factor b of up to three and n leaves. This number is given by a polynomial whose dominating term is $b^{log_b n}$—that is, it is linear in n, albeit with a rather large constant (since nodes correspond up to $3! = 6$ readings). For the relatively small n that we in practice need to cope with, this is still a lot of readings in the worst case.

However, the actual number of readings for real sentences will be very much lower, since it depends on how many true quantifiers are involved, and in exactly what configuration they occur. For example, the following three-quantifier sentence is predicted to have not $3! = 6$ but only 4 distinct readings, since the nonquantifiers *some dog* and *three rabbits* cannot alternate scope with each other independently of the truly quantificational dependency-inducing *Every boy*.[28]

(79) Every boy showed some dog three rabbits.

This is an important saving for the parser, as redundant syntactic analyses can be eliminated on the basis of identity of Logical Forms, a standard method of eliminating such "spurious ambiguities" (Karttunen 1989; Komagata 1999).

Similarly, as well as the restrictions that we have seen introduced by coordination, the SVO grammar of English means (for reasons discussed in Steedman 1996b) that embedded subjects in English are correctly predicted neither to extract nor take scope over their matrix subject in examples like the following:

(80) a. *a boy who(m) I know that admires John Coltrane
     b. Somebody knows that every boy admires some saxophonist.

Cooper (1983) and Williams (1986, (100)) argue that sentences like the latter have no readings where *every boy* takes scope over *somebody*. This three-quantifier sentence therefore has not $3! = 6$, not $2! * 2! = 4$, but only $2! * 1 = 2$ readings. Since such embeddings are crucial to obtaining proliferating readings, it is likely that in practice the number of available readings is usually quite small.

To the extent that the availability of wide scope readings for the true quantifiers depends upon syntactic derivability, we may expect to find interactions of phenomena like scope inversion with word order variation across languages of the kind discussed by Bayer (1996) and Kayne (1998). In particular, the failure of English complement subjects to take scope over their matrix generalizes to a wider class of embedded arguments in verb-final complements in languages like German and Dutch.

I will return to this point in chapters 6 and 7 in part II.

4.4.5 Disambiguation and Underspecification

It is interesting to speculate finally on the relation of the above account of the available scope readings with proposals to minimize search during processing by building "underspecified" Logical Forms by Kempson and Cormack (1981), Alshawi and Crouch (1992), Reyle (1992), Poesio (1995), Asher and Fernando (1997), Joshi and Vijay-Shanker (1999) and Willis and Manandhar (1999). There is a sense in which arbitrary individuals are themselves underspecified quantifiers, which are disambiguated by Skolemization. However, under the present proposal, they are disambiguated during the derivation itself.

The alternative of building a single underspecified Logical Form can under some circumstances dramatically reduce the search space and increase efficiency of parsing. However, few studies of this kind seem to have looked at the problems posed by the restrictions on available readings exhibited by sentences like (55b). If they are to be disambiguated efficiently, then the disambiguated representations must embody or include those restrictions. However, the restriction that Geach noted seems intrinsically disjunctive, and hence appears to threaten efficiency in both parsing and disambiguating underspecified representations.

The fact that relatively few readings are available and that they are so tightly related to Surface Structure and derivation means that the technique of incremental semantic or probabilistic disambiguation of fully specified partial Logical Forms mentioned earlier may be a more efficient technique for computing the contextually relevant readings. For example, in processing (81) (adapted from Hobbs and Shieber 1987), which Park 1995 claims to have only four readings, rather than the five predicted by their account, such a system can build both readings for the S/NP *every representative of three companies saw* and decide which is more likely, before building both compatible readings of the whole sentence and similarly resolving with respect to statistical or contextual support:

(81) Every representative of three companies saw some sample.

This is only possible because of the strictly monotone relation between Logical Form and syntactic derivation.

The above observations imply that among the so-called quantifier determiners in English, only those that can engender dependency-inducing scope-inversion have interpretations corresponding to genuine quantifiers. The others are not quantificational at all, but are various types of arbitrary individuals translated as Skolem terms. These give the appearance of taking narrow scope when they are bound to truly quantified variables, and of taking wide scope when they are unbound and therefore "take scope everywhere." In addition the plural arbitrary individuals can distribute over or bind other arbitrary objects that they c-command at the level of Logical Form. Available readings can be computed monotonically from the combinatorics of syntactic derivation alone. The notion of syntactic derivation embodied in CCG is the most powerful limitation on the number of available readings, and allows all logical-form level constraints on scope orderings to be dispensed with, a result related to, but more powerful than, that of Pereira (1990), as extended in Shieber, Pereira and Dalrymple (1996).

It is interesting to note in this connection that Baker (1995), Bittner (1995), Bittner and Hale (1995), Faltz (1995), Jelinek (1995), and Damaso Vieira

(1995), together with other papers in Bach et al. (1995), show that the universal involvement of generalized quantifiers in explaining scope phenomena assumed by Barwise and Cooper (1981) is not easy to reconcile with the properties of various nonconfigurational, pronominal-argument, or agglutinative languages including Mohawk, Warlpiri, Navajo, Lakhota, Straits Salish, and Asurini. It seems quite likely that further examination will reveal quantification in such languages to be mediated by explicitly nonquantificational devices similar to those proposed here for English.

4.5 Summary: Surface Structure and Interpretation

According to the theory of grammar proposed here (as 36 and 37 and the preceding discussion reveal), surface derivation is less closely tied to predicate-argument structure than we are used to assuming. There are in general several alternative surface derivations for any given reading of a sentence, in some of which the object may structurally command the subject as in (82b) (or may even command a subject in a higher clause)

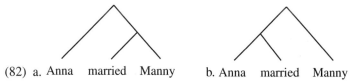

(82) a. Anna   married   Manny   b. Anna   married   Manny

At the same time, at the level of the interpretation all these derivations yield the same Logical Form, in which function-argument relations of dominance and command over subjects and other elements hold in pretty much their traditional form.

The proliferation of surface derivations in CCGs creates problems for the processor (to which I will return in part III), because it compounds the already grave problems of local and global ambiguity in parsing by introducing numerous semantically equivalent potential derivations for each reading. This has been referred to as the problem of "spurious" ambiguity by Wittenburg (1986). Although it clearly does not matter which member of any equivalence class the parser finds, the parser must find *some* member of *every* semantically distinct class of analyses. The danger is that the entire forest of possible analyses will have to be examined in order to ensure that all such analyses have been found. Since the number of distinct derivations (in the sense of distinct sequences of rule applications leading to a derivation) can grow as the Catalan function of the length of the sentence, the problem is potentially serious.

Nevertheless, this problem has been overstated. Standard PS grammars give rise to a similar proliferation of derivations, in the sense that for any syntactic structure there are many alternative orders in which rules can be applied in a derivation to yield the same tree. This fact tends to be forgotten, because of the isomorphism of trees representing syntactic structures and those representing derivations, but efficient parsing algorithms have to deal with this problem. They do so either by using a "normal form" algorithm (e.g. Earley's) that is guaranteed to find only one derivation per tree, or by making sure (as in the CKY parser discussed in chapter 9) that only one copy of each subtree is kept. These techniques will be discussed in chapter 9, where we will see that a variant of the latter technique originally proposed by Karttunen (1989) can be directly applied to CCG derivations.

In fact, the term "spurious ambiguity" is distinctly misleading. Far from being spurious this nondeterminism is simply a property of all natural languages. Any theory that captures the range of phenomena discussed here, in particular in respect of coordination, will necessarily encounter the same nondeterminism. Given the degree of ambiguity that is tolerated elsewhere in the language, it is not even particularly surprising to find that there is a bit more of it from this source.

To say this is not to deny that nondeterminism (of all kinds) remains a problem for processors. It is simply to deny that this particular nondeterminism indicates anything wrong in the combinatory categorial competence theory.

The architecture of this theory can be represented to a first approximation as in figure 4.1, which is a version of the transformationalists Y-diagram seen in figure 2.1 of 2, using the two derivations of one of the two interpretations of the sentence *Every boy admires some girl* as an example.

In the generative direction, according to this theory, derivations can be regarded as projected by the combinatory rules from the lexicon, which also pairs types or categories with interpretations or Logical Forms.[29]

In the analytic direction, combinatory derivations map Phonetic Form directly onto constituents, with a category consisting of a syntactic type and a Logical Form. The Logical Form associated with the S category that is monotonically specified as a result of the derivation is a quantified predicate-argument structure, which can be thought of as an unordered tree representing traditional dominance/command relations. We will see in chapter 5 that the interpretations of the immediate derivational antecedents of the root S node can be regarded as the elements of Information Structure and as identifying the content of topic/theme and comment/rheme. The corresponding structural

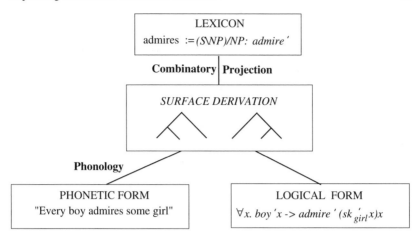

Figure 4.1
Architecture of a Combinatory Grammar, I

units directly coincide with phrasal intonational boundaries, where these are present, justifying the earlier identification of Surface Structure with Phonological Form. However, Surface Structure is strictly a record of the process of deriving such Logical Forms via combinatory operations that are type-driven, rather than structure-dependent. Surface Structure is therefore not a grammatical "level of representation" at all. To that extent, the theory is not only monotonic in the sense of never revising the structures it builds. It is also monostratal, in the sense that it builds only a single level of structure, namely, Logical Form.

Chapter 5

Structure and Intonation

Take care of the sense, and the sounds will take care of themselves.
Lewis Carroll, *Alice in Wonderland*

In chapter 2, (13), we considered the following exchange, in which intonation imposes a perceptual grouping of words in the spoken utterance into fragments that are inconsistent with traditional linguistic notions of syntactic constituency.[1]

(1) a. I know that Alice married Alan. But who did ANNA marry?
     b. (ANNA married) (MANNY).

The prosody informally indicated in (1b) by capitals (for stress) and parentheses (for intonational phrase boundaries) is one possibility (among others that we will come to later) for an answer to the question (1a). It consists in not only marking the focused information in the answer by the use of high pitch on the stressed first syllable of the word *MANNY*, but also in stressing the first syllable of *Anna*, using a high pitch-accent, and placing a final rise at the end of *married*, with lower pitch interpolated in between. This utterance might give rise to a pitch contour something like the sketch in figure 5.1, which is an idealized version of the actual pitch track shown in 5.2. This contour conveys the contrast between the previous topic concerning Alice's marriage and the new one concerning Anna's, and it imposes the perceptual grouping indicated by the brackets. Such a grouping cuts across the traditional syntactic analysis of the sentence as a subject and a predicate VP.

Many authorities, such as Chomsky (1971), Jackendoff (1972), Cooper and Paccia-Cooper (1980), Gee and Grosjean (1983), Kaisse (1985), and Croft (1995) have continued to argue, nevertheless, that intonation can be driven directly from Surface Structure. There is an immediate intuitive appeal to the idea, as noted in chapter 2, for it is hard to see why intonation should depart from the Constituent Condition on Rules in any language. However, the apparent complexities engendered by examples like (1) have led many others, such

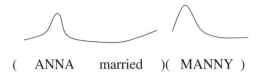

(ANNA   married   )(MANNY)

Figure 5.1
Idealized pitch contour for (1b)

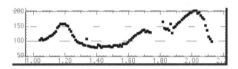

Figure 5.2
Actual pitch contour for (1b)

as Liberman (1975), Goldsmith (1976), Pierrehumbert (1980), Selkirk (1984), and Nespor and Vogel (1986), to postulate an autonomous level of "Intonation Structure" independent of Surface Structure and related only indirectly to Logical Form or function/argument structure, via Information Structure.

However compelling the logic of this argument may appear, we noted in chapter 2 that the involvement of two apparently autonomous levels of structure, related to two autonomous levels of meaning representation, complicates the theory considerably. The picture becomes even bleaker when it is realized that the two levels of structure must communicate, because of the presence of certain focusing constructions and operators, such as the English topicalization construction or the focusing particle *only*, the latter exemplified in the following sentence:

(2) John introduced only BILL to Sue.

Such constructions and particles, which have been discussed by Rooth (1985), von Stechow (1991), Hoeksema and Zwarts (1991), and others, have effects in both domains. These observations have seemed to demand the quite complex theoretical architecture shown in figure 2.3. Such a theoretical architecture offers a view of sentence structure as having an "autosegmental" topology which Halle influentially likened to that of a spiral-bound notebook (cf. Halle and Vergnaud 1987 p78-79). This notebook has phonetic segments arranged along the spine, and different autonomous levels of structure—prosodic, syntactic, and others—written on different leaves, each of which may refer to descriptions on other pages. As Zwicky and Pullum (1987, 4) have pointed out, such theories are potentially very unconstrained, in the absence of a principled statement about which of the pages may cross-refer, and why. The simplest possible constraint upon such a theory would be a demonstration that certain communicating levels involve isomorphic structural descriptions, for those levels at least could be combined upon a single page of the notebook.

However, a strong hint that a simplification might be possible seems to be provided by the observation that Intonation Structure is, despite its apparent partial independence from syntax, nonetheless constrained by meaning, and in particular by distinctions of focus, information, and propositional attitude toward concepts and entities in the discourse model. The intonation contour in the response in (1) seems to divide the utterance into a topic or theme to do with *Anna marrying*, and a comment or rheme *Manny*.[2] These terms will be defined formally below, but informally the theme can be thought of as denoting what the speaker assumes to be *the question under discussion* and the rheme can be thought of as what the speaker believes to be *the part of the utterance that advances the discussion*. Even in advance of a more formal definition, it will be convenient to refer to such partitions of the information in the proposition as the "Information Structure" of an utterance.

A theme in the present sense of the term can be more concretely exemplified as *that which is introduced into the discourse context by a* wh-*question*. By now we are familiar with the idea that such an entity can be expressed as a functional abstraction, as Jackendoff (1972) and Sag (1976) point out, equivalent in this case to the following λ-term:[3]

(3) $\lambda x.marry' x\ anna'$

Establishing a theme with content (3) in the context via a *wh*-question such as *Who did Anna marry?* is one way to make the intonation contour in (1) felicitous. (Of course, it is not claimed that an explicit mention, via a *wh-question* or otherwise, is necessary for interpreting the response. Nor does this *wh*-question uniquely determine this response—for example, for reasons that we will come to later, it is possible to answer the same question with the "fall-rise" contour confined to *Anna* and the boundary before the VP *married Manny*. There is also no claim that intonation contours in general determine Information Structure unambiguously. We return to these points in section 5.5.2 below.)

The close relation in English of Intonation Structure to Information Structure, first proposed by Halliday (1967a), has recently been endorsed by Selkirk

(1984, 284) as "The Sense Unit Condition" on intonational constituency, which says in essence that intonational constituents must have coherent translations at Information Structure.

However, we have seen in previous chapters that natural languages include a number of other constructions whose semantics is also reminiscent of functional abstraction. The most obvious and theoretically tractable class are Wh-constructions, in which many of the same fragments that can be delineated by a single intonation contour appear as the residue of the subordinate clause. Another and much more diverse class are the fragments resulting from the co-ordinate constructions discussed in previous chapters. The latter constructions are doubly interesting, because they and certain other sentence-fragmenting constructions, such as parentheticals, interact very strongly with intonation, on occasion making intonation breaks obligatory, rather than optional, as Downing (1970) and Bing (1979), among others, have noted. For example, the intonation indicated on the following ambiguous sentence forces one syntactic analysis with an absurd reading, and leaves the sensible analysis quite inaccessible (the example is from Pierrehumbert (1980), who attributes it to Mark Liberman):

(4) *(Harry likes the NUTS) (and bolts APPROACH).

It is therefore tempting to think that the nonstandard concept of Surface Structure and constituency that has been developed in earlier chapters in order to explain coordination and unbounded dependency might directly provide the notion of structure that is required to account for intonational prosody. If this conclusion is correct, then both the camps identified earlier are in a sense correct. Intonation can indeed be specified directly from surface syntactic structure, without the mediation of an autonomous Intonation Structure. However, the syntactic structure in question corresponds to Information Structure rather than traditional Surface Structure, and hence directly subsumes the Intonation Structure of English.

5.1 Surface Structure and Intonation Structure

According to the combinatory theory, conjoinable strings like *Anna married* and even *a policeman a flower* correspond to constituents in their own right, without syntactic operations of deletion or movement. It follows that they must also be possible constituents of simple noncoordinate sentences like *Give a policeman a flower* and (1b), *Anna married Manny*, as well. Such sentences have several Surface Structures, corresponding to different sequences of composition and application. As we have seen, the nonstandard derivation (5) is allowed for the latter sentence, as well as the traditional derivation (6):

(5)

Anna	married	Manny

$$\frac{\quad\quad\quad}{NP:anna'} \quad \frac{}{(S\backslash NP)/NP:marry'} \quad \frac{}{NP^{\uparrow}:manny'}$$

$$\frac{}{S/(S\backslash NP):\lambda f.f\ anna'}{>}\mathbf{T}$$

$$\frac{}{S/NP:\lambda x.marry'x\ anna'}{>}\mathbf{B}$$

$$\frac{}{S:marry'manny'anna'}{<}$$

(6)

Anna	married	Manny

$$\frac{\quad\quad\quad}{NP:anna'} \quad \frac{}{(S\backslash NP)/NP:marry'} \quad \frac{}{NP^{\uparrow}:manny'}$$

$$\frac{}{S/(S\backslash NP):\lambda f.f\ anna'}{>}\mathbf{T}$$

$$\frac{}{S\backslash NP:\lambda y.marry'manny'y}{<}$$

$$\frac{}{S:marry'manny'anna'}{>}$$

Such families of derivations form equivalence classes, for the semantics of the combinatory rules guarantees that all such derivations will deliver an interpretation determining the same function-argument relations—in this case, *marry'manny'anna'*. Moreover, the interpretation of the nonstandard constituent *Anna married* of type *S/NP* bears an interpretation equivalent to the abstraction (3).

It is therefore tempting to believe that these semantically equivalent derivations convey distinctions of discourse information and that they are on occasion distinguished by intonational markers in spoken language.[4]

For example, the following bracketings correspond to alternative CCG Surface Structures, arising out of different sequences of compositions and applications, each of which corresponds directly to a possible intonation contour:

(7) a. (I)(want to begin to try to write a play).
    b. (I want)(to begin to try to write a play).
    c. (I want to begin)(to try to write a play).
    d. (I want to begin to try)(to write a play).
    e. (I want to begin to try to write)(a play).

The leftmost element is in every case a fragment that can be coordinated. For example:

(8) *I wanted, and you expected,* to write a play.

Conversely, the following are at least as strange (and pragmatically demanding) as coordinations as they are as intonational phrases:

(9) a. ?(I want to BEGIN to), (try to write a PLAY).
    b. ?I wanted to, and you actually expected to, try to write a play.

(Examples like (7) and (9a) are used by Selkirk (1984, 294) to motivate a definition of the Sense Unit Condition in terms of a relation over the heads of constituents.) A stronger example emerges from comparing the following examples, in which the string *three mathematicians* is as hard to make an intonational phrase as it is to coordinate. (The unacceptability of (10a) is also used by Selkirk as evidence for the Sense Unit Condition.)[5]

(10) a. ?(Three MATHEMATICIANS) (in ten prefer MARGARINE).
     b. ?Three mathematicians, in ten prefer margarine, and in a hundred can cook a passable soufflé.

It is irrelevant to the present purpose to ask *how* sentences like (10b) might be excluded, or even to ask whether what is wrong with them is a matter of syntax, semantics, or pragmatics. The important point for present purposes is that the *same* constraint applies in syntactic and prosodic domains. That is, the Sense Unit Condition on prosodic constituents simply boils down to the Constituent Condition on Rules of grammar. This result is a very reasonable one, for what else but a constituent could we expect to be subject to the requirement of being a semantic unit?

It follows that we predict the strongest possible conspiracy between prosodic constituency and coordinate structure. Noncoordinate sentences typically have many equivalent combinatory derivations, because composition is optional and associative. These analyses can give rise to many different intonation contours. On the other hand, coordinate sentences, like relative clauses, have fewer equivalent analyses, because only analyses that make the conjuncts into constituents are allowed. Two predictions follow. First, we must expect that any substring that can constitute a prosodic constituent will also be able to coordinate. Second, of all the intonational tunes that distinguish alternative prosodic constituencies in noncoordinate sentences, we predict that only the ones that are consistent with the constituents demanded by the coordination rule will be allowed in coordinate sentences. Intonation contours that are appropriate to the alternative constituencies are syntactically ruled out. So for example, there are many prosodic constituencies for the example (7), *I want to begin to try to write a play*, realized by a variety of intonational contours. However, there are many fewer possible intonation contours for the following coordinate sentence, and they seem intuitively to be closely related to the ones that impose the corresponding bracketing (7e) in the simpler sentence:

(11) I want to begin to try to write, and you hope to produce, a musical based on the life of Sir Stafford Cripps.

Observations like the above make it seem likely intonation often determines which of the many possible bracketings permitted by the combinatory syntax of English is intended, and that the interpretations of the constituents are related to distinctions of information-structural significance among the concepts that the speaker has in mind. Thus, whatever problems for parsing written text arise from the profusion of equivalent alternative Surface Structures engendered by this theory, these "spurious" ambiguities seem to be to some extent resolved by prosody in spoken language. The theory therefore offers the possibility that prosody and syntax are one system, and that speech processing and parsing can be unified in a single process.[6]

This section and the next show that the combinatory rules of syntax that have been proposed in order to explain coordination and unbounded dependency in English do indeed induce Surface Structures that subsume the structures that have been proposed by Selkirk (1984) and others in order to explain the possible intonation contours for all sentences of English. The proof of this claim depends upon two results. First, it must be shown that the rules of combinatory grammar can be made sensitive to intonation contour, so as to limit the permissible derivations for spoken sentences like (1b). Second, it must be shown that the interpretations of the principal constituents of these derivations correspond to the Information Structure established by the context to which they are appropriate, such as (1a).

5.2 Two Intonation Contours and Their Functions

I will use a notation for intonation contours that is based on the theory of Pierrehumbert (1980), itself a development of proposals by Bruce (1977), Liberman (1975), and Goldsmith (1976). The version used here is roughly as presented in Selkirk 1984, Beckman and Pierrehumbert 1986, Pierrehumbert and Beckman 1988, and Pierrehumbert and Hirschberg 1990, although it will become clear below that I have extended Pierrehumbert's notation in a couple of minor respects. I have tried as far as possible to take my examples and the associated intonational annotations from those authors.

The advantage of this theory is that it specifies intonation contour independently of the string, in terms of just two kinds of fixed points or "tones." The contour between tones can be determined by interpolation. The first group of tones are the "pitch-accents," which are the substantial local pitch maxima and minima that coincide with perceived contrastive emphasis. The other group of tones are the "boundaries," that mark the right-hand edge of a prosodic phrase. I follow Pierrehumbert in assuming that intonation contours can be described in terms of two abstract or relative pitch levels, H and L, denoting high or low abstract pitch.

Of Pierrehumbert's six pitch accent tones, I will consider only two here, H* and L+H*.[7] The phonetic or acoustic realization of pitch accents is a complex matter. Roughly speaking, the L+H* pitch accent that is extensively discussed below in the context of the L+H* LH% melody generally appears as a maximum that is preceded by a distinctive low level and peaks later than the corresponding H* pitch accent when the same sequence is spoken with the H* LL% melody. (See Silverman 1988 for discussion. Nothing in the combinatory theory hinges on the precise identities of the pitch accent types. All that matters is that the two complete melodies are distinct, a matter on which all theories agree.)

The intonational constituents of interest here are made up of one or more pitch accents (possibly preceded by other material), followed by a boundary. In recent versions of the theory, Pierrehumbert and her colleagues distinguish two distinct levels of prosodic phrase: the intonational phrase proper and the "intermediate phrase." The intermediate phrase boundary is a bare phrasal tone, either L or H.[8] Intonational phrase boundaries are L or H phrasal tones plus an boundary tone written H% or L%. We will principally be concerned here with the intonational phrase boundaries that are written LH%, and the boundary L or LL%.

The intermediate phrase is distinguished in Pierrehumbert's theory as defining the domain of a phenomenon known as "downstep." If more than one pitch accent occurs without an intervening boundary—that is, within an intermediate phrase—then the entire pitch range of each successive pitch accent is shifted downward from its predecessor. At the intermediate phrase boundary (and therefore at any higher-level boundary including the intonational phrase boundary), the pitch levels are reset to the normal level. Although this aspect of the pitch contour is completely rule-governed, so that in Pierrehumbert's own notation, downstepped pitch accents are not distinguished, it is sometimes useful to include such a notation. On such occasions will use "!" as a prefix to the pitch accent type, a notation that originates with Ladd (1980) and has been included in the ToBI conventions, writing such sequences as follows:

(12) blueberries, bayberries, raspberries, mulberries, and brambleberries
      H*   !H*   !H*   !H*   !H* LL%

I have followed Beckman and Pierrehumbert in regarding boundaries of all kinds as confined to the right-hand end of the prosodic phrase. However, the position and nature of the phrasal tone is one of the more controversial details of the theory (Pierrehumbert and Beckman 1988, 236–237). The influence of, say, an L or LL% boundary on a preceding H* pitch accent is apparent immediately after the maximum, no matter how distant the right-hand boundary is. Pierrehumbert and Beckman point out that this influence may be apparent by the end of the word bearing the pitch accent preceding the boundary. Indeed, in the framework of the British School, the event corresponding to the phrasal tone component L or H of the boundary is considered to be part of the pitch accent, rather than part of the boundary event.

For all other regions of the prosodic phrase, notably the region before the (first) pitch accent, the regions between pitch accents, and the region between pitch accent and boundary, the pitch contour is merely interpolated. In Pierrehumbert's notation, such substrings therefore bear no indication of abstract tone whatsoever. It is sometimes convenient to regard such elements as bearing a "null" tone.[9]

Thus, according to this theory, the shape of a given pitch accent in a prosodic phrase, and of its phrase accent and the associated right-hand boundary, is essentially invariant. If the constituent is very short—say, a monosyllabic NP—then the whole intonation contour may be packed into that one syllable. If the constituent is longer, then the pitch accent will appear further to the left of the phrasal tone and boundary tone at the right-hand edge. The intervening pitch contour will merely be interpolated, as will any part of the contour preceding the pitch accent(s). In this way, the same tune can be spread over longer or shorter strings, in order to mark the corresponding constituents for the particular distinction of information and propositional attitude that the melody denotes.

Consider the prosody of the sentence *Anna married Manny* in the following pair of discourse settings, which are adapted from Jackendoff (1972, 260) and Steedman (1991a). To aid the exposition, words bearing pitch accents are printed in capitals, and prosodic phrase boundaries are explicitly marked in the sentences, using parentheses. (These devices are not part of Pierrehumbert's notation.)

(13) Q: Well, what about MANNY? Who married HIM?

    A: (ANNA) (married MANNY).
       H* L   L+H* LH%

(14) Q: Well, what about ANNA? Who did SHE marry?

    A: (ANNA married) (MANNY).
       L+H*   LH%   H* LL%

In these contexts the stressed syllables on both *Anna* and *Manny* receive a pitch accent, but a different one. In answer (13A) there is a prosodic phrase on *Anna* made up of the sharply rising pitch accent that Pierrehumbert calls H*, immediately followed by an L boundary, perceived as a rapid fall to low pitch. There is another prosodic phrase having the somewhat later- and lower-rising pitch accent called L+H* on *Manny*, preceded by null tone (and therefore interpolated low pitch) on the word *married*, and immediately followed by a rising "continuation" boundary, written LH%. (See Pierrehumbert and Hirschberg 1990, (33), for discussion of a similar example.)[10] In answer (14A) the two tunes are reversed (see figures 5.1 and 5.2): this time the tune with pitch accent L+H* and boundary LH% is spread across a prosodic phrase *Anna married*, and the other tune with pitch accent H* and boundary LL% is carried by the prosodic phrase *Manny*, again starting with an interpolated or null tone.[11]

The intuition that there is some systematic distinction in meaning between these tunes seems to be very compelling, though it has in the past proved hard to formalize. The tunes have been associated with such factors as social attitude (O'Connor and Arnold 1961; Merin 1983; Bartels 1997), illocutionary acts (Liberman and Sag 1974; Sag and Liberman 1975; Liberman 1975), propositional attitudes (Ward and Hirschberg 1985), maintenance of mutual belief (Pierrehumbert and Hirschberg 1990), and Information Structure (Halliday 1967a; Jackendoff 1972; Schmerling 1976; Ladd 1980; Gussenhoven 1983; Selkirk 1984; Terken 1984, Cormack 1992, Terken and Hirschberg 1994; Morel 1995; Rochemont 1986, 1998; Rochemont and Culicover 1990; Steedman 1991a,b; Zubizarreta 1998).

The present chapter concentrates on certain aspects of intonation that primarily concern Information Structure, in the sense of that term proposed by Valldví (1990), and Steedman (1991a), although these proposals differ in detail (see Valldví and Engdahl (1996) for a survey). These theorists follow Halliday (1967b, 1970) in assuming that there are two independent dimensions to

Information Structure that are relevant to intonation. The first corresponds to the distinction, informally introduced at the start of the chapter, between theme and rheme. In English we will see that this dimension of Information Structure determines the overall shape of the intonational tune or tunes imposed upon an utterance. The second dimension is one of salience or contrast. In English this dimension is reflected in the position of pitch accents on particular words. The presence of a pitch accent of any shape is generally agreed to assign salience or contrast independently of the particular shape or contour of the pitch accent or overall phrasal melody (see Pierrehumbert and Hirschberg 1990, 288-289). The next sections consider these two dimensions in turn.

5.3 Theme and Rheme

The λ-abstraction operator is closely related to the existential quantifier $\exists$. It is therefore natural to associate the notion of theme with the set of propositions among all those supported by the conversational context that could possibly satisfy the corresponding existential proposition. In the case of the exchange in (14) it is the following, in which $\diamond$ indicates possibility:

(15) $\exists x. \diamond marry' x \ anna'$

This might be a set like the following:

$$(16) \quad \left\{ \begin{array}{l} \diamond marry' alan' anna' \\ \diamond marry' fred' anna' \\ \diamond marry' manny' anna' \\ \quad \ldots \end{array} \right\}$$

This extensional interpretation of the notion theme resembles the Alternative Semantics approach to presupposition and focus of Karttunen and Peters (1979), Rooth (1985, 1992), and Kratzer (1991), and the related analysis of German intonational meaning of Büring (1995, 1997). Specifically, the alternative set in question is the one that Rooth and Büring call C, the "contextual" alternative set. Since all alternative sets are contextual, I will refer to it here as the "rheme" alternative set.

Alternative sets are of course in many cases not exhaustively known to hearers, and in practice one would want to compute with something more like the quantified expression (15) or the λ-term itself, as in the structured-meanings approach of Cresswell (1985) and others. However, alternative sets are easy to grasp and are used here for reasons of exposition.

In semantic terms the theme and rheme can therefore be characterized as follows:

(17) a. The Theme *presupposes* the rheme alternative set.

   b. The Rheme *restricts* the rheme alternative set.

The sense in which a theme "presupposes" the rheme alternative set is much the same as that in which a definite expression presupposes the existence of its referent. That is to say, there is a pragmatic presupposition that the relevant alternative set is available in the contextual "mental model" (Johnson-Laird 1983) or database. The presupposition may be "accommodated" in the sense of Lewis (1979)—that is, be added by the hearer after the fact of utterance to a contextual model that is consistent with it.

5.3.1 Update Semantics for Theme and Rheme

One way of making such referents available is to think of the theme of an utterance as *updating* or having side-effects on the context or discourse model.[12] Following Jacobs (1991) and Krifka (1991), it can be characterized as in general causing one or more existing referents or "facts" such as $(\theta'\lambda x.marry'x\ anna')$, where θ marks the λ-term as a theme, to be *retracted* or removed from the context model, and causing a new thematic referent or fact to be *asserted* or added. If the theme is unmarked by any accent, then it will simply be the corresponding thematic referent that is retracted and asserted. Unless a fact of the appropriate form is already present in (or is at least consistent with) the context, the first of these effects will cause the discourse to fail. Otherwise, the thematic referent will be reasserted.

The rheme should also be thought of as updating the context with a similar type of referent, which may become the theme of a subsequent utterance. However, the rheme does not require a preexisting referent or cause any existing thematic referents to be retracted (although we will see that it may have other effects on the database, via the entailments and implicatures discussed above).

The exact form of the retracted and/or asserted informational referents in all of the above examples depends upon the location of focus and pitch accents in the utterance and is determined in a manner discussed in section 5.4.

Noncompositional, procedural notions like assertion and retraction must eventually be declarativized, if we are to be able to prove anything about the expressive power of this theory. However, procedural descriptions can be very transparent, probably because they remain very close to what is actually going on in our heads, and for the moment it will be helpful to think of the problem in these terms.[13]

The claim that the L+H* LH% tune when present marks the theme in one or the other of these closely related senses is implicit in the accounts of Jackendoff (1972), Ladd (1980), and others, but it remains controversial. Pierrehumbert and Hirschberg (1990, 294–297) propose a compositional semantics for intonational tunes that is based on scalar values on dimensions of propositional attitude such as certainty concerning relevance and degree of commitment to belief revision. According to their account, the L+H* pitch accent is used "to convey that the accented item—and not some alternative related item—should be mutually believed" (p. 296).

As an example, Pierrehumbert and Hirschberg discuss the following dialogue (adapted from Jackendoff (1972, 258–265), and also discussed by Ladd (1980, 157–159), and Steedman (1991a)), which is isomorphic to (13):

(18) Q: What about the beans? Who ate THEM?
       A: Fred ate the BEANS.
          H* L   L+H*LH%

In support of their claim that the L+H* pitch accent evokes a set of alternatives besides the accented item, they correctly observe that the utterance implicates the possibility that other people may have eaten other things. However, this particular alternative set has already been introduced into the context by the question, and in the absence of such a question (or some other utterance establishing a context that supports or is at least consistent with this theme), the intonation contour is inappropriate. The example therefore does not exclude the possibility that the L+H* LH% tune evokes this set of alternatives by marking a part of the theme.

The following minimal pair of dialogues will be helpful in deciding between these claims, because it appears at first glance to raise problems for both.

(19) Q: Does Mary like corduroy?
       A: Mary likes BOMBAZINE.
              H* LL%

(20) Q: Does Mary like corduroy?
       A: Mary likes BOMBAZINE.
          L+H* LH%

In (19), the entire response is marked with the H*LL% tune that we have identified as marking the rheme, constituting what the speaker believes the hearer needs. Depending on the context, the speaker may thereby be committed by the usual Gricean principles to a number of conversational implicatures. For example, if liking bombazine entails hating corduroy, then this response implicates denial. If on the other hand liking bombazine entails liking corduroy, then the response implicates affirmation. Either way, the speaker's intonation commits them only to the claim that *bombazine* is the rheme—that is, that it restricts the set of alternatives to just one—rather than to a particular change in belief.

More specifically in both cases, the rheme of the yes-no question adds a theme *theme'* (*like'corduroy'mary'*) to the facts making up the respondent's context. (The alternative set here is confined to the proposition and its negation.) The respondent then constructs the corresponding query and evaluates it with respect to the context. If the query immediately succeeds, or fails altogether, then it is appropriate to respond with a direct yes or no. If the query succeeds but a step of inference involving the respondent's rule that *Everyone who likes bombazine likes corduroy* and the respondent's knowledge that *Mary likes bombazine* is needed to establish the answer, then one of the following cases may apply. If the respondent's discourse model implies that the questioner knows neither the rule nor the truth of the premise, then the respondent should state them both, as in the extended example (23). On the other hand, if the discourse model implies that the respondent knows the rule, but not the premise, then the response should be either as in (19) or as in (20). If there is reason to believe that this is the only relevant difference between the questioner's knowledge and the respondent's own, then stating the premise as a rheme, as in (19), is appropriate, since the respondent can sincerely claim that it is everything the questioner needs. But if the respondent has reason to suspect that there may be other differences and therefore cannot sincerely claim that the questioner can make this inference, then the respondent should mark the premise as a theme, as in (20), and leave the questioner to derive the rheme or not, as the case may be.

As is often the case, the respondent may for reasons of politeness or other pragmatic footwork use an utterance of an isolated theme to conversationally implicate lack of willingness to commit to the adequacy of their information, simultaneously being perfectly certain of the outcome. Nearly all speech acts like the response in (20) have the smell of indirection about them, and we should not expect to capture them in terms of literal meaning alone.

Example (20), which is of a kind discussed by Jackendoff (1972, 264–265), Liberman and Sag (1974), and Ladd (1980, 146–148), appears at first glance to be almost equivalent. In particular, the possibilities for conversational implicature of either affirmation or denial seem identical. Any difference seems to lie in the degree of conviction that the utterance constitutes an answer to the question.

Since in other respects the two utterances seem similar, there is a temptation to believe that the L+H* LH% tune in this case might mark a rheme, rather than a theme, differing from the standard H*LL% rheme tune in terms of the degree of commitment to whether it does in fact restrict the set of rheme alternatives sufficiently.

However, it is also possible to believe that this utterance is in fact a theme and that what the respondent has actually done is to offer a new set of alternatives, without stating a rheme at all, leaving the other party to supply the rheme. This would certainly explain the lack of commitment to whether the utterance restricts the rheme alternative set, since that is exactly what a theme does not do. It is also likely that the effect of not taking responsibility for a rheme in this utterance will be that of *conversationally implicating* a lack of confidence in either the relevance of the theme or the certainty of the inference that might be drawn. But that would not be a matter of literal or conventional meaning of the utterance or the intonation contour itself.

This is essentially the analysis proposed by Ladd (1980, 153-156), who relates "fall-rise" contours to the function of evoking a set of alternatives established by the preceding context—a notion I have identified with the notion of theme and have interpreted above in terms of the Alternative Semantics of Karttunen and Peters (1979) and Rooth (1985).

In the case of answer (20A) the new theme is simply the following:

(21) *like′ bombazine′ mary′*

Since this is a fully saturated proposition, with no λ-bound variables, the corresponding rheme alternative set is a singleton:

(22) {*like′ bombazine′ mary′*}

Since it contains only one member, it also entails an answer to the question via exactly the same chain of inference from shared beliefs as (19).

Further support for the claim that the L+H* LH% tune marks theme in (20), establishing a new set of alternatives, and that any effect of lack of commitment arises by conversational implicature, can be found in the fact that this intonation remains appropriate when the step of inference that generates the rheme itself is explicitly spelled out, as in the following deliberately exaggerated example, in which *liking bombazine* is necessarily distinct from the rheme:

(23) Q: Does Mary like corduroy?
      A: Well, she likes   BOMBAZINE,
                                 L+H* LH%
      And people who like   BOMBAZINE like CORDUROY.
                                 L+H* LH%   H*LL%
      So I am sure that Mary likes   CORDUROY.
                                 H*LL%

(Note that *likes bombazine* in the first conjunct could equally well be uttered with an H*L% rheme accent, but in the second it really must be marked as a theme. Under most circumstances the first and third conjuncts could be omitted entirely, as being implicated by the second.)

Still more evidence for the claim that L+H* LH% invariably marks a theme can be found in the fact that when a similarly implicative reply states a law from which the conclusion necessarily follows, so that there is no plurality of alternatives, then only the rheme tune is felicitous, as in the following minimal pair:

(24) Q: Will Mary come to the meeting on time?
      A: Mary is ALWAYS on time.
                H*   LL%

(25) Q: Will Mary come to the meeting on time?
      A: #Mary is ALWAYS on time.
                L+H*   LH%

Conversely, if the content of the response necessarily implicates a plurality of alternatives, then the position is reversed: only the theme tune is felicitous:

(26) Q: Will Mary come to the meeting on time?
      A: Mary is USUALLY on time.
                L+H*   LH%

(27) Q: Will Mary come to the meeting on time?
      A: #Mary is USUALLY on time.
                H*   LL%

It is clear that the L+H*LH% tune in the latter example indicates no lack of commitment to the probabilistic claim about Mary's punctuality; rather, it indicates a lack of commitment to the adequacy of this information to fully answer the question.

5.3.2 Unmarked Themes

Extravagantly informative intonation contours like those in (13) and (14) are the exception. It is only appropriate to mark the theme with an L+H* pitch accent when it stands in contrast to a preceding different theme. If the rheme alternative set that a theme presupposes is unambiguously established in the context, it is common to find that the theme is deaccented throughout—in Pierrehumbert's terms, without any pitch accent or obvious boundary, as in the following exchange:

(28) Q: Who did Anna marry?
     A: (Anna married) (MANNY).
                  H* LL%

We would be missing an important semantic generalization if we failed to note that examples (14) and (28) are identical in Information Structure as far as the theme-rheme division goes. We will therefore need to distinguish the "marked" theme in the former from the "unmarked" theme in the latter. Unmarked intonation, unlike the marked variety, is always ambiguous with respect to Information Structure. In the following context the same contour will have the Information Structure of (13):

(29) Q: What do you know about Anna?
     A: (Anna) (married MANNY).
               H* LL%

In these terms it is clear that the context-establishing questions in (13) and (14) can also be analyzed in terms of a theme and a rheme. In both cases, as Prevost (1995) points out, the *wh*-item constitutes the theme. Usually such themes are prosodically unmarked, but they may also bear the marked L+H*LH% theme tune. In either case the phrase *who*, *what*, or *which man* translates as an abstraction such as the following:

(30) $\lambda p.\lambda x.man'x \wedge px$

Such a theme defines a very unspecific set of alternatives, namely, the set of all contextually supported predicates applying to persons, things, men, or whatever. However, the remainder of the *wh*-question, which must bear the H*LL% rheme tune, restricts this set to one particular predicate. It is this predicate that typically becomes the theme of the answer.

5.3.3 Multiple Themes and Rhemes

It is quite possible for an utterance to mark more than one disjoint segment as either theme or rheme. An example of a multiple or discontinuous theme can be found in the following exchange:

(31) Q: I know which team Mary EXPECTS to LOSE. But which one does she WANT to WIN?

    A: (Mary   WANTS) (IPSWICH) (to   WIN.)
               L+H* LH%   H* L   L+H* LH%

The theme established by the question is *Which one Mary wants to win.* That is:[14]

(32) $\exists x.\Diamond *want'(*win'(ana'x))x\,mary'$

We may assume that the rheme alternative set includes propositions like the following:

(33) $\left\{ \begin{array}{l} \Diamond want'(win'(ana'watford'))watford'mary' \\ \Diamond want'(win'(ana'ipswich'))ipswich'mary' \\ \Diamond want'(win'(ana'sunderland'))sunderland'mary' \end{array} \right\}$

In the answer the words *wants* and *win* get L+H* pitch accents, because the theme alternative set includes the previous theme, *Which one Mary expects to lose,* or $\exists x.\Diamond want'(lose'(ana'x))x\,mary'$. Since elements of the theme are separated by the rheme *Ipswich* (which of course has its own H* pitch accent and boundary), there are two L+H* LH% theme tunes. These fragments work independently to have the effect of a "discontinuous theme." The first presupposes that the rheme alternative set consists entirely of propositions of the form $want'x\,y\,mary'$; the second presupposes that it consists of propositions of the form $p(win'(ana'y))y\,z$. Both presuppositions are compatible with the same rheme alternative set, so together they require that it consists of propositions of the form $want'(win'(ana'x))x\,mary'$, just as if they constituted a single discontinuous theme.

5.4 Focus and Background

The possibility of such unmarked themes, lacking any pitch accent, draws attention to a second independent dimension to discourse Information Structure that affects intonational tune. In (14) the L+H* LH% tune is spread across the entire substring of the sentence corresponding to the theme in the above

sense—that is, over the substring *Anna married*.[15] In (13) the same tune L+H*
LH% is confined to the object of the theme *married Manny*, because the intonation of the original question indicates that marrying Manny *as opposed to
someone else* is the new topic or theme. In (28) and (29) there is no L+H* LH%
tune at all.

The position of the pitch accent in the phrase has to do with a further dimension of Information Structure *within both theme and rheme*, corresponding to
a distinction between *the interesting part(s)* of either information unit, and the
rest. Halliday (1967b), who was probably the first to identify the orthogonal nature of these two dimensions, called it "new" information, in contrast to
"given" information (cf. Brown 1983). The term "new" is not entirely helpful,
since (as Halliday was aware) the relevant part of the theme need not be novel
to the discourse, as in the examples to hand. Here I will follow the phonological literature and Prevost (1995) in calling the information marked by the pitch
accent the "focus," distinguishing theme focus and rheme focus where necessary, and use the term "background" for the part unmarked by pitch accent or
boundary. Again there are a number of other taxonomies, most of which are
fairly straightforwardly compatible with the present proposal.[16]

The following example serves to illustrate the full range of possibilities for
the distribution of focus and background within the theme and the rheme.

(34) Q: I know that Mary envies the man who wrote the musical. But who does
         she ADMIRE?

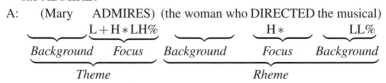

Here the theme is something that I will call *Mary admires*, as an informal
shorthand referring to the translation of that part of the utterance as the abstract proposition λx.*admires′x mary′*. Only the word *admires* is emphasized,
because the previous theme was also about Mary. The presence of pitch accents in themes like that in (34) is marked by distinguishing the corresponding
constant in the translation *admires′* with an asterisk:

(35) ∃x.◇*admires′x mary′*

Unless a compatible prior theme—that is, one that matches (35) when
admires′ is replaced by some other constant, as in (36)—can be retrieved or
accommodated, the utterance is simply infelicitous, and the analysis will fail
at this point:

(36) $\exists x. \Diamond like' x \, mary'$

The set of alternative themes in this case is the following:

(37) $\left\{ \begin{array}{l} \exists x. \Diamond admires' x \, mary' \\ \exists x. \Diamond like' x \, mary' \end{array} \right\}$

The set of alternative themes is closely related to Büring's (1995) Q, or "question" alternative set. Here I will call it the "theme" alternative set, in contrast to the earlier rheme alternative set.

The rheme alternative set presupposed by the theme is therefore a set of propositions about Mary admiring various people. The rheme is *the woman who directed the musical*, where only the word *directed* is contrasted.

It is important to note that it is all and only the material marked by the pitch accent(s) that is contrasted. This applies when there is more than one pitch accent, as the reader can verify by observing the effect of adding a further pitch accent on the word *musical*. Anything not so marked, including the material between the pitch accent(s) and the boundary, is background. Examples like this suggest that the focusing property of pitch accents applies at the level of words and their interpretations, not at the level of larger constituents, unlike the theme/rheme distinction.

However, there is an asymmetry between the "prenuclear" background material *the woman who ...* that precedes the pitch accent on *directed*, and the background material that succeeds it (*the musical*). The fact that there is no pitch accent on the latter seems to demand that all individuals in the context have the property of having something to do with this particular musical. It would actually be wrong in this context to have a pitch accent. However, the lack of accent on the former does not seem similarly to demand that all the individuals that we are restricting over are women, and in fact in the example they are not. The implication is that in this context the property of directing the musical is sufficient to distinguish the individual uniquely—the fact that this individual is *also* unique by virtue of being a woman need not be marked.[17]

Why does this asymmetry hold? Could it work the other way around? Prevost (1995) has proposed that pitch accents are assigned to words corresponding to properties that successively limit the extension of an NP to the desired referent. If we assume that the order in which these predicates are successively evaluated is "bottom up" with respect to some kind of interpretation or predicate-argument structure, then we predict that if a modifier like the relative clause *who directed the musical* completely specifies the extension, then words corresponding to predicates higher up the predicate-argument structure, such as the head noun, need not be stressed.[18] Thus, the pragmatic difference between prenuclear and postnuclear background material arises from the relation of word order to predicate-argument structure in English.

5.5 Grammar and Information Structure

What is the relation of such Intonation Structures to syntax and semantics, and how is Information Structure computed? Many of the intonational constituents that we have just been examining—such as the string *Anna married*—do not correspond to traditional syntactic constituents. Jacobs (1991) and Krifka (1991, sec. 4.8) have pointed out the problems that ensue for the semantics of focus.

Such "nonconstituent" intonational units are very widespread and can cooccur with other intonational tunes, including the H*+L rheme tune considered here. Consider the following utterance (adapted from Ladd 1980—see below), uttered in the context of a question like *I know that Harry keeps up with the newspapers, but has he read* War and Peace*?*:

(38) Harry doesn't READ BOOKS!
　　　 H*L L+H* LH%

Here the theme seems to be *books*, marked because the concept stands in contrast to *newspapers*. The rheme seems to be *Harry not reading something*, with the usual final H*L tune on *read*. The theme can also be unmarked, even in this context, as in Ladd's original example:[19]

(39) Harry doesn't READ books.
　　　 H*　　 LL%

The interest of such derivations for present purposes will be obvious. The claim is simply that the nonstandard Surface Structures that are induced by the combinatory grammar to explain coordination in English subsume the Intonation Structures that are postulated by Pierrehumbert and her colleagues to explain the possible intonation contours for sentences of English. The claim is that in spoken utterances, intonation helps to determine which of the many possible bracketings permitted by the combinatory syntax of English is intended, and that the interpretations of the constituents that arise from these derivations, far from being "spurious," are related to distinctions of Information Structure and discourse focus among the topics that the speaker has in mind and the comments that the speaker has to contribute.

The proof of this claim lies in showing that the rules of combinatory grammar can be made sensitive to intonation contour, which limits their application in spoken discourse. We must also show that the major constituents of intonated utterances like (14), under the analyses that are permitted by any given intonation, correspond to the Information Structure required by the context to which the intonation is appropriate. A preliminary proposal, to which the next section proposes a revision and an extension, was sketched in Steedman 1991a,b, and Prevost and Steedman 1994.

5.5.1 Combinatory Prosody

The papers just cited followed Pierrehumbert and colleagues in taking an "autosegmental" approach to the tones, in the sense of the term introduced by Goldsmith (1976), assigning a distinct prosodic CG category to all elements of the sentence, as well as a grammatical one. Like grammatical categories, prosodic categories could be either functions or arguments and could apply to or compose with one another. Syntactic combination was made subject to intonation contour by the assumption of a "Prosodic Constituent Condition", which only permitted combination of syntactic categories via a syntactic combinatory rule if their result was also a prosodic constituent.

The present version of the theory takes a different approach, integrating prosodic information with the standard grammatical categories to more directly capture Intonation Structure, together with its interpretation as Information Structure, in CCG.

We have already noted that the focus-marking property of pitch accents seems to belong at the level of the word, whereas the theme/rheme-marking property seems to belong at the level of phrasal constituents. We therefore begin by assuming that pitch accents both mark (some element of) the interpretation of the words they occur on for focus or contrast, and mark the syntactic category in a way that "projects" theme-rheme status to elements with which the word combines. Although eventually we will certainly want to do this by morphological rule, for present purposes we will regard this compiled out into distinct lexical entries like the following categories for the verb *ate* bearing the two pitch accents under discussion here. before syntax gets to work on them:[20]

(40) ate $:=\ (S_\theta \backslash NP_\theta)/NP_\theta : *ate'$
   L+H*

(41) ate $:=\ (S_\rho \backslash NP_\rho)/NP_\rho : *ate'$
   H*

The subscript symbols θ and ρ are mnemonic for theme and rheme respectively, and are a shorthand for a value on a feature of the whole category that I will call *INFORMATION*. A category like (40) ensures that any argument that combines with it must be phonologically compatible with being part of a theme.

The "null tone," which I will follow Pierrehumbert in leaving without any annotation in strings, does not affect the interpretation of a word that carries it, and leaves the syntactic category unspecified as to the value of the feature *INFORMATION*. It can therefore conveniently be written without any annotation, as before:

(42) ate := $(S\backslash NP)/NP : ate'$

Since the value of *INFORMATION* is unspecified, this category can combine with either θ, ρ, or unmarked categories. However, it is important to remember that the unspecified values on arguments and result are the *same* unspecified value of the same attribute *INFORMATION*. In the first two cases, this *INFORMATION* value becomes specified for all arguments and the result, by the usual unification mechanism, and subsequent combinations must be compatible with that value.[21]

Prosodically annotated categories of this kind allow the influence of the pitch accent to spread over arbitrarily large constituents. For example, in analyzing the first two words of the sentence *Fred ate the beans*, uttered in response to a question like *I know what Harry ate. But what did FRED eat?*, the following partial derivation can occur:

(43)

$$
\frac{\dfrac{\text{FRED}}{\text{L}+\text{H}*} \qquad \dfrac{\text{ate}}{} \qquad \text{the BEANS} \quad \text{LH\%} \quad \text{H}* \quad \text{LL\%}}{}
$$

$$
\frac{S_\theta/(S_\theta\backslash NP_\theta) : \lambda p.p\ *fred' \quad (S\backslash NP)/NP : \lambda x.\lambda y.ate'xy}{S_\theta/NP_\theta : \lambda x.ate'x\ *fred'} {>}\mathbf{B}
$$

The L+H* pitch accent on *FRED* marks all elements of the raised subject category as θ on the *INFORMATION* feature. The verb bears the null tone, but when the subject composes, all occurrences of the verb's own *INFORMATION* feature come to bear the value θ by the unification mechanism. Hence the object in the category that results from composition also bears the *INFORMATION* value θ.

In contrast to the version in Steedman 1991a, the present theory assumes that boundary tones, unlike pitch accents, are not associated with words, but are elements of the string in their own right, much like the punctuation marks that, on occasion, represent them in the orthography. Like the pitch accents, the boundary tones affect both the syntactic and the semantic components of categories. The grammatical category of a boundary is that of a function from categories marked as θ, ρ, or unspecified, into phonological phrasal categories, distinguished by a value ϕ.[22]

The boundary tones must also mark the informational units at the level of the interpretation, so that the combination of a constituent bearing a boundary tone with another including a pitch accent semantically defines the major informational elements such as the theme and the rheme.

For present purposes, the full categories for the three boundary tones under discussion here are written in full using the following notation.[23]

(44) L, LL%, LH% := $S\$_\phi \backslash S\$_\eta : \lambda f.\eta' f$

The variable $S\$$ ranges as usual over a set $\{S\$\}$ of categories including S and all functions into members of $\{S\$\}$—that is, it includes S, S/NP, and all verbs and type-raised arguments of verbs, but not nouns and the like. The subscript η, which can be thought of as a variable ranging over the two *INFORMATION* values θ and ρ, further specifies it as ranging over correspondingly marked categories S_θ, S_θ/NP_θ, $(S_\rho \backslash NP_\rho)/NP_\rho$), etc. When it combines with such a function, it has the effect of replacing its θ or ρ marking with a distinct marker ϕ (for "phrasal"), which can only unify with itself. Such a category can only combine with other ϕ-marked prosodically phrasal categories.

Semantically, the boundary categories apply a corresponding thematic or rhematic function θ' or ρ' to the interpretation of the category with which they combine, via a corresponding variable category η'. In terms of the Logical Form, θ' or ρ' are identity functions that effectively vanish from the predicate-argument structure when they apply. However, they are assumed to cause the appropriate alternative set to be evoked from the database, and to be accompanied by the updates discussed in section 5.3.1 Until they do apply, they block any further reduction of the interpretation to the canonical predicate-argument structure.

This specification of boundaries allows them to combine with either pitch accent, consistent with Pierrehumbert's own system, in which all pitch accents and boundaries can combine freely. For example, low boundaries can combine with L+H* pitch accents, as in the following sentence, from Ladd 1996, 96-7:

(45) THAT's the whole POINT of the exercise!
     H* L   L+H*   LL%

The implicit claim that the boundaries also project θ or ρ marking from the pitch accent, so that the phrase *the whole point of the exercise* is a theme in the above example (as it would be if it bore an LH% boundary), is more controversial, and will not be discussed here. Nevertheless, we will see later that at least one variety of theme, the unmarked variety, does bear low boundaries.

To say that the boundary projects the category of the pitch accent is not to exclude a more active role in the semantics for the boundary, analogous to a specifier such as a determiner, contributing distinctively to information structural content along the lines suggested by Pierrehumbert and Hirschberg (1990).

Since they bear exactly the same category as L boundaries, LL% boundaries are free in the present system to occur utterance-medially, in contrast to earlier versions of the theory which were criticized on this point by Beckman (1996, 63-64). Utterance medial LL% boundaries do not figure much in the examples discussed in the present chapter (although see (75) below and the discussion of example (60) in chapter 7). In particular it does not appear to be possible to substitute them freely for L intermediate phrase boundaries in examples like (13) (a fact upon which Beckman does not comment). By the same token, the present system allows L boundaries to occur utterance-finally, which is impossible. We will assume for present purposes that these details are to do with finer distinctions between the boundaries, and in particular with the distinction between intermediate and intonational phrases. The question of whether LL% boundaries are or are not categorically distinct from intermediate phrase L boundaries is a matter of some dispute among phonologists, and we will continue to pass over it here.

The following example, which completes the derivation of the theme of the earlier sentence *FRED ate the BEANS*, demonstrates the effect of the boundary tone:

(46)   FRED   ate   the BEANS
        L+H*   LH%   H*   LL%

$$\frac{S_\theta/(S_\theta\backslash NP_\theta)}{:\lambda p.p \; *fred'} \quad \frac{(S\backslash NP)/NP}{:\lambda x.\lambda y.ate'xy} \quad \frac{S\$_\phi\backslash S\$_\eta}{:\lambda f.\theta'f}$$

$$\frac{S_\theta/NP_\theta : \lambda x.ate'x \; *fred'}{}{>}\mathbf{B}$$

$$\frac{S_\phi/NP_\phi : \theta'(\lambda x.ate'x \; *fred')}{}{<}$$

The second prosodic phrase in (46) bears the H*LL% rheme tune, parallel to (14) above. The complete derivation is as follows:

(47)

FRED	ate		the	BEANS	
L+H*		LH%		H*	LL%

$$S_\theta/(S_\theta\backslash NP_\theta) \quad (S\backslash NP)/NP \quad S\$_\phi\backslash S\$_\eta \quad NP^\uparrow/N \quad N_\rho \quad S\$_\phi\backslash S\$_\eta$$
$$: \lambda p.p *fred' \quad : \lambda x.\lambda y.ate'xy \quad : \lambda f.\theta'f \quad : \lambda x.\lambda p.p(the'x) \quad : *beans \quad : \lambda f.\rho'f$$

$$\frac{\qquad\qquad\qquad}{S_\theta/NP_\theta : \lambda x.ate'x *fred'}{>}\mathbf{B} \qquad\qquad \frac{\qquad\qquad\qquad}{NP_\rho^\uparrow : \lambda p.p(the' *beans')}{>}$$

$$\frac{\qquad\qquad\qquad\qquad\qquad}{S_\phi/NP_\phi : \theta'(\lambda x.ate'x *fred')}{<} \qquad \frac{\qquad\qquad\qquad\qquad\qquad}{NP_\phi^\uparrow : \rho'(\lambda p.p(the' *beans'))}{<}$$

$$\frac{\qquad\qquad\qquad\qquad\qquad\qquad\qquad}{S_\phi : \rho'\lambda p.p(the' *beans')(\theta'\lambda x.ate'x *fred')}{<}$$

$$\frac{\qquad\qquad\qquad\qquad\qquad\qquad\qquad}{S_\phi : ate'(the' *beans') *fred'}$$

No *other* division into a theme and a rheme is possible for this intonation contour.[24]

It is only once the functions θ' and ρ' have applied that the final semantic reduction or normalization can take place, to yield the canonical predicate-argument structure. As far as the interpretation goes, these are just the identity function, but we have assumed that they are accompanied by side effects of assertion or retraction on the database. The reduction of θ' and ρ' can occur at any point in a derivation.

The division of the utterance into a property constituting the theme and an argument constituting the rheme is appropriate to a context parallel to that established in (14)—say, by the *wh*-question *What did FRED eat?* uttered in the context of a discussion of what somebody else (say, Harry) ate and a prior theme such as the following:

(48) $\theta'\lambda x.ate'x harry'$

The theme in derivation (47), $\theta'\lambda x.ate'x *fred'$, is a member of the theme alternative set in the earlier sense.[25] The new theme presupposes a rheme alternative set of propositions about Fred eating things, which the rheme $\rho'\lambda p.p(the' *beans')$ reduces to a single proposition, $ate'(the'beans')fred'$.

Since categories bearing the null tone can compose either with others bearing null tone, or with those bearing pitch accents, intonational phrasal tunes like L+H* LH% can spread unboundedly across any sequence that forms a grammatical constituent according to the combinatory grammar. For example, if the answer to *What did FRED eat?* is *MARY says he ate BEANS*, then the tune will typically be spread over *Mary says he ate . . .* as in the (incomplete) derivation (49), in which the semantics has been suppressed in the interests of brevity:

(49)   MARY   says   he   ate
         L+H*   LH%   ...

$\underline{S_\theta/(S_\theta\backslash NP_\theta)}$ $\underline{(S\backslash NP)/S}$ $\underline{S/(S\backslash NP)}$ $\underline{(S\backslash NP)/NP}$ $\underline{S\$_\phi\backslash S\$_\eta}$

$\underline{\hspace{3cm}}$>**B**

$\underline{S_\theta/S_\theta}$

$\underline{\hspace{5cm}}$>**B**

$\underline{S_\theta/(S_\theta\backslash NP_\theta)}$

$\underline{\hspace{6cm}}$>**B**

$\underline{S_\theta/NP_\theta}$

$\underline{\hspace{7cm}}$<

S_ϕ/NP_ϕ

A number of derivations are permitted for more complex rheme NPs like *the green beans* with a final pitch accent, represented by the following bracketings:

(50) a. (the green) (BEANS)
              H*   LL%

      b. (the) (green BEANS)
              H*   LL%

The same derivational ambiguity is characteristic of a further intonation contour, in which the H* pitch accent is applied to the word *green*, making that word alone contrasted:

(51) Q: Did Fred eat the green beans or the yellow beans?

      A: (FRED   ate) (the GREEN beans.)
         L+H* LH%   H*   LL%

It also applies when both words are marked for rheme accent with H* pitch accents, in a context in which both elements of the noun group *green beans* are contrasted or informative:

(52) Q: Did Fred eat the green beans or the yellow squash?

      A. (FRED   ate) (the GREEN BEANS.)
         L+H* LH%   H*   !H* LL%

Example (52) needs further comment. First, the rheme includes more than one H* pitch accent. These pitch accents belonging to the same intonational/intermediate phrase would be seen in a pitch track to be downstepped— that is, to have successively lower peaks and baselines for approximately the same pitch range. The ToBI conventions (Silverman et al. 1992) again offer a convenient notation for downstep, extending Pierrehumbert's system with the prefix "!". However, as in Pierrehumbert's original theory, words bearing downstepped pitch accents bear identical categories to non-downstepped accents. The !-notation is redundant, and the effect on pitch-contour can be determined automatically.

Downstepped pitch accents can therefore compose, to allow derivations like the following:

(53)

FRED ate	the	GREEN	BEANS	
L+H* LH%		H*	!H*	LL%

$$S_\phi/NP_\phi \qquad NP/N \quad N_\rho/N_\rho \quad N_\rho \quad S\$_\phi\backslash S\$_\eta$$
$$: \theta'(\lambda x.ate'x *fred') \quad : the' \quad : *green \quad : *beans' \quad : \lambda f.\rho'f$$

$$\frac{\qquad\qquad}{NP_\rho/N_\rho} {>}\textbf{B}$$
$$: \lambda x.the'(*green'x)$$

$$\frac{\qquad\qquad\qquad}{NP_\rho : (the'(*green' * beans'))} {<}$$

$$\frac{\qquad\qquad\qquad}{S_\rho\backslash(S_\rho/NP_\rho)} {<}\textbf{T}$$
$$: \lambda f.f(the'(*green' * beans'))$$

$$\frac{\qquad\qquad\qquad}{S_\phi\backslash(S_\phi/NP_\phi)} {<}$$
$$: \rho'(\lambda f.f(the'(*green' * beans')))$$

$$\frac{\qquad\qquad\qquad\qquad}{S_\phi : \rho'\lambda f.f(the'(*green' * beans'))(\theta'\lambda x.ate'x *fred')} {<}$$

$$S_\phi : ate'(the'(*green' * beans'))*fred'$$

This time, there is another derivation for the rheme in (53). In fact, both derivations illustrated in (50) are permitted for all three stress patterns. The sentences differ only in the elements of the interpretation that are marked for contrast. These observations reinforce the earlier suggestion that the effect of the pitch accents applies at the level of words words and their interpretations, rather than at higher levels of derivation, unlike the effect of boundary tones.

Many impossible intonation contours correctly remain excluded by the fact that CCG conflates prosodic structure and syntactic structure, including examples of the kind that motivated Selkirk's Sense Unit Condition. For example, the following are disallowed because their Intonation Structure is not compatible with any syntactic analysis, owing to island constraints:

(54) a. *(FRED ate the green) (BEANS.)
      L+H*   LH% H* LL%

    b. *(My OLDER) (sister ate the green BEANS.)
       L+H* LH%   H* LL%

5.5.2 Unmarked Themes

So far I have only considered sentences that include a theme and rheme that both include words marked for contrast by pitch accents. Such sentences are relatively unambiguous with regard to their Information Structure. However, sentences like the following, which in Pierrehumbert's terms consist of a single intonational phrase, are much more common:

(55) (Mary wrote a book about BATS.)

                 H* LL%

Such sentences are notoriously ambiguous with respect to the theme they presuppose (cf. Selkirk 1995). For example, (55) seems equally appropriate as a response to any of the following questions:

(56) a. What did Mary write a book about?
        b. What did Mary write?
        c. What did Mary do?
        d. What's new?

Such questions could in more contrastive contexts give rise to themes marked by the L+H* LH% tune, bracketing the sentence as follows:

(57) a. (Mary wrote a book about)$_{Theme}$(BATS.)$_{Rheme}$
        b. (Mary wrote)$_{Theme}$(a book about BATS.)$_{Rheme}$
        c. (Mary)$_{Theme}$(wrote a book about BATS.)$_{Rheme}$
        d. (Mary wrote a book about BATS.)$_{Rheme}$

It is therefore a virtue in the grammar as it stands that it already allows all of the implicit derivations for the sentence in which the theme is unmarked, while the various possible rhemes are marked as such in the derivation.

     Such unmarked themes can be made explicit in the theory as follows. The boundary categories (44) are already defined so as to allow them to combine with unmarked categories, on the assumption that an unspecified *INFORMATION* value can unify with or match the variable η in the boundary category.

     If we further assume that an L boundary is phonetically indistinguishable from the null tone, then such a boundary tone may be postulated anywhere there is null tone (and low pitch). Such a tactic nondeterministically allows all of the derivations indicated in (57). For example:

(58)

$$
\begin{array}{c}
\cfrac{
\cfrac{
\cfrac{\begin{array}{c} S/NP \\ : \lambda x.write'(a'(book'(about'x)))mary' \end{array} \quad \cfrac{S\$_\phi \backslash S\$_\eta}{: \lambda f.\eta' f}}{\cfrac{S_\phi/NP_\phi}{: \eta'(\lambda x.write'(a'(book'(about'x)))mary')}}^{<} \quad \cfrac{S_\phi \backslash (S_\phi/NP_\phi)}{: \rho'(\lambda p.p * bats')}
}{
S_\phi : \rho'(\lambda p.p * bats')(\eta'(\lambda x.write'(a'(book'(about'x)))mary'))
}^{<}
}{
S_\phi : write'(a'(book'(about' * bats')))mary'
}
\end{array}
$$

Mary wrote a book about   L   BATS H*   LL%

On the reasonable assumption that an unspecified η' has the same effect as a value of θ' in the interpretation, apart from necessarily applying to an argument lacking any * marker of contrast, then the representation of theme and rheme in the interpretation is exactly as in the earlier examples.

As Steedman 1991a points out, this nondeterminism can be eliminated for processing purposes by taking advantage of the fact that the unmarked theme is exclusively used when the hearer is assumed to already know the theme. Thus, the appropriateness of applying the rule to a given category can be directly decided by referring to the discourse model to see whether it supports the presupposition that the corresponding referent is theme, background, or whatever. (See Straub 1997 for experimental evidence for the systematic omission of explicit prosodic boundaries by speakers when alternative sources of disambiguating information, including contextual, are present.)

The ambiguity of such contours with respect to Information Structure appears to be correctly constrained by the assumption that Information Structure and syntactic structure must coincide. That is, the following do not appear to be possible Information Structures, because, like the related examples in (54), they are not possible syntactic structures.[26]

(59) a. *(Fred ate the green)$_{Theme}$(BEANS)$_{Rheme}$
      b. *(My older)$_{Theme}$(sister ate the green BEANS)$_{Rheme}$

The trick of nondeterministically assuming an invisible boundary to null themes may seem unnecessarily clumsy, and to compromise the theory by introducing phonological entities that have no phonetic realization, as Croft (1995) and Ladd (1996) have suggested. I will return to this point below. However, the device captures an important generalization concerning the relation of these unmarked themes to the corresponding marked ones, and to another variety of unmarked theme which *does* have an explicit boundary.

In English (as opposed to many other languages—see Ladd 1996; Zubizarreta 1998) unmarked themes can occur utterance-finally, and when they do, they end with an LL% boundary, as in the following example:[27]

(60) Q: Who ate the beans?
      A: (FRED) (ate the beans).
         H* L   LL%

If the rheme *FRED* is to be a well-formed intonational phrase distinct from the unmarked theme, it must end in an L intermediate phrase boundary. Again postulating such a boundary introduces a nondeterminism—but again this nondeterminism arises only in contexts where the theme in question is entirely given, or background, and hence is recoverable by the hearer. (When evaluated, such themes must by definition yield a set of alternative propositions identical to the background set. I will return to this point.)

However, an intonational-phrase-final LL% tone cannot always be analyzed in this way. It may just be background information in the rheme. To take an old example from Schmerling (1976), one may announce the death of Nixon in the absence of any prior discourse by saying the following:

(61) NIXON died.
       H*   LL%

The second word is then part of the rheme, which of course is allowed by the grammar, and the utterance is felicitous just in case dying is a background possibility for the individual in question. (If not, as Schmerling points out, one has to say something like *Nixon DIED*.)

The other, apparently phonetically indistinguishable analysis for this sentence, with an unmarked theme, is of course still available and is appropriate to a situation where the question is *Who died?*, as Ladd (1980, 53) points out. It is this analysis that is at work in Ladd's own example (39), repeated here in the revised notation, uttered in the context of a question *Has Harry read* War and Peace*?*:

(62) Harry doesn't READ books.
                 H* L LL%

Although the analysis proposed here is quite different from Ladd's, he supports a view of the Information Structure according to which the utterance is "about a book" (Ladd 1980, 52)—in present terms, where *books* is the theme.

5.6 Intonation and the Simplex Clause

Jackendoff (1972) exhaustively examines the effect of all possible assignments of the two tunes considered here to a simple transitive clause, *Fred ate the beans*, and it is instructive to do the same within the present framework.

In contrast to the intonation in the derivation (47), the intonation contour on (18) prevents the composition of subject and verb, because under the forward prosodic composition rule the subject is not allowed to combine with the verb. It follows that a derivation parallel to the earlier one (and the formation of the corresponding theme) is not allowed. On the other hand, the following derivation *is* allowed for (18):

(63)
$$
\begin{array}{c}
\text{Fred}\\
H*
\end{array}
\qquad
\begin{array}{c}
\\
L
\end{array}
\qquad\qquad
\begin{array}{c}
\text{ate}\\
\end{array}
\qquad
\begin{array}{c}
\text{the}\\
\end{array}
\qquad
\begin{array}{c}
\text{beans}\\
L+H*
\end{array}
\quad
\begin{array}{c}
\\
LH\%
\end{array}
$$

$$
\begin{array}{c}
S_\rho/(S_\rho\backslash NP_\rho)\\
:\lambda p.p \ *fred'
\end{array}
\quad
\begin{array}{c}
S\$_\phi\backslash S\$_\eta\\
:\lambda f:\rho'f
\end{array}
\quad
\begin{array}{c}
(S\backslash NP)/NP\\
:\lambda x.\lambda y.ate'xy
\end{array}
\quad
\begin{array}{c}
NP^\uparrow/N\\
:\lambda x.(the'x)
\end{array}
\quad
\begin{array}{c}
N_\theta\\
:*beans'
\end{array}
\quad
\begin{array}{c}
S\$_\phi\backslash S\$_\eta\\
:\lambda f:\theta'f
\end{array}
$$

$$
\overline{S_\phi/(S_\phi\backslash NP_\phi):\rho'\lambda p.p \ *fred'}\ {}^{<}
\qquad\qquad
\overline{NP^\uparrow_\theta:the'*beans'}\ {}^{>}
$$

$$
\overline{\qquad S_\phi:\rho'\lambda p.p \ *fred'(\theta'\lambda y:ate'(the'*beans')y)\qquad}\ {}^{>}
$$

$$
\overline{S_\phi:ate'(the'*beans')*fred}
$$

Again no other analysis is allowed, and again the division into rheme and theme, and the associated interpretations, are consistent with the context given in (18).

The effect of the above derivation is to annotate the entire predicate as theme, just as if the tune L+H* LH% had been spread across the whole constituent.

Other cases considered by Jackendoff are accepted under the same assumptions and in every case yield unique and contextually appropriate interpretations, as follows. (The derivations themselves are suggested as an exercise.) The first two yield derivations parallel to (63), in that the fundamental division of the sentence is into a traditional subject and predicate (again these are the only analyses that the rules permit):

(64) Q: What about FRED? What did HE do to the beans?

    A: (FRED)   (ATE the beans.)
        L+H* LH% H*   LL%
        Theme   *Rheme*

(65) Q: I know who COOKED the beans. But then, who ATE them?

    A: (FRED) (ATE the beans.)
        H* L L+H*   LH%
        Rheme   *Theme*

The other two cases considered by Jackendoff yield derivations parallel to (47), in which the fundamental division of the sentence is orthogonal to the traditional subject-predicate structure:

(66) Q: I know what Fred COOKED. But then, what did he EAT?

    A: (Fred   ATE) (the BEANS.)
        L+H* LH%   H* LL%
        Theme   *Rheme*

(67) Q: Well, what about the BEANS? What did Fred do with THEM?

  A: (Fred ATE) (the BEANS.)
     H* L L+H* LH%
    Rheme   *Theme*

In the case of (66) at least, it seems obvious that the theme established by the context is indeed the one corresponding to the bracketing. In the case of (67) it is less obvious. However, the treatment of relative clauses below will show that this analysis must at least be available.

The following further derivation for (67) is also allowed, as is a parallel derivation for (66), in which *Fred* is a background component of a discontinuous theme, rather than a background part of the rheme:

(68) Q: Well, what about the BEANS? What did Fred do with THEM?

  A: (Fred) (ATE) (the BEANS.)
    L H* L L+H* LH%
   Theme Rheme *Theme*

There seems to be little to distinguish the alternatives on pragmatic or phonetic grounds. It is the context that determines which Information Structure is felicitous.

Two further cases, which are parallel to (63) and (47) except that the theme and rheme tunes are exchanged, are also accepted, again yielding unique, contextually appropriate analyses. The first is the following:

(69) Q: I know that ALICE read a BOOK. But what about FRED? What did
   HE do?

  A: (FRED) (ate the BEANS.)
   L+H* LH%   H* LL%
   Theme   *Rheme*

The contour on the response here is also a coherent response in the context used in (43). This possibility (which may be the one intended in Jackendoff's 1972 discussion of the example) appears to arise from an ambiguity in the context itself. However, the converse does not apply: the intonation on the response in (64) is not felicitous in the above context, as the following example shows:[28]

(70) Q: I know that ALICE read a BOOK. But what about FRED? What did
   HE do?

  A: #(FRED ate) (the BEANS.)
   L+H* LH% H* LL%
   Theme   *Rheme*

There is one final possibility, which Jackendoff does not distinguish from (63). It is intuitively less obvious than the others, because its discourse meaning is better expressed (at least in the written language) by a left dislocation, *As for the BEANS, FRED ate them*, or even a passive *The BEANS were eaten by FRED*, uttered with the same assignment of pitch accents to *the beans* and *Fred*. Again the use of a second pitch accent on the verb *ate* in the rheme would also improve the example. Its place in the scheme of things will become clearer in section 5.7.2.

(71) Q: Well, what about the BEANS? What happened to THEM?

      A: (FRED ate) (the BEANS.)
          H*   L   L+H* LH%
        Rheme   *Theme*

5.7 Intonation in Complex Constructions

The number of possible intonation contours for complex sentences is naturally even larger than those that have just been demonstrated for simple transitive sentences, and the contextual conditions that are required to make them felicitous are even more abstruse. The following sections are necessarily restricted to showing that the theory makes correct predictions concerning the complex constructions in which forward composition is necessarily implicated in syntax (in particular, reduced coordinate sentences and relative clauses), rather than merely allowing alternative derivations.

5.7.1 Coordinate Sentences

Since the coordinate sentence (72a) below necessarily involves composition of the (type-raised) subject with the verb, whereas (72b) necessarily does not, it is predicted that the intonation contours that they permit will be more restricted than for the non coordinate sentence (72c):

(72) a. Bill cooked, and Fred ate, the beans.
      b. Fred ate the beans, and drank the wine.
      c. Fred ate the beans.

For example, among other alternatives, we would expect the intonation contour (73) to be possible for (72a). (The example assumes the mechanism for multiple pitch accents of section 3.3. It is a possible answer to the question *What did Bill and Fred do with the beans?*)

(73) (Bill COOKED and Fred ATE) (the BEANS.)
             H*   !H*L   L+H* LH%

By contrast, intonational tunes that assign categories that are not consistent
with the crucial syntactic compositions block derivation:

(74) a. *(Bill cooked and   FRED)   (ate the BEANS.)
                             H*L   L+H* LH%
      b. *(Bill cooked and   FRED)   (ate the BEANS.)
                          L+H*LH%   H* LL%

This effect is sufficiently strong for garden paths to be forced under the same
principle, as we saw earlier:

(75) *(Harry likes the NUTS) (and bolts APPROACH.)
                       H*LL%   H* LL%

5.7.2 Relative Clauses

Since relative clauses, like the coordinate structures of section 4.1, also force
the involvement of functional composition, a similar conspiracy with intonation is predicted for them as well. And indeed, all the possible intonational
tunes that appeared in Jackendoff's (1972) examples on the fragment *Fred
ate*—that is, all those that allow syntactic composition under the Prosodic Constituent Condition—can also appear on the same fragment when it occurs as
the residue in a relative clause:

(76)   the beans that Fred   ate
      a.   L+H*   LH%
      b.   L+H*LH%
      c.   H*   LL%
      d.   H*LL%

(The null tone is of course also allowed on the relative clause.) Each alternative
conveys different presuppositions concerning the context. Since the cleft construction is often used with the *wh*-clause marked with the theme tune, L+H*
LH%, (77) and (78) show one way of making the first two alternatives—(76a)
and (76b) respectively—felicitous:

(77) Q: FRED didn't eat the POTATOES. HARRY ate THEM.

      A: (It was the BEANS) (that FRED ate.)
                   H* L   L+H* LH%

(78) Q: Fred didn't eat the POTATOES. He threw THEM AWAY.

     A: (It was the BEANS) (that Fred   ATE.)
           H* L   L+H*LH%

The H* LL%tune, which marks the rheme, is frequently used on restrictive relatives, so (79) and (80) may serve to make the remaining two cases—(76c) and (76d) respectively—felicitous. (I have assumed an analysis with an unmarked theme, but this detail is not crucial.)

(79) Q: It wasn't the beans that HARRY ate that looked so delicious.

     A: (It was) (the beans that FRED ate.)
                    H* LL%

(80) Q: It wasn't the beans that Fred COOKED that looked so delicious.

     A: (It was) (the beans that Fred ATE.)
                   H*LL%

The converse also holds. As in the case of coordination, tone sequences that are consistent with no CCG derivation are forbidden from appearing on the relative clause. Thus, we predict that (81a,b) are intonationally disallowed, for the same reason that (81c) is ruled out:

(81) a. *(The beans that   FRED)   (ate were DELICIOUS.)
                    H*L   L+H* LH%
     b. *(The beans that   FRED)   (ate were DELICIOUS.)
                    L+H*LH%   H* LL%
     c. *The beans that I, and squash that you, cooked were delicious

Thus a condition akin to Selkirk's Sense Unit Condition emerges as a theorem of the assumptions inherent in CCG, without independent stipulation.

5.8 Conclusion

At this point it should be clear that we can simply subsume both Intonation Structure and Surface Structure under a single notion of Information Structure. Such a view of Intonation Structure involves a richer structural representation than the one invoked under that name by Pierrehumbert and others, since Information Structure includes many constituent boundaries that do not have any phonetic realization. This should not seem a strange conclusion to reach. It simply means that information-structural boundaries are no more (and no less) completely specified by tones than syntactic boundaries are specified by words.

This observation means that Ladd's (1996, 224) criticism of earlier version of this account as being "compromised by its dependence on entities whose presence cannot be independently [phonetically] verified" and Croft's (1995, 856) related suggestion that it "leaves unexplained the mismatch between prosody and information structure" both rather miss the point. One might as well criticize standard syntactic theories for using lexically unattested brackets. There *is* no "mismatch" between interpretable structure and its surface markers such as function words and tones. These markers are simply rather ambiguous and highly elliptical, just like everything else in natural language.

If Information Structure boundaries and surface syntactic boundaries coincide in this way, then there are a number of other prosodic effects that should depend upon the Surface Structures afforded by CCG in as direct a manner as English intonation contour. Some obvious candidates are such vowel-harmonic effects as French *liaison* (Selkirk 1972), American English flapping (Nespor and Vogel 1986), the Rhythm Rule (Gussenhoven 1983; Selkirk 1984), Bengali /r/ assimilation (Hayes and Lahiri 1991), and Italian *raddoppiamento syntattico* (Napoli and Nespor 1979; Kaisse 1985; Nespor and Vogel 1986; Vogel 1994). The last authors in particular show information-structural effects of focus that seem likely to be capturable in this way. These phenomena would then be brought under the category of "superficial" constraints of syntax on phonology called for by Pullum and Zwicky (1988), since Surface Structure now completely specifies the input to phonology and relation to the metrical grid (Liberman and Prince 1977; Prince 1983; Hayes 1995). In fact, in the sense in which Pullum and Zwicky intend the term, the present theory of syntax is "phonology-free," although in another sense CCG syntax actually subsumes prosodic structure.

More speculatively, it seems likely that many of the "end-based" effects of syntax upon phonology argued for by Selkirk (1986, 1990), Selkirk and Shen (1990), Hirst (1993), and Truckenbrodt (1995, 1999), according to which intonation-structural boundaries coincide with either left or right edges of syntactic constituents, but not necessarily both, are artifacts of the syntactic theories within which they are being framed. That is to say, English appears to be a left-edge language because a traditional right-branching account of its Surface Structure just doesn't offer phonologists enough right brackets to work with. The present theory simply claims that those right brackets are there in the syntax, in left-branching structures like (5). Under this interpretation of Surface Structure it is unnecessary to postulate an additional independent prosodic structure, as does Selkirk, and as do Nespor and Vogel (cf. Vogel and Kenesei

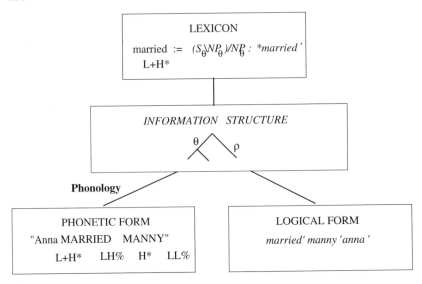

Figure 5.3
Architecture of a combinatory grammar, II

1990; Zec and Inkelas 1990). We should instead adopt a more liberal notion of syntactic structure, one that is directly compatible with the boundaries that the phonologists observe.[29]

However, the status of Surface Structure in such a theory is very different from the status of the related concepts in GB and earlier theories such as the "annotated surface structures" of Chomsky (1971) and Jackendoff (1972). To understand this point, it will again be helpful to consider the architecture of the present theory of grammar in terms of the traditional "T" or "Y" diagram, as in figure 5.3, which includes an example of an object of the kind represented in each structural module for the following sentence:

(82) Anna MARRIED   MANNY.
            L+H*   LH%   H*   LL%

According to the present theory, the lexicon associates category-interpretation pairs with (the phonological specification of) each word of the language. Derived objects or constituents also pair (the phonological specification of) strings with category-interpretation pairs, which are projected in parallel from (ordered multisets of) lexical entries, via derivations using combinatory rules. In the case of both lexical items and derived objects, the category is, strictly speaking, redundant, since under the Principle of Categorial Type Transparency, it is presumed to be entirely predictable from (a) the type of the interpretation, (b) X-bar theory, and (c) a parametric description of the language specifying position of heads relative to complements. In effect, the CG category "compiles out" this information, in the sense that it represents explicitly information that could be derived. Therefore, the category-interpretation pairs really count as a single level of representation.[30]

Surface Structure does not figure at all as a level of representation in the theory. Although I have described the combinatory derivations that map phonological strings onto such category-interpretation pairs (and vice versa) in terms of structures, I have never predicated any rule or relation over such structures. They are merely a history or record of how an algorithm might get from the string to the interpretation (or vice versa). Although it is convenient to write such structures down and refer to them as Surface Structures, precisely in order to make the point that no rules of domination, deletion, or movement apply to those structures, they do not constitute a grammatical level of representation at all. No rule ever needs to know how a category that it applies to was derived.

It is the combinatory derivations that correspond to Intonation Structure in the extended sense of the term defined above, as well as capturing coordinate structure and the effects of relativization. Surface Structure or derivation in the present sense therefore subsumes some functions of S-Structure, and all those of Intonation Structure, together with some of the role of PF as it is understood in GB. Phonetic Form in present terms really is no more than an abstract specification of speech segments.

The interpretation the derivation associates with a constituent of category S (or any other derived constituent) directly reflects such information-structural distinctions as those between theme and rheme and between focus and ground.[31] Such information-structural elements are evaluated with respect to alternative sets in the contextual database, and they may be discontinuous.

The present realization of Surface Structure as Information Structure conspicuously fails to represent traditional notions of dominance and command, including c-command. However, relations of dominance and command *are* represented in the canonical predicate-argument structure that results from the trivial procedure of normalizing or "β-reducing" the alternative Information Structures yielded by the alternative derivations of a given proposition, as discussed in connection with examples (5) and (6), and as implicitly assumed in derivations throughout the chapter. It follows that all grammatical relations that depend upon c-command, notably including binding and control and such related phenomena as crossover, must be treated as properties of predicate-argument structure, not Surface Structure, a suggestion consistent with the observations of Lasnik and Saito (1992).

By incorporating the finer distinction between focus and background within both theme and rheme, the present grammar opens up further possibilities of addressing a range of questions in semantics that have been explained in terms of various notions of focus (see Chomsky 1971; Jackendoff 1972; Rooth 1985; Rochemont 1986; von Stechow 1991; Jacobs 1991; Hoeksema 1991; Kratzer 1991; Krifka 1991). In particular, one may expect some light to fall on certain phenomena that have been identified in semantic accounts of particles like *only*, which are claimed to "associate with focus" and which, as Jacobs (1991) and Krifka (1991, sec. 4.8) have noted, interact with intonation in puzzling ways. They are exemplified in sentences like the following:

(83) a. Freeman even introduced HARDY$_{H*}$ to Willis$_{LL\%}$.
     b. Freeman only introduced HARDY$_{H*}$ to WILLIS$_{!H* \ LL\%}$.

One might have expected that availability of quantifier scope alternations in scope-ambiguous sentences like *Some boy admires every saxophonist* might be affected by intonation, since we saw in chapter 4 that scope alternations are limited by syntactic derivation, and we have seen in the present chapter that intonation may limit combinatory derivation. Such an expectation would be in line with the claims of the Prague School that Information Structure determines scope—see Hajičová, Partee and Sgall (1998) for discussion. However, the lexical mechanism for quantifier scope advanced in chapter 4, motivated by examples like (55), makes scope entirely independent of which combinatory derivation is involved, just as long as there is one.

This means that according to the theory of scope ambiguities sketched in section 4.4, the effects of intonation on availability of readings are essentially limited to changes in the relative preference or salience of the readings that the competence grammar makes syntactically and semantically available, a conclusion that appears to be consistent with the observations on both sides of the debate in Hajičová, Partee and Sgall (1998), although it remains somewhat unclear what the facts in this area actually are.

Much further work remains to be done to complete this picture of the interface between grammar and speech. Nothing has been said here about the way metrically related phenomena of rhythm, timing, and lengthening are to be accommodated. (It should be obvious nevertheless that the theory offered here is consistent with more or less any of the available theories.)

Serious difficulties also attend the automatic identification of prosodic boundaries in speech. The phonetic realizations of elements such as pitch accents and boundary tones are subject to coarticulation effects, like all phonological segments, and are hard to recognize. In fact, it is highly likely that the process of identifying them cannot be separated from that of recognizing the words that carry them. This observation might seem daunting, since current techniques for word recognition, although improving dramatically, are nonetheless not very good. However, it is likely that the task of recognizing words and intonation together will turn out to be easier than doing either task in isolation, as Pierrehumbert (1993) points out.

The problem of so-called spurious ambiguity engendered by combinatory grammars now appears in a different light. Although the semantic properties of the rules (notably the associativity of functional composition) indeed allow alternative analyses that are equivalent in terms of the function-argument structure to which their interpretations reduce, the corresponding distinctions in surface constituency are nonetheless meaning-bearing. To call them "spurious" is very misleading, for they are genuine ambiguities at the level of Information Structure. Any theory that actually addresses the range of prosodic phenomena and coordinate constructions considered here must implicate exactly the same nondeterminism.

However, the question remains, how does the parser cope with structural ambiguity in general, and with this kind in particular? Sometimes of course intonation uniquely specifies structure. But very often it does not. PP attachment ambiguities, of the kind exhibited in the following sentence, are not usually disambiguated by intonation:

(84) Put the block in the box on the table.

Moreover, in the discussion in section 5.5.2 of the null tone on unmarked themes, we saw that Information Structure boundaries need not be disambiguated by intonation either.

The pragmatic nature of sentences with unmarked themes actually provides a strong suggestion about the nature of a mechanism for resolving not only the nondeterminism inherent in the null tone, but also other structural ambiguities such as PP attachment.

The null tone is found on the theme precisely when the corresponding theme is entirely ground information—that is, when it is already established in the context and known to the listener, and when nothing else in the context stands in contrast to it. That is to say, this particular ambiguity is only permitted when the theme is already in the listener's model of the discourse. In the case of (55) this means that at successive positions in a left-to-right analysis of the string *Mary wrote a book about BATS*, the property corresponding to *Mary*, *Mary wrote*, and *Mary wrote a book about* can be derived and can be compared with the one(s) present in the model, so that choices between syntactic alternatives such as composing or not composing can be made accordingly. What is more, since the combinatory grammar allows more or less any leftmost substring to be treated as a constituent, complete with an interpretation, there exist very simple parsing algorithms that will permit incremental analysis of this kind, consistent with the strict competence hypothesis.

This may be the most significant practical benefit of the combinatory theory. In the past, syntax and semantics on the one hand, and phonology and discourse information on the other, have appeared to demand conflicting structural analyses and to require processing more or less independently. The present theory shows them to be in harmony. Processors may more easily be devised that use all these sources of information at once, potentially simplifying both problems. The fact that the combinatory notion of syntactic structure and interpretation stands in the closest possible relation both to the prosodic structure of the signal itself and to the concepts, referents, and themes represented in the discourse context should make it easier to use all of these higher-level sources of information to filter out the ambiguities that will inevitably continue to arise from processing at lower levels.

I will return to this architecture and to the question of how to process these grammars in part III (to which the more psycholinguistically or computationally inclined reader might well turn directly). But first it is important to look more deeply into the linguistic justification for the grammars proposed here. Part II presents two related case studies, which examine in detail the extent to which the theory generalizes to more complex constructions, including further varieties of coordination in English and other languages, and to their interaction with quantifier scope and intonation.

PART II
Coordination and Word Order

Chapter 6

Cross-Serial Dependencies in Dutch

"Bluebirds and thrushes work beautifully together," said Bravura.
Raymond Smullyan, *To Mock a Mockingbird*

To see how the theory sketched in part I generalizes to other languages and other linguistic phenomena, it is interesting to begin with Dutch.[1] Although Dutch and German are predominantly SOV or verb-final languages, they are very close relatives of English in historical terms. A good theory of English should therefore be convertible into a theory of either language with minimal changes. Ideally, one would hope that little more would be necessary than a change in the directional specifications in the lexicon, at least for those constructions where the lexical heads are most closely related semantically.

This observation presents a challenge for any theory of grammar, since Dutch and German differ dramatically from English in word order and the constraints upon the long-distance dependencies that are involved in relative clauses, coordinate constructions, and infinitival complementation in raising and control constructions. In particular, as we saw for example (20) in chapter 2, Dutch is notable for allowing cross-serial dependencies in certain "verb-raising" sentences that translate directly into English and German sentences in which the dependencies entirely nest.

Intersecting or cross-serial dependencies arise when the elements of a discontinuous constituent (such as a relative-pronoun and the verb that governs it in a relative clause) are intercalated in the surface string with elements of another discontinuous constituent.

The Dutch construction is illustrated by the following subordinate clauses:

(1)   ... omdat   ik Cecilia de nijlpaarden   zag voeren.
       ... because I Cecilia the hippopotamuses saw feed

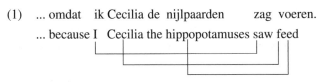

      '... because I saw Cecilia feed the hippopotamuses.'

(2)   ... omdat   ik Cecilia Henk de nijlpaarden   zag helpen voeren.
      ... because I Cecilia Henk the hippopotamuses saw help   feed

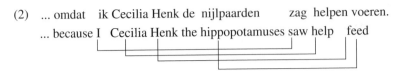

'... because I saw Cecilia help Henk feed the hippopotamuses.'

The connecting lines indicate the dependencies between NPs and verbs that are generally assumed to be represented in the semantics of these sentences, as reflected in Deep Structure or the equivalent. The construction—which is commonly used—will be examined in detail below, but it is worth noting that for these particular verbs, although some dialects allow some variation (Evers 1975; Zaenen 1979), the orders shown in (1) and (2) are preferred and in most cases obligatory. The phenomenon is therefore of intense interest, both because of its strength and because it arises in a language so closely related to English. This chapter shows how the theory originally proposed to account for extraction and coordination in English will also account for these crossed dependencies, for the somewhat greater freedom of order in the related infinitival "equi" construction, and for the extraction possibilities that these constructions allow. The related question of the coordinate structures that these constructions allow is mainly deferred until chapter 7.

Context-free grammars are known not to be adequate to capture crossed dependencies (Wall 1972). The phenomenon therefore provides an important case to consider in choosing among the various mildly context-sensitive extensions to context-free grammar that are on offer. Interestingly enough, crossed dependencies remain in a distinct minority, a fact that prompted Fodor (1978) to propose a performance-related Nested Dependency Constraint (NDC) on natural languages, and that others have taken to be evidence that natural language competence grammar is some rather minimal generalization of context-free grammar. Nevertheless, many (and perhaps all) natural languages undoubtedly do include constructions with intersecting dependencies.

The argument in this chapter will go as follows. Section 6.1 briefly reviews the basic facts of clause constituent order in Dutch and German with particular attention to the construction introduced above. Sections 6.2–6.6 then anatomize the subordinate-clause orders.

First, section 6.2 shows that the way in which the bare infinitival complement verbs in Dutch and German form a cluster in advance of combination with their arguments can be captured via (a) rules of functional composition of the kind already invoked for English and (b) a systematic difference in the directionality of the lexical categories for these verbs. This section also shows that it is a prediction rather than a stipulation that the dependencies in Dutch can cross, whereas the corresponding dependencies in German generally nest. However this section leaves open the question of why the Dutch dependencies for these verbs *must* in general cross, and it leaves some overgeneralization still to be excluded. Section 6.3 then argues that this degree of freedom is in fact necessary to capture the freer word order of the closely related equi verbs like *proberen* 'to try,' so that it is reasonable to expect to capture the difference via minor featural differences between types, and to defer this question until further problems regarding the preverbal argument sequence have been dealt with in section 6.4.

Section 6.4 uses coordination and extraction data to elucidate the structure of the preverbal NP sequence, arguing that Dutch NPs are obligatorily type-raised by the same order-preserving rules as English. Possibilities for argument cluster coordination (identical to that in English apart from being on the left of the subordinate verb cluster rather than the right) arise from the involvement of a suitably restricted composition rule. Detailed consideration of further cases of coordination of contiguous fragments of the Dutch subordinate clause is deferred until chapter 7. The fact that arguments are type-raised finally provides the means to further limit the constituent orders allowed by bare infinitival complement verbs, while still permitting greater freedom for the equi verbs.

Section 6.5 then analyzes the relative clause in greater depth, using only the apparatus already invoked for English relative clauses to correctly limit extraction and exclude scrambling in Dutch. Section 6.6 shows that the lack of a subject-object extraction asymmetry in Dutch, as manifested in the equivalent of the English Fixed-Subject Condition or *that*-trace effect (Bresnan 1972; Chomsky and Lasnik 1977), is a prediction, as claimed in chapter 4.

Section 6.7 then shows that this apparatus generalizes to the main-clause orders, including topicalization to sentence-initial position. (The further question of coordination is again deferred to chapter 7). Section 6.8 looks at some ways in which Dutch and German word order limits quantifier ambiguities under the account sketched in chapter 4. The concluding section 6.9 briefly reviews the question of the conditions under which crossed dependencies can arise, and why they should be rarer than the nested variety. An appendix summarizes the assumptions and corresponding notations that are progressively introduced, for reference as the chapter proceeds.

6.1 Word Order in Dutch

As examples (1) and (2) suggest, the grammatical orders of constituents in the Dutch clause to some extent resemble those of German. In subordinate clauses all the verbs generally occur in a clause-final group, with arguments such as NPs and adverbials preceding the verb group in the sentence. In main clauses, although the same verb-final pattern generally holds, the tensed verb itself (which may of course be the only verb) must occur in first or second position in the sentence. (This constraint, which is somewhat confusingly called the "verb-second" or V2 constraint, is widespread among Germanic languages, although the English topicalized clause constitutes an exception.) Dutch differs from German in that the left-to-right order of the auxiliaries and other nonmain verbs in the clause-final verb group is predominantly the same as in English. Thus, the basic orders for a Dutch clause including a subject, a tensed modal, a main verb, and an NP complement are as follows:

(3) a. Hij moet appels eten.   (Declarative)
       He must apples eat
       'He must eat apples.'
    b. Moet hij appels eten?   (Interrogative)
    c. Appels moet hij eten!   (Topicalization and Obj. Question)
    d. (...dat) hij appels moet eten.   (Subordinate Clause)
    e. (appels) die hij moet eten   (Obj. Relative)

German predominantly requires the verbs to be in the mirror-image order, with the tensed verb rightmost as in the following example, in contrast to (3d):

(4) (...daß) er Äpfel [essen muß].
    (...that) he apples [eat   must]
    '(...that) he must   eat   apples.'

(There are many systematic exceptions to this generalization, some of which are discussed below.)

It is because of this combination of verb-finality with the English verb order that Dutch frequently exhibits crossed dependencies between verbs and the NPs that they govern in nested infinitival complements of certain verbs of perception and causation, like *zien*, 'to see' and *helpen*, 'to help' (see Seuren 1985; Evers 1975; Huybregts 1976, 1984; Zaenen 1979; de Haan 1979; Bresnan et al. 1982; Shieber 1985). In subordinate clauses the constructions introduced in (1) and (2) result. (Again, there are systematic exceptions to this generalization, some of which are discussed below.)

The following are in some sense the standard orders for the parallel German sentences.

(5)   ... weil   ich Cecilia die Nilpferde   füttern sah.

      ... because I   Cecilia the hippopotamuses feed   saw

'... because I saw Cecilia feed the hippopotamuses.'

(6)   ... weil   ich Cecilia Hans die Nilpferde   füttern helfen sah.

      ... because I   Cecilia Hans the hippopotamuses feed   help   saw

'... because I saw Cecilia help Hans feed the hippopotamuses.'

Evers (1975, 51), following Bech (1955), notes that in German sentences including multiple infinitives, there is a strong tendency for all but the two most deeply embedded verbs to occur in the Dutch tensed-first order. This propensity reinforces the observation first made by Evers and since confirmed experimentally by Bach, Brown and Marslen-Wilson (1986) that, far from being strained or unnatural, the dependency-crossing version of the construction is at least as natural in Dutch as the nested version is in German.[2]

Because the construction can embed, indefinitely many crossed dependencies are allowed in Dutch.[3] In most dialects the alternative in which the verb group is in the German order is actually disallowed (see Zaenen 1979, fn. 3), and in all dialects it appears to be uncommon, particularly when there are more than two verbs:

(7) a. ?... omdat ik Cecilia de nijlpaarden voeren zag.

    b. *... omdat ik Cecilia Henk de nijlpaarden voeren helpen zag.

That this option can be excluded or dispreferred is remarkable, for it would restore the nested dependencies exhibited in the corresponding German constructions (5) and (6) between the verbs and their complements. In no dialect are sentences allowed that have any of the NP dependencies in the reversed, nesting order, except when these NPs are clitic pronouns, which are ignored here.[4]

The verbs that demand the construction are all verbs of perception and causation, plus a few that probably also belong under the causation heading, such as *helpen* 'to help' and *leren* 'to teach'. The rather similar verbs such as *besluiten* 'to decide', *schijnen* 'to seem', and *toelaten* 'to allow', which take

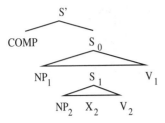

Figure 6.1
Generic underlying structure for Germanic verb raising

the other Dutch infinitive with the particle *te* (cf. English *to*), behave similarly in that they allow crossing, but differently in that they allow certain alternative orders as well (Zaenen 1979).

In the sections 6.2–6.4 the syntax of these two types of verb group and the preverbal NP sequence will be considered at length. The assumptions and corresponding notations introduced in these sections are summarized in the appendix to the chapter, for ease of reference.

6.2 Verb Raising as Composition

Although there is continuing controversy surrounding the Surface Structure of sentences (1) and (2) with which the chapter begins, all the authors cited above agree that the entire verb group *zag . . . voeren* constitutes a surface constituent of type V. There is less agreement about how this constituent is structured internally, and how the NP sequence is structured, but there is a similar consensus that the predicate-argument structure underlying (2) (however expressed) is the one shown in figure 6.1. This of course is the structure that in the German version of this construction seems to be straightforwardly compatible with the surface word order. Again, there is considerable disagreement over how this underlying structure maps onto Dutch surface order.

Within the present theory the entity closest to traditional Deep Structure is the interpretation associated with each category. One set of lexical categories that could deliver predicate-argument structures corresponding to (unordered versions of) structures like figure 6.1 for German subordinate clauses, using functional application alone, is the fragment of the German lexicon shown in (8), in which all infinitival verbs are functions from whatever the verb takes as complement into functions-from-NPs-into-infinitival-Ss, and all tensed verbs are as usual functions from the verb's complement into the predicate category $S\backslash NP$. The entries in (8) are constructed on the (not uncontroversial) assumption that the German stem *seh-* of *sah* and *sehen* is an object control verb, as *see* is in English and as the accusative case of the NP suggests, and on the assumption that everything else has the obvious category.:[5]

(8) sah := $((S_{+SUB}\backslash NP)\backslash NP)\backslash VP$
     sehen, helfen := $(VP\backslash NP)\backslash VP$
     füttern := $VP\backslash NP$

The result S in the first of these categories is distinguished as a tensed subordinate clause, S_{+SUB}, since the order that it gives rise to is not a legal German main clause.

These categories are quite systematically related to those of the corresponding English verbs, except that the latter take all their nonsubject arguments to the right. As in all verb-initial constructions, the order of combination specified over the rightward arguments by the English lexicon is the *reverse* of that of the corresponding German/Dutch leftward category. (In Bach's (1979; 1980) terms, the English rightward argument(s) "wrap," although the present grammar captures this in the fact that the predicate-argument structures for the English verbs are identical to those of the corresponding verbs in Dutch and German.) We noted in chapter 4 that this constraint seems to be a very widespread property of verb-initial constructions crosslinguistically. Thus, the following are the corresponding categories for English main and subordinate clauses:

(9) saw := $((S\backslash NP)/VP)/NP$
     see, help := $(VP/VP)/NP$
     feed := VP/NP

Like their German counterparts, these are object control verbs, analogous to *persuade*, example (41) in chapter 4. They can be written in full with their interpretations as follows:[6]

(10) saw := $((S\backslash NP)/VP)/NP : \lambda x.\lambda p.\lambda y.saw'(p(ana'x))xy$
      see := $(VP/VP)/NP : \lambda x.\lambda p.\lambda y.see'(p(ana'x))xy$
      feed := $VP/NP : \lambda x.\lambda y.feed'xy$

(The interpretations "wrap" the rightward arguments, as any SVOX language must in the terms of chapter 4.)

The German categories in (8) allow the derivation of the relevant German subordinate clauses, using functional application alone, as in (11). The dependencies between NPs and the functions that take them as arguments are indicated using subscripts. (These subscripts are included purely for ease of reading; the grammar itself does not include or require them. Note also that the subscripts identify *surface syntactic* dependencies, not the deep-structural or semantic dependencies discussed before.) To further simplify the exposition, I will begin by representing NPs as un-type-raised, although I will later replaced them type-raised categories, as in the earlier analysis of English.

(11)   … daß   ich   Cecilia   die Nilpferde   füttern   sah

$\overline{S'_{+SUB}/S_{+SUB}}$ $\overline{NP_1}$ $\overline{NP_2}$ $\overline{NP_3}$ $\overline{VP\backslash NP_3}$ $\overline{((S_{+SUB}\backslash NP_1)\backslash NP_2)\backslash VP}$

$$\frac{\qquad\qquad\qquad}{VP}{<}$$

$$\frac{\qquad\qquad\qquad\qquad\qquad\qquad}{(S_{+SUB}\backslash NP_1)\backslash NP_2}{<}$$

$$\frac{\qquad\qquad\qquad\qquad}{S_{+SUB}\backslash NP_1}{<}$$

$$\frac{\qquad\qquad}{S_{+SUB}}{<}$$

(These categories do not permit the German main-clause word orders. I return to the question of main-clause order in section 6.7.)

On the reasonable assumption that the Dutch lexicon is identical in most respects to that of German except in directionality of the infinitival complements themselves, so that the stem *zie-* of *zag* and *zien* is a raising/control verb taking its infinitival to the right, we get the following corresponding fragment of the Dutch lexicon:[7]

(12) zag := $((S_{+SUB}\backslash NP)\backslash NP)/VP_{-SUB}$
       zien, helpen := $(VP\backslash NP)/VP_{-SUB}$
       voeren := $VP\backslash NP$

Again, the result of the tensed verb category is marked as a subordinate clause. The reason for marking the VP complement of such verbs as *zien* as $-SUB$ will become apparent later, but it is important to notice that the VP *result* of infinitival verbs is unmarked or unspecified on this feature; that is, it is compatible with either $+SUB$ or $-SUB$.[8]

Although for the most part I will take semantics as read in what follows, the corresponding fully interpreted categories can be specified as in (13), with semantic interpretations identical to those of the corresponding English verbs in (10), apart from the fact that they do not wrap arguments, as must in the terms of chapter 4 be the case for any SOV language:

(13) zag := $((S_{+SUB}\backslash NP)\backslash NP)/VP_{-SUB} : \lambda p.\lambda x.\lambda y.saw'(p(ana'x))xy$

zien := $(VP\backslash NP)/VP_{-SUB} : \lambda p.\lambda x.\lambda y.see'(p(ana'x))xy$

voeren := $VP\backslash NP : \lambda x.\lambda y.feed'xy$

With application alone, these categories do not give rise to correct Dutch subordinate clauses for the verbs in question. However, with the inclusion of a single further rule of functional composition, the grammar will accept Dutch subordinate-clause orders on these elements. The rule in question is the *crossed* version of forward composition, which I will provisionally schematize as follows using the most general version of the $ convention (32) of chapter 3 over functions with n arguments for some small finite n:[9]

(14) *Dutch forward crossed composition I* ($> \mathbf{B}^n{}_\times$)

$X/Y \quad (Y\backslash Z)\$ \quad \Rightarrow_{\mathbf{B}^n} \quad (X\backslash Z)\$$

where $Y = VP_{-SUB}$

The restriction on this rule is more specific than the parallel restriction on the English backward crossed rule (24) in chapter 4. It will turn out later to be crucially involved in limiting the Dutch version to infinitival complement constructions. In particular, it prevents type-raised categories from composing into verbs (see discussion of example (60)). It permits derivations on the following patterns, in which the verbs and their NP arguments lie on a right-branching spine:

(15) dat ik Cecilia de nijlpaarden zag voeren

$$
\begin{array}{cccccc}
\overline{NP_1} & \overline{NP_2} & \overline{NP_3} & \overline{((S_{+SUB}\backslash NP_1)\backslash NP_2)/VP_{-SUB}} & \overline{VP\backslash NP_3} \\
& & & \multicolumn{2}{c}{\overline{\qquad\qquad\qquad\qquad\qquad}}{}_{>\mathbf{B}_\times} \\
& & & \multicolumn{2}{c}{((S_{+SUB}\backslash NP_1)\backslash NP_2)\backslash NP_3} \\
& & \multicolumn{3}{c}{\overline{\qquad\qquad\qquad\qquad\qquad\qquad\qquad}}{}_< \\
& & \multicolumn{3}{c}{(S_{+SUB}\backslash NP_1)\backslash NP_2} \\
& \multicolumn{4}{c}{\overline{\qquad\qquad\qquad\qquad\qquad\qquad\qquad\qquad}}{}_< \\
& \multicolumn{4}{c}{S_{+SUB}\backslash NP_1} \\
\multicolumn{5}{c}{\overline{\qquad\qquad\qquad\qquad\qquad\qquad\qquad\qquad\qquad}}{}_< \\
\multicolumn{5}{c}{S_{+SUB}}
\end{array}
$$

(16) dat ik Cecilia Henk de nijlpaarden zag helpen voeren

$$
\begin{array}{ccccccc}
\overline{NP_1} & \overline{NP_2} & \overline{NP_3} & \overline{NP_4} & \overline{((S_{+SUB}\backslash NP_1)\backslash NP_2)/VP_{-SUB}} & \overline{(VP\backslash NP_3)/VP_{-SUB}} & \overline{VP\backslash NP_4} \\
& & & & & & {}_{>\mathbf{B}_\times} \\
& & & & & (VP\backslash NP_3)\backslash NP_4 \\
& & & & & & {}_{>\mathbf{B}^2_\times} \\
& & & & (((S_{+SUB}\backslash NP_1)\backslash NP_2)\backslash NP_3)\backslash NP_4 \\
& & & & & {}_< \\
& & & ((S_{+SUB}\backslash NP_1)\backslash NP_2)\backslash NP_3 \\
& & & & {}_< \\
& & (S_{+SUB}\backslash NP_1)\backslash NP_2 \\
& & & {}_< \\
& S_{+SUB}\backslash NP_1 \\
& & {}_< \\
S_{+SUB}
\end{array}
$$

These surface orders are only accepted because the grammar includes the forward crossed composition rule. This rule is the *only* rule that the theory allows us to specify that will combine the verbal categories into a single constituent.

The rule has the inevitable consequence that *functions that combine under this rule will necessarily produce as their composition a function that demands its arguments in the crossed rather than the nested order.*

In the case of (16), there is a second possible derivation. Here the verbs combine by two compositions in the opposite order, to yield a left-branching structure, and the NPs remain as before:

(17)

dat	ik	Cecilia	Henk	de nijlpaarden	zag	helpen	voeren

$$\overline{NP_1} \quad \overline{NP_2} \quad \overline{NP_3} \quad \overline{NP_4} \quad \overline{((S_{+SUB}\backslash NP_1)\backslash NP_2)/VP_{-SUB}} \quad \overline{(VP\backslash NP_3)/VP_{-SUB}} \quad \overline{VP\backslash NP_4}$$

$$\cfrac{(((S_{+SUB}\backslash NP_1)\backslash NP_2)\backslash NP_3)/VP_{-SUB}}{} {}_{>\mathbf{B}^2_\times}$$

$$\cfrac{(((S_{+SUB}\backslash NP_1)\backslash NP_2)\backslash NP_3)\backslash NP_4}{} {}_{>\mathbf{B}_\times}$$

$$\cfrac{((S_{+SUB}\backslash NP_1)\backslash NP_2)\backslash NP_3}{} {}_<$$

$$\cfrac{(S_{+SUB}\backslash NP_1)\backslash NP_2}{} {}_<$$

$$\cfrac{S_{+SUB}\backslash NP_1}{} {}_<$$

$$\cfrac{S_{+SUB}}{} {}_<$$

Because of the associativity of composition, the result is the semantically identical verb cluster of type $(((S_{+SUB}\backslash NP_1)\backslash NP_2)\backslash NP_3)\backslash NP_4$. This order of composition is the one that would be preferred by a maximally incremental left-to-right parser. Whether such derivations should be permitted by the grammar depends upon consideration of the following coordinate sentences:

(18) a. dat ik Cecilia Henk de paarden zag helpen voeren en   hoorde leren wassen.
          that I   Cecilia Henk the horses   saw help   feed   and heard   teach wash
          'that I saw Cecilia help Henk feed the horses and heard her teach him to wash them'.

      b. dat ik Cecilia Henk de paarden zag helpen voeren en leren wassen.

      c. dat ik Cecilia Henk de paarden zag helpen en hoorde leren voeren.

Sentence (18c) is somewhat odd. A parallel example receives a *? rating from Bresnan et al. (1982) and is used to justify the assumption of a right-branching Surface Structure for the verb group, following Evers (1975). In the earlier work I found that some informants would allow it, and I suggested that the source of its anomaly lies in the pragmatics of right node raising, which tends to make the rightmost element a rheme or comment, rather than in syntax. The rule (14) follows the earlier paper in allowing the verbs to combine in either left- or right-branching fashion and in allowing all of (18a–c). However, a more restrictive version of the present theory, conforming to the judgments reported by Evers and Bresnan et al., can be obtained by replacing the forward crossed rule (14) by the following version, using the \$ instance of the $ convention.

(19) *Dutch forward crossed composition I (alternative)* ($>\mathbf{B}^n_\times$)

$X/Y \quad (Y\backslash Z)\backslash\$ \quad \Rightarrow_{\mathbf{B}^n} \quad (X\backslash Z)\backslash\$$

where $Y = VP_{-SUB}$

This version allows (16) but excludes (17) and hence (18c). All remaining examples and derivations in this chapter are compatible with the more restricted grammar.

The grammar permits neither the marginal case (7a) nor the ungrammatical case (7b) of the "German-style" Dutch orderings. (I return to the first of these below.)

The corresponding German construction, which contains the same elements but where the corresponding verbs occur in the mirror-image order and the dependencies nest, is accepted in exactly the same way, using exactly the same categories, as in (16). The only difference is that the verb group must be assembled by (a suitably restricted form of) the backward composition rule $<\mathbf{B}$. For example:

(20) daß ich Cecilia Henk die Nilpferde füttern helfen sah

$$\overline{NP_1} \quad \overline{NP_2} \quad \overline{NP_3} \quad \overline{NP_4} \quad \overline{VP\backslash NP_4} \quad \overline{((VP\backslash NP_3)\backslash VP} \quad \overline{((S_{+SUB}\backslash NP_1)\backslash NP_2)\backslash VP}$$

$$\cfrac{(VP\backslash NP_3)\backslash NP_4}{\,}{}_{<\mathbf{B}}$$

$$\cfrac{(((S_{+SUB}\backslash NP_1)\backslash NP_2)\backslash NP_3)\backslash NP_4}{\,}{}_{<\mathbf{B}^2}$$

$$\cfrac{((S_{+SUB}\backslash NP_1)\backslash NP_2)\backslash NP_3}{\,}{}_{<}$$

$$\cfrac{(S_{+SUB}\backslash NP_1)\backslash NP_2}{\,}{}_{<}$$

$$\cfrac{S_{+SUB}\backslash NP_1}{\,}{}_{<}$$

$$\cfrac{S_{+SUB}}{\,}{}_{<}$$

(As in the Dutch example, there is an alternative analysis, in which the verbs compose in another order. The order shown here is the one that would be favored by a maximally incremental left-to-right processor combining as rapidly as possible. Again the existence of the different constituent structures needs to be tested by coordination possibilities.)[10] The rule in question is the following (again the $ schematization is given in the most general form, but a more restricted version schematized as $(Y\backslash Z)\backslash\$$ is compatible with the examples here):

(21) *Dutch/German backward composition* ($<\mathbf{B}^n$)

$(Y\backslash Z)\$ \quad X\backslash Y \quad \Rightarrow_{\mathbf{B}^n} \quad (X\backslash Z)\$$

Since this rule is order-preserving, it simply provides alternative derivations such as (20) for sentences like (6). However, the availability of these alternatives is crucial to the constructions considered in section 6.4.

The Dutch fragment does not permit the following ungrammatical orders, because verbs such as *zien* are defined as functions over *NP* and *VP*, rather than over "small clauses" of type S^{-IP}:[11]

(22) *...omdat ik zag [Cecilia Henk de nijlpaarden helpen voeren.]$_{S_{INF}}$

(23) *...omdat ik zag Cecilia helpen [Henk de nijlpaarden voeren.]$_{S_{INF}}$

(24) *...omdat ik zag [Cecilia Henk helpen de nijlpaarden voeren.]$_{S_{INF}}$

However, in order to prevent overgeneralization to the following word order, in which the embedded VP includes its object, we must do something more:

(25) *...omdat ik Cecilia [zag]$_{((S_{+SUB}\backslash NP)\backslash NP)/VP_{-SUB}}$ [de nijlpaarden voeren.]$_{*VP_{-SUB}}$

I return below to the question of what exactly prevents *de nijlpaarden voeren* from becoming a VP_{-SUB}. However, there is good reason to believe that this should be left as a question of fine-tuning, because a closely related family of raising verbs does allow orders parallel to (25). (In fact, some informants seem to feel that (25) is not as bad as (22)–(24)).

6.3 Equi Verbs

The "equi" verbs like *proberen* 'to try' (Zaenen 1979; Seuren 1985) allow greater freedom of word order. In particular, the tensed equi verb may occur either at the front of the final group, as in (26a) or in second position in a subordinate clause, as in (26b). The alternatives (26c,d) are also grammatical (Seuren 1972). A more questionable pattern is (26e) (starred in Seuren 1972).[12]

(26) a. ...omdat   ik Jan het lied probeer te leren (*te) zingen.
         ...because I Jan the song try   to teach (*to) sing
         '...because I try to teach Jan to sing the song.'
     b. ...omdat ik probeer Jan het lied te leren (*te) zingen.
     c. ...omdat ik probeer Jan te leren het lied te zingen.
     d. ...omdat ik Jan probeer te leren het lied te zingen.
     e. ?...omdat ik Jan probeer het lied te leren (*te) zingen

An important detail about this construction that is likely to create complications for any theory lies in the apparently perverse conditions on the presence or absence of the particle *te* with the embedded infinitival. It is obligatory in (26c and d), but disallowed in (26a,b,e).

Given the present account of infinitives and the possibility of (26c and d), the Dutch equi verbs such as *proberen* must when tensed bear the category $(S_{+SUB}\backslash NP)/VP^{TE}$, where VP^{TE} abbreviates $S_{?SUB}^{+TE,-IP}\backslash NP$ and *VP* abbreviates $S_{?SUB}^{-TE,-IP}\backslash NP$. The particle *te* is VP^{TE}/VP so that *te*-infinitive verbs bear categories parallel to those of bare infinitives. To summarize:

(27) zag := $((S_{+SUB}\backslash NP)\backslash NP)/VP_{-SUB}$
      probeer := $(S_{+SUB}\backslash NP)/VP^{TE}$
      zien, leren, helpen := $(VP\backslash NP)/VP_{-SUB}$
      voeren := $VP\backslash NP$
      te := VP^{TE}/VP

Readers may easily satisfy themselves that the augmented fragment accepts (26a) and (26b). For example:

(28)

dat	ik	Jan	het lied	probeer	te leren	(∗te) zingen
	$\overline{NP}$	$\overline{NP}$	$\overline{NP}$	$\overline{(S_{+SUB}\backslash NP)/VP^{TE}}$	$\overline{(VP^{TE}\backslash NP)/VP}$	$\overline{VP\backslash NP}$

$$\frac{\qquad\qquad}{(VP^{TE}\backslash NP)\backslash NP} >\mathbf{B}_\times$$

$$\frac{\qquad\qquad\qquad}{((S_{+SUB}\backslash NP)\backslash NP)\backslash NP} >\mathbf{B}_\times^2$$

$$\frac{\qquad\qquad\qquad}{(S_{+SUB}\backslash NP)\backslash NP} <$$

$$\frac{\qquad\qquad}{S_{+SUB}\backslash NP} <$$

$$\frac{\qquad}{S_{+SUB}} <$$

(29)

dat	ik	probeer	Jan	het lied	te leren	(∗te) zingen
	$\overline{NP}$	$\overline{(S_{+SUB}\backslash NP)/VP^{TE}}$	$\overline{NP}$	$\overline{NP}$	$\overline{(VP^{TE}\backslash NP)/VP}$	$\overline{VP\backslash NP}$

$$\frac{\qquad\qquad}{(VP^{TE}\backslash NP)\backslash NP} >\mathbf{B}_\times$$

$$\frac{\qquad\qquad\qquad}{VP^{TE}\backslash NP} <$$

$$\frac{\qquad\qquad}{VP^{TE}} <$$

$$\frac{\qquad\qquad}{S_{+SUB}\backslash NP} >$$

$$\frac{\qquad}{S} <$$

In order to capture syntactically the subtle alternation between bare and *te*-infinitivals typified in sentences like (26b–d), there seems to be no alternative to brute force. I therefore include the following additional lexical category for the complementizer as a stipulation:[13]

(30) *The* Te *Category Brute Force Stipulation*:
      te := $(VP^{TE}\$/VP_{+SUB}^{TE})/(VP\$/VP_{-SUB})$

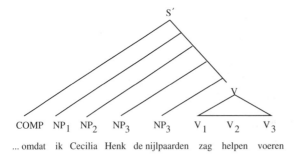

... omdat   ik   Cecilia   Henk   de nijlpaarden   zag   helpen   voeren

Figure 6.2
Not the Right Surface Structure

This turns *te leren* into a category that can apply to but not compose with *te*-infinitival VPs. It has the effect of allowing (26c,d) without also allowing the starred *te* particles in the earlier cases, a problem that was not solved in the earlier paper. For example:

(31) dat ik   probeer   Jan   te leren   het lied te zingen

$$\underbrace{}_{NP}\ \underbrace{}_{(S_{+SUB}\backslash NP)/VP^{TE}}\ \underbrace{}_{NP}\ \underbrace{}_{(VP^{TE}\backslash NP)/VP_{+SUB}}\ \underbrace{}_{NP}\ \underbrace{}_{VP^{TE}\backslash NP}$$

The fragment as it stands still overgenerates examples like the following, in which a bare complement verb applies to an entire VP rather than composing with the verb;

(32) *... dat ik Cecilia zag de nijlpaarden voeren.

To see how such overgenerations are excluded, we must first look more closely at the preverbal argument sequence.

6.4 Argument Cluster Composition

Derivations like those in (16) might seem to commit us to the kind of combinatory Surface Structure shown in figure 6.2, in which the triangle schematizes over the multiple derivations for the verb group.   In conjunction with the argument structures provided in the lexicon for the fully interpreted categories given in (13), the semantics of functional composition will ensure that this derivation yields a predicate-argument structure that might be written as follows:

(33) $see'(help'(feed'hippos'(ana'harry'))harry'(ana'cecilia'))cecilia'me'$

Thus, apart from the assumption that argument structure is order-free, forward crossed composition has much the same effect as a verb raising adjunction transformation (see Evers 1975; Haegeman 1992), "reanalysis" (Lasnik and Kupin 1977; Haegeman and van Riemsdijk 1986), the unification mechanism of LFG (Johnson 1988; Netter 1988; Zaenen and Kaplan 1995), or certain TAG analyses (Kroch and Santorini 1991; Rambow 1994a). The difference is that the CCG derivation is entirely type-driven, rather than structure-driven.

However, as far as derivation or Surface Structure goes, coordination and extraction phenomena reveal that the structure shown in figure 6.2 for the NP sequence, corresponding to the simple backward application of the verb composite, is misleading. As in the case of the verb group, there are several Surface Structures for the same NP sequence, all again yielding the same predicate-argument structure.

6.4.1 Coordination and Extraction
First, contiguous subsequences or "clusters" of arguments can coordinate, just like their English counterparts in the *give a policeman a flower* sentences (see (40) of chapter 3), albeit that in Dutch subordinate clauses these arguments are to the *left* of the verb:

(34) Ik denk dat ik [Cecilia de appels en Henk de peren] zag plukken.
       I think that I Cecilia the apples, and Henk the pears, saw pick
       'I think that I saw Cecilia pick the apples, and Henk the pears.'

Within the present framework, this phenomenon (to which I return at length in chapter 7) means that the NP sequences must be constituents.

Second, any of the NPs (and other arguments) in the preverbal sequence may extract under relativization, disrupting the normal cross-serial order of the sequence.[14] For example (trace notation is used to indicate the intended reading):

(35) (de appels) die ik het meisje   zag plukken.
       (the apples) that$_i$ I the girl t_i saw pick
       '(the apples) that I saw the girl pick.'

The sentence is not accepted by the grammar of section 6.2, because the verb complex *zag plukken* is separated from the relative-pronoun *die* by the NP sequence *ik het meisje* and from the subject *ik* by the NP *het meisje*. The phenomenon is quite independent of the infinitival construction and the earlier account of the verb sequence. It is a quite general problem in Dutch/German syntax. For example, either object of a ditransitive can extract from the preverbal NP sequence in a simple relative clause:

(36) a. de appels die ik het meisje gaf.
        the apples that I the girl   gave
        'the apples that I gave the girl.'

     b. het meisje dat ik appels gaf.
        the girl   that I apples gave
        'the girl that I gave apples.'

Whatever category we choose for the verb, one of these extractions will block for the same reason.

The general problem of relativizing preverbal NPs (and other arguments) in German and Dutch can be stated as follows. The construction has n NPs (or whatever), followed by a number of verbs requiring them as arguments. The ith NP, say, is extracted and placed as a relative-pronoun to the left of the subject. The verbs can be composed into a single verblike entity $(\ldots((S_{+SUB}\backslash NP_1)\backslash \ldots)\backslash NP_n$, wanting the NPs as in section 6.2. (In Dutch the composition is the crossed forward variety, and in German it is the backward variety. The end result is the same, only the linear order of the verbs varying.) The general form of the German/Dutch relative clause can therefore be written as follows (trace notation is again used to indicate the intended reading):

(37) $(N\backslash N)/(S_{+SUB}\backslash NP_i), NP_1,\ldots,NP_h, t_i, NP_j,\ldots,NP_n, (\ldots(S_{+SUB}\backslash NP_1)\backslash \ldots)\backslash NP_n$

The verb group can pick up the NPs n down to j in the usual way by backward application, to yield (38):

(38) $(N\backslash N)/(S_{+SUB}\backslash NP_i), NP_1\ldots NP_h, t_i, ((\ldots((S_{+SUB}\backslash NP_1)\backslash NP_2)\backslash \ldots)\backslash NP_h)\backslash NP_i$

But at this point, the construction blocks.

Within the present framework there is only one way that any extraction can ever be accommodated. Under the Principle of Adjacency, all material between the *wh*-item $(N\backslash N)/(S_{+SUB}\backslash X)$ and the verb that wants X as an argument must be composed by the combinatory rules into a single entity $S_{+SUB}\backslash X$. In the case of a relativized NP$_i$, the implication is that the arguments 1 to h, and the complex that includes NPs j to n and the verb group, must combine into a single entity $S_{+SUB} \backslash NP_i$. Since there may be arbitrarily many NPs preceding the extraction site, they must all be type-raised functions, and they must combine by functional composition.

6.4.2 Type-raising

If type-raising can apply to English NPs and other arguments, turning them into functions that can in turn compose, thus capturing the phenomena of extraction and coordination in English discussed in chapters 3 and 4, then we are free to suppose that in Dutch and German all arguments such as NPs are rightward-looking functions whose domain is leftward verbal functions that take such arguments, and whose range is that of their results. As in sections 6.2 and 6.3, we will begin with a simple but overgeneralizing proposal, and then restrict it slightly. Since there is more than one kind of verbal function that takes an NP complement to its left, we need a variable T that ranges over categories. We can therefore regard all NPs as undergoing the rightward type-raising rule of chapter 4 (10) to yield the following familiar category, similarly constrained:

(39) *The verb-final clause NP complement category (simplified)*
    $T/(T \backslash NP)$

Each instance of the polymorphic variable over categories, written T, is again *unique* to each individual instance of the raised category. The syntactic restrictions that this category requires will become apparent when we consider its behavior under the combinatory rules. Its semantics is simply to apply the function matching $T \backslash NP$ to the original unraised NP, to yield T, its result.

As in English, I will assume that other arguments of verbs, such as subcategorized prepositional and adverbial phrases, can bear analogous categories of the form $T/(T \backslash X)$, where X is *PP*, *ADV*, and the like. As in the earlier chapters on English, I will often suppress the step of type-raising in derivations to save space, and I may on occasion abbreviate the raised categories themselves as $NP^\uparrow$ and the like when it simplifies the presentation.

The combinatory rules act on the raised categories as follows.

6.4.2.1 Forward Application of Type-Raised Arguments Type-raised NPs including object NPs of the form $T/(T \backslash NP)$ can combine with verbs and the verb groups that result from composition by the forward application rule. For example, the Dutch complement . . . *dat Jan appels at* ' . . . that Jan ate apples' is accepted as follows:

(40) dat   Jan   appels   at
      $\overline{T/(T\backslash NP)}$ $\overline{T/(T\backslash NP)}$ $\overline{(S_{+SUB}\backslash NP)\backslash NP}$
                                   $\underline{\qquad\qquad\qquad\qquad}$>
                                   $S_{+SUB}\backslash NP$
      $\underline{\qquad\qquad\qquad\qquad\qquad\qquad\qquad}$>
                          S_{+SUB}

The application of the forward application rule with the raised category under
the interpretation of rules set out in chapter 3 matches the metavariable T with
$S\backslash NP$. Because of the semantics of type-raising, the result of this process is
the same as the corresponding earlier derivation using backward application.
That is, the interpretation f of $(S_{+SUB}\backslash NP)\backslash NP$ is applied to that of the NP, a,
and yields $S_{+SUB}\backslash NP : fa$. It is therefore simplest to assume that all leftward
arguments of the verb group including the subject must bear raised categories
like (39), and only that category. It follows that NP arguments in subordinate
clauses must combine with the verb group by *forward* rules.

If it were not for the inclusion of functional composition rules, such a fragment would be strongly equivalent to the earlier one. That is, the derivations
of the infinitival sentences can proceed as before, except that the verb complex
is combined with the preverbal type-raised arguments by the forward application rule, rather than by the backward one. For example, derivation (16) now
appears as follows. (Subscripts are as usual included for the reader's guidance
only.)

(41) dat   Jan   Cecilia   Henk   de nijlpaarden   zag helpen voeren
     $\overline{T/(T\backslash NP_1)}$ $\overline{T/(T\backslash NP_2))}$ $\overline{T/(T\backslash NP_3)}$ $\overline{T/(T\backslash NP_4)}$ $\overline{(((S_{+SUB}\backslash NP_1)\backslash NP_2)\backslash NP_3)\backslash NP_4}$
                                                          $\underline{\qquad\qquad\qquad\qquad\qquad\qquad\qquad\qquad}$>
                                                          $((S_{+SUB}\backslash NP_1)\backslash NP_2)\backslash NP_3$
                                               $\underline{\qquad\qquad\qquad\qquad\qquad\qquad\qquad\qquad}$>
                                               $(S_{+SUB}\backslash NP_1)\backslash NP_2$
                                   $\underline{\qquad\qquad\qquad\qquad\qquad}$>
                          $(S_{+SUB}\backslash NP_1)$
          $\underline{\qquad\qquad\qquad\qquad\qquad\qquad\qquad\qquad}$>
                          S_{+SUB}

Because of the semantics of the raised categories, the result is the same as
in (16) using the simple NP category and the backward application rule. In
particular, the illegal sentences (22) and (23) are still excluded.

In order to allow the word orders associated with the *proberen* class of verbs,
while still disallowing the corresponding word orders with the *zien* class, we
should recall that the earlier categories of infinitival complements of the *zien*
class were distinguished from those of the *te*-infinitival complements of the
proberen class by restriction to VP_{-SUB} as follows (cf. 27):

(42) zag := $((S_{+SUB}\backslash NP)\backslash NP)/VP_{-SUB}$
probeer := $(S_{+SUB}\backslash NP)/VP^{TE}$
zien, leren, helpen := $(VP\backslash NP)/VP_{-SUB}$
voeren := $VP\backslash NP$
te := VP^{TE}/VP

Crucially, the complement of the *zien* class is distinguished as non-verb-final, in contrast to the *te*-complement of the *proberen* class, which is unspecified on this attribute. The results of all infinitivals including *zien, te zien*, and so on are also unspecified on the feature *SUB*.

If we further assume that the variable T in the order-preserving raised NP category is a typed variable that can only match (tensed or untensed) categories of the form $S_{+SUB}^{-CP,?IP}\$$, then it will not only be able to partake in verb-final tensed and untensed clauses, but also have the important effect of causing infinitival VPs to become specified as $+SUB$. Such an effect can be achieved by writing the forward category in full as follows, though for obvious reasons I will continue to abbreviate it as $T/(T\backslash X)$:

(43) *The verb-final NP complement category (full)*:

$$T/(T\backslash X) \equiv S_{+SUB}^{-CP,?IP}\$/(S_{+SUB}^{-CP,?IP}\$\backslash X)$$

This stratagem will have the important effect of permitting complements like [*het lied te leren zingen*]$_{VP_{+SUB}}$ for verbs like *proberen*$_{VP/VP^{TE}}$, while forbidding those like [*de nijlpaarden voeren*]$_{VP_{+SUB}}$ for verbs like *zien*$_{(VP\backslash NP)/VP_{-SUB}}$.

Thus, the freer word order characteristic of equi verbs like *proberen* is still permitted (cf. (26)), as in the following derivations:

(44) dat   ik   Jan   het lied   probeer   te leren   (∗te) zingen

dat	ik	Jan	het lied	probeer	te leren	(∗te) zingen
	$T/(T\backslash NP)$	$T/(T\backslash NP)$	$T/(T\backslash NP)$	$(S_{+SUB}\backslash NP)/VP^{TE}$	$(VP^{TE}\backslash NP)/VP_{-SUB}$	$VP\backslash NP$

$(VP^{TE}\backslash NP)\backslash NP$ $>\mathbf{B}_\times$

$(VP^{TE}\backslash NP)\backslash NP$ $>\mathbf{B}_\times^2$

$((S_{+SUB}\backslash NP)\backslash NP)\backslash NP$

$(S_{+SUB}\backslash NP)\backslash NP$ $>$

$S_{+SUB}\backslash NP$ $>$

S_{+SUB} $>$

(45) dat   ik   probeer   Jan   het lied   te leren   (∗te) zingen

dat	ik	probeer	Jan	het lied	te leren	(∗te) zingen
	$T/(T\backslash NP)$	$(S_{+SUB}\backslash NP)/VP^{TE}$	$T/(T\backslash NP)$	$T/(T\backslash NP)$	$(VP^{TE}\backslash NP)/VP_{-SUB}$	$VP\backslash NP$

$>\mathbf{B}_\times$

$(VP^{TE}\backslash NP)\backslash NP$

$VP^{TE}\backslash NP$ $>$

VP^{TE} $>$

$S_{+SUB}\backslash NP$ $>$

S_{+SUB} $>$

Because of stipulation (30), (26c, d) are also permitted:

(46) dat   ik   probeer   Jan   te leren   het lied   te zingen

$$\underline{T/(T\backslash NP)} \quad \underline{(S_{+SUB}\backslash NP)/VP^{TE}} \quad \underline{T/(T\backslash NP)} \quad \underline{(VP^{TE}\backslash NP)/VP^{TE}_{+SUB}} \quad \underline{T/(T\backslash NP)} \quad \underline{VP^{TE}\backslash NP}$$

$$\overline{\qquad\qquad\qquad\qquad\qquad VP^{TE}_{+SUB} \qquad\qquad\qquad\qquad\qquad}{}^{>}$$

$$\overline{\qquad\qquad\qquad\qquad\qquad VP^{TE}\backslash NP \qquad\qquad\qquad\qquad\qquad}{}^{>}$$

$$\overline{\qquad\qquad\qquad\qquad VP^{TE}_{+SUB} \qquad\qquad\qquad\qquad}{}^{>}$$

$$\overline{\qquad\qquad\qquad S_{+SUB}\backslash NP \qquad\qquad\qquad}{}^{>}$$

$$\overline{\qquad\qquad S_{+SUB} \qquad\qquad}{}^{>}$$

(47) dat   ik   Jan   probeer   te leren   het lied   te zingen

$$\underline{T/(T\backslash NP)} \quad \underline{T/(T\backslash NP)} \quad \underline{(S_{+SUB}\backslash NP)/VP^{TE}} \quad \underline{(VP^{TE}\backslash NP)/VP^{TE}_{+SUB}} \quad \underline{T/(T\backslash NP)} \quad \underline{VP^{TE}\backslash NP}$$

$$\overline{\qquad\qquad\qquad\qquad\qquad VP^{TE}_{+SUB} \qquad\qquad\qquad\qquad\qquad}{}^{>}$$

$$\overline{\qquad\qquad\qquad\qquad\qquad VP^{TE}\backslash NP \qquad\qquad\qquad\qquad\qquad}{}^{>}$$

$$\overline{\qquad\qquad\qquad (S_{+SUB}\backslash NP)\backslash NP \qquad\qquad\qquad}{}^{>\mathbf{B}_{\times}}$$

$$\overline{\qquad\qquad S_{+SUB}\backslash NP \qquad\qquad}{}^{>}$$

$$\overline{\qquad S_{+SUB} \qquad}{}^{>}$$

However, the doubtful example (26e) is now excluded, as Seuren (1972) claims it should be, since *het lied te leren zingen* is $VP^{TE}_{+SUB}\backslash NP$ and cannot be composed into as follows:

(48) ?dat   ik   Jan   probeer   het lied   te leren   zingen

$$\underline{T/(T\backslash NP)} \quad \underline{T/(T\backslash NP)} \quad \underline{(S_{+SUB}\backslash NP)/VP^{TE}} \quad \underline{T/(T\backslash NP)} \quad \underline{(VP^{TE}\backslash NP)/VP_{-SUB}} \quad \underline{VP\backslash NP}$$

$$\overline{\qquad\qquad\qquad\qquad (VP^{TE}\backslash NP)\backslash NP \qquad\qquad\qquad\qquad}{}^{>\mathbf{B}_{\times}}$$

$$\overline{\qquad\qquad\qquad VP^{TE}_{+SUB}\backslash NP \qquad\qquad\qquad}{}^{>}$$

$$\overline{\qquad\qquad VP^{TE}_{+SUB}\backslash NP \qquad\qquad}{}^{*>\mathbf{B}_{\times}}$$

The type restriction on T implicit in in the type-raised category also eliminates a number of potential overgeneralizations noted earlier, including (25), repeated here as (49a), since the object *de nijlpaarden* specifies the bare infinitival and past participial VPs as $+SUB$:

(49)   a.   *... omdat ik Cecilia [zag]$_{((S_{+SUB}\backslash NP)\backslash NP)/VP_{-SUB}}$
        [de nijlpaarden voeren.]$_{VP_{+SUB}}$

      b.   *... omdat ik probeer Jan [te leren]$_{(VP^{TE}_{+SUB}\backslash NP)/VP_{-SUB}}$ [de nijlpaarden
        voeren.]$_{VP_{+SUB}}$

      c.   *... omdat ik [heb]$_{(S_{SUB}\backslash NP)/VP^{PPL}_{-SUB}}$ [de nijlpaarden gevoerd.]$_{VP^{PPL}_{+SUB}}$

Since verb-final bare infinitival VP complements are essential to the analysis of main clauses like the following, we must anticipate that main-clause *zag*, *heeft*, and the like must require VP_{+SUB} complements:

(50) Hij zal [de nijlpaarden   voeren.]$_{VP_{+SUB}}$
      He will the hippopotamuses feed
      'He will feed the hippopotamuses.'

(51) Ik heb [de nijlpaarden   gevoerd.]$_{VP_{en_{+SUB}}}$
      I have the hippopotamuses fed
      'I fed the hippopotamuses.'

(52) Ik zag Cecilia [de nijlpaarden   voeren.]$_{VP_{+SUB}}$
      I saw Cecilia the hippopotamuses feed
      'I saw Cecilia feed the hippopotamuses.'

Although I have so far ignored the problem of main-clause order, it is important to realize that this assumption is a forced move anyway under present assumptions, and corresponds to the lexicalist's version of base generation for the main-/subordinate-clause word order alternation. I will continue to defer detailed discussion of main-clause order until section 6.7.

6.4.2.2 Forward composition of Type-Raised Arguments   Since type-raised argument categories of the form $T/(T\backslash X)$ are functions, they can potentially take part in functional composition. For example, a subject may compose into an object under the (noncrossing) forward composition rule, to yield a function that can apply to the verb:

(53) dat   Jan   appels   at
$$\frac{\dfrac{\overline{T/(T\backslash NP_1)}\quad \overline{T/(T\backslash NP_2)}}{T/((T\backslash NP_1)\backslash NP_2)}{}^{>\mathbf{B}}\qquad \overline{(S_{+SUB}\backslash NP_1)\backslash NP_2}}{S_{+SUB}}{}^{>}$$

However, we still need to prevent the following case of ordinary harmonic composition, since the sentence is disallowed under the relevant reading:[15]

(54) ∗dat   het lied   Jan   probeert   te zingen
$$\frac{\overline{T/(T\backslash NP_2)}\quad \dfrac{\dfrac{\overline{T/(T\backslash NP_1)}\quad \overline{(S_{+SUB}\backslash NP_1)/VP^{TE}}}{S_{+SUB}/VP^{TE}}{}_{*>\mathbf{B}}\quad \overline{VP^{TE}\backslash NP_2}}{S_{+SUB}\backslash NP_2}{}^{>\mathbf{B}_{\times}}}{S_{+SUB}}{}^{>}$$

One way to do so is to restrict the noncrossing forward rule to composition into nominal type-raised categories, as follows:

(55) *Dutch forward composition I* (>**B**)

$$X/Y \quad Y/(Y\backslash Z) \quad \Rightarrow_{\mathbf{B}} \quad X/(Y\backslash Z)$$

where $Y = S$

Because of the semantics of the combinatory rules and the type-raised NP complement category, the interpretation that results from the derivation (53) involving composition of type-raised categories is exactly the same as was produced in (40) by two forward applications. The result of such a composition can in turn compose with a further NP bearing the novel category, and this process can iterate indefinitely. Because the composition is order-preserving, no new orderings of the arguments are allowed. The result of such iterated composition is a function over exactly the kind of verbal functions that were produced from the composition of the verb group in section 6.2. It can therefore combine with the verb group by a forward application, as follows:

(56) dat   Jan   Cecilia   Henk   de nijlpaarden   zag helpen voeren

$$
\begin{array}{cccccc}
& \overline{T/(T\backslash NP_1)} & \overline{T/(T\backslash NP_2)} & \overline{T/(T\backslash NP_3)} & \overline{T/(T\backslash NP_4)} & \overline{(((S_{+SUB}\backslash NP_1)\backslash NP_2)\backslash NP_3)\backslash NP_4} \\
& \multicolumn{2}{c}{\overline{T/((T\backslash NP_1)\backslash NP_2)}^{>\mathbf{B}}} & & & \\
& \multicolumn{3}{c}{\overline{T/(((T\backslash NP_1)\backslash NP_2)\backslash NP_3)}^{>\mathbf{B}}} & & \\
& \multicolumn{4}{c}{\overline{T/((((T\backslash NP_1)\backslash NP_2)\backslash NP_3)\backslash NP_4)}^{>\mathbf{B}}} & \\
& \multicolumn{5}{c}{\overline{S_{+SUB}}^{>}} \\
\end{array}
$$

The Surface Structure of the NP sequence that is induced by composition into the novel category is *left*-branching.[16] It is therefore directly compatible with incremental semantic interpretation of the NP sequence in advance of processing the verb group, a point to which we return in chapter 9.

Additional derivations such as the following are possible for such sentences.

(57) dat   Jan   Cecilia   Henk   de nijlpaarden   zag helpen voeren

$$
\begin{array}{cccccc}
& \overline{T/(T\backslash NP_1)} & \overline{T/(T\backslash NP_2)} & \overline{T/(T\backslash NP_3)} & \overline{T/(T\backslash NP_4)} & \overline{(((S_{+SUB}\backslash NP_1)\backslash NP_2)\backslash NP_3)\backslash NP_4} \\
& & \multicolumn{2}{c}{\overline{T/((T\backslash NP_2)\backslash NP_3)}^{>\mathbf{B}}} & & \\
& & \multicolumn{3}{c}{\overline{T/(((T\backslash NP_2)\backslash NP_3)\backslash NP_4)}^{>\mathbf{B}}} & \\
& \multicolumn{4}{c}{\overline{T/((((T\backslash NP_1)\backslash NP_2)\backslash NP_3)\backslash NP_4)}^{>\mathbf{B}}} & \\
& \multicolumn{5}{c}{\overline{S_{+SUB}}^{>}} \\
\end{array}
$$

Such alternative derivations are harmless because the composition rule is order-preserving, and because all the derivations are semantically equivalent, owing to the associativity of functional composition. Moreover, the alternative constituencies that these derivations permit are necessary, in order to capture in the grammar the fact that all of the nonstandard constituents that they engender can coordinate with similar sequences. These and a number of other possibilities for coordination that have sometimes misleadingly been described under the heading of "gapping" are discussed in chapter 7.

6.5 Relative Clauses

The grammar now includes almost everything necessary to permit relative clauses, which take the following general form repeated from (37) (trace notation is again used to indicate the intended reading):

(58) $(N\backslash N)/(S_{+SUB}\backslash NP_i), NP_1, \ldots, NP_h, t_i, NP_j, \ldots, NP_n, (\ldots(S_{+SUB}\backslash NP_i)\backslash\ldots)\backslash NP_n$

What we would *like* to happen with a Dutch relative clause meaning *who Jan saw Cecilia help feed the hippopotamuses* is the following:

(59)

die	Jan	Cecilia	de nijlpaarden	zag helpen voeren
$(N\backslash N)/(S_{+SUB}\backslash NP)$	$T/(T\backslash NP_1)$	$T/(T\backslash NP_2)$	$T/(T\backslash NP_4)$	$(((S_{+SUB}\backslash NP_1)\backslash NP_2)\backslash NP_3)\backslash NP_4$

$$\frac{T/((T\backslash NP_1)\backslash NP_2)}{}{}^{>B}$$

$$\frac{((S_{+SUB}\backslash NP_1)\backslash NP_2)\backslash NP_3}{}{}^{>}$$

$$\frac{S_{+SUB}\backslash NP_3}{}{}^{>B_\times}$$

$$\frac{N\backslash N}{}{}^{>}$$

First the subject *Jan* $T/(T\backslash NP_1)$ would compose with the object *Cecilia*, which bears the category $T/(T\backslash NP_2)$, to yield $T/((T\backslash NP_1)\backslash NP_2)$. (The subscripts are as usual included for guidance only.) Next, the object *de nijlpaarden*, $T/(T\backslash NP_4)$, would combine with the verb group, $(((S\backslash NP_1)\backslash NP_2)\backslash NP_3)\backslash NP_4$, by simple forward application. The entity *Jan Cecilia*, $T/((T\backslash NP_1)\backslash NP_2)$, resulting from the earlier composition would then compose with the new result *de nijlpaarden zag helpen voeren*, $((S\backslash NP_1)\backslash NP_2)\backslash NP_3$, to give *Jan Cecilia de nijlpaarden zag helpen voeren*, $S\backslash NP_3$, a function to which the relative-pronoun could simply apply as usual.

However, the crucial composition of *Jan Cecilia* with *de nijlpaarden zag helpen voeren* is not allowed by the crossed composition rule (14), because of the restriction on Y in that rule to the category VP_{-SUB}. Nor can we permit the composition by relaxing this constraint without also allowing overgeneralizations like (60) and (61), in which objects are "scrambled" over subjects, which (as de Roeck (1984) and Janeaway (1991) noted) the earlier account wrongly permitted:[17]

(60) a. **... dat Jan Cecilia zag zwemmen.*
    ... that Jan Cecilia saw swim
    '... that Jan saw Cecilia swim.'

  b.

*dat	Jan	Cecilia	zag	zwemmen
	$T/(T\backslash NP_2)$	$T/(T\backslash NP_1)$	$((S_{+SUB}\backslash NP_1)\backslash NP_2)/VP$	VP

$$\frac{(S_{+SUB}\backslash NP_1)\backslash NP_2}{}{}^{>}$$

$$\frac{S_{+SUB}\backslash NP_2}{}{}^{>B_\times}$$

$$\frac{S_{+SUB}}{}{}^{*}$$

(61) a. *... dat Jan de nijlpaarden   Cecilia zag voeren.
         ... that Jan the hippopotamuses Cecilia saw feed
         '...that Jan saw Cecilia feed the hippopotamuses.'

b.
$$
\begin{array}{ccccc}
*\text{dat} & \text{Jan} & \text{de nijlpaarden} & \text{Cecilia} & \text{zag voeren} \\
& \underline{T/(T\backslash NP_1)} & \underline{T/(T\backslash NP_3)} & T/(T\backslash NP_2) & ((S_{+SUB}\backslash NP_1)\backslash NP_2)\backslash NP_3
\end{array}
$$

We also need to exclude overgenerations like the following:

(62) a. *Ik denk ze dat het heeft gedaan
         I think she that it has done

b.
$$
\begin{array}{ccccc}
*\text{Ik denk} & \text{ze} & \text{dat} & \text{het} & \text{heeft gedaan} \\
\underline{S/S'_{+SUB}} & T/(T\backslash NP) & S'_{+SUB}/S_{+SUB} & T/(T\backslash NP) & (S_{+SUB}\backslash NP)\backslash NP
\end{array}
$$

c.
$$
\begin{array}{ccccc}
*\text{Ik denk} & \text{ze} & \text{dat} & \text{het} & \text{heeft gedaan} \\
\underline{S/S'_{+SUB}} & T/(T\backslash NP) & S'_{+SUB}/S_{+SUB} & T/(T\backslash NP) & (S_{+SUB}\backslash NP)\backslash NP
\end{array}
$$

In order to permit the desired derivation (59) without such overgeneralizations allowing "real" NPs to combine in "scrambled" orders, we must mark the extracting argument in the same way that we distinguished extractable subjects in chapter 4, using the feature value $+ANT$ in the following instance of the crossed composition rule, and the earlier assumption that type-raised categories (which for conciseness I continue to write as $T/(T\backslash NP)$) are written in full as $T/(T\backslash NP_{-ANT})$:

(63) *Dutch forward crossed composition II* ($>\mathbf{B}_\times$)
     $X/Y \quad Y\backslash Z_{+ANT} \quad \Rightarrow_\mathbf{B} \quad X\backslash Z_{+ANT}$
     where $Y = S\backslash\$$

The extraction is then permitted, as follows:[18]

(64)
$$
\begin{array}{ccccc}
\text{die} & \text{Jan} & \text{Cecilia} & \text{de nijlpaarden} & \text{zag helpen voeren} \\
(N\backslash N)/(S_{+SUB}\backslash NP) & T/(T\backslash NP_1) & T/(T\backslash NP_2) & T/(T\backslash NP_4) & (((S_{+SUB}\backslash NP_1)\backslash NP_2)\backslash NP_3)\backslash NP_4
\end{array}
$$

The general case (37) can be accepted in an analogous fashion. That is, the subject and complement NPs 1 to h that precede the site of extraction can combine by successive forward compositions into a function of the form $T/((\ldots(T\backslash NP_1)\backslash\ldots)\backslash NP_h)$. (As the (64) shows, the processor somehow has to cope with the problem of deciding where the extraction site actually is, but that is not a problem of grammar.) The complement NPs j to n that follow the extraction site can combine with the verb complex by successive forward compositions and/or applications into a single entity $((\ldots(S_{+SUB}\backslash NP_1)\backslash\ldots)\backslash NP_h)\backslash NP_i$. These two entities can then compose by the crossed composition rule (63), "canceling" $(\ldots((S_{+SUB}\backslash NP)\backslash NP_1)\ldots)\backslash NP_h$, to give a single entity $S'_{+SUB}\backslash NP_{i+ANT}$, to which the relative-pronoun $(N\backslash N)/(S'_{+SUB}\backslash NP_{+ANT})$ can finally apply to yield the N modifier category $N\backslash N$. At every stage the interpretations of the object category $T/(T\backslash NP)$ of the combinatory rules ensure that the correct dependencies are established in predicate-argument structure. Exactly the same apparatus will allow either NP in (36), but not both, to extract.

Nevertheless, the potential overgenerations (60)–(62) arising from the interaction of crossed composition and the type-raised categories are prevented by the restriction of the residue of relativization to "antecedent government," or combination with arguments other than the relative-pronoun, via the $+ANT$ feature and the fact that the standard order-preserving type-raised categories are an abbreviation for $T/(T\backslash NP_{-ANT})$:

(65) *dat   Jan   Cecilia   zag   zwemmen

$$\cfrac{\cfrac{\cfrac{T/(T\backslash NP_2)\quad T/(T\backslash NP_1)\quad \cfrac{((S_{+SUB}\backslash NP_1)\backslash NP_2)/VP \quad VP}{(S_{+SUB}\backslash NP_1)\backslash NP_2}>}{(S_{+SUB}\backslash NP_1)\backslash NP_2}>\mathbf{B}_\times}{S_{+SUB}\backslash NP_{2+ANT}}}{}*$$

(66) *dat   Jan   de nijlpaarden   Cecilia   zag voeren

$$\cfrac{\cfrac{T/(T\backslash NP_1)\quad T/(T\backslash NP_3)}{T/((T\backslash NP_1)\backslash NP_3)}>\mathbf{B}\qquad \cfrac{T/(T\backslash NP_2)\quad ((S_{+SUB}\backslash NP_1)\backslash NP_2)\backslash NP_3}{(S_{+SUB}\backslash NP_1)\backslash NP_{3+ANT}}>\mathbf{B}_\times}{}*$$

(67) *ik denk   ze   dat   het   heeft gedaan

$$\cfrac{\cfrac{S/S'_{+SUB}\quad T/(T\backslash NP)\quad S'_{+SUB}/S_{+SUB}\quad \cfrac{T/(T\backslash NP)\quad \cfrac{(S_{+SUB}\backslash NP)\backslash NP}{S_{+SUB}\backslash NP}>}{S'_{+SUB}\backslash NP_{+ANT}}>\mathbf{B}_\times}{}*>}{S'_{+SUB}}$$

(68) *ik denk   ze   dat   het   heeft gedaan

$$\cfrac{\cfrac{S/S'_{+SUB}\quad T/(T\backslash NP)}{S/(S'_{+SUB}\backslash NP)}{}^{>\mathbf{B}}\quad S'_{+SUB}/S_{+SUB}\quad \cfrac{T/(T\backslash NP)\quad (S_{+SUB}\backslash NP)\backslash NP}{\cfrac{S_{+SUB}\backslash NP}{S'_{+SUB}\backslash NP_{+ANT}}{}^{>\mathbf{B}_{\times}}}{}^{>}}{}^{*>}$$

6.6 Subject and Object Extraction from Embedded Clauses

Relativization of the kind described above can of course be unbounded, as in (69):

(69) het nijlpaard   dat ik denk dat Jan Cecilia zag voeren
      the hippopotamus that I think that Jan Cecilia saw feed
      'the hippopotamus that I think that Jan saw Cecilia feed'

Moreover, as noted in chapter 4, the present theory predicts that the asymmetry in extractability of subjects and objects found in English depends upon the differential directionality of these arguments, and that it will not be characteristic of verb-final or verb-initial languages. The asymmetry does indeed fail to occur in Dutch (Maling and Zaenen 1978; Koster 1986, 206). Both subject and object extractions are permitted by the rules introduced above, as follows:

(70) a. de arts   die ik denk dat het werk heeft gedaan.
          the doctor who I think that the work has   done
          '*the doctor who I think that did the work.'

      b. (de arts)   die   ik denk   dat   het werk   heeft gedaan

$$\cfrac{(N\backslash N)/(S\backslash NP)\quad S_{+SUB}/S'_{+SUB}\quad S'_{+SUB}/S_{+SUB}\quad \cfrac{T/(T\backslash NP)\quad (S\backslash NP)\backslash NP}{\cfrac{S_{+SUB}\backslash NP}{\cfrac{S'_{+SUB}\backslash NP_{+ANT}}{S_{+SUB}\backslash NP_{+ANT}}{}^{>\mathbf{B}_{\times}}}{}^{>\mathbf{B}_{\times}}}{}^{>}}{N\backslash N}$$

(71) a. het werk dat ik denk dat ze   heeft gedaan
          The work that I think that she has   done
          "the work that I think that she did'

      b. (het werk)   dat   ik denk   dat   ze   heeft gedaan

$$\cfrac{(N\backslash N)/(S\backslash NP)\quad S_{+SUB}/S'_{+SUB}\quad S'_{+SUB}/S_{+SUB}\quad \cfrac{T/(T\backslash NP)\quad (S\backslash NP)\backslash NP}{\cfrac{S_{+SUB}\backslash NP_{+ANT}}{\cfrac{S'_{+SUB}\backslash NP_{+ANT}}{S_{+SUB}\backslash NP_{+ANT}}{}^{>\mathbf{B}_{\times}}}{}^{>\mathbf{B}_{\times}}}{}^{>\mathbf{B}_{\times}}}{N\backslash N}$$

The earlier claim that the English subject/object extraction asymmetry is a consequence of the way the combinators project directionality from its SVO lexicon, rather than of an autonomous Empty Category Principle or a value on the pro-drop parameter is therefore sustained (Steedman 1997, 55).[19]

6.7 Dutch Main-clause Order

The account of Dutch word order given so far has ignored the main-clause orders exemplified in (3a—c). In terms of the standard movement metaphor, these orders are related to the corresponding subordinate-clause order, (3d) by *bounded* movement. In a lexical grammar this translates into the assumption that the main-clause orders arise from a single additional lexical entry for each verb in the language. (Of course, for Dutch inversion, unlike English inversion, we must eventually expect to capture this pattern via a lexical rule. However, I will ignore the question of how to do this here.) I will assume the following additional main-clause categories for Dutch tensed intransitive, transitive, and ditransitive verbs:[2021]

(72) wint 'wins' $:= S_{-SUB}/NP$
   at 'ate' $:= (S_{-SUB}/NP)/NP$
   gaf 'gave' $:= ((S_{-SUB}/NP)/NP)/NP$

The feature $-SUB$ identifies the VSO clause as a main clause, in contrast to the SOV category.

The tendency noted in chapter 4 for rightward arguments to "wrap" with respect to the Logical Form means that the first of these arguments is the subject, as revealed by agreement and the interpretation in the following full categories:

(73) wint 'wins' $:= S_{-SUB}/NP_{3s} : \lambda x.wins'x$
   at 'ate' $:= (S_{-SUB}/NP)/NP_{agr} : \lambda x.\lambda y.eat'yx$
   gaf 'gave' $:= ((S_{-SUB}/NP)/NP)/NP_{agr} : \lambda x.\lambda y.\lambda z.give'zyx$

(Details of agreement will usually be omitted from derivations.)

I will assume that sentence-initial arguments in Dutch, including subjects, extract by the same mechanism as the English topicalized sentences discussed in note 8 to chapter 4 and the relative-pronouns discussed in chapter 3 and section 6.5. That is, they have categories parallel to example (43) of chapter 3, as in (74) below. (As in the case of the English topicalized categories, I assume that the Dutch categories are assigned only to leftmost elements of sentences.)

(74) a. $S'_{-SUB}/(S_{-SUB}\backslash NP)$

   b. $S'_{-SUB}/(S_{-SUB}/NP)$

   c. $(S'_{-SUB}/X)/((S_{-SUB}/X)/NP)$

As usual, S'_{-SUB} abbreviates S^{+CP}_{-SUB}, a main-clause CP in which the feature-value $+CP$ distinguishes the topicalized clause from the untopicalized clause S_{-SUB}, and the feature-value $-SUB$ distinguishes both from the corresponding subordinate SOV clause types.

This category permits the following main-clause orders for the simple tensed transitive verb:

(75) a. At Jan appels?

   b. Appels at Jan!

   c. Jan at appels.

I assume that NPs on the right of the verb undergo order-preserving type-raising, an assumption supported by the similar possibilities for argument cluster coordination, as in *Hij gaf de leraar een appel en de politieman een bloem* 'He gave the teacher an apple, and the policeman, a flower' (see below). It is important for future developments that these leftward-raised categories do not restrict T on the *SUB* feature as the rightward ones do (see (43)). For example:

(76)

Appels	at	Jan
$S'_{-SUB}/(S_{-SUB}/NP_2)$	$(S_{-SUB}/NP_2)/NP_1$	$T\backslash(T/NP_1)$

$$\frac{\quad\quad\quad\quad\quad\quad\quad\quad S_{-SUB}/NP_2 \quad\quad\quad\quad\quad\quad}{\quad\quad\quad\quad\quad\quad\quad\quad\quad\quad S'_{-SUB}\quad\quad\quad\quad\quad\quad\quad\quad\quad}{}^{<}_{>}$$

Such extractions can be unbounded:

(77) Appels denk ik dat Jan heeft gegeten
   Apples think I that Jan has eaten
   'Apples, I think that John has eaten.'

(78)

Appels	denk ik	dat	Jan	heeft gegeten
$S'_{-SUB}/(S_{-SUB}\backslash NP)$	S_{-SUB}/S'_{+SUB}	S'_{+SUB}/S_{+SUB}	$S_{+SUB}/(S_{+SUB}\backslash NP)$	$(S_{+SUB}\backslash NP)\backslash NP$

$$\frac{S'_{+SUB}/S_{+SUB}}{}{}^{>B}\quad\quad\quad \frac{S_{+SUB}\backslash NP_{+ANT}}{}{}^{>B_{\times}}$$

$$\frac{S'_{-SUB}/S_{+SUB}}{}\quad\quad\quad\quad \frac{S'_{-SUB}\backslash NP_{+ANT}}{}{}^{>B_{\times}}$$

$$\frac{\quad\quad\quad\quad\quad\quad\quad\quad\quad S' \quad\quad\quad\quad\quad\quad\quad\quad\quad}{}{}^{>}$$

By contrast, the derivation of SVO order (and in general of fronting of any argument except the most oblique) crucially involves the same backward crossed composition rule as the English rule (33) and the nonperipheral extraction examples (28) of chapter 4, which we can write as follows:

(79) *Dutch backward crossed composition I* ($<\mathbf{B}_\times$)

$$Y/Z_{-SHIFT,+ANT} \quad X\backslash Y \quad \Rightarrow_{\mathbf{B}} \quad X/Z_{-SHIFT,+ANT}$$

where $Y = S_{-SUB}/NP$

We must also assume that in Dutch main verbs, subcategorized nonperipheral rightward arguments bear the feature-value $-SHIFT$, like English dative NP arguments of ditransitives (see (32a) of chapter 4, although I will usually suppress this feature-value by convention in the notation):

(80) a. at $:= (S/NP)/NP_{-SHIFT}$

b. gaf $:= (S/NP/NP_{-SHIFT})/NP_{-SHIFT}$

Subjects can then front as follows:

(81)

Jan	at	appels
$S'_{-SUB}/(S_{-SUB}/NP_1)$	$(S_{-SUB}/NP_2)/NP_{1-SHIFT}$	$T\backslash(T/NP_2)$

$$\frac{S_{-SUB}/NP_{1-SHIFT,+ANT}}{} {}^{<\mathbf{B}_\times}$$

$$\frac{S'_{-SUB}}{} {}^{>}$$

The $+ANT$ restriction on the argument Z in rule (79) marks it for antecedent government only, and as incompatible with any normal in situ argument NP. In this respect the rule is exactly parallel to the Forward Crossed Composition rule II (63) used in relative clauses. Examples like the following are thereby prevented:

(82) a. *[At appels]$_{S_{-SUB}/NP_{-SHIFT,+ANT}}$ het meisje.

Ate apples   the girl

'The girl ate apples.'

b. *[Gaf hij appels]$_{S_{-SUB}/NP_{-SHIFT,+ANT}}$ het meisje.

Gave he apples   the girl

'He gave the girl apples.'

c. *[Gaf hem appels]$_{S_{-SUB}/NP_{-SHIFT,+ANT}}$ het meisje.

Gave him apples   the girl

'The girl gave him apples.'

For example:

(83)

$*$At	appels	het meisje
$(S_{-SUB}/NP_2)/NP_1$	$T\backslash(T/NP_2)$	$T\backslash(T/NP_{1-ANT})$

$$\frac{S/NP_{1+ANT}}{} {}^{<\mathbf{B}_\times}$$

$$\frac{}{} {}^{*}$$

To the extent that heavy NP shift over nonarguments is allowed in Dutch, as in examples like the following, the other English instance of the backward crossed composition rule (31) restricted to arguments compatible with $+SHIFT$ must be included in Dutch as well.

(84) Jan zag gisteren   een vlucht regenwulpen.
     Jan saw yesterday a   flock whimbrels
     'Jan saw a flock of whimbrels yesterday.'

The rule is the following:

(85) *Dutch backward crossed composition II* ($<\mathbf{B}_\times$)
$$Y/Z_{+SHIFT} \quad X\backslash Y \quad \Rightarrow_{\mathbf{B}} \quad X/Z_{+SHIFT}$$
where $Y = S_{-SUB}/NP$

German appears to allow examples parallel to (83), so it presumably has the more general backward crossed composition rule (24) of chapter 4.[22]

The generalization implicit in the above analysis of leftward-extraction is that fronting of a preverbal element in Dutch is the mirror-image of unbounded extraction in Dutch relative clauses, as exemplified in (64). That is, any arguments that lie between the canonical position of the extracted argument and the verb combine normally with the verb. Any arguments that lie on the other side of the extraction site combine with each other by a simple composition rule. The two fragments then combine to create the clause residue of extraction by a crossed composition rule, to form the argument of the topicalized element. The following ditransitives illustrate the point:

(86)   Hij   geeft   de politieman   een bloem
$\overline{S'_{-SUB}/(S_{-SUB}/NP_1)}$ $\overline{((S_{-SUB}/NP_3)/NP_2)/NP_1}$ $\overline{T\backslash(T/NP_2)}$ $\overline{T\backslash(T/NP_3)}$
                                                                       $\underline{\qquad\qquad\qquad\qquad}_{<\mathbf{B}}$
                                                                       $T\backslash((T/NP_3)/NP_2)$
                                                   $\underline{\qquad\qquad\qquad\qquad\qquad\qquad}_{<\mathbf{B}_\times}$
                                                   $S_{-SUB}/NP_{1_{+ANT}}$
$\underline{\qquad\qquad\qquad\qquad\qquad\qquad\qquad\qquad\qquad\qquad}_{>}$
                         S'_{-SUB}

(87)   De politieman   geeft   hij   een bloem
$\overline{S'_{-SUB}/(S_{-SUB}/NP_2)}$ $\overline{((S_{-SUB}/NP_3)/NP_2)/NP_1}$ $\overline{T\backslash(T/NP_1)}$ $\overline{T\backslash(T/NP_3)}$
                               $\underline{\qquad\qquad\qquad\qquad\qquad\qquad}_{<}$
                               $(S_{-SUB}/NP_3)/NP_2$
                                $\underline{\qquad\qquad\qquad\qquad\qquad\qquad\qquad\qquad}_{<\mathbf{B}_\times}$
                                $S_{-SUB}/NP_{2_{+ANT}}$
$\underline{\qquad\qquad\qquad\qquad\qquad\qquad\qquad\qquad\qquad\qquad}_{>}$
                    S'_{-SUB}

(88)

Een bloem	geeft	hij	de politieman
$S'_{-SUB}/(S_{-SUB}/NP_3)$	$((S_{-SUB}/NP_3)/NP_2)/NP_1$	$T\backslash(T/NP_1)$	$T\backslash(T/NP_2)$

$$\frac{\qquad\qquad}{(S_{-SUB}/NP_3)/NP_2}<$$

$$\frac{\qquad\qquad\qquad\qquad}{S_{-SUB}/NP_3}<$$

$$\frac{\qquad\qquad\qquad\qquad\qquad}{S'_{-SUB}}>$$

Similarly, we can assume the following verb-initial categories for the modal *zal* 'shall/will', the perfect *heeft* 'has', and the tensed causative *zag* 'saw'. (Note that these categories also obey the lexical wrapping universal.)

(89) $zal := (S_{-SUB}/VP_{+SUB})/NP$

$heeft := (S_{-SUB}/VP^{PPL}_{+SUB})/NP$

$zag := ((S_{-SUB}/VP_{+SUB})/NP)/NP$

The interpreted categories can be written in full as follows:

(90) $zal := (S_{-SUB}/VP_{+SUB})/NP : \lambda x.\lambda p.shall'px$

$heeft := (S_{-SUB}/VP^{PPL}_{+SUB})/NP : \lambda x.\lambda p.has'px$

$zag := ((S_{-SUB}/VP_{+SUB})/NP)/NP : \lambda x.\lambda y.\lambda p.saw'pyx$

In such main-clause tensed-verb categories, the VP complements are distinguished as having OV order—that is, as $+SUB$, in contrast to the corresponding complements of the related SOV verbs. We saw in connection with (49), repeated here, that OV VPs are not permitted as complements of verbs like *zien* in subordinate clauses:

(91) a. *... omdat ik Cecilia [zag]$_{((S_{+SUB}\backslash NP)\backslash NP)/VP_{-SUB}}$
[de nijlpaarden voeren.]$_{VP_{+SUB}}$

b. *... omdat ik probeer Jan [te leren]$_{(VP^{TE}\backslash NP)/VP_{-SUB}}$
[de nijlpaarden voeren.]$_{VP_{+SUB}}$

c. *... omdat ik [heb]$_{(S_{SUB}\backslash NP)/VP_{EN,-SUB}}$
[de nijlpaarden gevoerd.]$_{VP_{EN,+SUB}}$

VP_{+SUB} and VP^{PPL}_{+SUB} are as usual abbreviations for predicate categories $(S_{+SUB}\backslash NP)$ and $(S^{PPL}_{+SUB}\backslash NP)$.

It will be recalled that the order-preserving forward type-raised category is restricted via the variable T to combination with $+SUB$ categories. It follows that all of the following main-clause orders are allowed:[23]

(92) a. $\text{Jan}_{(S'_{-SUB}/X)/((S_{-SUB}/X)/NP)}$ $\text{zal}_{(S_{-SUB}/VP_{+SUB})/NP}$ [appels eten.]$_{VP_{+SUB}}$

    b. [Zal Jan]$_{S_{-SUB}/VP_{+SUB}}$ [appels eten?]$_{VP_{+SUB}}$

    c. Appels$_{S'_{-SUB}/(S_{-SUB}\backslash NP)}$ [zal   Jan]$_{S_{-SUB}/VP_{+SUB}}$ [Cecilia

    geven.]$_{VP_{+SUB}\backslash NP_{+ANT}}$

All of the following are excluded as main clauses:

(93) a. *Jan appels zal eten.

    b. *Appels Jan zal eten.

    c. *Zal appels Jan eten.

Similarly, the main clauses in (94) are permitted, but those in (95) are not:

(94) a. Jan heeft [appels gegeten.]$_{VP^{PPL}_{+SUB}}$

    b. Ik zag Cecilia [de paarden voeren.]$_{VP_{+SUB}}$

(95) a. *Jan appels heeft gegeten.

    b. *Ik Cecilia de paarden zag voeren.

Finally (although we will continue to ignore the details of binding theory here, directing the reader to Steedman 1996b for a fuller account), it is clear that the binding of reflexives will behave correctly, because the main-clause verb categories as usual wrap their arguments into the predicate-argument structure.

The above analysis of main clauses in Dutch makes some strong predictions concerning coordinate sentences, including nonconstituent and gapping varieties. Discussion of these predictions is deferred until chapter 7.

6.8 Interaction of Word order and Quantifier Scope

Although a full treatment of quantification remains beyond the scope of the present book, the brief outline in chapter 4 touched on the fact that, as Kayne (1983) and others have argued, embedded SVO subjects in English and several Romance languages disallow the wide scope readings that objects and more oblique arguments permit. In CCG this is a necessary consequence of the fact that subjects are leftward arguments. I noted in passing that related disallowed scope inversions are strongly predicted for verb-final constructions in German, in which many more arguments are leftward.

Kayne (1998), following Bayer (1990, 1996), points out that, although German does allow scope alternations in sentences like (96), examples like (97) do not, unlike their English counterparts:

(96) (Weil) irgendjemand auf jeden   gespannt ist.   *(Ambiguous)*
      (Since) someone   on everybody curious   is
      'Since someone is curious about everybody.'

(97) (Weil) jemand   versucht hat jeden   reinzulegen.   *(Unambiguous)*
      (Since) someone tried   has everyone cheat
      'Since someone has tried to cheat everyone.'

In present terms, this asymmetry arises because in (96), *gespannt ist* can form by composition and the quantifier *auf jeden* can then combine with the whole thing to take scope over the tensed verb. The referential *jemand* can then combine to yield the scope-inverted reading. By contrast, in (97), although *versucht hat* can similarly compose, it cannot combine with *reinzulegen* until *jeden* has combined with it. *Jeden* therefore cannot take wide scope with respect to tense, and hence cannot take inverse scope over *jemand*.

Haegeman and van Riemsdijk (1986, 444-445), and Haegeman (1992, 202), cite a number of related effects of "Verb Projection Raising" on scope in West Flemish Dutch and Zurich German subordinate clauses (see Koster 1986, 286-288 for discussion). For example both "verb raising" word order (98a) and "verb projection raising" word order (98b) are allowed for the following West Flemish subordinate clause:

(98) a. (da) Jan vee   boeken hee willen lezen   *(Ambiguous)*
          (that) Jan many books   has wanted read
          'that Jan wanted to read many books'

      b. (da) Jan hee willen   vee   boeken lezen   *(Unambiguous)*
          (that) Jan has wanted many books   read
          'that Jan wanted to read many books'

Only (98a) is ambiguous and allows "many books" to take wider scope than "wanted," yielding the reading where there are many books such that Jan wanted to read them.

Similar results apply for the equi verbs, which allow related word order alternations in standard dutch:

(99) a. (omdat)   Jan veel   liederen probeert te zingen   *(Ambiguous)*
          (because) Jan many songs   tries   to sing
          'because Jan tries to sing many songs'

      b. (omdat)   Jan probeert veel   liederen te zingen   *(Unambiguous)*
          (because) Jan tries   many songs   to sing
          'because Jan tries to sing many songs'

We therefore correctly predict that these verbs under the latter word order will limit scope inversion similarly to Bayer's (97), making (100b) unambiguous in comparison to (100a):

(100) a. (omdat) iemand alle   liederen probeert te zingen   *(Ambiguous)*
         (because) someone every song   tries   to sing
         'because someone tries to sing every song'

      b. (omdat) iemand probeert alle   liederen te zingen *(Unambiguous)*
         (because) someone tries   every song   to sing
         'because someone tries to sing every song'

6.9 On the Rarity of Crossing Dependencies

The above Dutch fragment suffers from a number of omissions. Many important questions, including certain idiosyncrasies of clitic pronoun placement and the placement of adverbials and negation, have been passed over and await future work. However, I hope to have shown that the facts of Dutch grammar confirm a number of the assumptions that were made in formulating the grammar of English. First, the extraction and coordination possibilities in Dutch confirm the assumption that NPs and other arguments should bear order-preserving type-raised functor categories. The claim that type-raising is related to the phenomenon of case and that even nonexplicitly cased languages like English and Dutch have implicit case is borne out. Second, the existence of crossed dependencies in a language with the lexicon of Dutch is predicted, and continues to support the controversial inclusion of "slash crossing" rules of functional composition in the theory.[24]

One might ask at this point why crossing or intercalating dependencies remain comparatively rare. Although it seems to be the case that many, and perhaps all, natural languages include a few crossing dependencies, no configurational language entirely crosses dependencies, or even crosses a majority of them. The question of why they are relatively rare therefore remains crucial for any theory that allows them at all.[25]

Grammars of the kind proposed here allow crossed dependencies only when they include (a) function categories that combine with some of their arguments to one side, and with others to the other side, and (b) combinatory rules that "cross" directionality in their operands. It is well known from studies by Greenberg (1963), Vennemann (1973), Lehmann (1978), Comrie (1981), Hawkins (1982), and Mallinson and Blake (1981) that there is a strong crosslinguistic tendency for constituent types that are closely related (say, in terms of the $\bar{X}$-theory), such as VP and PP, to have a consistent order of head and complement, a suggestion that has been recast by Dryer (1992) in terms of consistent ordering of phrasal and nonphrasal elements. German and Dutch are rather unusual in going against this trend, which is generally supposed to originate in semantic similarities between such categories, and a requirement for natural grammars to be as transparent a reflection of the semantics as possible. The latter requirement is equally widely supposed to stem in turn from requirements of ease of learning, or processing, or both.

In the terms of the present theory, this observation translates into a tendency for semantically related function categories—for example, verbs—to find their arguments consistently to one side or the other, as has been noted within other categorial approaches to Universal Grammar (Vennemann 1973; Keenan and Faltz 1978; Flynn 1983) and as seems consistent with Dryer 1992. It follows that the conditions under which crossed dependencies can arise according to the present theory are known for independent reasons to be relatively rare.

Appendix: Summary of the Dutch Fragment

Certain details of the categories and rules in the following summary of the grammar fragment developed so far for Dutch anticipate further discussion of Dutch in chapter 7.

Category Abbreviations
The following abbreviations are used:

$S = S^{-CP,+IP}$ (a tensed clause or IP)

$S' = S^{+CP,+IP}$ (a tensed clause or CP)

$VP = S^{-CP,-IP,-TE}\backslash NP$ (a bare infinitival VP)

$VP^{TE} = S^{-CP,-IP,+TE}\backslash NP$ (a te-infinitival VP)

Verb Categories
Four types of Dutch clause are distinguished, using the categories (tensed) S and (infinitival, participial, etc.) VP, and the feature SUB(ordinate), which may take the value + (plus), − (minus), or ? (either). Thus:

S_{-SUB} is a tensed main clause.

S_{+SUB} is a tensed subordinate clause.

VP_{+SUB} is an infinitival (etc.) VP yielding S_{+SUB}.

To avoid clutter, $VP_{?SUB}$ is often abbreviated as VP. VP can be further distinguished by minor superscript features such as TE (*te*-infinitival) and PPL (participial).

Verbs have distinct categories as heads of main and subordinate clauses, unlike their English counterparts (other than the auxiliaries). Main-clause verbs take all arguments to the right and "wrap" them into Logical Form. All other verbs take NP, PP, and the like. on the left, and S, VP, and the like. on the right. All such arguments are $?ANT$—unspecified on the feature ANT—although this detail is left implicit to save clutter. For example, *zien* 'to see' has the following categories:

zag $:= ((S_{-SUB}/VP_{+SUB})/NP)/NP$ (head of main clause)

zag $:= ((S_{+SUB}\backslash NP)\backslash NP)/VP_{-SUB}$ (head of subordinate clause)

zien $:= (VP\backslash NP)/VP_{-SUB}$ (head of infinitival)

te zien $:= (VP^{TE}_{+SUB}\backslash NP)/VP_{-SUB}$ (head of *te*-infinitival)

te zien $:= (VP^{TE}\backslash NP)/VP^{TE}_{+SUB}$ (head of *te*-infinitival)

(The last of these arises from the brute force *te* category stipulation (30).) *Voeren* 'to feed' has the following categories:

voerde $:= (S_{-SUB}/NP)/NP$ (head of main clause)

voerde $:= (S_{+SUB}\backslash NP)\backslash NP$ (head of subordinate clause)

voeren $:= VP\backslash NP$ (head of infinitival)

te voeren $:= VP^{TE}_{+SUB}/NP$ (head of *te*-infinitival)

NPs and Other Argument Categories

Order-preserving type-raised categories allow noun complements and verb groups to form complex constituents. Restrictions on possible type-raised categories encode the syntactic difference between infinitival verbs and full VPs. V2 main-clause order is the result of topicalization. $S\$$ is frequently abbreviated as T. All arguments except topics and relative-pronouns are $-ANT$. The latter are unmarked on this feature, and this is reflected in the raised categories, although in derivations this detail is usually suppressed (see "Rules" below). For example:

de nijlpaarden $:= S\$\backslash(S\$/NP_{-ANT})$ (main-clause argument)

de nijlpaarden $:= S_{+SUB}\$/(S_{+SUB}\$\backslash NP_{-ANT})$(subordinate-clause argument)

de nijlpaarden $:= S'_{-SUB}\$/(S_{-SUB}\$/NP_{?ANT})$ (mainclause topic)

die/dat $:= (N\backslash N)\$/(S_{+SUB}\$\backslash NP_{?ANT})$ (relative-pronoun)

Rules

Composition rules distinguish type-raised categories from others, and restrictions on composition using the feature *ANT* prevent scrambling but enable wh-movement.

a. *Forward application*

$X/Y \quad Y \quad \Rightarrow \quad X$

b. *Backward application*

$Y \quad X\backslash Y \quad \Rightarrow X$

c. *Forward composition I* ($>$**B**) (55)

$X/Y \quad Y/(Y\backslash Z) \quad \Rightarrow_\mathbf{B} \quad X/(Y\backslash Z)$

where $Y = S$

d. *Forward composition II* ($>$**B**)—see chapter 7, example (25)

$X/Y \quad Y/Z \quad \Rightarrow_\mathbf{B} \quad X/Z$

where $Y = S_{-SUB}/\$$

e. *Forward crossed composition I* ($> \mathbf{B}^n{}_\times$) (14)/(19)

$X/Y \quad (Y\backslash Z)\$ \quad \Rightarrow_{\mathbf{B}^n} \quad (X\backslash Z)\$$

where $Y = VP_{-SUB}$

f. *Forward crossed composition II* ($>$**B**$_\times$) (63)

$X/Y \quad Y\backslash Z_{+ANT} \quad \Rightarrow_\mathbf{B} \quad X\backslash Z_{+ANT}$

where $Y = S\backslash \$$

g. *Backward composition* ($<$**B**^{n}) (21)

$(Y\backslash Z)\$ \quad X\backslash Y \quad \Rightarrow_{\mathbf{B^n}} \quad (X\backslash Z)\$$

h. *Backward crossed composition I* ($<$**B**$_\times$) (79)

$Y/Z_{-SHIFT,+ANT} \quad X\backslash Y \quad \Rightarrow_\mathbf{B} \quad X/Z_{-SHIFT,+ANT}$

where $Y = S_{-SUB}/NP$

i. *Backward crossed composition II* ($<$**B**$_\times$) (85)

$Y/Z_{+SHIFT} \quad X\backslash Y \quad \Rightarrow_\mathbf{B} \quad X/Z_{+SHIFT}$

where $Y = S_{-SUB}/NP$

j. *Forward type-raising* ($>$**T**)

$X \quad \Rightarrow_\mathbf{T} \quad T/(T\backslash X_{-ANT})$

where $T\backslash X$ is a parametrically licensed category, and $T = S_{+SUB}\$$

k. *Backward type-raising* ($<$**T**)

$X \quad \Rightarrow_\mathbf{T} \quad T\backslash(T/X_{-ANT})$

where $T\backslash X$ is a parametrically licensed category, and $T = S_{?SUB}\$$

Two further rules corresponding to the combinator **S**, which in Steedman 1996b are used to capture parasitic gaps in Dutch, are not discussed here.

Chapter 7

Gapping and the Order of Constituents

'O where are you going?'
Said reader to rider,
'That valley is fatal where furnaces burn,
Yonder's the midden whose odours will madden,
That gap is the grave where the tall return.'

W. H. Auden, *Five Songs, V*

The Dutch pattern of argument cluster coordination in subordinate clauses—briefly introduced in section 6.4.1 and discussed in greater depth in section 7.1—is a case of the more general universal identified by Ross (1970) noted in chapter 2, concerning the tendency of argument cluster coordination to conserve or "project" the directionality of the lexicon across SOV, VSO, and SVO languages and/or constructions (see Koutsoudas 1971; Lehmann 1978; and Mallinson and Blake 1981):

(1) a. SOV: *SOV and SO, SO and SOV
     b. VSO: VSO and SO, *SO and VSO
     c. SVO: SVO and SO, *SO and SVO

The SOV and VSO cases are essentially symmetrical, and are discussed in sections 7.1 and 7.2. Certain cases of Dutch main-clause argument cluster coordination fall under the VSO heading, as the choice of a VSO category for main-clause verbs predicts (see chapter 6). These are also discussed in section 7.2.

The remainder of the chapter explains gapping in SVO languages like English, as in *Dexter ate bread and Warren, potatoes*, and the related cases of forward gapping in Dutch and other Germanic languages, in terms of the combinatory theory. In particular, the theory predicts Ross's generalization that verb-medial languages and constructions necessarily pattern with the verb-initial ones rather than the verb-final ones in permitting forward, but not backward, gapping, as in (1c) above, and explains why certain SOV languages like Dutch and certain VSO languages like Zapotec show exceptions to the above pattern.[1]

Although the basic SOV and VSO cases reduce to argument cluster coordination, and (as Maling (1972) pointed out in different terms) do not require a distinctive rule of gapping as such, I will argue that SVO gapping is also, in a sense, argument cluster coordination. For that reason, I will continue to refer informally to this whole collection of phenomena as "gapping."

7.1 Gapping and SOV Word Order

As we saw, type-raising arguments over an SOV verb, composing them, and then conjoining the resulting nonstandard constituents permits the "backward gapping" construction characteristic of coordinate clauses in SOV languages. Thus, in Japanese a subject and an object NP can not only combine with the verb by forward application, but also forward-compose as follows, via forward type-raising over the following SOV verb:

(2) $\text{tazuneta}_{SOV} := (S \backslash NP_{nom}) \backslash NP_{acc} : \lambda x. \lambda y. visit' xy$

(3) a. Ken-ga   Naomi-o   tazuneta.
         Ken-NOM Naomi-ACC visit-PAST.CONCL
         'Ken visited Naomi.'

   b.
$$\cfrac{\cfrac{\text{Ken-ga}}{S/(S \backslash NP_{nom})}{}^{>T} \quad \cfrac{\cfrac{\text{Naomi-o}}{(S \backslash NP_{nom})/((S \backslash NP_{nom}) \backslash NP_{acc})}{}^{>T} \quad \cfrac{\text{tazuneta}}{(S \backslash NP_{nom}) \backslash NP_{acc}}}{S/((S \backslash NP_{nom}) \backslash NP_{acc})}{}^{>B}}{S}{}^{>}$$

The resulting nonstandard constituent *Ken-ga Naomi-o* can therefore conjoin:

(4) [Ken-ga Naomi-o],   [Erika-ga Sara-o]   tazuneta.
      $S/((S \backslash NP_{nom}) \backslash NP_{acc})$ $S/((S \backslash NP_{nom}) \backslash NP_{acc})$ $(S \backslash NP_{nom}) \backslash NP_{acc}$
      Ken-NOM Naomi-ACC Erika-NOM Sara-ACC visit-PAST.CONCL
      'Ken visited Naomi, and Erika, Sara.'

What is more, the Principles of Adjacency, Consistency, and Inheritance, together with the order-preserving constraint on type-raising that is the sine qua non of an order-dependent language, again limit the possible constituent orders. They do not permit any raised categories or rules of composition that would produce a *leftward*-looking function, so that the corresponding "forward gapping" construction is disallowed on the SOV lexicon:[2]

(5) *Ken-ga   Naomi-o   tazunete,   Erika-ga   Sara-o
        Ken-NOM Naomi-ACC visit-PAST.ADV Erika-NOM Sara-ACC
        'Ken visited Naomi, and Erika, Sara.'

As noted earlier, this asymmetry tends to be characteristic of strictly SOV languages. However, a number of important qualifications to the generalization have to be made. Most importantly, like other Germanic languages, Dutch *does* allow coordinations on the above pattern in subordinate-clause conjunctions:

(6) ...dat Maaike aardappels eet en Piet bonen
    ...that Maaike potatoes   eats and Piet beans
    '...that Maaike eats potatoes and Piet beans.'

We will see that this exception to the SOV pattern is related to the fact that these languages possess an SVO main-clause constituent order as well, which Japanese lacks.

Japanese also allows OSV word order, as in (7):

(7) Naomi-o   Ken-ga   tazuneta.
    Naomi-ACC Ken-NOM visit-PAST.CONCL
    'Ken visited Naomi.'

However, the temptation to allow this by introducing forward crossed composition, so that the raised Japanese subject could compose with the Japanese verb, as in the following derivation, should be resisted:

(8)

$$\frac{\dfrac{\text{Naomi-o}}{(S\backslash NP_{nom})/((S\backslash NP_{nom})\backslash NP_{acc})}\text{>T} \quad \dfrac{\dfrac{\text{Ken-ga}}{S/(S\backslash NP_{nom})}\text{>T} \quad \dfrac{\text{tazuneta}}{(S\backslash NP_{nom})\backslash NP_{acc}}}{S\backslash NP_{acc}}\text{*>B}_\times}{S}\text{>}$$

Such crossed composition, besides introducing a whole new combinatory rule schema into the grammar, would immediately need to be heavily constrained if it were not (for reasons familiar from chapter 4) to give rise to very free word order indeed, including non-clause-bounded scrambling. Moreover, such an analysis would fail to account for the fact that OS order can also give rise to constituent cluster coordination parallel to (4), as in (9):

(9) [Naomi-o Ken-ga,]   [Sara-o Erika-ga]   tazuneta
    $S/((S\backslash NP_{acc})\backslash NP_{nom})$ $S/((S\backslash NP_{acc})\backslash NP_{nom})$ $(S\backslash NP_{acc})\backslash NP_{nom}$
    Naomi-ACC Ken-NOM, Sara-ACC Erika-NOM visit-PAST.CONCL
    'Ken visited Naomi and Erika, Sara.'

Although the generalized type-raised categories can compose in OS order to yield such OS argument clusters, the order-preserving nature of the rules concerned forces them to deliver a cluster demanding a different OSV category for the verb, as the agreement features in (9) reveal, rather than the SOV verb standardly assumed for Japanese.

It is therefore tempting under present assumptions to regard so-called scrambling constituent orders in Japanese as lexically specified, either via multiple verb categories or via explicitly unordered leftward categories, a move that is in keeping with the observation that scrambling (as distinct from true extraction) is clause-bounded. However, I will not pursue the question of OS order in Japanese any further here.[3] Under the analysis presented in the chapter 6, Dutch subordinate clauses are predicted to exhibit the SOV pattern (1a). For example, the entire preverbal argument cluster can coordinate:

(10) a. . . . dat [Jan de kinderen en Marie de nijlpaarden] zag zwemmen.
　　　　. . . that [Jan the children and Marie the hippos] 　saw swim
　　　　'. . . that Jan saw the children swim and Mary saw the hippos swim.'

　　 b. . . . dat [Jan Marie en Cecilia Henk] de kinderen zag helpen
　　　　. . . that [Jan Marie and Cecilia Henk] the children saw help
　　　　zwemmen.
　　　　swim
　　　　'. . . that Jan saw Marie and Cecilia saw Henk help the children swim.'

　　 c. . . . dat [Jan Marie de kinderen en Henk Cecilia de nijlpaarden] zag
　　　　. . . that [Jan Marie the children and Henk Cecilia the hippos] 　saw
　　　　helpen zwemmen.
　　　　help　swim
　　　　'. . . that Jan saw Marie help the children swim and Henk saw Cecilia help the hippos swim.'

Example (10b) is related to the following "backward gapping" example, due to van Oirsouw (1982, 555, example (8b)), apart from the fact that in the latter case the verbs are in the "German" order, as is common in standard Dutch with the auxiliary *hebben*:

(11) Ik geloof dat Jan *Syntactic Structures* en Piet *Aspects* gelezen heeft.
　　 I believe that Jan *Syntactic Structures* and Piet *Aspects* read 　has
　　 'I believe that Jan has read *Syntactic Structures* and Piet *Aspects*.'

The grammar also allows contiguous preverbal argument sequences that do not include the subject to compose, so the following examples are also allowed, on the assumption that the dative PP *aan Henk* has the category $T/(T\backslash PP_{DAT})$ and that one category of the stem *geef-* 'give' is $(VP\backslash NP)\backslash PP_{DAT}$:

(12) ...dat Jan de kinderen [een treintje aan Piet en   een pop aan Henk] zag
      ...that Jan the children [a   train   to Piet and a   doll to Henk] saw
      geven.
      give.
      '...that Jan saw the children give a train to Piet and a doll to Henk.'

(13) ...dat Jan [de meisjes een treintje aan Piet en de jongens een pop aan
      ...that Jan [the girls   a   train   to Piet and the boys   a   doll to
      Henk] zag geven.
      Henk] saw give
      '...that Jan saw the girls give a train to Piet and the boys give a doll to
      Henk.'

(14) ...dat Jan [de meisjes een treintje en   de jongens een pop] aan Henk
      ...that Jan [the girls   a   train   and the boys   a   doll] to Henk
      zag   geven.
      saw   give
      '...that Jan saw the girls give a train and the boys give doll to Henk.'

Sentence (12) is completely acceptable (cf. Bresnan et al. 1982, 619). The
grammaticality of a sentence parallel to the second of these is questioned by
by Bresnan et al. in the course of justifying a rather different account of the
NP sequence. It seems to be accepted by some informants. The third is not
discussed by Bresnan et al., but seems to be also accepted.

Similarly since the complete verb sequence can combine by forward application with preverbal NPs in the crossed order, any subsequence that includes
all of the verbs and some rightmost subsequence of the preverbal NP sequence
can be a constituent, and may also conjoin. Examples are:

(15) a. ...dat ik Henk [de nijlpaarden zag voeren en de olifanten hoorde
         ...that I Henk the hippos   saw feed   and the elephants heard
         wassen.]
         wash]
         '...that I saw Henk feed the hippos and heard him wash the elephants.'

     b. ...dat ik [Cecilia de nijlpaarden zag voeren en Henk de olifanten
         ...that I Cecilia the hippos   saw feed   and Henk the elephants
         hoorde wassen.]
         heard wash]
         '...that I saw Cecilia feed the hippos and heard Henk wash the ele-
         phants.'

Unless such conjuncts include the entire verb group, the combination with the NPs will not be possible with the rules as set out above. It follows that sentences like the following are excluded by the present grammar:

(16) a. ?...dat   ik Cecilia [de nijlpaarden zag en de olifanten hoorde]
     ...that I Cecilia [the hippos   saw and the elephants heard]
     wassen.
     wash
     '...that I saw Cecilia wash the hippos and heard her wash the elephants.'

   b. ?...dat ik [Cecilia de nijlpaarden zag en Henk de olifanten hoorde]
      ...that I Cecilia the hippos   saw and Henk the elephants heard
      wassen.
      wash
      '...that I saw Cecilia wash the hippos and heard Henk wash the elephants'

Some informants seem prepared to tolerate such examples. Whatever their status, it is striking that so much freedom is allowed in Dutch, and that it can be accounted for within the same degrees of freedom that are required for English grammar.

7.2 Gapping and VSO Word Order

As Dowty (1988) was the first to point out, the position is reversed for verb-initial languages such as Irish. Again, subject and object can raise and compose with each other and with adjuncts in an order-preserving way to yield a single function over a transitive verb like *chonaic* 'saw', this time via leftward type-raising and composition; and again, the nonstandard constituent can coordinate:[4]

(17) chonaic$_{VSO}$:= $(S/NP)/NP : \lambda x.\lambda y.see'yx$

(18) a. Chonaic Eoghan Siobhán.
        saw   Eoghan Siobhán
        'Eoghan saw Siobhán.'

   b.   Chonaic   Eoghan   Siobhán
      $\overline{(S/NP)/NP}$ $\overline{(S/NP)\backslash((S/NP)/NP)}^{<\mathbf{T}}$ $\overline{S\backslash(S/NP)}^{<\mathbf{T}}$
                        $\overline{\qquad S\backslash((S/NP)/NP) \qquad}^{<\mathbf{B}}$
              $\overline{\qquad\qquad\qquad S \qquad\qquad\qquad}^{<}$

(19) Chonaic   [Eoghan Siobhán] agus [Eoghnaí Ciarán].
$(S/NP)/NP\ S\backslash((S/NP)/NP)$ $S\backslash((S/NP)/NP)$
saw   Eoghan Siobhán and Eoghnaí Ciarán
'Eoghan saw Siobhán, and Eoghnaí, Ciarán.'

Again the three principles exclude the "backward gapping" construction that Ross (1970) held to be generally disallowed in strictly verb-initial languages:

(20) *[Eoghan Siobhán] agus chonaic   [Eoghnaí Ciarán].
$S\backslash((S/NP)/NP)$ $(S/NP)/NP\ S\backslash((S/NP)/NP)$
Eoghan Siobhán and saw   Eoghnaí Ciarán

As in the case of Dutch and SOV, there are exceptions to Ross's generalization for VSO languages. Later we will examine the case of Zapotec (Rosenbaum 1977), a VSO language that allows backward gapping and that like Dutch, will turn out to do so because it allows other constituent orders in main clauses.

The derivation and the category for the VSO transitive verb assume that the subject—that is, the NP corresponding to the least oblique element x at predicate-argument structure—is the *first* argument of the VSO verb, not the last, as in the Germanic languages. As a result, the object commands the subject in a purely applicative context-free derivation. This assumption is an instance of the generalization noted at the end of chapter 4 and is forced by the present theory. However, objects may *always* c-command subjects in CCG derivations, even in SVO languages. And the separation of predicate-argument structure from derivations and surface categories (which is crucial to the present analysis of binding in English) allows us to capture the fact that binding phenomena in VSO languages and constructions strongly parallel those in SVO languages and all others with respect to the obliqueness hierarchy (see Keenan 1988).[5]

VOS word orders do not arise in general in Irish. See Baldridge 1999 for an argument parallel to that given earlier for Japanese OSV orders to the effect that VSO languages that do allow VOS orders (such as Tagalog) do so via base generation.

Many coordination phenomena in Dutch main clauses conform to the pattern of VSO languages and are predicted by the fragment presented in chapter 6 and the assumption that main-clause verbs have VSO categories. Such phenomena include examples like the following, parallel to English argument cluster coordination and VSO complement cluster coordination (van Oirsouw 1987, 58):

(21) Wil$_{S-SUB/NP/NP}$ [jij een ijsje   en Marietje limonade?]$_{T\backslash(T/NP)/NP}$
        want   you an ice-cream and Marietje lemonade
        'Do you want an ice-cream, and Marietje lemonade?'

This example is simply the mirror-image of the "backward gapping" subordinate clauses discussed in section 7.1. Because of the involvement of the backward crossed composition rule (79) of chapter 6, VP coordination is also captured:

(22) a. Hij [at aardappels en   dronk bier.]$_{S/NP_{+ANT}}$
            he ate potatoes   and drank beer

      b. Hij [gaf Marie appels en   verkocht Hendrik peren.]$_{S/NP_{+ANT}}$
            he gave Mary apples and sold   Harry   pears

To capture the full variety of constituent coordinations in Dutch main and subordinate clauses, we must apply the same generalization as in English to the relative-pronoun and the topic categories, using the $ convention to schematize over functions of up to four arguments, as in the appendix to chapter 6:

(23) a. $(N\backslash N)\$/(S_{+SUB}\$\backslash NP)$
      b. $S'_{-SUB}\$/(S_{-SUB}\$/NP)$

All of the following are then predicted to be grammatical; their derivations are suggested as an exercise:

(24) a. [Hendrik kocht   en Wim at]$_{S'_{-SUB}/NP}$ de aardappels.
            Hendrik bought and Wim ate   the potatoes

      b. [Hendrik kan en Karel moet]$_{S'_{-SUB}/VP_{+SUB}}$ aardappels eten.
            Hendrik can and Karel must   potatoes   eat
            Hendrik can and Karel must eat potatoes.'

      c. aardappels die Hendrik kocht   en Wim at
            potatoes   that Hendrik bought and Wim ate

      d. Hij geeft [de politieman een bloem en   de leraar   appels.]$_{T\backslash((T/NP)/NP)}$
            he gave the policeman a   flower and the teacher apples

We also need the following version of forward composition (25) (see appendix to chapter 6) to encompass coordinations like (26) (from van Oirsouw 1987, 253).

(25) *Forward composition II* ($>$**B**)
        X/Y Y/Z $\Rightarrow_B$ X/Z
        where $Y = S_{-SUB}/\$$

(26) De hond voer en de kat aai   ik.
    the dog feed and the cat stroke I
    'I feed the dog and stroke the cat.'

The earlier examples are unaffected by these generalizations, although in many cases alternative derivations are made available.

7.3 Gapping and SVO Word Order

According to the combinatory theory, VSO "forward gapping," SOV "backward gapping," and "right node raising" in all three major word order groups, reduce to simple constituent coordination, as Maling (1972) implies they should when she equates "backward" and "forward" gapping with varieties of node raising, rather than with deletion or copying. But what about sentence-*medial* ellipsis in SVO languages like English and in Dutch/German SVO main clauses? I will begin by reviewing some salient properties of this remarkable construction.[6]

7.3.1 The Natural History of Gapping in English

Gapping in English is unlike all other varieties of constituent coordination in being almost completely insensitive to agreement. In this respect it bears some resemblance to truly elliptical constructions like VP ellipsis. (Ross 1967). Compare the following examples:

(27) a. *I cook beans and eats potatoes.
      b. Harry eats beans, and I, potatoes.
      c. Harry eats beans, and I do too.

However, as Jackendoff (1971) notes, gapping differs from VP ellipsis in being strictly restricted to root sentences. Hence, (28a,b) are very bad indeed, unlike VP ellipsis, (28c), and the related "pseudogapping" construction, (28d), both of which involve explicit anaphoric verbal elements:[7]

(28) a. *I know that Dexter read *Ulysses* and you say that Warren, *Dr. Zhivago.*
      b. *I know that Dexter read *Ulysses* and that Warren, *Dr. Zhivago.*
      c. I know that Dexter read *Ulysses* and you say that Warren did too.
      d. I know that Dexter read *Ulysses* and you say that Warren did *Dr. Zhivago.*

A large number of apparent further constraints on the gapping construction have been proposed within transformational frameworks by Jackendoff (1971),

Hankamer (1971), Langendoen (1975), Stillings (1975), Hankamer and Sag (1976), and Sag (1976), reviewed by Neijt (1979). Examples like the following have been held by some of these authors to be ungrammatical under the readings indicated by the brackets:

(29) a. Dexter [went to] London, and Warren, Detroit.
　　 b. Dexter [will give] an apple to the teacher, and Warren, a flower to a policeman.

However, Kuno (1976) has pointed out that the acceptability of gapped sentences is highly dependent upon discourse context. Sentences (29a, b) are acceptable when preceded by sentences establishing appropriate themes, presuppositions, and "open propositions" (in the sense of Wilson and Sperber 1979, Prince 1986, and Levin and Prince 1986), such as the following questions, which we will assume are asked in the context of a discussion of Dexter and Warren:

(30) a. Which city did each man go to?
　　 b. Which man will give what to whom?

Even the most basic gapped sentence, like *Warren ate bread, and Dexter, bananas*, is only really felicitous in contexts that support (or can accommodate) the presupposition that the question under discussion is *Who ate what?* Conversely, contexts that establish a *different* open proposition cause gapping to fail. For instance, the following example (from Williams 1978) fails because by the time the putative gap is encountered, the theme is $\lambda x.hit'\ bill'\ x$, rather than $\lambda x.\lambda y.hit'xy$:

(31) Fred hit Bill. *Then Alice did too, and Bert, Tom.

　　Kuno (1976) shows that many other apparent constraints noted by earlier authors supposedly prohibiting gapping of strings that are in present terms surface constituents, as evidenced by the fact that they can be coordinated, are equally sensitive to context and to the inclusion of materials that are compatible with the discourse functions associated with gapping:[8]

(32) a. Twenty percent of the population [wants the president] to raise taxes, and eighty percent, to lower them.
　　 b. Twenty percent of the population [keeps coal] in the cellar, and eighty percent, in the bath.
　　 c. Twenty percent of the population [believes that the country is run] by madmen, and eighty percent, by crooks.

Kuno suggests on the basis of related examples and their sensitivity to island conditions that there is a close relation between gaps and residues of relativization (Kuno 1976, 317, n.29). Since in present terms the residue of relativization is a constituent, and island constraints arise when it is impossible to build such a constituent, this observation suggests that—unlike some other elliptical constructions—gapping is closely related to surface syntax.

However, not only does the "residue" of the gapping process in the rightmost conjunct appear to correspond to a discontinuous part of the leftmost conjunct—the gapped part of the leftmost conjunct may also be discontiguous:

(33) Dexter wants Watford to win, and Warren, Ipswich.

Discontinuous gapping of this kind is even more widespread in German and Dutch main-clause coordinations, like the following, because of the "V2" requirement:

(34) Jacob *heeft* appels *gegeten*, en   Hendrik, peren.
      Jacob *has*   apples *eaten*,   and Hendrik, pears
      'Jacob has eaten apples and Hendrik, pears.'

Gapping therefore appears to involve something more than surface grammar, which under present assumptions is subject to the Principle of Adjacency.

Nevertheless, CCG already affords almost everything we need to account for the above phenomena. For example, the residues and the gapped element itself in each of the well-known family of gapped sentences mentioned in chapter 2 are all constituents under one or another of the possible analyses of *you want to try to begin to write a play*:

(35)   I want to try to begin to write a novel, and . . .
      a. you, to try to begin to write a play.
      b. you,   to begin to write a play.
      c. you,   to write a play.
      d. you,   a play.

Conversely, when failure of coordination suggests that a substring cannot be a constituent, even in this extended sense, it cannot be a gap either. Compare (36a) (see (17) of chapter 1) with (36b) under the intended reading:

(36) a. *Three cats in twenty like velvet and in ten prefer corduroy.

      b. *Three cats in twenty like velvet, and two dogs, corduroy.

In all of the earlier examples the coordination of argument sequences was brought under the general mechanism of constituent coordination by type-raising the arguments and composing to yield a function over verbal and sentential functors—as in the English argument cluster coordination example (40) of chapter 3, repeated here:

(37) Give$_{(VP/NP)/NP}$ [a teacher an apple]$_{VP\backslash((VP/NP)/NP)}$ and [a policeman a flower]$_{VP\backslash((VP/NP)/NP)}$

It is therefore tempting to believe that the sequence of arguments that is left behind by gapping is also a constituent assembled by order-preserving type-raising and composition, that coordinates with an adjacent category of the same type. Gapping would be an instance of constituent coordination under the extended sense of the term implicated in combinatory grammar. Such a constituent would semantically be a function over a tensed verb, so its syntactic category would have to follow suit, as in (38):

(38) (A teacher likes an apple, and) [a policeman, a flower.]$_{S\backslash((S\backslash NP)/NP)}$

The theory of SVO gapping presented below has two components. First, I will show that gapped right conjuncts like *Warren, potatoes* also have the status of constituents under the present theory, just like argument sequences in SOV and SVO languages, and just as in argument cluster coordination. In particular, like argument cluster conjuncts, the gapped constituent has an interpretation that enables it to combine with the missing verbal component to yield a correct interpretation for the whole. Moreover, no rule that will produce a backward-gapped rightward-looking function from the English type-raised argument categories is permitted by the universal Principles of Adjacency, Consistency, and Inheritance that were in earlier chapters claimed to constrain combinatory rules, together with the "order-preserving" constraint on the type-raised categories that are allowed in an SVO language.

More controversially, I will propose, following Steedman 1990, that the "gapped" conjunct is coordinated with a "virtual" constituent of the same type in the ungapped left conjunct. The second part of the argument suggests a way to recover this virtual constituent, together with another virtual constituent corresponding to the gap, even though neither may be a derivational constituent—or even a contiguous substring—of the left conjunct. The possibility arises because *associativity* of functional composition induces semantic equivalence over certain classes of derivations. Furthermore, the *parametric neutrality* of combinatory rules like composition and application allows the recovery in a restricted sense of certain constituents under one derivation from the result of another.

7.3.2 The Category of the Right Conjunct[9]

I have assumed so far that leftward type-raising in English yields the following quite general category:

(39) $T\backslash(T/NP)$

On the assumption that English auxiliaries bear the category of VSX verbs as in (40a) and that coordinations like (40b) are allowed, it must be the case that subjects, including explicitly nominative pronominal ones, also bear this category, schematizing over functions over S/NP, $(S/NP)/NP$, $(S/PP)/NP$, and so forth, as they do in the German and Dutch main clauses discussed in chapter 6.

(40) a. are := $(S_{inv}/NP)/NP_{2s}$

b. Are you now, or have you ever been, a member of the Friends of the Legume Film Society?

It follows that we already have in the form of the backward composition rule (41) of chapter 3 a rule that will make a nonstandard constituent out of the gapped right conjunct, complete with an impeccable semantic interpretation, as in the derivation in (41) below.

(41) Dexter eats beans,   and   Warren,   potatoes
$$\underbrace{}_{CONJ}\ \underbrace{}_{T\backslash(T/NP_1)}{}^{<\mathbf{T}}\ \underbrace{}_{T\backslash(T/NP_2)}{}^{<\mathbf{T}}$$
$$\underline{}_{T\backslash((T/NP_2)/NP_1)}{}^{<\mathbf{B}}$$

The resultant argument cluster category is specified as needing to combine with a VSO verb, which do not in general exist in English. As a consequence, the category will be unable to take any further part in any normal derivation. This much is desirable, as it correctly prevents the following from being accepted in English, unlike the related examples in Dutch and German:

(42)   *Eats   Warren   potatoes
$$\underbrace{}_{(S\backslash NP)/NP}\ \underbrace{}_{T\backslash(T/NP_1)}{}^{<\mathbf{T}}\ \underbrace{}_{T\backslash(T/NP_2)}{}^{<\mathbf{T}}$$
$$\underline{}_{T\backslash((T/NP_2)/NP_1)}{}^{<\mathbf{B}}$$
$$\underline{}_{*}$$

Nevertheless, we have at least found a way to make the gapped conjunct a constituent, which is the first step toward making grammatical rules apply to it under the Constituent Condition on Rules.

It is striking that related derivations of illegal gapped clauses like (28a–d) are ruled out for the same reason as the Fixed-Subject Condition violations discussed in chapter 4, because of the continued exclusion from the grammar of English of the Forward Crossed Composition rule:

(43) $*$Warren eats beans,   and   I believe that   Dexter, potatoes

$\underline{}$ $\underline{}$ $\underline{}$ $\underline{}$

$\qquad\qquad CONJ \qquad S/S \qquad T\backslash((T/NP)/NP)$

$$\underline{}_{*}$$

(44) $*$Warren eats beans,   and   I believe that Dexter,   potatoes

$\underline{}$ $\underline{}$ $\underline{}$ $\underline{}$

$\qquad\qquad CONJ \qquad\qquad S/(S\backslash NP) \qquad\qquad T\backslash(T/NP)$

$\qquad\qquad\qquad : \lambda p.believe'(p\ dexter')me' \quad : \lambda p.p\ potatoes'$

$$\underline{}_{*}$$

For the same reason, gaps within the scope of a complementizer are blocked:

(45) $*$I believe that Warren eats beans,   and   that   Dexter, potatoes

$\underline{}$ $\underline{}$ $\underline{}$ $\underline{}$

$\qquad\qquad S \qquad\qquad\qquad CONJ \quad S'/S \quad T\backslash((T/NP)/NP)$

$$\underline{}_{*}$$

(46)   I believe that Warren eats beans,   and   Dexter, potatoes

$\underline{}$ $\underline{}$ $\underline{}$

$\qquad\qquad S \qquad\qquad\qquad CONJ \quad T\backslash((T/NP)/NP)$

Thus, we correctly capture the restriction of gapping to clauses immediately dominated by the conjunct.[10]

On the assumption that adjuncts bear the category $(S\backslash NP)\backslash(S\backslash NP)$, the following derivation will block, because backward composition will deliver a fragment that is incompatible with any analysis of the left conjunct:[11]

(47) Dexter ran quickly,   and   Warren,   slowly

$\underline{}$ $\underline{}$ $\underline{}$ $\underline{}$

$\qquad S \qquad\quad CONJ \quad T\backslash(T/NP_1) \quad (S\backslash NP_2)\backslash(S\backslash NP_2)$

$$\underline{}_{<\mathbf{B}}$$

$$S\backslash((S\backslash NP_2)/NP_1)$$

This is in fact a desirable result, because if *Warren slowly* were to come in general to bear a gap-permitting category, it would threaten to allow examples like the following to mean something like *Dexter ran and Warren ran quickly* (see discussion in Sag 1976 and Wood 1988):

(48) $*$Dexter ran,   and   Warren,   quickly

$\underline{}$ $\underline{}$ $\underline{}$ $\underline{}$

$\quad S \qquad CONJ \quad T\backslash(T/NP_1) \quad (S\backslash NP_2)\backslash(S\backslash NP_2)$

$$\underline{}_{<\mathbf{B}}$$

$$S\backslash((S\backslash NP_2)/NP_1)$$

We must instead assume that examples like (47) arise from the tendency noted in section 4.3.2 for verbs to behave as if they subcategorized for certain types of adverbs, to allow derivations like the following for sentences like *Dexter ran quickly, and Warren, slowly*, while continuing to exclude examples like **Ran Warren slowly*:

(49) Dexter ran quickly,   and   Warren,   slowly

$$\frac{\overline{CONJ}\quad \overline{T\backslash(T/NP)}\quad \overline{T\backslash(T/ADV)}}{T\backslash((T/ADV)/NP)}{}^{<\mathbf{B}}$$

Although we have yet to see how a gapped verb *ran* of category $(S/ADV)/NP$ can be accessed in such examples, it is clear that such a verb cannot be involved in examples like (48).

The schema $T\backslash(T/NP)$ merely abbreviates categories raised over the categories of English grammar that are permitted under the Principle of Categorial Type Transparency, as informally defined in chapter 3. It follows that the present mechanism for constructing gapped right conjuncts by composing leftward type-raised arguments will permit such conjuncts only when they preserve the linear order of subject, object, and more oblique arguments.

The rule allows several more complex types of gapped right conjunct. For example, it allows (50), adapted from Aoun et al. 1987:[12]

(50) Dexter gave a teacher an apple,   and   Warren,   a policeman a flower

$$\frac{}{S}\qquad \frac{\overline{CONJ}\quad \overline{T\backslash(T/NP_1)}\quad \overline{T\backslash((T/NP_3)/NP_2)}}{T\backslash(((T/NP_3)/NP_2)/NP_1)}{}^{<\mathbf{B}}$$

On the assumption that subject phrases like *which woman* also bear the leftward type-raised category, as they must when in situ, as in *What book did which woman buy?*, the following example (also of a kind discussed in Aoun et al. 1987) is accepted:

(51) I wonder   which man met Dexter,   and   which woman,   Warren

$$\frac{}{S/S_{iq}}\qquad \frac{}{S_{iq}}\qquad \frac{\overline{CONJ}\quad \overline{T\backslash(T/NP_1)}\quad \overline{T\backslash(T/NP_2)}}{T\backslash((T/NP_2)/NP_1)}{}^{<\mathbf{B}}$$

Parallel derivations are allowed for *I wonder which teacher you gave an apple, and which policeman, a flower*, and *Which apple did you give to the teacher, and which flower to the policeman?*

However, the rule correctly excludes all of the following, because the arguments in the gapped conjunct are not in canonical order:[13]

(52) a. *Which man did Dexter invite, and which woman, Warren?

      b. *Which   man   did   Dexter   introduce   to   Warren,   and   [which
          woman,$]_{(S/PP)\backslash((S/PP)/NP)}$ [Gilbert,$]_{((S/PP)/NP)\backslash(((S/PP)/NP)/NP)}$ [to
          George?$]_{S\backslash(S/PP)}$

      c. *Freeman   wondered   what   Hardy   gave   to   Willis,   and
          [what$]_{(S/PP)/((S/PP)/NP)}$ [Gilbert,$]_{((S/PP)/NP)\backslash(((S/PP)/NP)/NP)}$ [to
          George.$]_{S\backslash(S/PP)}$

Examples (52b) and (52c) are also of a kind considered by Aoun et al. 1987,
(12-13).

Finally, the theory correctly predicts that the gap may be discontinuous, as
in (33) (repeated here), since the second NP has the same category as any NP
complement.

(53) Dexter wants Watford to win, and Warren$_{T\backslash(T/NP)}$, Ipswich$_{T\backslash(T/NP)}$.

These possibilities for gapping are a direct corollary of the way in which
the permitted combinatory rules project directionality from the English SVO
lexicon. It is also a corollary of the Principles of Adjacency, Consistency, and
Inheritance, and the fact that English verb are confined to SVX and VSX patterns, that no forward combining gapped constituent over tensed verbs can be
constructed. In particular, the Principle of Inheritance ensures that the composite function will be *backward* looking, just as in the case of a VSO language
(see (17) and (19)).[14]

Now if only (41) had the following analysis, we would have an answer to the
question of why SVO languages pattern with the VSO alternative in gapping
on the right:

(54) *eats$_{((S/NP)/NP)}$ [Dexter   beans$]_{S\backslash((S/NP)/NP)}$ and   [Warren
      potatoes$]_{S\backslash((S/NP)/NP)}$

The nonstandard constituent is leftward-looking, so it must occur to the right
of the verb. That fact would enable the coordination rule to apply to yield the
effect of a gap on the right. A gap on the left would be impossible with this
category, just as it is in VSO languages.

Of course, (54) is *not* a possible surface analysis of (41), and we still need
to say how both the gap and the appropriate nonstandard gapped constituent
can be recovered, in the face of the fact that both the putative conjunct and the
gap itself may correspond to discontinuous substrings of the sentence. But the
directionality result, coupled with capturing several empirical constraints that

set gapping apart from other elliptical constructions, is a strong argument. It suggests that we should resist any solution to this problem that extends the calculus by compromising the Principle of Adjacency. The next sections propose one possible alternative. It will be convenient to refer to the two putative virtual constituents as the "virtual gap" and the "virtual left conjunct," respectively.

7.3.3 A Hypothesis Concerning the Left Conjunct

It is important that any proposal for revealing "virtual" adjacent nonstandard constituents in the left conjunct should conform to the Principles of Adjacency, Consistency, and Inheritance, if it is not to compromise the claims of earlier sections concerning Universal Grammar. Interestingly, there is a way of using the rules of the grammar itself to yield the virtual constituent, so that the grammar as a whole continues to respect the basic constituent order specified in the lexicon in the way it has up to this point, even though the subject and the object are not contiguous in the string.

The device in question depends on a property of the combinatory rules that was first identified by Pareschi (1986, see Pareschi and Steedman 1987) as providing a possible basis for a technique for parsing in the face of so-called spurious ambiguity, a topic to which I will return in part III. I will call this property "parametric neutrality." It can be described as follows:

(55) *Parametric neutrality*

Specifying the syntactic type of any two categories that are related by a given combinatory rule determines the syntactic type of the third.

For example, we normally think of a rule like application as taking a function of type X/Y or $X\backslash Y$ and an argument of type Y as input parameters, and combining them to yield the result X. But because any two categories between them specify all the information that is required to determine the type of the third, we can consider *any two* of the three categories that such a rule relates as the input parameters and use the rule to determine the type of the third. For example, we can define the argument type Y and the result type X of application to determine the type of the third category X/Y.

The observation holds for all of the combinatory syntactic rules, as may be verified by inspecting the three familiar rule types exemplified here.

(56) *Application* $\quad X/Y \quad Y \qquad\quad \Rightarrow \quad X$
$\quad\;$ *Composition* $\;X/Y \quad Y/Z \qquad \Rightarrow_{\mathbf{B}} \quad X/Z$
$\quad\;$ *Substitution* $\;\,Y/Z \quad (X\backslash Y)/Z \quad \Rightarrow_{\mathbf{S}} \quad X/Z$

This observation concerning syntactic types does not extend without qualification to their interpretations. In Pareschi and Steedman 1987 we assumed that categories were matched to rules via first order unification of the kind familiar from the programming language Prolog in which λ-terms have to be simulated, in a manner discussed at length by Pereira and Shieber (1987). In this framework the related nonstandard invocations yield only "dummy" constant functions. For example, consider the gapped sentence *Dexter eats apples, and Warren, pears*, and consider instantiating the backward application rule with Y as the "virtual" VSO verb category $(S/NP)/NP : v$ and X as the left conjunct $S : eats' apples' dexter$. First-order unification would yield the following constant function as the value of $X \backslash Y : f$:

(57) $S \backslash ((S/NP)/NP) : \lambda v.eats' apples' dexter$

Crucially, although this virtual category can only reduce to yield the same proposition we started with, it can first coordinate with the semantically non-vacuous right conjunct, since it has the same type. If the gapped verb is somehow made available, the whole coordinate fragment can then combine to yield an S with the following interpretation, as desired:

(58) $S : and' (eats' warren' pears')(eats' apples' dexter')$

Crucially, the verbal argument must be to the left.

However, mere first-order unification will not yield a verb that can combine in this way. It will again yield only a dummy category, which again will semantically be a constant function that either will refuse to combine with the right conjunct, blocking the derivation, or will yield an incorrect meaning. Accordingly, the analysis in Steedman 1990 used unification only to specify the syntactic type of the verb. The claim was that its interpretation was obtained from an extra sentential discourse context including representations of elements such as given information or background, via anaphora rather than via the unification process itself.

Although we have already noted an interesting relation between possibilities for gapping and the state of the discourse context, reflected to some extent in intonation, the sententially bound nature of gapping suggests that this information must in fact be obtained from the left conjunct rather than from extra sentential context.

One mechanism for the kind of abstraction or matching that appears to be involved that has recently received attention in the literature is higher-order unification. Pareschi (1989) has proposed a number of applications for higher-order unification in natural language grammar, and Dalrymple, Shieber and Pereira (1991) and Shieber, Pereira and Dalrymple (1996) show how a generalization of the technique described above could be applied more generally to a wide variety of elliptical and anaphoric constructions, via higher-order unification over *typed* λ-terms (Hindley and Seldin 1986) using Huet's algorithm (Huet 1975; Huet and Lang 1978).

This observation is interesting for present purposes, since interpretations are coupled in CCG with a syntactic category that is simply their semantic type plus some directional information. CCG categories are themselves in effect typed λ-terms. Higher-order unification and other implementations of matching or abstraction therefore remain interesting possibilities to explore as a basis for gap retrieval. In particular, the fact that gaps exhibit the same ambiguities between "strict" and "sloppy" anaphora as VP ellipsis suggests a common mechanism:

(59) a. Dexter fed his cat chicken, and Warren did too.
      b. Dexter fed his cat chicken, and Warren, tunafish.

Nevertheless, higher-order unification is equivalent to quite general abstraction over typed terms and will deliver spurious interpretations including vacuous abstractions and interpretations that violate the generalization that rightward arguments in English must "wrap," discussed in chapter 4. Dalrymple, Shieber and Pereira (1991) and Shieber, Pereira and Dalrymple (1996) filter these spurious Logical Forms via structural criteria of "primary occurrence," domination, and identification of "source parallel elements." Many of these structural criteria replicate parts of the grammar itself, and for the present purpose we must seek a more purely grammatical mechanism.

These observations provide a strong motivation for trying to exploit the property of parametric neutrality within the competence grammar itself to subsume gapping to ordinary constituent coordination.

One way to do this is to assume that the gap is interpreted as the theme of the left conjunct, made available from the interpretation of the left conjunct via a discourse mechanism related to Kuno's (1976, 310) Functional Sentence Perspective Principle.

Mats Rooth (personal communication) has suggested that the following kind of exchange presents problems for the idea that the gap is a theme, and for information-structure based proposals for gap recovery in general:

(60) Q: Do Sid and Nancy like Dexter and Warren?
      A: No! Sid LOATHES Dexter, and NANCY, WARREN.

However, the example is at least compatible with an L+H* pitch accent on *loathes* and a mid-sentential LL% boundary, and it is therefore possible to argue in the terms of chapter 5 that it involves the accommodation of a marked theme $\lambda x.\lambda y.loathe'xy$, standing in contrast to the alternative theme $\lambda x.\lambda y.like'xy$.

The theme of the left conjunct can be made available to the right conjunct by defining the term $\theta''left$ as an anaphor that picks out the theme that the left conjunct has established along lines described in chapter 5. This term is introduced grammatically via the following production, related to backward application:[15]

(61) *Virtual conjunct–revealing rule (<dcomp)*
$\quad$ $X : left \quad \Longrightarrow \quad Y : \theta''left \quad X\backslash Y : \lambda y.left$
$\quad$ where $Y = S/\$$

The interpretation of the revealed function $X\backslash Y$ is defined as a constant function, rather than as applying y to the discontinuous rheme of $left'$, since the latter would eventually yield $left'$ anyway.

Although the rule as written is nondeterministic, in a parser we would arrange to constrain the category $X\backslash Y$ to be that of the right conjunct.[16] It will be convenient to refer to such a use of combinatory rules in the grammar as "category decomposition." The application of this rule in derivations will be indicated by a *dotted* underline and an index $<dcomp$, identifying the combinatory rule involved as backward application.

For example, rule (61) can be used to deliver the following categories from a nonstandard invocation of backward application in which the result category X is set to $S : eats'bread'dexter'$, the function type $X\backslash Y$ among the inputs is specified as the same type as the right conjunct $S\backslash((S/NP)/NP)$, and the decomposition forces the revealed verb to be a "virtual" VSO verb:

(62)

$$
\begin{array}{ccc}
\underline{\hspace{3cm}} & & \\
\text{Dexter eats bread,} & \text{and} & \text{Warren, potatoes} \\
\hline
S & CONJ & S\backslash((S/NP)/NP) \\
: eats'bread'dexter' & & : \lambda f.f\ potatoes'warren' \\
\end{array}
$$

$\overline{\hspace{2cm}}$ $<dcomp$

$$
\begin{array}{cc}
((S/NP)/NP) & S\backslash((S/NP)/NP) \\
: \theta''(eats'bread'dexter') & : \lambda y.eats'bread'dexter' \\
\end{array}
$$

$\overline{\hspace{5cm}}$ $<\Phi>$

$$
S\backslash((S/NP)/NP) \\
: \lambda f.and'(f\ potatoes'warren')(eats'bread'dexter')
$$

$\overline{\hspace{6cm}}$ $<$

$$
S : and'(\theta''(eats'bread'dexter')potatoes'warren')(eats'bread'dexter') \\
= S : and'(eats'potatoes'warren')(eats'bread'dexter')
$$

The attraction of category decomposition is that it exploits exactly the same rules as the original grammar and therefore preserves the projection of lexical directionality from the lexicon under coordination.

The prediction that gapping in English and every other SVO language is *forward* gapping (see section 7.3.2) remains in force when category decomposition is included. Even though an English subject and object can raise and compose on the left of a conjunct, backward gapping on the SOV pattern as in (63) is excluded by universal principles. The recovery of the virtual conjunct would require a rule of decomposition that violated the Principle of Consistency, and it would yield a result requiring a similarly illegal rule to recombine.

(63) *Warren, potatoes   and   Dexter bought bread
$$\underline{\qquad\qquad\qquad\qquad}\quad\underline{\quad}\quad\underline{\qquad\qquad\qquad\qquad\qquad\qquad}$$
$$S\backslash((S/NP)/NP)\quad CONJ \qquad\qquad\qquad S$$
$$\overline{\qquad\qquad\qquad\qquad\qquad\qquad\qquad\qquad\qquad}*dcomp$$
$$S\backslash((S/NP)/NP)\ (S/NP)/NP$$

Nor could this example be permitted in a language like English by composing forward type-raised categories and including a forward virtual conjunct-revealing rule, as in the following illegal derivation:

(64) *Warren,   potatoes   and   Dexter bought bread
$$\underline{\qquad\quad}\quad\underline{\qquad\quad}\quad\underline{\quad}\quad\underline{\qquad\qquad\qquad\qquad}$$
$$T/(T\backslash NP)\ \ T/(T\backslash NP)\ \ CONJ \qquad\qquad\qquad S$$
$$\overline{\qquad\qquad\qquad\qquad\qquad\qquad}*{>}\mathbf{B}\qquad\overline{\qquad\qquad\qquad\qquad\qquad\qquad\qquad}{>}dcomp$$
$$S/((S\backslash NP)\backslash NP)\qquad\qquad\quad S/((S\backslash NP)\backslash NP)\ (S\backslash NP)\backslash NP$$
$$\overline{\qquad\qquad\qquad\qquad\qquad\qquad\qquad\qquad\qquad}{<}\Phi{>}$$
$$S/((S\backslash NP)\backslash NP)$$

The crucial composition of the two forward–type-raised subjects is ruled out for English (though not for German and Dutch) by the restrictions on type-raising to raising to parametrically licensed categories permitted by Type Transparency, discussed in earlier chapters, as shown in example (42) of chapter 3.

Nor does the inclusion of category decomposition in the theory permit "anti-gapping"—that is, overgenerations of the following kind, in which the *leftmost* product of decomposition is made available for coordination on the pattern of a VSO language, rather than the rightmost, because virtual VSO verbs bear a different category from real SVO verbs and inverting auxiliaries like (40a):[17]

(65)   *Cooks,   and   Dexter eats beans
$$\underline{\qquad\qquad}\quad\underline{\quad}\quad\underline{\qquad\qquad\qquad\qquad}$$
$$(S\backslash NP)/NP\ \ CONJ \qquad\qquad\qquad S$$
$$\overline{\qquad\qquad\qquad\qquad\qquad\qquad\qquad}{<}dcomp$$
$$(S/NP)/NP\ \ S\backslash((S/NP)/NP)$$
$$\overline{\qquad\qquad\qquad\qquad\qquad\qquad}*{<}\Phi{>}$$

The same technique will reveal nonconstituent virtual gaps as well. Consider example (41), repeated here:

(66) Dexter will buy bread, and Warren, potatoes.

The gapped right conjunct can be assembled in the usual way into a leftward-looking function over transitive verbs, of the following category:

(67) $S\backslash((S/NP)/NP) : \lambda p.p\ potatoes'warren'$

By assumption, the left-conjunct-revealing rule (61) can decompose the S on the left into a category with the type of a transitive verb and a category of the same type as the right conjunct. The entire sentence can then be syntactically derived as follows (semantics is omitted, since the real work is done by the anaphoric θ'' anaphor):

(68)

Dexter will buy bread,	and	Warren, potatoes

$$\underline{S} \qquad CONJ \quad S\backslash((S/NP)/NP)$$

$$\overline{(S/NP)/NP \quad S\backslash((S/NP)/NP)}\ ^{<dcomp}$$

$$\overline{S\backslash((S/NP)/NP)}\ ^{<\Phi>}$$

$$\overline{S}\ ^{<}$$

On the assumption that the anaphoric operator θ'' can reveal discontinuous themes of the kind discussed in section 5.3.3, examples like (69) will also be accepted with appropriate interpretations:[18]

(69)

Dexter wants Ipswich to win	and	Warren, Watford

$$\underline{S} \qquad CONJ \quad S\backslash((S/NP)/NP)$$

$$\overline{(S/NP)/NP \quad S\backslash((S/NP)/NP)}\ ^{<dcomp}$$

$$\overline{S\backslash((S/NP)/NP)}\ ^{<\Phi>}$$

$$\overline{S}\ ^{<}$$

For the same reason, discontinuous gapping is not subject to the same Fixed-Subject Condition as extraction. For example, related sentences with non-nominative second NPs in the gapped conjunct seem much better than those with nominatives like (53b). For example, consider the following, uttered in a context in which the question at issue is which team each of the men claim to have won the Cup:

(70) Dexter said (that) Watford won, and Warren, Ipswich.

This exemption from the Fixed-Subject Condition constitutes a major objection to any purely syntactic account of gapping, as it does for pronoun binding and quantifier scope.[19]

As noted earlier, multiple or discontinuous gapping of the kind illustrated in (69) is even more common in German and Dutch main clauses, so it is time to return to the earlier analysis of Dutch and see how the main-clause grammar emerges from the same generalization.

7.3.4 Verb Gapping in Dutch Main Clauses

Gapping in Dutch and German is even simpler than gapping in English, because the category of main-clause verbs is VSO. It follows that the simple backward composition rule, (21) of chapter 6, repeated here as (72), can apply to the order-preserving backward type-raised categories to deliver gapped right conjuncts like *Hendrik peren* in sentences like the following:

(71) Jacob heeft appels gegeten en   Hendrik peren.
       Jacob has   apples eaten   and Hendrik pears
       'Jacob ate apples, and Hendrik, pears.'

(72) *Dutch/German backward composition* ($<\mathbf{B}^n$)
       $(Y\backslash Z)\$ \quad X\backslash Y \quad \Rightarrow_{\mathbf{B}^n} \quad (X\backslash Z)\$$

It follows that if we further assume that Dutch has the same virtual conjunct–revealing rule (61) that English has, limited to Dutch VSO main verbs as in (73), then identical main-clause gapping is allowed, as in (74):

(73) *Dutch virtual conjunct–revealing rule I ($<dcomp$)*
       $X : left \quad \Longrightarrow \quad Y : \theta'' left \quad X\backslash Y : \lambda y.left$
       where $Y = S/\$$

(74)

Jacob heeft appels gegeten	en	Hendrik	peren

$$\frac{\dfrac{\overline{S'_{-SUB}}}{\cdots\cdots\cdots\cdots\cdots\cdots\cdots\cdots\cdots\cdots\cdots\cdots_{<dcomp}}}{(S_{-SUB}/NP_2)/NP_1)_{+ANT}\ \ S'_{-SUB}\backslash((S'_{-SUB}/NP_2)/NP_1)_{+ANT}}\quad CONJ\ \ \dfrac{T\backslash(T/NP_1)\ \ \dfrac{T\backslash(T/NP_2)}{T\backslash((T/NP_2)/NP_1)_{+ANT}}_{<\mathbf{B}}}{}_{<\Phi>}$$

$$\frac{S'_{-SUB}\backslash((S'_{-SUB}/NP)/NP)_{+ANT}}{S'_{-SUB}}_<$$

As in the case of English gaps like (33), the gapped material is discontinuous, a possibility that again stems from the assumption that the virtual verb translation is recovered via Information Structure as a discontinuous theme.

The variable T in the Dutch backward type-raised category $T\backslash(T/NP)$ is free to match the topicalized main-clause category S'_{-SUB} in the above derivation, despite the fact that there are no "real" verbs of category $(S'_{-SUB}/NP)/NP$, on the assumption that such categories are consistent with the directional parameterization of the language. Since such a category is distinct from that of a real main verb, the following potential overgeneration is blocked:

(75) *Kocht$_{(S/NP)/NP}$ en [Hendrik at appels.]$_{S'}$

However, by the same token, T can match S_{+SUB}, the subordinate-clause category, to precipitate a similar decomposition in a subordinate left conjunct. This correctly allows rightward gapping in Dutch embedded clauses, as in the following sentence from van Oirsouw (1982, 555, (8c)), despite the involvement of SOV order in the left conjunct and the absence from the Dutch lexicon of "real" verbs of category $(S_{+SUB}/NP)/NP$:

(76)
Ik geloof dat	Jan *Syntactic Structures* gelezen heeft	en	Piet	*Aspects*

$$
\begin{array}{c}
\text{Ik geloof dat} \quad \underline{\text{Jan \textit{Syntactic Structures} gelezen heeft}} \quad \text{en} \quad \text{Piet} \quad \textit{Aspects} \\
S'_{-SUB}/S_{+SUB} \qquad\qquad S_{+SUB} \qquad\qquad\qquad\quad CONJ \quad T\backslash(T/NP) \quad T\backslash(T/NP) \\
\underline{((S_{+SUB}/NP)/NP)_{+ANT} \quad S_{+SUB}\backslash((S_{+SUB}/NP)/NP)_{+ANT}}^{<dcomp} \qquad \underline{T\backslash((T/NP)/NP)_{+ANT}}^{<\mathbf{B}} \\
\underline{S_{+SUB}\backslash((S_{+SUB}/NP)/NP)_{+ANT}}^{<\Phi>} \\
\underline{S_{+SUB}}^{<} \\
S'_{-SUB}
\end{array}
$$

This analysis implies the following claim. According to this theory, the SOV+SO pattern of gapping is allowed in Dutch only because the directional parametric specification of legal categories for the Dutch lexicon includes VSO main verbs, which in turn allow arguments to be raised over them to give backward raised categories. If Dutch were a "pure" SOV language, like Japanese, it would not license $T\backslash(T/NP)$ categories, and would be predicted not to allow forward gapping on the SOV+SO pattern, as is indeed the pattern with more strictly SOV languages like Japanese.[20]

Of course, predictions cut both ways. If we predict that when an SOV language like Dutch allows VSO/SVO main-clause order, it may allow SOV+SO gapping as well as the usual SO+SOV, then we necessarily also predict that a VSO/SVO language that allows SOV as a main-clause order may allow SO+VSO/SVO as well as the standard VSO/SVO+SO.

Zapotec (Rosenbaum 1977) appears to be exactly such a language, the mirror image in this respect of Dutch. It is clearly a VSO language, since indirect questions and other subordinate clauses require that order. However, it also allows SVO, OVS, and SOV as intonationally and pragmatically marked main-clause orders. It allows SO+VSO/SVO gapping, as well as the VSO/SVO+SO order that Ross's (1970) generalization would predict. Tojolabal (Furbee 1974) appears to be a similar case.

Zapotec and Tojolabal have often been cited, following Rosenbaum and Furbee themselves, as counterexamples to Ross's basic generalization. However, once it is understood how true discontinuous gapping actually works, it is clear that these languages only appear to violate the generalization because they are not purely verb-initial, and include verb-final lexical entries for verbs, which in turn determine the categories of type-raised arguments. If Ross's generalization is restated in the following form, then they are entirely consistent with it:

(77) *Ross's generalization (revised)*
   The possibility of "rightward gapping" in a given language depends on the availability to its lexicon of rightward-combining verbs (and hence the possibility of rightward categories raised over them), and the possibility of "Leftward Gapping" depends on the availability to its lexicon of leftward-combining verbs (and the associated raised categories).

7.4 Other Elliptical Phenomena

The assumption that gapping arises in languages like English via the availability of a backward type-raised category for subjects as well as other arguments, and of the revealing rule (61), predicts that a subject or any other argument alone should be able to coordinate with a sentence in the same way, giving rise to the construction that Ross called "Stripping," illustrated in the following examples:[21]

(78) a. Dexter ran away, and Warren (too).
   b. Dexter ran away, but not Warren.

(79) a. Dexter gave a flower to a policeman, and chocolates (too).
   b. Dexter sent a flower to a policeman, but no chocolates.

(80) a. Dexter gave a policeman a flower, and a judge (too).
   b. Dexter gave every policeman a flower, but no judge.

For example:[22]

(81)
$$
\begin{array}{ccccc}
\text{Dexter} & \text{ran away,} & \text{and} & \text{Warren} \\
\hline
\multicolumn{2}{c}{S} & CONJ & S\backslash(S/NP) \\
\end{array}
$$

$$
\frac{\cdots\cdots\cdots <dcomp}{S/NP \quad S\backslash(S/NP)}
$$

$$
\frac{}{S\backslash(S/NP)} {<}\Phi{>}
$$

(82) Dexter gave a flower to a policeman   and   chocolates

$$\underbrace{\overbrace{\underbrace{S/NP}\qquad\overbrace{S\backslash(S/NP)}}^{S}}_{\underset{<\Phi>}{S\backslash(S/NP)}}\;\;\overbrace{CONJ}\;\overbrace{S\backslash(S/NP)}$$

As would be expected under the assumption that Information Structure is involved, acceptability is helped by appropriate contextual questions, such as "Which boys ran away?" and "What presents did Dexter give to a policeman?," as well as by discourse-linking particles like *too* and contrastive conjunctions like *but not*.

   The implication that gapping and stripping are related seems to be empirically correct. As Morgan (1973) points out, they both share the curious restriction to root subjects, which was explained in the case of gapping by the fact that fragments like *I believe that Dexter* do not bear the category of a VSO subject: this explanation generalizes correctly to stripping:

(83) a. *Dexter likes apples and I think that Warren pears.

      b. *Dexter likes apples and I think that Warren (too).

Chao (1987) offers extensive crosslinguistic evidence that languages like English and French that allow gapping, also allow stripping, while those that do not, like Chinese (which otherwise seems qualified to allow rightward gapping), do not allow stripping either.

   Sluicing (84a) and VP ellipsis (84b) do not appear to be amenable to analysis in the same syntactic terms as stripping and gapping, since the requisite categories are not otherwise present in the grammar and/or the requisite rules would violate the Principle of Consistency, even on the optimistic assumptions about the categories of the elided conjuncts embodied here:

(84) a. [Dexter did something with the beans,]$_S$ but [I don't know what.]$_{S/(S/NP)}$

      b. [Somebody has to do the job,]$_S$ but [I know that I won't.]$_{S/VP}$

Under present assumptions such constructions must be regarded as being mediated by a quite separate, presumably purely anaphoric mechanism, as their freedom to occur outside the context of coordination suggests, rather than as being syntactically mediated, as gapping and stripping are according to the present theory.[23] Their constituent categories are presumably the following, which trivially conform to the assumption made here that only like types can coordinate:

(85) a. [Dexter did something with the beans,]$_S$ but [I don't know what.]$_S$

      b. [Somebody has to do the job,]$_S$ but [I know that I won't.]$_S$

The suggestion that they are mediated by anaphoric processes rather than syntactic ones is borne out by the absence of word order-dependent constraints parallel to those noted by Ross for gapping. (That is, we do not find "backward VP anaphora" and "backward sluicing" predominating in verb-final languages, but rather the same "forward" varieties that predominate in English.)

The conclusion that gapping is syntactically unrelated to sluicing and VP-ellipsis is contrary to Hankamer and Sag's (1976) and Sag and Hankamer's (1984) claim that all three fall into their "surface anaphoric" or "elliptical" class of constructions, as opposed to their other class of elliptical constructions mediated by the "deep" or "model-interpretive" anaphora that is characteristic of pronouns. However, see Williams 1977, Schachter 1977, and Chao 1987, 112–127, for further arguments that support the present proposal, according to which VP ellipsis and sluicing are mediated by model-interpretive anaphora, like pronouns, and their more restricted character arises from the special nature of their antecedents. Gapping and Stripping, by contrast, are claimed here to be under the control of syntax, pragmatically specialized though they are.

7.5 A Cautious Conclusion

The introduction of rules of decomposition is a radical departure. It involves an appeal to discourse context to determine Logical Form and potentially threatens the constrained nature of the core CCG. Such rules should not be invoked lightly, and they are not needed in the chapters that remain. If something more purely grammatical will do the job, then it should be welcomed. Nevertheless, the widespread involvement of noncontinuous gapping, particularly in Germanic languages, makes it seem certain that something more than pure combinatory rules will be needed, at least in semantic terms.

If we adopt the hypothesis that rules of decomposition are to be allowed in syntax, then medially gapped sentences arise from the coordination of two nonstandard constituents—in descriptive terms, two gapped sentences—and their combination with a third constituent—the virtual gap. In this respect the present proposal is akin to theories in which gapping arises from the restoration of the gapped conjunct to the status of a standard clause, the gapped material being accessed via processes of anaphora or structure copying. The advantage of the present approach is that an analysis, including an interpretation, can be achieved by combining elements that are strictly adjacent by strictly syntactic type-driven operations. The theory thus explains why constituent order under coordination exhibits Ross's (1970) universals, as presently revised. According to the present theory, as with related categorial analyses that similarly extend the notion of constituent (e.g. Stump 1978; van der Zee 1982; Cremers 1983; Oehrle 1987; Dowty 1988; Moortgat 1988a; Morrill 1988; Wood 1988; Hepple 1990; Solias 1992; Solias Aris 1996; Morrill and Solias 1993; Houtman 1994; Hendriks 1995; and Versmissen 1996), everything that can coordinate, including medially "gapped" conjuncts, is a constituent under the generalized definition of that notion that is afforded by categorial grammars.

Within the framework of CCG the twin principles of Consistency and Inheritance to which combinatory rules are subject predict the observations of Ross and Maling concerning the dependency of forward and backward "gapping" in coordinate structures upon the lexical specification of clause constituent orders in any given language, including the observation that SVO patterns with VSO in forbidding the backward variety. These principles further predict that languages like Dutch/German and Zapotec that are not "purely" verb-final or verb-initial may allow both forward *and* backward gapping, a fact that has hitherto been supposed to controvert Ross's generalization. On the contrary, such languages merely underline the fact that Ross's generalization should be thought of as applying to parametrically specified *lexicons* specifying verbs as having one or more orders such as VSO, SOV etc., rather than as applying to languages via a single "underlying" word order, a notion the present theory entirely avoids.

PART III

Computation and Performance

Chapter 8

Combinators and Grammars

"I once asked Bravura whether there were any Kestrels in his forest. He seemed somewhat upset by the question, and replied in a strained voice: 'No! Kestrels are not allowed in this forest!'"
Raymond Smullyan, *To Mock a Mockingbird*

What does the theory presented in the earlier chapters actually tell us? Why should natural grammars involve combinatory rules, rather than the intuitively more transparent apparatus of the λ-calculus? Why are the combinators in question apparently confined to Smullyan's Bluebird, Thrush, and Starling— that is, to composition, type-raising, and substitution? Why are the syntactic combinatory rules further constrained by the Principles of Consistency and Inheritance? What expressive power does this theory give us? How can grammars like this be parsed?

8.1 Why Categories and Combinators?

There is a strong equivalence between (typed and untyped) combinatory systems and the (typed and untyped) λ-calculi, first noted by Schönfinkel (1924), elaborated by Curry and Feys (1958), and developed and expounded by Rosenbloom (1950), Stenlund (1972), Burge (1975), Barendregt (1981), Smullyan (1985, 1994), and Hindley and Seldin (1986). Even quite small collections of combinators of the kind already encountered are sufficient to define applicative systems of expressive power equal to that of the λ-calculus, as will be demonstrated below.

The difference between the λ-calculi and the combinatory systems is that the latter avoid the use of bound variables. One interest of this property lies in the fact that bound variables can be a major source of computational overhead— for example in the evaluation of expressions in programming languages related to the λ-calculus, such as LISP. The freedom that their users demand to use the same identifier for variables that are logically distinct in the sense of having distinct bindings to values in distinct environments means that all the various bindings must be stored during the evaluation. This cost is serious enough that considerable ingenuity is devoted to minimizing it by the designers of such "functional" programming languages. One tactic, originating with Turner (1979b), is to avoid the problem entirely, by compiling languages like LISP into equivalent variable-free combinatory expressions, which can then be evaluated by structural, graph reduction techniques akin to algebraic simplification. We will see that there some rather striking similarities between the combinatory system that Turner proposes and the one that is at work in natural languages.

However, it seems quite unlikely that a pressure to do without variables for reasons of computational efficiency is at work in natural language interpretation.[1] The computational advantage of the combinatory systems is highly dependent upon the precise nature of the computations involved, and it is far from obvious that these particular types of computation are characteristic of linguistic comprehension (although the extensive involvement of higher-order functions in CCG is one property that does exacerbate the penalties incurred from the use of bound variables). Furthermore, the wide acceptance of the idea that the pronoun in sentences like *Every farmer in the room thinks he is a genius* is semantically a bound variable, as assumed in the analysis of such phenomena in section 4.4 in chapter 4, suggests that there is no overall prohibition against such devices at the level of Logical Form or predicate-argument structure. The binding conditions, and in particular Condition C, which are discussed in terms of CCG in Chierchia 1988 and Steedman 1997, are also phenomena that are most naturally thought of in terms of scope (although it has to be said that they do not look much like the properties of the *usual* kind of variables).[2]

It seems more likely that natural grammars reflect a combinatory semantics because combinator-like operations such as composition are themselves cognitively primitive and constitute a part of the cognitive substrate from which the language faculty has developed. Such primitive and prelinguistic cognitive operations as learning how to reach one's hand around an obstacle to a target have many of the properties of functional composition, if elementary movements are viewed as functions over locations. The onset of the ability to construct such composite motions appears to immediately precede the onset of language in children (Diamond 1990, 653–655). Similarly, a notion very like type-raising seems to be implicit in the kind of association between objects and their characteristic roles in actions that is required in order to use those objects as tools in planned action. (The idea that tool use and motor planning are immediate precursors of language goes back to de Laguna's (1927) observations on Köhler's's (1925) work on primate tool use and has been investigated more recently by Bruner (1968), Greenfield, Nelson and Saltzman (1972), Greenfield (1991), and Deacon (1988, 1997), among many others.)

To the extent that languages adhere to the Principle of Head Categorial Uniqueness and project unbounded dependencies from the same categories that define canonical word order, the presumed universal availability of combinatory operations in principle allows the child to acquire the full grammar of the language on the basis of simple canonical sentences alone, on the assumption of chapter 2, that the child has access (not necessarily error-free, and not necessarily unambiguously) to their interpretations. (We will return briefly to the problems induced by exceptions to Head Categorial Uniqueness in chapter 10.)

To see whether this hypothesis is reasonable, we must begin by examining the specific combinators that have been identified above—composition, type-raising, and Schönfinkel's **S**—and ask what class of concepts can be defined using them.

8.2 Why Bluebirds, Thrushes, and Starlings?

The equivalence between combinatory systems and the λ-calculus is most readily understood in terms of a recursive algorithm for converting terms in the λ-calculus into equivalent combinatory expressions. Surprisingly small collections of combinators can be shown in this way to completely support this equivalence. One of the smallest and most elegant sets consists of three combinators, **I**, **K**, and the familiar **S** combinator. The algorithm can be represented as three cases, as follows:[3]

$$
\begin{aligned}
(1) \quad \lambda x.x \ &= \ \mathbf{I} \\
\lambda x.y \ &= \ \mathbf{K}y \\
\lambda x.AB \ &= \ \mathbf{S}(\lambda x.A)(\lambda x.B)
\end{aligned}
$$
where x is not free in y

The combinators **I** and **K** have not been encountered before, but their definitions can be read off the example: **I** is the identity operator, and **K**, Smullyan's Kestrel, is vacuous abstraction or the definition of a constant function. This algorithm simply says that these two combinators represent the two ground conditions of abstracting over the variable itself and abstracting over any other variable or constant, and that the case of abstracting over a compound term consisting of the application of a function term A to an argument B is the Starling combinator **S** applied to the results of abstracting over the function and over the argument. (Given the earlier definition of **S**, it is easy to verify that this equivalence holds.) Since the combinator **I** can in turn be defined in terms of the other two combinators (as **SKK**), the algorithm (attributed in origin to Rosser (1942) in Curry and Feys 1958, 237) is often referred to as the "**SK**" algorithm. It is obvious that the algorithm is complete, in the sense that it will deliver a combinatory equivalent of any λ-term. It therefore follows that any combinator, including composition and type-raising, can be defined in terms of **S** and **K** alone.

The **SK** algorithm is extremely elegant, and quite general, but it gives rise to extremely cumbersome combinatory expressions. Consider the following examples, adapted from Turner 1979b. The successor function that maps an integer onto the integer one greater might be defined as follows in an imaginary functional programming language:

(2) $succ = \lambda x.plus \ 1 \ x$

The obvious variable-free definition of this trivial function is the following:

(3) $succ = plus \ 1$

However, the **SK** algorithm produces the much more cumbersome (albeit entirely correct) expression shown in the last line of the following derivation:

(4) $succ$ = $\lambda x.plus \ 1 \ x$
    ⇒   **S**$\lambda x.plus \ 1\lambda x.x$
    ⇒   **S**(**S**$\lambda x.plus\lambda x.1$)**I**
    ⇒   **S**(**SK***plus***K***1*)**I**

The following is the familiar recursive definition of the factorial function (where *cond A B C* means "if A then B else C"):[4]

(5) $fact = \lambda x.cond(equal \ 0 \ x)1(times \ x(fact(minus \ x \ 1)))$

It yields the following monster:

(6) **S**(**S**(**S**(**K** *cond*) (**S**(**S**(**K** *equal*)(**K** 0))**I**))(**K** 1))
     (**S**(**S**(**K** *times*)**I**)(**S**(**K** *fact*)
     (**S**(**S**(**K** *minus*)**I**)(**K** 1))))

What is wrong with the **SK** algorithm is that it fails to distinguish cases in which either the function or the argument or both are terms in which the variable *x* does not occur (is not free) from the general case in which both function and argument are terms in *x*. It is only in the latter case that the combinator **S** is appropriate. Curry and Feys (1958, 190–194) offer the following alternative algorithm:[5]

(7) a. $\lambda x.x$ $\quad = \quad$ **I**
   b. $\lambda x.y$ $\quad = \quad$ **K**y
   c. $\lambda x.fx$ $\quad = \quad$ f
   d. $\lambda x.fA$ $\quad = \quad$ **B**$f(\lambda x.A)$
   e. $\lambda x.Ay$ $\quad = \quad$ **C**$(\lambda x.A)y$
   f. $\lambda x.AB$ $\quad = \quad$ **S**$(\lambda x.A)(\lambda x.B)$
   where x is not free in f, y

This algorithm distinguishes the case (7c) (corresponding to η-reduction), in which the expression to be abstracted over consists of a function term that does not contain the variable and an argument term that *is* the variable. This case immediately preempts a great many applications of **K** (to constants), **I** (for the variable), and **S** (for the application). For example, it immediately gives us what we want for the successor function:

(8) $succ$ $\quad = \quad$ $\lambda x.plus\ 1\ x$
        $\Rightarrow \quad plus\ 1$

The new algorithm also distinguishes the cases (7d) and (7e), where either the argument term or the function term do not include the variable. These cases correspond to the familiar functional composition combinator **B**, and the "commuting" combinator **C**, which has not been encountered in natural syntax before, but whose definition is as follows:[6]

(9) **C**fxy $\quad \equiv \quad$ fyx

This algorithm gives rise to much terser combinatory expressions. For example, the earlier definition of factorial comes out as follows:

(10) **S**(**C**(**B**$cond(equal\ 0)$) 1)(**S**$times$(**B**$fact$(**C**$minus\ 1$)))

Like the **SK** set, this set of combinators is complete with respect to the λ-calculi. This result is obvious, since it includes **S** and **K**. More interestingly, in includes other subsets that are also complete. The most interesting of these is the set **BCSI**. This set is complete with respect to the λ-calculus with the single exception that **K** itself is not definable. This set therefore corresponds to the λ-calculus without vacuous abstraction, which is known as the λ_I-calculus (Church 1940), as distinct from the λ_K-calculus. Vacuous abstraction is the operation that figured as an irrelevant side effect of Huet's unification algorithm in the discussion in chapter 7 of work by Dalrymple, Shieber, and Pereira (1991; see also Shieber, Pereira and Dalrymple 1996), who used it as an operation on predicate-argument structures, to recover interpretations for VP ellipsis. It is therefore interesting to note the existence of calculi and combinatory systems that exclude it, corresponding to linear, relevance, and intuitionistic logics, and to recall that it is not represented among the syntactic combinatory rules either.

Turner (1979a,b) and others have proposed further cases to optimise and extend similar translations of λ-terms into combinatory equivalents, including combinators corresponding to **T**, the type-raising combinator (which is a natural partner to **C** in (7)), to Curry's Φ, the combinator that is implicit in the coordination rule proposed earlier, and to the "paradoxical" fixed-point combinators that are required to complete the combinatory definition of recursive functions like (10).

What then can we say concerning the nature and raison d'être of the combinatory system **BTS** that we have observed in natural language syntax? The most obvious question is whether this set of combinators is complete. To begin with, note that the linguistic combinatory rules, unlike the systems discussed in most of the literature cited above (but see Church 1940; Barendregt 1981, app. A; Hindley and Seldin 1986), are a *typed* combinatory system. That is to say, rules like the forward composition rule of chapter 3 are defined in terms of (variables over) the types of the domain and range of the input functions and the function that results. Indeed, the syntactic categories of a categorial grammar are precisely types, in that sense. So we are talking about completeness with respect to the simply typed λ^τ-calculi. Since mathematicians and computer scientists usually think of functions in this way, the typed λ-calculi are useful and interesting objects.

Interestingly, the paradoxical combinators such as Curry's **Y** and Smullyan's $\lambda x.xx$ are not definable in the typed systems. Since the existence of such fixed-point combinators is what allows the definition of recursion within the pure λ-calculus, recursive functions like *fact* cannot be defined within the pure λ^τ-calculi. There is also an interesting relation (discussed by Fortune, Leivant and O'Donnell 1983) to type systems in programming languages like PASCAL and ML.

Exactly the same correspondence holds between typed combinators and the typed λ-calculi as we have seen for the untyped versions. In particular, the **SK** system is complete with respect to the λ^τ_K-calculus. The **BCSI** system is similarly complete with respect to the λ^τ_I-calculus. Since the type-raising combinator **T** is equivalent to the combinatory expression **CI**, and since the linguistically observed set **BTS** includes **B** and **S**, it seems highly likely that **BTS** is related to **BCSI** and hence also to the λ^τ_I-calculus. Certainly **C** is definable in terms of **T** and **B**, as shown by Church (see Smullyan 1985, 113).[7]

The only qualification to the correspondence that I have been able to identify is that the combinator **I** itself does not appear in general to be definable in terms of **BTS**. A combinator corresponding to a special case of **I**, of type $(\alpha \to \beta) \to (\alpha \to \beta)$, can be defined as **CT**. This is not the true **I** combinator, for it will not map an atom onto itself. Nevertheless, **CT** constitutes the identity functional for first-order functions and all higher types, so this does not seem a very important deviation. We may assume that the λ_I^τ-calculus constitutes an upper bound on the expressive power of the **BTS** system and that the two are essentially equivalent.[8]

It follows immediately that all of the important constraints on the system as a theory of natural grammars stem from directional constraints imposed upon syntactic combinatory rules by the twin Principles of Consistency and Inheritance, discussed in chapter 4. This observation raises the further question of the expressive or automata-theoretic power of CCG.

8.3 Expressive Power

The way the Dutch cross-serial verb construction was captured in examples like (2) of chapter 6 suggests that CCG is of greater strong generative power than context-free grammar.[9] The Dutch construction intercalates the dependencies between arguments and verbs, rather than nesting them, and therefore requires this greater power, at least for strongly adequate capture. Whether standard Dutch can be shown on the basis of this construction not to be a weakly context-free *language* is of course another question. Huybregts (1984) and Shieber (1985) have shown that a related construction in related dialects of Germanic is not even weakly context-free. It is therefore clear that Universal Grammar has more than context-free power, and the further question of whether standard Dutch happens to exploit this power in a way that makes the *language* non-context-free (as opposed to the strongly adequate grammar) is of only technical interest.

The question is, how *much* more power do cross-serial dependencies demand and does CCG offer? An interesting class of languages to consider is the class of indexed grammars, which are discussed by Gazdar (1988) with reference to the Dutch construction. More recently Vijay-Shanker and Weir (1990, 1994) have argued that several apparently unrelated near-context-free grammar formalisms, including the present one, are weakly equivalent to the least powerful level of indexed grammars, the so-called linear indexed grammars.[10]

This section presents an informal version of their argument.

Indexed grammars (IGs) are grammars that, when represented as phrase structure rewriting systems, allow symbols on both sides of a production to be associated with features whose values are *stacks*, or unbounded pushdown stores. We can represent such rules as follows, where the notation [...] represents a stack-valued feature under the convention that the top of the stack is to the left, and where α and β are nonterminal symbols and W_1 and W_2 are strings of nonterminals and terminals, in the general case including nonterminals bearing the stack feature:

(11) $\alpha_{[...]} \rightarrow W_1 \ \beta_{[...]} \ W_2$

Such rules have the effect of passing a feature encoding arbitrarily many long-range dependencies from a parent α to one or more daughters β. The rules are allowed to make two kinds of modification to the stack value: an extra item may be "pushed" or added on top of the stack, or the topmost item already on the stack may be "popped" or removed. These two types of rule can be represented as similar schemata, as follows:

(12) a. "pushing:" $\alpha_{[...]} \rightarrow W_1 \ \beta_{[i,...]} \ W_2$

     b. "popping:" $\alpha_{[i,...]} \rightarrow W_1 \ \beta_{[...]} \ W_2$

In general, IGs may include rules that pass stack-valued features to more than one daughter. The most restrictive class of indexed grammars, linear indexed grammars (LIGs), allows the stack-valued feature to pass to only one daughter; that is, W_1 and W_2 are restricted to strings of terminals and nonterminals *not* bearing the stack feature.

It is easy to show that Linear Indexed Grammar (LIG) offers a formalism that will express cross-serial dependencies. I will simplify the Dutch problem for illustrative purposes and assume that the goal is to generate a language whose strings all have some number of nouns on the left, followed by the same number of verbs on the right, with the dependencies identified by indices in the grammar. The following simple grammar (adapted from Gazdar 1988) will do this.

(13) $S_{[...]} \rightarrow n \quad S_{[v,...]}$

     $S_{[...]} \rightarrow S'_{[...]}$

     $S'_{[v,...]} \rightarrow S'_{[...]} \ v$

     $S'_{[\ ]} \rightarrow \varepsilon$

The derivation tree for the string $n_1 \ n_2 \ n_3 \ v_1 \ v_2 \ v_3$ is shown in figure 8.1.

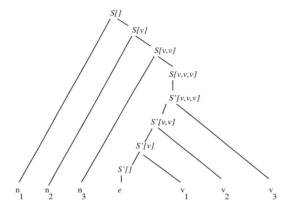

Figure 8.1
LIG derivation for n^3v^3

This is rather reminiscent of the structure produced by the (linguistically incorrect) CCG derivation using crossed composition but lacking type-raised categories shown in figure 6.2. While this particular grammar is weakly equivalent to a context free grammar (since a^nb^n is a context-free language, although a context-free grammar assigns different dependencies), it is equally easy to write a related grammar for the language $a^nb^nc^n$, which is not a context-free language.

Vijay-Shanker and Weir (1990, 1994) identify a characteristic automaton for these grammars, and show on the basis of certain closure properties that it defines what they call an "abstract family of languages" (AFL), just as the related pushdown automaton does. They provide polynomial time recognition and parsing results, of the order of n^6. These results crucially depend upon the linearity property, because it is this property that ensures that two branches of a derivation cannot share information about an unbounded number of earlier steps in the derivation (Vijay-Shanker and Weir 1994, 591–592). This fact both limits expressivity and permits efficient divide-and-conquer algorithms to apply.

Weir (1988) and Weir and Joshi (1988) were the first to observe that there is a close relation between linear indexed rules and the combinatory rules of CCG. Function categories like *give* and *zag helpen voeren* can be equated with indexed categories bearing stack-valued features, as follows:

(14) give := $(VP/NP_2)/NP_1$ $\equiv$ $VP_{[NP_1,NP_2]}$

zag helpen voeren := $(((S\backslash NP_4)\backslash NP_3)\backslash NP_2)\backslash NP_1$ $\equiv$ $S_{[NP_1,NP_2,NP_3,NP_4]}$

Note that the LIG categories no longer encode directionality—it is up to the LIG rules to do that.

Combinatory rules can be translated rather directly in terms of such categories into sets of LIG productions of the form shown on the right of the equivalences in (15) and (16). Since LIG categories do not capture directionality, the grammar for a particular language will be made up of more specific instances of these schemata involving just those categories that do in fact combine in the specified order for that language.[11]

(15) $X/Y \quad Y \quad \Rightarrow \quad X \quad \equiv \quad X'_{[\ldots]} \quad \rightarrow \quad X'_{[Y,\ldots]} \quad Y_{[\,]}$

(16) $X/Y \quad Y/Z \quad \Rightarrow \quad X/Z \quad \equiv \quad X'_{[Z,\ldots]} \quad \rightarrow \quad X'_{[Y,\ldots]} \quad Y_{[Z]}$

Rule (15) is forward application, realized as a binary LIG rule of the "push" variety. Rule (16) is first-order forward composition, **B**, and involves both pushing a Y and popping a Z. Crucially, the stack, represented as $\ldots$, is passed to only one daughter. The same is true for the substitution rule:

(17) $Y/Z \quad (X\backslash Y)/Z \quad \Rightarrow \quad X/Z \quad \equiv \quad X'_{[Z,\ldots]} \quad \rightarrow \quad Y_{[Z]} \quad X'_{[Z,Y,\ldots]}$

The same linearity property also holds for the rules corresponding to $\mathbf{B}^2, \mathbf{B}^3$ and so on, because the set of arguments of the function into Y is bounded. It would *not* hold for an unbounded schema for a rule corresponding to $\mathbf{B}^n$. This rule, which can be written in the present notation as follows, involves *two* stack-valued features, written $\ldots_1$ and $\ldots_2$:

(18) $X/Y \quad Y/Z\$ \quad \Rightarrow \quad X/Z\$ \quad \equiv \quad X'_{[\ldots_1,Z,\ldots_2]} \quad \rightarrow \quad X'_{[Y,\ldots_2]} \quad Y_{[\ldots_1,Z]}$

It is not currently known precisely what strong generative power such generalized rules engender. They may not take us to the full power of IGs, because the translation from CCG forces us to regard the left-hand side of the rule as bearing a *single* stack feature, which the production nondeterministically breaks into two stack fragments that pass to the daughters. This is not the same as passing the same stack to two daughters—crucially, the two branches of the derivation that it engenders do not share any information, and therefore seem likely to permit efficient divide-and-conquer parsing techniques.

Weir and colleagues treat type-raising as internal to the lexicon, rather than as a rule in syntax, However, Hoffman (1993, 1995b) has pointed out that a similar increase in power over LIG follows from the involvement of type-raised categories like $T/(T\backslash NP)$ if T is regarded as a true variable, rather than a finite schematization. To a first approximation, the indexed category corresponding to a type-raised category looks like this:

(19) $T/(T\backslash Y) \equiv X'_{[X'_{[Y,\ldots_1]},\ldots_1]}$

Again, the LIG category does not capture the order information, and in particular the order-preserving character, of the original. That has to be captured in the LIG productions, in such facts as that for every instance of rule (15) there is a rule like the following:

(20) $X'_{[\ldots_1]} \rightarrow X'_{[X'_{[Y,\ldots_1]},\ldots_1]} \ X'_{[Y,\ldots_1]}$

The LIG equivalent of a raised category has two copies of the stack $\ldots_1$. However, as far as functional application goes, it is simply a function like any other—that is, an instance of $\alpha_{[\beta,\ldots]}$. It follows that this rule is simply another instance of (15). Again, no information is shared across branches of the derivation.

However, by the same reasoning, when *two* of the raised categories compose, even via the first-order composition rule (16), so that Y is $T_{[X,\ldots]}$, their two distinct stack variables give rise to a nonlinear production, as follows:

(21) $X_{X_{[Z,\ldots_1,\ldots_2]}} \rightarrow X_{[X_{[Y,\ldots_2]},\ldots_2]} \ X_{[Z,X_{[Y,\ldots_1]},\ldots_1]}$

This composition has the characteristic noted earlier of nondeterministically partitioning a single stack feature on the left-hand side into two fragments, passed as stack features to the daughters. In effect, the variable transforms bounded composition into the unbounded variety. Again no information is shared across the two branches of the derivation.

Hoffman shows how the language $a^n b^n c^n d^n e^n$ (which is outside the set of linear-indexed languages) can be defined by exploiting this behavior of variables in type-raised categories. It is therefore known that if this property is allowed in CCGs, it raises their power strictly beyond LIG. What is not currently known is how *much* beyond LIG it takes us, or whether CCLs so defined are a subset of IL, the full set of indexed languages.

Alternatively, we can, as suggested earlier, confine ourselves to LIG power by eschewing the general interpretation of composition and type-raising and by interpreting the variables involved in each as merely finite schemata. Such a limitation allows all derivations encountered in parts I and II of the book and keeps CCG weakly equivalent to LIG.[12]

The advantages of keeping to such a limitation are potentially important, as Vijay-Shanker and Weir (1990, 1994) show. As noted earlier, because LIGs pass the stack to only one branch, they limit expressive power and allow efficient algorithms to apply. As a result, Vijay-Shanker and Weir have been able to demonstrate polynomial worst-case complexity results for recognizing and parsing CCGs and TAGs, which are also weakly equivalent to LIGs. It is currently unclear whether similar advantages obtain for the more general class of CCGs. The important fact that neither generalised composition nor variables in type-raised categories pass any one stack feature to more than one daughter gives reason to suppose that they too may be polynomially recognizable using divide-and-conquer techniques.

As Gazdar (1988) has pointed out, it is not clear that the linguistic facts allow us to keep within either of these bounds. The full generality of the Dutch verb-raising construction in noncoordinate sentences can be captured with weakly LIG-equivalent rules, but they allow functions of arbitrarily high valency to be grown. If such functions can coordinate, then we need the full power of IG. This result follows immediately from the fact that the unbounded coordination combinator Φ^n corresponds to a production that passes the same stack feature to two daughters:

(22) $X_{[...l]} \rightarrow X_{[...l]} \ CONJ \ X_{[...l]}$

The crucial cases for Dutch are those in which unboundedly long sequences of nouns or verbs of unbounded valency coordinate. However, once the valency or number of arguments gets beyond four, the limit found in the Dutch and English lexicon, the sentences involved become increasingly hard to process, and hard to judge.

Rambow (1994a) makes a similar argument for the translinear nature of scrambling in German. However, this argument depends on the assumption that unbounded scrambling is complete to unbounded depth of embedding. Because these sentences also go rapidly beyond anything that human processors can handle, any argument that either kind of sentence is grammatical depends on assumptions about what counts as a "natural generalization" of the construction, parallel to a famous argument of Chomsky's (1957) concerning the non-finite-state nature of center embedding.

Joshi, Rambow and Becker (to appear) have made the point that this analogy may not hold. They note that all such arguments—including Chomsky's—fall if a lesser automaton or AFL that covers all and only the acceptable cases is ever shown to exist. The status of any residual marginal cases is then decided by that automaton. It is only because no one has yet identified such a finite-state automaton that Chomsky's claim that context-free grammars constitute a lower bound on competence still stands, and is unlikely ever to be overthrown.[13]

It follows that if LIG alone can be shown to be of sufficient power to provide strongly adequate grammars for the core examples, or alternatively if unbounded composition rules and variable-based type-raising are indeed of lesser power than IG, and if a class of automata characterizing an AFL can be identified, the question of whether that lesser power provides an upper bound on natural complexity comes down to the question of whether some exceedingly marginal coordinations and scramblings are acceptable or not. If an automaton exists that is strongly adequate to recognize all and only the sentences that we are certain about, then we might well let that fact decide the margin, in the absence of any other basis for claiming a natural generalization. This is a question for further research, but however it turns out, CCG should be contrasted in this respect with multimodal type-logical approaches of the kind reviewed by Moortgat (1997), which Carpenter (1995) shows to be much less constrained in automata-theoretic terms.

8.4 Formalizing Directionality in Categorial Grammars

In chapter 4, I claimed that the Principles of Adjacency, Consistency, and Inheritance are simple and natural restrictions for rules of grammar. In chapters 6 and 7, I claimed that a number of well-known crosslinguistic universals follow from them. We have just seen that low automata-theoretic power and a polynomial worst-case parsing complexity result also follow from these principles. So quite a lot hinges on the claim that these principles *are* natural and nonarbitrary.

The universal claim further depends upon type-raising's being limited (at least in the case of configurational languages) to the following schemata:[14]

(23) $X \Rightarrow_T T/(T\backslash X)$

$X \Rightarrow_T T\backslash(T/X)$

If the following patterns (which allow constituent orders that are not otherwise permitted) were allowed, the regularity would be unexplained. In the absence of further restrictions, grammars would collapse into free order:

(24) $X \Rightarrow_T T/(T/X)$

     $X \Rightarrow_T T\backslash(T\backslash X)$

But what are the principles that limit combinatory rules of grammar, to include (23) and exclude (24)? And how can we move type-raising into the lexicon without multiplying NP categories unnecessarily?

The intuition here is that *we want to make type-raising sensitive to the directionality of the lexically defined functions that it combines with.* However, the solution of combining type-raising with the other combination rules proposed by Gerdeman and Hinrichs (1990) greatly expands their number.[15]

The fact that directionality of arguments is inherited under the application of combinatory rules, according to the Principle of Inheritance, strongly suggests that directionality is a property of arguments themselves, just like their categorial type, *NP* or whatever, as suggested in Steedman 1987, and as in Zeevat, Klein and Calder 1987 and Zeevat 1988.

Our first assumption about the nature of such a system might exploit a variant of the notation used in the discussion of LIGs above (cf. Steedman 1987), in which a binary feature marks an argument of a function as "to the left" or "to the right." In categorial notation it is convenient to indicate this by subscripting the symbol $\leftarrow$ or $\rightarrow$ to the argument in question. Since the slash in a function will now be nondirectional, both $\backslash$ and $/$ can be replaced by a single nondirectional slash, also written $/$, so that for example the transitive verb category is written as follows:[16]

(25) enjoys $:= (S/NP_{\leftarrow})/NP_{\rightarrow}$

(The result *S* has no value on this feature until it unifies with a function as its argument, so it bears no directional indication. It is just an unbound variable.)

In this notation the (noncrossed) forward composition rule is written as follows:

(26) *Forward composition*

    $X/Y_{\rightarrow}$ $Y/Z_{\rightarrow}$ $\Rightarrow_B$ $X/Z_{\rightarrow}$ $(> \mathbf{B})$

The forbidden rule (6) of chapter 4, which violates the Principle of Inheritance, would be written as follows:

(27) $X/Y_{\rightarrow}$ $Y/Z_{\rightarrow}$ $\nRightarrow$ $X/Z_{\leftarrow}$

However, given the definition of directionality as a feature of Z, this is not a rule of composition at all. As long as the combinatory rules are limited to operations like composition, only rules obeying the Principle of Inheritance are permitted.

The feature in question does not have the equally desirable effect of limiting type-raising rules to the order-preserving kind in (23). Those rules are now written as follows:

(28) $X \Rightarrow_T T/(T/X_\leftarrow)_\rightarrow$

$X \Rightarrow_T T/(T/X_\rightarrow)_\leftarrow$

Since the input to the rule, X, is unmarked on this feature, there is nothing to stop us from writing the order-*changing* rules in (24):

(29) $X \Rightarrow_T T/(T/X_\rightarrow)_\rightarrow$

$X \Rightarrow_T T/(T/X_\leftarrow)_\leftarrow$

This is very bad. Although we can easily exclude the latter rules to define grammars for languages like English, we could with equal ease exploit the same degree of freedom to define a language in which *only* order-changing type-raising is allowed, so that the directionality of functions in the lexicon would be systematically overruled. Thus, we could have a language with an SVO lexicon, but OVS word order. Worse still, we could equally well have a language with one of each kind of type-raising rule—say, with an SVO lexicon but a VOS word order. Such languages seem unreasonable, and would certainly engender undesirably cynical attitudes toward life in any child faced with the task of having to acquire them.

Zeevat, Klein and Calder (1987) and Zeevat (1988) offer an ingenious, but partial, solution to this problem. Of the two sets of rules (28) and (29), it is actually the order-*changing* pair in (29) that looks most reasonable, in that the raised function can at least be held to inherit the *same* directionality as its argument. That is, both rules are instances of a schema in which the directionality value is represented as a variable, say, D. In the present notation they can both be conveniently represented by the following single rule:

(30) $X \Rightarrow_T T/(T/X_D)_D$

This rule has the attractive properties of being able to combine with either rightward- or leftward-combining arguments and of inheriting its own directionality from them. Since it therefore *only* combines to the left with leftward arguments and to the right with rightward ones, it offers a way around the problem of having multiple type-raised categories for arguments. We can simply apply this rule across the board to yield one type for NPs. In fact, we can do this off-line, in the lexicon, as Zeevat, Klein, and Calder propose.

However, there is a cost in theoretical terms. As noted earlier, since this is the direction-changing rule, the lexicon must reverse the word order of the language. An SVO language like English must have an OVS lexicon. This is in fact what Zeevat, Klein and Calder (1987) propose (see Zeevat 1988, 207–210).

Despite this disadvantage, there is something very appealing about this proposal. It would be very nice if there were a different treatment of the directionality feature that preserved its advantages without implicating this implausible assumption about the lexicon. Of course, as a technical solution we might encode the values $\rightarrow$ and $\leftarrow$ as list structures $[0,1]$ and $[1,0]$, and write a similar single order-preserving rule as follows, using variables over the elements:

(31) $X \Rightarrow_T T/(T/X_{[x,y]})_{[y,x]}$

But such a move explains nothing, for we could equally well exploit this device to write the order-changing rule or, by using constants rather than variables, define any mixture of the two. What is wrong is that directionality is being represented as an abstract feature, without any grounding in the properties of the string itself. If instead we define the feature in question in terms of string positions, in a manner that is familiar from the implementation of definite clause grammars (DCGs) in logic programming, we can attain a more explanatory system, in which the following results emerge:

1. The Principle of Inheritance is explained as arising from inheritance of this feature under unification of categories.

2. A single order-preserving type-raised category combining either to the right or to the left can be naturally specified.

3. No comparable single order-*changing* type-raised category can be specified (although a completely order-free category can).

Since these matters are somewhat technical, and since they impinge very little upon linguistics, this whole discussion is relegated to an appendix to the present chapter, which many readers may wish to skip entirely. Since the notation becomes quite heavy going, it is emphasised here that *it is not a proposal for a new CCG notation*. It is a semantics for the metagrammar of the *present* CCG notation.

Appendix: Directionality as a Feature

This appendix proposes an interpretation, grounded in string positions, for the symbols / and \ in CCG. This interpretation is easiest to present using unification as a mechanism for instantiating underspecified categories and feature value bundles, a mechanism that has been implicit at several points in the earlier discussion.

For a full exposition of the concept of unification, the reader is directed to Shieber 1986. The intuition behind the notion is that of an operation that amalgamates compatible terms and fails to amalgamate incompatible ones. The result of amalgamating two compatible terms is the most general term that is an instance of both the original terms. For example, the following pairs of terms unify, to yield the results shown:

$$(32)\quad
\begin{array}{llll}
x & a' & \Longrightarrow & a' \\
f'(g'a') & x & \Longrightarrow & f'(g'a') \\
f'x & f'(g'y) & \Longrightarrow & f'(g'y) \\
f'a'x & f'yy & \Longrightarrow & f'a'a'
\end{array}$$

The following pairs of terms do not unify:

$$(33)\quad
\begin{array}{llll}
a' & b' & \Longrightarrow & \textit{fail} \\
f'x & g'y & \Longrightarrow & \textit{fail} \\
f'a'b' & f'yy & \Longrightarrow & \textit{fail}
\end{array}$$

(Constants are distinguished from variables in these terms by the use of primes.)

Besides providing a convenient mechanism for number and person agreement, unification-based formalisms provide a convenient way of implementing combinatory rules in which X, Y, and so on, can be regarded as variables over categories that can be instantiated or given values by unification with categories like NP or $S \backslash NP$. This observation provides the basis for a transparent implementation of CCG in the form of definite clause grammar (DCG; Pereira and Warren 1980) in programming languages like Prolog (and its higher-order descendant λ-Prolog), and in fact such an implementation has been implicit at a number of points in the exposition above—for instance in the discussion of agreement in chapter 3. A example of a simple (but highly inefficient) program of this kind for use as a proof checker for the feature-based account of directionality that follows is given in Steedman 1991c.

The unification-based implementation has the important attraction of forcing the Principle of Combinatory Type Transparency to apply to combinatory rules interpreted in this way, because of the resemblance between a model-theoretic semantics for unification and the set-theoretic representations of categories (see van Emden and Kowalski 1976; Stirling and Shapiro 1986; Miller 1991, 1995).

One form of DCG equivalent of CFPSG rewrite rules like (34a) is the Prolog inference rule (34b), in which : − is the Prolog leftward logical implication operator, and P0, P1, P are variables over string positions. such as the positions 1, 2, and 3, in (34c) (see Pereira and Shieber 1987 for discussion):

(34) a. $S \;\rightarrow\; NP \; VP$
   b. s(P0,P) : − np(P0,P1),vp(P1,P).
   c. $_1$ dexter $_2$ walks $_3$

The Prolog clause (34b) simply means that there is a sentence between two string positions P0 and P if there is an NP between P0 and some other position P1, and a VP between the latter position and P. This device achieves the effect of declarativizing string position and has the advantage that, if lists are used to represent strings, the Prolog device of difference-list encoding can be used to represent string position implicitly, rather than explicitly as in (34c) (see Pereira and Warren 1980; Stirling and Shapiro 1986).

The basic form of a combinatory rule under the Principle of Adjacency is $\alpha \, \beta \;\Rightarrow\; \gamma$. However, this notation leaves the linear order of α and β implicit. We therefore temporarily expand the notation, replacing categories like *NP* by 4-tuples, of the form $\{\alpha, DP_\alpha, L_\alpha, R_\alpha\}$, comprising (a) a *type* such as *NP*; (b) a *distinguished position*, which we will come to in a minute; (c) a *left-end position*; and (d) a *right-end position*. The latter two elements are the exact equivalent of the DCG positional variables.

The Principle of Adjacency then finds expression in the fact that all legal combinatory rules must have the form in (35), in which the right-end of α is the same as the left-end of β:

(35) $\{\alpha, DP_\alpha, P_1, P_2\} \;\; \{\beta, DP_\beta, P_2, P_3\} \;\; \Rightarrow \;\; \{\gamma, DP_\gamma, P_1, P_3\}$

I will call the position P_2, to which the two categories are adjacent, the "juncture."

The distinguished position of a category is simply the one of its two ends that coincides with the juncture when it is the "canceling" term Y, which from now on we can refer to as the "juncture term" in a combination. A rightward combining function, such as the transitive verb *enjoy*, specifies the distinguished position of its argument (here underlined for salience) as being that argument's *left*-end. So this category is written in full as in (36a), using a *nondirectional slash* /:

(36) a. enjoy := $\{\{VP, DP_{vp}, L_{vp}, R_{vp}\} / \{NP, \underline{L_{np}}, \underline{L_{np}}, R_{np}\}, DP_{verb}, L_{verb}, R_{verb}\}$
   b. enjoy := $\{VP / \{NP, \underline{L_{np}}, \underline{L_{np}}, R_{np}\}, \text{-}, L_{verb}, R_{verb}\}$

The notation in (36a) is rather overwhelming. When positional features are of no immediate relevance in such categories, they will be suppressed, either by representing the whole category by a single symbol or by representing anonymous variables whose identity and binding is of no immediate relevance as "$\_$".[17] For example, when we are thinking of such a function *as* a function, rather than as an argument, we will write it as in (36b), where *VP* stands for $\{VP, DP_{vp}, L_{vp}, R_{vp}\}$ and the distinguished position of the verb is written $\_$. It is important to note that although the binding of the NP argument's distinguished position to its left-end L_{np} means that *enjoy* is a rightward function, the distinguished position is *not* bound to the actual right-end of the verb, R_{verb}, as in the following version of (36b):

(37) *enjoy $:= \{VP/\{NP, \underline{R_{verb}}, \underline{R_{verb}}, R_{np}\}, \_, L_{verb}, \underline{R_{verb}}\}$

It follows that the verb can potentially combine with an argument elsewhere, just so long as it is to the right. This property was crucial to the earlier analysis of heavy NP shift. Coupled with the parallel independence in the position of the result from the position of the verb, it is the point at which CCG parts company with the directional Lambek calculus, as we will see.

In the expanded notation the rule of forward application is written as follows:

(38) $\{\{X, DP_x, P1, P3\}/\{Y, P2, P2, P3\}, \_, P1, P2\}$ $\{Y, P2, P2, P3\}$ $\Rightarrow$ $\{X, DP_x, P1, P3\}$

The fact that the distinguished position must be one of the two ends of an argument category, coupled with the requirement of the Principle of Adjacency, means that *only* the two order-preserving instances of functional application can exist, and only consistent categories can unify with those rules.

A combination under this rule proceeds as follows. Consider example (39), the VP *enjoy musicals*. (In this example the elements are words, but they could be any constituents.)

(39) 1   enjoy   2   musicals   3
$\{VP/\{NP, L_{arg}, L_{arg}, R_{arg}\}, \_, L_{fun}, R_{fun}\}$ $\{NP, DP_{np}, L_{np}, R_{np}\}$

The derivation continues as follows. First the positional variables of the categories are bound by the positions in which the words occur in the string, as in (40), which in the first place we will represent explicitly, as numbered string positions:[18]

(40) 1   enjoy   2   musicals   3
$\{VP/\{NP, L_{arg}, L_{arg}, R_{arg}\}, \_, 1, 2\}$ $\{NP, DP_{np}, 2, 3\}$

Next the combinatory rule (38) applies, to unify the argument term of the function with the real argument, binding the remaining positional variables including the distinguished position, as in (41) and (42):

(41) 1 $\qquad$ enjoy $\qquad$ 2 $\qquad$ musicals $\qquad$ 3

$$\{VP/\{NP,L_{arg},L_{arg},R_{arg}\},\_,1,2\} \qquad \{NP,DP_{np},2,3\}$$
$$\{X/\{Y,P2,P2,P3\},\_,P1,P2\} \qquad \{Y,P2,P2,P3\}$$

(42) 1 $\qquad$ enjoy $\qquad$ 2 $\qquad$ musicals $\qquad$ 3

$$\frac{\{VP/\{NP,2,2,3\},\_,1,2\} \qquad \{NP,2,2,3\}}{\{VP,1,3\}}$$

At the point when the combinatory rule applies, the constraint implicit in the distinguished position must actually hold. That is, the distinguished position must be adjacent to the functor.

Thus, the Consistency property of combinatory rules follows from the Principle of Adjacency, embodied in the identification of the distinguished position of the argument terms with the juncture $P2$, the point to which the two combinands are adjacent, as in the application example (38).

The Principle of Inheritance also follows directly from these assumptions. The fact that rules correspond to combinators like composition forces directionality to be inherited, like any other property of an argument such as being an NP. It follows that only instances of the two very general rules of composition shown in (43) are allowed, as a consequence of the three principles:

(43) a. $\{\{X,DP_x,L_x,R_x\}/\{Y,P2,P2,R_y\},\_,P1,P2\} \quad \{\{Y,P2,P2,R_y\}/\{Z,DP_z,L_z,R_z\},\_,P2,P3\}$

$\qquad \Rightarrow_{\mathbf{B}} \quad \{\{X,DP_x,L_x,R_x\}/\{Z,DP_z,L_z,R_z\},\_,P1,P3\}$

b. $\{\{Y,P2,L_y,P2\}/\{Z,DP_z,L_z,R_z\},\_,P1,P2\} \quad \{\{X,DP_x,L_x,R_x\}/\{Y,P2,L_y,P2\},\_,P2,P3\}$

$\qquad \Rightarrow_{\mathbf{B}} \quad \{\{X,DP_x,L_x,R_x\}/\{Z,DP_z,L_z,R_z\},\_,P1,P3\}$

To conform to the Principle of Consistency, it is necessary that L_y and R_y, the ends of the canceling category Y, be distinct positions—that is, that Y not be coerced to the empty string. This condition has always been explicit in the Principle of Adjacency (Steedman 1987, 405, and see above), although in any Prolog implementation such as that in Steedman 1991c it has to be explicitly imposed. These schemata permit only the four instances of the rules of composition proposed in Steedman 1987 and Steedman 1990, and chapter 4, repeated here as (44) in the basic CCG notation:

(44) *The possible composition rules*

a. $X/Y \quad Y/Z \quad \Rightarrow_{\mathbf{B}} \quad X/Z$ $\qquad\qquad\qquad\qquad$ ($>\mathbf{B}$)

b. $X/Y \quad Y\backslash Z \quad \Rightarrow_{\mathbf{B}} \quad X\backslash Z$ $\qquad\qquad\qquad\qquad$ ($>\mathbf{B}_\times$)

c. $Y\backslash Z \quad X\backslash Y \quad \Rightarrow_{\mathbf{B}} \quad X\backslash Z$ $\qquad\qquad\qquad\qquad$ ($<\mathbf{B}$)

d. $Y/Z \quad X\backslash Y \quad \Rightarrow_{\mathbf{B}} \quad X/Z$ $\qquad\qquad\qquad\qquad$ ($<\mathbf{B}_\times$)

"Crossed" rules like (44b,d) are still allowed (because of the nonidentity noted in the discussion of (36) between the distinguished position of arguments of functions and the position of the function itself). They are distinguished from the corresponding noncrossing rules by further specifying DP_z, the distinguished position on Z.[19] However, no rule violating the Principle of Inheritance, like (27), is allowed: such a rule would require a *different* distinguished position on the two Zs and would therefore not be functional composition at all.[20] This is a desirable result: as shown in the earlier chapters, the non-order-preserving instances (44b, d) are required for the grammar of English and Dutch. In configurational languages like English they must of course be carefully restricted with regard to the categories that may unify with Y.

The implications of the present formalism for the type-raising rules are less obvious. Type-raising rules are unary, and probably lexical, so the Principle of Adjacency does not obviously apply. However, as noted earlier, we only want the *order-preserving* instances (23), in which *the directionality of the raised category is the reverse of that of its argument.* But how can this reversal be anything but an arbitrary property?

Because the directionality constraints are defined in terms of string positions, the distinguished position of the subject argument of a predicate *walks*—that is, the right-edge of that subject—is equivalent to the distinguished position of the predicate that constitutes the argument of an order-preserving raised subject *Dexter*—that is, the *left*-edge of that predicate. It follows that both of the order-preserving rules are instances of the single rule (45) in the extended notation:

(45) $\underline{\{X, DP_{arg}, L_{arg}, R_{arg}\}}$

$\Rightarrow \{T/\{T/\{X, \underline{DP_{arg}, L_{arg}, R_{arg}}\}, DP_{arg}, L_{pred}, R_{pred}\}, -, \underline{L_{arg}, R_{arg}}\}$

The crucial property of this rule, which forces its instances to be order-preserving, is that *the distinguished-position variable DP_{arg} on the argument of the predicate in the raised category is the same as that on the argument of the raised category itself.* (The two distinguished positions are underlined in (45).) Notice that this choice forces the raised NP and its argument to be string adjacent; it is exactly the opposite choice from the one that we took in allowing lexical categories like (36) to unify with arguments anywhere in the specified direction.[21] Of course, the position is unspecified at the time the rule applies, and it is simply represented as an unbound unification variable with an arbitrary mnemonic identifier. However, when the category combines with a predicate, this variable will be bound by the directionality specified in the predicate itself. Since this condition will be transmitted to the raised category, *it will have to coincide with the juncture of the combination.* Combination of the categories in the nongrammatical order will therefore fail, just as if the original categories were combining without the mediation of type-raising.

Consider the following example. Under rule (45), the categories of the words in the sentence *Dexter walks* are as shown in (46), before binding.

(46) 1   Dexter   2   walks   3
$\{S/\{S/\{NP,DP_g,L_g,R_g\},DP_g,L_{pred},R_{pred}\},-,L_g,R_g\}$ $\{S/\{NP,R_{np},L_{np},R_{np}\},DP_w,L_w,R_w\}$

Binding of string positional variables yields the categories in (47).

(47) 1   Dexter   2   walks   3
$\{S/\{S/\{NP,DP_g,1,2\},DP_g,L_{pred},R_{pred}\},-,1,2\}$ $\{S/\{NP,R_{np},L_{np},R_{np}\},DP_w,2,3\}$

The combinatory rule of forward application (38) applies as in (48), binding further variables by unification. In particular, DP_g, R_{np}, DP_w, and $P2$ are all bound to the juncture position 2, as in (49):

(48) 1   Dexter   2   walks   3
$\{S/\{S/\{NP,DP_g,1,2\},DP_g,L_{pred},R_{pred}\},-,1,2\}$ $\{S/\{NP,R_{np},L_{np},R_{np}\},DP_w,2,3\}$
$\{X/\{Y,P2,P2,P3\},-,P1,P2\}$ $\{Y,P2,P2,P3\}$

(49) 1   Dexter   2   walks   3
$\{S/\{S/\{NP,2,1,2\},2,2,3\},1,2\}$ $\{S/\{NP,2,1,2\},2,2,3\}$
───
$\{S,1,3\}$

By contrast, the same categories in the opposite linear order fail to unify with any combinatory rule. In particular, the backward application rule fails, as in (50):

(50) 1   *Walks   2   Dexter   3
$\{S/\{NP,R_{np},L_{np},R_{np}\},-,1,2\}$ $\{S/\{S/\{NP,DP_g,2,3\},DP_g,L_{pred},R_{pred}\},-,2,3\}$
$\{Y,P2,P1,P2\}$ $\{X/\{Y,P2,P1,P2\},-,P2,P3\}$

(Combination is blocked because 2 cannot unify with 3.)

On the assumption implicit in (45), the only permitted instances of type-raising are the two rules given earlier as (23). The earlier results concerning word order universals under coordination are therefore captured. Moreover, we can now think of these two rules as a single underspecified order-preserving rule directly corresponding to (45), which we might write less long-windedly as follows, augmenting the original simplest notation with a vertical "order-preserving" slash | to distinguish it from the undifferentiated nondirectional slash /:

(51) *The Order-preserving type-raising rule*
$$X \quad \Rightarrow_T \quad T|(T|X)$$

The category that results from this rule can combine in either direction, but will always preserve order. Such a property is extremely desirable in a language like English, whose verb requires some arguments to the right and some to the left, but whose NPs do not bear case. The general raised category can combine in both directions, but will still preserve word order. Like Zeevat's (1988) rule, it thus eliminates what was earlier noted as a worrying extra degree of categorial ambiguity. As under that proposal, the way is now clear to incorporate type-raising directly into the lexicon, substituting categories of the form $T|(T|X)$, where X is a category like *NP* or *PP*, directly into the lexicon in place of the basic categories, or (more readably, but less efficiently), to keep the basic categories and the rule (51), and exclude the base categories from all combination. Most importantly, we avoid Zeevat's undesirable assumption that the English lexicon is OVS, thus ensuring continued good relations with generations of language learners to come.

Although the order-preserving constraint is very simply imposed, it is in one sense an additional stipulation, imposed by the form of the type-raising rule (45). We could have used a unique variable—say, DP_{pred}—in the crucial position in (45), unrelated to the positional condition DP_{arg} on the argument of the predicate itself, to define the distinguished position of the predicate-argument of the raised category, as in (52):

(52) $*\{X, DP_{arg}, L_{arg}, R_{arg}\} \Rightarrow$
      $\{T/\{T/\{X, \underline{DP_{arg}}, L_{arg}, R_{arg}\}, \underline{DP_{pred}}, L_{pred}, R_{pred}\}, -, L_{arg}, R_{arg}\}$

However, this tactic would yield a completely unconstrained type-raising rule, whose result category could not merely be substituted throughout the lexicon for ground categories like *NP* without grammatical collapse. (Such categories immediately induce totally free word order—for example, permitting (50) on the English lexicon.)

Although it is conceivable that such non-order-preserving type-raised categories might figure in grammars for extremely nonconfigurational languages, such languages are usually characterized by the presence of *some* fixed elements. It seems likely that type-raising is universally confined to the order-preserving kind and that the sources of so-called free word order lie elsewhere.[22]

Such a constraint can therefore be understood in terms of the present proposal simply as a requirement for the lexicon itself to be consistent. It should also be observed that a single uniformly order-*changing* category of the kind proposed by Zeevat (1988) is not possible under this theory.

That is not to say that more specific order-changing categories cannot be defined in this notation. As noted earlier, in a non-verb-final language such as English the object relative-pronoun must have the category written in the basic notation as $(N\backslash N)/(S/NP)$, which is closely related to a type-raised category. In the extended notation, and abbreviating $N\backslash N$ as R, this category is the following:

(53) whom := $\{R/\{T/\{X, \underline{L_{arg}}, L_{arg}, R_{arg}\}, \underline{L_{pred}}, L_{pred}, R_{pred}\}, \text{-}, L_{arg}, R_{arg}\}$

In fact, provided we constrain forward crossed composition correctly, as we must for any grammar of English, the following slightly less specific category will do for the majority dialect of English in which there is no distinction between subject and object relative-pronouns *who*, or for the un-case-marked relative-pronoun *that*:

(54) who/that := $\{R/\{T/\{X, \underline{DP_{arg}}, L_{arg}, R_{arg}\}, \underline{L_{pred}}, L_{pred}, R_{pred}\}, \text{-}, L_{arg}, R_{arg}\}$

In the former category both the complement function and its argument are specified as being on the right. In the latter, the directionality of the complement argument is unspecified. Thus, we need look no further than the relative-pronouns of well-attested dialects of English to see exploited in full all the degrees of freedom that the theory allows us to specify various combinations of order-preserving and non-order-preserving type-raising in a single lexical category.

The account of pied-piping proposed by Szabolcsi (1989), to which the reader is directed for details, is also straightforwardly compatible with the present proposal.[23]

Chapter 9
Processing in Context

[After the second word of Tom wanted to ask Susan to bake a cake*] we have in the semantics a function, which we might call (*Tom want*). …If the parser is forced to make a choice between alternative analyses, it may make reference in this choice to semantics.*
John Kimball, "Predictive Analysis and Over-the-Top Parsing"

To account for coordination, unbounded dependency, and Intonation Structure, strictly within the confines of the Constituent Condition on Rules, we have been led in parts I and II of the book to a view of Surface Structure according to which strings like *Anna married* and *thinks that Anna married* are constituents in the fullest sense of the term. As we have repeatedly observed, it follows that they must also potentially be constituents of noncoordinate sentences like *Anna married Manny* and *Harry thinks that Anna married Manny*. For moderately complex sentences there will in consequence be a large number of nonstandard alternative derivations for any given reading.

We should continue to resist the natural temptation to reject this claim out of hand on the grounds that it is at odds with much linguistic received opinion. We have already seen in earlier chapters that on many tests for constituency— for example, the list cited in (1) of chapter 2—the combinatory theory does better than most. The temptation to reject the proposal on the basis of parsing efficiency should similarly be resisted. It is true that the presence of such semantic equivalence classes of derivations engenders rather more nondeterminism in the grammar than may have previously been suspected. Although this makes writing parsers a little less straightforward than might have been expected, it should be clear that this novel form of nondeterminism really is a property of English and all other natural languages and will be encountered by any theory with the same coverage with respect to coordination and intonational phenomena. It is also worth remembering that natural grammars show no sign of any pressure to minimize nondeterminism elsewhere in the grammar. There is therefore no a priori reason to doubt the competence theory on these grounds.

The only conclusion we can draw from the profusion of grammatical nondeterminism is that the mechanism for coping with it must be very powerful.

This chapter will argue that the most important device for dealing with nondeterminism in the human processor is a process of eliminating partial analyses whose interpretation is inconsistent with knowledge of the domain under discussion and the discourse context.

The chapter will also claim that combinatory grammars are particularly well suited to the incremental, essentially word-by-word assembly of semantic interpretations, for use with this "interactive" parsing tactic. Any attempt to argue for the present theory of competence and against any other on the basis of this last observation alone would be fallacious. The methodological priority of competence arguments remains unassailable, and none of the theories currently on offer, including this one, have yet come close to descriptive adequacy as competence theories. Since all of them are compatible in principle with incremental interpretation in this sense of the term, all bets are off until the question of descriptive adequacy has been settled.

Nevertheless, we can draw the following weaker conclusion. If the program sketched in this book is ultimately successful, and CCG, together with the view of constituency and syntactic structure that it implicates, is in the end vindicated as a descriptively adequate theory of competence grammar, then it is likely that it will also be very simply and directly related to the parser as well. In other words, if it is descriptively adequate, then it is probably explanatorily adequate as well.

9.1 Anatomy of a Processor

All language-processors can be viewed as made up of three elements. The first is a grammar, which defines how constituents combine to yield other constituents. The second is an algorithm for applying the rules of the grammar to a string. The third is an oracle, or mechanism for resolving nondeterminism. The oracle decides which rule of grammar to apply at points in the analysis where the nondeterministic algorithm allows more than one rule to apply. The following sections briefly discuss these elements in turn.[1]

9.1.1 Grammar
The strong competence hypothesis as originally stated by Bresnan and Kaplan (1982) assumes that the grammar that is used by or implicit in the human sentence processor is the competence grammar itself. It is important to be clear that this is an assumption, not a logical requirement. The processors that we design ourselves (such as compilers for programming languages) quite often

do not exhibit this property. There is no logical necessity for the structures involved in processing a programming language to have anything to do with the structures that are implicated by its competence grammar—that is, the syntactic rules in the reference manual that are associated with its semantics. The compiler or interpreter can parse according to a quite different grammar, provided that there exists a computable homomorphism mapping the structures of this "covering grammar" onto the structures of the competence grammar. If the homomorphism is simple, so that the computational costs of parsing according to the covering grammar plus the costs of computing the mapping are less than the costs of parsing according to the competence grammar, then there may be a significant practical advantage in this tactic. For this reason, it is quite common for compilers and interpreters to parse according to a weakly equivalent covering grammar, mapping to the "real" grammar via a homomorphism under concatenation on a string representing the derivation under the covering grammar. For example, programming language compilers sometimes work like this, when a parsing algorithm that is desirable for reasons of efficiency demands grammars in a normal form that is not adhered to by the grammar in the reference manual (see Gray and Harrison 1972; Nijholt 1980). Such a situation also arises in artificial parsers for natural languages, when it is desired to use top-down algorithms, which can be ill suited to the left-recursive rules that commonly occur in natural grammars (see Kuno 1966 for an early example). As Berwick and Weinberg (1984, esp. 78-82) note, there is therefore no logical necessity for the structures involved in human syntactic processing to have anything to do with the structures that are implicated by the competence grammar—that is, the structures that support the semantics.

Nevertheless, similar considerations of parsimony in the theory of language evolution and language development to those invoked earlier might also lead us to expect that, as a matter of fact, a close relation is likely to hold between the competence grammar and the structures dealt with by the psychological processor, and that it will in fact incorporate the competence grammar in a modular fashion. One reason that has been frequently invoked is that language development in children is extremely fast and gives the appearance of proceeding via the piecemeal addition, substitution, and modification of individual rules and categories of competence grammar. Any addition of, or change to, a rule of competence grammar will not in general correspond to a similarly modular change in a covering grammar. Instead, the entire ensemble of competence rules will typically have to be recompiled into a new covering grammar. Even if we assume that the transformation of one grammar into another is determined by a language-independent algorithm and can be computed each time at negligible cost, we have still sacrificed parsimony in the theory and increased the burden of explanation on the theory of evolution. In particular, it is quite unclear why the development of either of the principal components of the theory in isolation should confer any selective advantage. The competence grammar is by assumption unprocessable, and the covering grammar is by assumption uninterpretable. It looks as though they can only evolve as a unified system, together with the translation process. This is likely to be harder than to evolve a strictly competence-based system.[2]

Indeed, the first thing we would have to explain is why a covering grammar was necessary in the first place. The reference grammars of programming languages are constrained by human requirements rather than the requirements of the machines that process them. Such grammars can be ill suited to parsing with the particular algorithms that we happen to be clever enough to think of and to be able to implement on that kind of machine. It is we humans who find requirements like Greibach Normal Form tedious and who prefer grammars with left-recursive rules, forcing the use of covering grammars on some artificial processors. If convenience to the available computing machinery were the only factor determining the form of computer languages, then their grammars would take a form that would not require the use of a covering grammar at all. It is quite unclear what external force could have the effect of making natural grammars ill-matched to the *natural* sentence processor.[3]

It is important to note that the strong competence hypothesis as stated by Bresnan and Kaplan imposes no further constraint on the processor. In particular, it does not limit the structures built by the processor to fully instantiated constituents. However, the Strict Competence Hypothesis proposed in this book imposes this stronger condition.[4] The reasoning behind this strict version is again evolutionary. If in order to process sentences we need more than the grammar itself, even a perfectly general "compiler" that turns grammars into algorithms dealing in other structures, then the load on evolution is increased. Similar arguments for the need for the grammar and processor to evolve in lockstep mean that a theory that keeps such extras to the minimum is preferred.

This strict version of the strong competence hypothesis has the effect of generalizing the Constituent Condition on Rules to cover the processor. The claim is that the constituents that are recognized in the grammar (and their interpretations) will be the only structures the processor will give evidence of. Anything else we are forced to postulate is an extra assumption and will require an independent explanation if it is not to count against the theory. Of course, such an explanation may be readily forthcoming. But if it is not, then it will remain a challenge to explanatory adequacy.

9.1.2 The Algorithm

If we believe that the natural processor must incorporate the competence grammar directly, what more must it include? According to the assumptions with which this section began, it must include a nondeterministic algorithm that will apply the rules of the grammar to accept or reject the string, together with some extra apparatus for simultaneously building a structure representing its analysis. Provided that the competence grammar is monotonic, this structure can be the semantic translation itself, rather than a strictly syntactic structure. Under this view (which has been standard in computational linguistics at least since Woods's (1970) ATN), a syntactic derivation is simply a trace of the way in which this interpretable structure was built.

The processor must also include an oracle (dealt with in section 9.1.3) to resolve the nondeterminism that the grammar allows (or at least rank the alternatives) for the algorithm. A theory will be successful to the extent that both of these components can be kept as minimal and as language-independent as possible. For this reason, we should be very careful to exclude the possibility that either the algorithm or the oracle covertly embeds rules of a grammar other than the competence grammar.

There are of course a great many algorithms for any given theory of grammar, even when we confine ourselves to the simpler alternatives. They may work top-down and depth-first through the rules of the grammar, or work bottom up from the string via the rules, or employ some mixture of the two strategies. For obvious reasons, most parsers with any claim to psychological realism work from the earliest elements of the sentence to the last, or (for the present orthography) leftmost-first, but alternatives are possible here, too.

Such algorithms require an automaton, including a working memory such as the chart mechanism discussed below, in addition to the competence grammar and a mechanism for eliminating nondeterminism. For context-free grammars the automaton is a pushdown automaton. For the classes of grammars treated in this book, it is Vijay-Shanker and Weir's (1990; 1994) generalization of the same device, the extended pushdown automaton, also discussed below. The question we must ask under the strict competence hypothesis is, how little more can we get away with? In particular, can we get away with nothing more than the theoretical minimum—that is, an algorithm that does not need to know about anything except rules of grammar, the string, and the state of the stack and the working memory, subject to the adjudication of the oracle?

CCGs are very directly compatible with one of the simplest classes of algorithm, namely, the binary-branching bottom-up algorithms. They are most easily understood by considering in turn: (a) a nondeterministic shift-reduce parser, and (b) a chart-based deterministic left-right incremental version of the Cocke-Kasami-Younger (CKY) algorithm (Cocke and Schwartz 1970; Harrison 1978).[5]

The nondeterministic leftmost-first shift-reduce algorithm can be stated as follows:

(1) 1. Initialize the stack to the empty stack and make a pointer point to position 0 in the string, before the first word.

2. As long as there are any words left in the string or a combinatory rule can apply to the topmost item(s) on the stack **either:**

   a. Put on the stack (shift) a category corresponding to the word that starts at the pointed-to position, **or:**

   b. Apply the combinatory rule to the topmost categories on the stack and replace them by its result (reduce).

For a simple sentence, *Thieves love watches,* this algorithm allows an analysis via the sequence shift, shift, reduce, shift, reduce (for simplicity, NPs are shown as lexically raised):

(2)

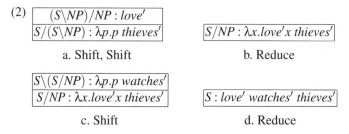

$$(S\backslash NP)/NP : love'$$
$$S/(S\backslash NP) : \lambda p.p\ thieves'$$

a. Shift, Shift

$$S/NP : \lambda x.love'x\ thieves'$$

b. Reduce

$$S\backslash(S/NP) : \lambda p.p\ watches'$$
$$S/NP : \lambda x.love'x\ thieves'$$

c. Shift

$$S : love'\ watches'\ thieves'$$

d. Reduce

One (very bad) way of making this algorithm deterministic is to choose a default strategy for resolving shift-reduce ambiguities—say, "reduce-first"— and to keep a trail of parse states including alternatives not taken, backtracking to earlier states and trying the alternatives when the analysis blocks. This will cope with the fact that all three words in the sentence are ambiguous between nouns and verbs. However, if we want to be sure that we have found not only *an* analysis, but in fact *all possible* analyses of the sentence, we must restart the process and backtrack again until all possible avenues have been examined and no choices are left on the trail. Because naive backtracking parsers examine all possible paths in the search space, they are time-exponential in the number of words in the sentence. The source of this exponential cost lies in the algorithm's tendency to repeat identical analyses of the same substring, as when, the algorithm having mistakenly chosen the auxiliary category for the first word of the following sentence and having failed to find an analysis at the word *take*, the entire analysis of the arbitrarily complex subject NP has to be unwound and then repeated once the alternative of analyzing the first word as a main verb is taken (the example is from Marcus (1980)):

(3) Have *the students who missed the exam* take the makeup.

Because of the extra nondeterminism induced by type-raising and the associative composition rules, there is even more nondeterminism in CCG than in other grammars, so even for quite small fragments, particularly those that involve coordination, naive backtracking parsers are in practice unusable. Unlike standard grammars and parsing algorithms, because of the associativity of functional composition and the semantics of combinatory rules, CCG derivations fall into equivalence classes, with several derivations yielding identical interpretations.[6] Of course, it does not matter which member of any equivalence class we find, so long as we find some member of each. However, the search space is unacceptably large, and to ensure that we have found at least one member of all possible equivalence classes of derivation for a string of words, we are still threatened by having to search the entire space.

Karttunen (1989), Pareschi and Steedman (1987), and Pareschi (1989) discuss the use of a "chart" (Kay 1980) to reduce the search space for combinatory parsers. Chart parsing is by origin a technique for parsing CFPSG using a data structure in which all constituents that have been found so far are kept, indexed by the position of their left and right edge or boundary in the string. Each chart entry identifies the type of the constituent in question. It is common to refer to chart entries as "arcs" or "edges" and to represent the chart as a graph or network. We will be interested in the possibility that the chart may also associate other information with an arc or entry, such as the predicate-argument structure of the constituent. (For a sentence of length n, this chart can be conveniently represented as an $n \times n$ half-matrix with sets of categories as entries.)

Using a chart overcomes the main source of exponential costs in naive backtracking, arising from repeated identical analyses of a given substring. In the case of mere recognition, it is enough to make one entry in the table for a constituent of a given type spanning a given substring. For the task of finding all distinct parses of a sentence, the chart must include an entry for each distinct analysis spanning that substring.

Since even context-free grammars can approach bracketing completeness, and do so in practice for constructions like multiple noun compounding, to similarly reduce the worst-case complexity of the parsing problem to n^3 requires the use of structure-sharing techniques to produce a "shared forest" of analyses using linked lists (see Cocke and Schwartz 1970; Earley 1970; Pratt 1975; Tomita 1987; Billot and Lang 1989; Dörre 1997).

As noted earlier, because of the associative nature of function composition, CCG parsers will potentially deliver structurally distinct derivations for a constituent of a given type and interpretation spanning a given substring—the property that is misleadingly referred to as "spurious" ambiguity.[7] If multiple equivalent analyses are entered into the chart, then they too will engender an explosion in computational costs. To the extent that CCGs approximate the bracketing completeness of the Lambek calculus version, the number of derivations will proliferate as the Catalan function of the length of the sentence—essentially exponentially.

Pareschi, following Karttunen, proposed to eliminate such redundancies via a check for constituents of the same type and interpretation, using unification. Any new constituent resulting from a reduction of existing constituents whose predicate-argument structure was identical to one already existing in the chart would not be added to it. This reduces the worst-case complexity of combinatory parsing/recognition for the context-free case to the same as that for standard context-free grammars without "spurious" ambiguity—that is, to n^3, with the same proviso that interpretation structures are shared, and with a constant overhead for the redundant reductions and for the unification-based matching entry check.[8]

Vijay-Shanker and Weir (1994) discuss the problem of generalizing the context-free algorithms to mildly context-sensitive formalisms including the present one. Because such grammars potentially introduce infinitely many nonterminal categories, generalizing the CKY algorithm discussed below to deal with them potentially makes it worst-case exponential, unless a technique of structure sharing of category entries that they describe is used. It should not be forgotten that this is strictly a worst-case complexity result. As always, caution is needed in drawing conclusions for practical average-case complexity. Komagata (1997a) suggests that average-case recognition complexity for significant practical grammar fragments for Japanese and English is roughly cubic, so that the overhead of Vijay-Shanker and Weir's technique may not be worthwhile in practical applications.

As a first step toward defining a psychologically reasonable parser, it is instructive to see a trace of an algorithm of this kind, the left-to-right breadth-first bottom-up context-free chart parser. This can be defined in terms of an algorithm that can be informally stated as follows.[9]

(4) 1. Initialize the chart to the empty chart, and make a pointer point to position 0 in the string, before the first word.
  2. Until the end of the sentence is reached:
     a. Add entries corresponding to all categories of the word that starts at the pointed-to position. Make the pointer point to the next position in the sentence.
     b. As long as there is a pair of entries in the chart that can reduce, do the reduction and add an entry representing the result to the chart, unless the matching-entry test reveals that an equivalent entry is already present.

Since by definition shifting a new lexical category for the jth word can only induce new reductions to give categories whose right boundary is at position j in the sentence, an efficient way of carrying out step 2 is to ask for all i where $0 \leq i \leq (j - 2)$ whether there are any such reductions. This in turn means asking for all k where $i < k < j$ whether there are entries spanning (i, k) and (k, j) that reduce. Since adding a new entry (i, j) during this process may itself enable further reductions, it is necessary to compute the new entries (i, j) bottom up—that is, by starting with $i = j - 2$ and stepping down to $i = 0$. Hence, we can state the algorithm more completely and formally as follows, where *present* is the test for a matching entry already in the table, and A, B, C are category-interpretation pairs of the form $\Sigma : \Lambda$ where Σ is a syntactic category such as *NP* or *S/NP*, and Λ is a predicate-argument structure:

(5) 1. **for** $j := 1$ **to** n **do**
     begin
     $t(j - 1, j) := \{A | A \text{ is a lexical category for } a_j\}$
  2. **for** $i := j - 2$ **down to** 0 **do**
     begin
  3. $t(i, j) \quad := \quad \{A | \text{there exists } k, i < k < j, \text{ such that } B\ C \Rightarrow A \text{ for some}$
     $\qquad\qquad\qquad B \in t(i, k), C \in t(k, j), \text{ and not } present(A, i, j)\}$
     end
     end

This algorithm is complete, in the sense that it finds all possible grammatical constituents and all complete analyses for the sentence.

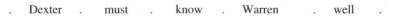

Figure 9.1
The start-state: string and empty chart

Figure 9.2
Shift *Dexter*, shift *must*, reduce

Imagine that such a parser is faced with the sentence *Dexter must know Warren well*, and suppose (simplifying) that all words have a unique category, including the adverb *well* which is a VP modifier with the single category *VP\VP*. The reduce-first strategy goes through the following stages. Since the chart is initially empty, as in figure 9.1, nothing can happen until categories have been shifted to the chart for the first two words, *Dexter must*. At that point a single reduction is possible via the composition rule, leaving the chart in the state shown in figure 9.2. No further reductions are possible, so we shift a category for the next word, *know*. Two new reductions are now permitted, again via the composition rule. One of these is with the previously shifted modal, $(S\backslash NP)/VP$, and one with the result of the previous reduction, S/VP. The first induces a result that can further reduce with the subject, but this yields a result equivalent to the second in predicate-argument structural terms, so one or the other is detected to be redundant. No further reductions are possible, so the state is as in figure 9.3. We must shift a category for the word *Warren*, a shift that precipitates reductions and new entries as shown in figure 9.4. These include a number of redundant constituents that will take part in no grammatical analysis, including the *S, Dexter must know Warren*. Many of them have multiple analyses that must be detected by the matching check (or preempted by some other mechanism such as the normal form parsers that Hepple and Morrill (1989), Hendriks (1993), König (1994), and Eisner (1996) have proposed). Finally we shift a category for the adverb and halt in the state shown with a single S spanning positions 0 through 5, as in figure 9.5.

This derivation reveals the tendency for bottom-up parsers to build unnecessary constituents, here typified by the spurious *S, Dexter must know Warren*. Even the comparative simplicity of the derivation described above is mislead-

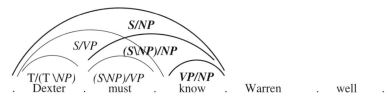

Figure 9.3
Shift *know*, reduce, reduce

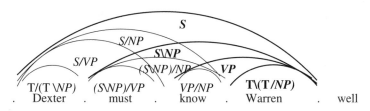

Figure 9.4
Shift *Warren*, reduce, reduce, reduce

ing in this respect. There is at least one other category for *Warren* (namely, the *subject* type-raised category), and it can combine with another category for *know* (namely, VP/S). In more complex sentences such fruitless analyses will proliferate.

However, this example serves to reify some of the main components of a practical parser, in preparation for the discussion of how this sort of device could be made more like a human processor. Human beings are rarely aware of lexical or global syntactic ambiguity in the sentences that they process, and they rarely encounter difficulty arising from nondeterminism in the grammar. How can this be? There was a broad hint in chapter 5, where we saw that intonational boundaries can on occasion reduce the ambiguity of CCG derivation. Although such indicators are frequently missing, the occasions on which they *are* missing can plausibly be argued to be exactly the occasions on which the Information Structure, and therefore some important aspects of Surface Structure, can be assumed to be known to the hearer. Perhaps there are other sources of information that mean that redundant structure building and proliferation of categories exemplified above can be eliminated for the benefit of the parser.

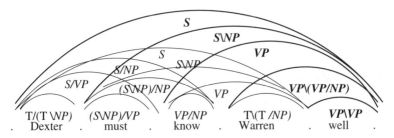

Figure 9.5
Shift *well*, reduce, reduce, halt

9.1.3 The Oracle

Nothing about the expected close relation between syntax and semantics entails that the mapping should be unambiguous, even though the grammars for artificial languages we design ourselves typically permit only the most local of nondeterminism, because they are designed for use as formal calculi. Expressions in natural languages seem to be remarkably free with ambiguity, both global and local, as in the following famous examples;

(6) Flying planes can be dangerous.

(7) a. Have the students taken the exam?
    b. Have the students take the exam!

In the latter example, from Marcus 1980, the substring *have the students* is (syntactically and semantically) locally ambiguous, in the sense that a processor cannot immediately know which rule of grammar to apply after encountering it. Human beings seem to be remarkably adept at resolving such ambiguities, which are astonishingly profuse in natural language.[10]

Probably for the same reason, we do as a matter of fact tend to design our artificial languages in ways that make their symbols "locally" ambiguous, either in terms of which rule of syntax should apply, or in terms of which rule of semantics should apply. (An example of the latter is the "overloading" of an operator like + to denote distinct operations applying to integers, real numbers, and complex numbers.) The one lesson that we can derive from our experience with artificial languages and processors like compilers is that such ambiguities must be resolvable quickly and locally if the computational complexity of processing is to be contained.

In order to facilitate this requirement, programming languages are invariably carefully designed so that local ambiguity can be resolved immediately, either syntactically by examining the next symbol in the string, or semantically by examining the types of functions and arguments (as in the case of overloading above). However, natural language shows no sign of any such constraint from within grammar. For example, although the locally ambiguous substring *Have the students* ... in (7) is disambiguated by the phrase *take/taken the exam*, an indefinite amount of further linguistic material may intervene between the ambiguous substring and the disambiguating information, as when the sentences begin *Have the students who were late with the homework* ..., *Have the students who were late with the homework that I assigned last Monday* ..., and so on. This apparent nondeterminism in the grammar is an anomaly that requires further explanation, for if we allow the ambiguities to proliferate, then the costs of maintaining the alternatives will explode. Indeed, as Marcus points out, we must be able to eliminate all but some bounded number of alternative paths on the basis of purely local evidence, since there is no evidence that processing load increases as a worse-than-linear function of sentence length. I will call the device that eliminates nondeterminism, and decrees which rule of the grammar should be invoked at any point in the derivation, an "oracle." However this device works, it is clear that it must be very effective in order to deal with the degree of nondeterminism that natural grammars exhibit. Moreover, as noted earlier, it must also be entirely language-independent, if it is not to compromise the parsimony and modularity of the theory of the processor.

Most accounts of the human sentence-processing mechanism have assumed that local attachment ambiguity resolution is based on structural criteria, such as parsing "strategies" (Fodor, Bever and Garrett 1974; Kimball 1973), structural preferences (Frazier 1978), rule orderings (Wanner 1980), lexical preferences (Ford, Bresnan and Kaplan 1982), or lookahead (Marcus 1980). Such accounts have been claimed to explain a wide range of sentence-processing phenomena, the most spectacular of which is undoubtedly the identification by Bever (1970) of the "garden path phenomenon"—that is, the existence of sentences like the following, for which a local ambiguity is *mis*resolved in a way that makes a perfectly grammatical sentence unanalyzable:

(8) The horse raced past the barn fell.

However, such accounts have generally been characterized either by empirical shortcomings or by proliferation of devices and degrees of freedom in the theory (see e.g. the exchange between Frazier and Fodor (1978), and Wanner

(1980)). In particular, since the earliest stages of the inquiry, it has been clear that all human parsing phenomena are extremely sensitive to the influence of semantics and especially referential context. Bever (1970) notes a difference in the strength of the garden path effect in minimal pairs of sentences analogous to the following, raising the possibility of an influence either from different word transition probabilities or from the related differing pragmatic plausibility of analyzing the initial NP as a subject of the ambiguous verb/participle *sent*:

(9) a. The doctor sent for the patient arrived.
     b. The flowers sent for the patient arrived.

Various computational proposals have been made for how pragmatic plausibility might have this effect via a "weak" interaction between syntax and semantics, using a filtering process of comparing rival partial analyses on the basis of their success or failure in referring to entities in the model or discourse context (see Winograd 1972 and Hirst 1987). In particular, Crain and Steedman (1985) and Altmann and Steedman (1988) proposed a criterion for selecting among analyses called the "Principle of Parsimony," which can be stated as follows:

(10) *The Principle of Parsimony*
      The analysis whose interpretation carries fewest unsatisfied but accommodatable presuppositions or consistent entailments will be preferred.

These authors use the term "presupposition" in the "pragmatic" sense of Stalnaker (1974) and Lewis (1979), and explain this principle in terms of the associated notion of accommodation of unsatisfied presuppositions. They point out that the two analyses of sentence (8), which differ according to whether it begins with a simple NP *the horse* or a complex NP *the horse raced past the barn*, also differ in the number of horses whose existence in the model they presuppose (one or more than one) and in the number of properties that they assume to distinguish them—none in the case of the singleton horse, and being caused to race along a given path in contrast to some other property in the case of multiple horses. They argue that contexts which already support one or the other set of presuppositions—say, because a single horse has previously been mentioned, or several horses and some racing—will favor the related analysis at the point of ambiguity and thereby either induce or eliminate the garden path for this sentence under the Principle of Parsimony. Crucially, they also argue that the empty context, in which *no* horses and no racing have been mentioned, will favor the simplex NP analysis, because its interpretation carries fewer unsatisfied but consistent presuppositions and is therefore easiest to accommodate. The principle accordingly predicts a garden path in the empty context.

In support of this view, Crain and Steedman (1985) offer experimental evidence that attachment preferences are under the control of referential context. Subjects were presented with minimal pairs of target sentences displaying local attachment ambiguities, preceded by contexts that established either two referents, respectively with and without a distinguishing property, or one referent with that property. Examples (modified from the original) are as follows:

(11) a. *Contexts:*
         i. A psychologist was counseling two women. He was worried about one of them, but not about the other.
        ii. A psychologist was counseling a man and a woman. He was worried about one of them, but not about the other.
      b. *Targets:*
         i. The psychologist told the woman that he was having trouble with *her husband.*
        ii. The psychologist told the woman that he was having trouble with *to visit him again.*

Both target sentences have a local ambiguity at the word *that*, which is resolved only when the italicized words are encountered. Frazier's (1978) Minimal Attachment Principle would predict that the second target would always cause a garden path. In fact, however, this garden path effect is eliminated when the sentence is preceded by the first context, which satisfies the presupposition of the relative-clause analysis. Moreover, a garden path effect is induced in the first target when it is preceded by the same context, because by the same token it fails to support the presupposition that there is a unique woman. Crain and Steedman (1985) also confirmed certain related predictions concerning the effect of definiteness on garden paths in the null context. The experiments were repeated and extended with improved materials by Altmann (1988) and Altmann and Steedman (1988), and the effect has been show to be robust across a number of experimental measures of processing load including brain-imaging and Event-Related Potential (ERP) measures (van Berkum, Brown and Hagoort 1999).

Whereas examples like (9) are compatible with an alternative explanation based on word transition probabilities and higher-order statistics of the language, these experiments showing effects of referential context with minimal pairs of targets are much harder to plausibly account for in this way.

The majority of early psycholinguistic experiments on processing loads used only empty contexts, and therefore failed to control for this sort of effect. However, more recent experiments (see e.g. Carroll, Tanenhaus and Bever 1978; Tanenhaus 1978; Marslen-Wilson, Tyler and Seidenberg 1978; Swinney 1979; Tanenhaus, Leiman and Seidenberg 1979; Crain 1980; Altmann 1985; Trueswell, Tanenhaus and Kello 1993; Trueswell, Tanenhaus and Garnsey 1994; Spivey-Knowlton, Trueswell and Tanenhaus 1993; Sedivy and Spivey-Knowlton 1993; and van Berkum, Brown and Hagoort 1999) have now built up a considerable body of evidence that effects of semantics, knowledge-based plausibility, and referential context are extremely strong. Indeed, almost all theories of performance nowadays admit that some such component, in the form of a "thematic processor" (Frazier 1989), "construal" (Frazier and Clifton 1996), or the equivalent, can intervene at an early stage of processing. The only remaining area of disagreement is whether anything *else* besides this potentially very powerful source of ambiguity resolution is actually required. (See the exchange between Clifton and Ferreira (1989) and Steedman and Altmann (1989)). For, if interpretations are available at every turn in sentence processing, then there is every reason to suppose that the local syntactic ambiguities that abound in natural language sentences may be resolved by taking into account the appropriateness of those interpretations to the context of utterance, even when the rival analyses are in traditional terms incomplete. Indeed, the possibility that human language-processors are able to draw on the information implicit in the context or discourse model seems to offer the only mechanism powerful enough to handle the astonishing profusion of local and global ambiguities that human languages allow and to explain the fact that human language users are so rarely aware of them. Such a selective or "weak" interaction between syntactic processing and semantic interpretation is entirely modular, as J.A. Fodor (1983, 78 and 135) points out.

If interpretation in context is the basis of local ambiguity resolution, then a number of further properties of the parser follow. The felicity of an interpretation with respect to a context is not an all-or-none property, comparable to syntactic well-formedness. Utterances are often surprising—indeed, they are infelicitous if they are *not* at least somewhat novel in content. It follows that evaluation in context can only yield information about the *relative* good fit of various alternatives. We might therefore expect the parser to use a tactic known as "beam-search," whereby at a point of local ambiguity, all alternative analyses permitted by the grammar are proposed in parallel, and their interpretations are then evaluated in parallel. Readings that fail to refer or are otherwise implausible are discarded or ranked lower than ones that are consistent with what is known, along the lines suggested earlier (see Gibson 1996; Collins 1997, 1998; Charniak, Goldwater and Johnson 1998.) The parsing process then proceeds with the best candidate(s), all others being discarded or interrupted. (A similar tactic is widely used in automatic speech processing to eliminate the large numbers of spurious candidates that are thrown up in word recognition; see Lee 1989).

On the assumption that the number of alternative analyses that can be maintained at any one time is strictly limited, we can also assume that the process of semantic filtering occurs very soon after the alternatives are proposed. It should at least be completed before the next point of local ambiguity, for otherwise we incur the penalties of exponential growth in the number of analyses. Given the degree of nondeterminism characteristic of natural grammars, this means that the interplay of syntactic analysis and semantic adjudication must be extremely intimate and fine-grained. Since most words are ambiguous, semantic adjudication will probably be needed almost word by word.

For example, consider (9), repeated here:

(12) a. The doctor sent for the patient arrived.
      b. The flowers sent for the patient arrived.

The garden path effect in (12a) is reduced in (12b), because flowers, unlike doctors, cannot send for things. The very existence of a garden path effect in (12a) suggests that this knowledge must be available early. If the processor were able to delay commitment until the end of the putative clause *the flowers sent for the patient*, then it would have got to the point of syntactic disambiguation by the main verb, and there would be no reason not to expect it to be able to recover from the garden path in (12a). It follows that to explain the lack of such an effect in (12b), we must suppose that the interpretation of an *incomplete* proposition *the flowers sent for . . .* is available in advance of processing the rest of the PP, so that its lack of an extension can cause the garden path analysis to be aborted.[11]

However, the proposal to resolve nondeterminism by appeal to such interpretations immediately leads to an apparent paradox. If the processor resolves nondeterminism in midsentence, more or less word by word, on the basis of contextual appropriateness of interpretations, then those interpretations must be available in mid-sentence, also more or less word by word. However, under the rule-to-rule hypothesis and the strict competence hypothesis, only *constituents* have interpretations, and only constituents are available to the processor. Now, there is no particular problem about constructing a grammar according to which every leftmost string is a constituent, so that processing can proceed in this incremental fashion. Any left-branching grammar provides an example. For such grammars, the assumption of a rule-to-rule compositional semantics means that, for each terminal in a left-to-right pass through the string, as soon as it is syntactically incorporated into a phrase, the interpretation of that phrase can be provided. And since the interpretation is complete, it may also be evaluated; for example, if the constituent is a noun or an NP, then its extension or referent may be found.

A right-branching context-free grammar, on the other hand, does not have this property for left-to-right processors. In the absence of some further apparatus going beyond rule-to-rule processing and rule-to-rule semantics, all comprehension must wait until the end of the string, when the first complete constituent is built and can be interpreted. Until that point any processor that adheres to the strict competence hypothesis must simply pile up constituents on the stack. It therefore seems that we should, under the strict competence hypothesis, expect the languages of the world to favor left- branching constructions, at least wherever incremental interpretation is important for purposes of resolving nondeterminism. However, the languages of the world make extravagant use of *right*-branching constructions—the crucial clause in (12), *The flowers sent for the patient*, being a case in point. The availability of an interpretation for what are in traditional terms nonconstituents (e.g. *the flowers sent . . .* and/or *the flowers sent for . . .*) therefore contradicts the strict competence hypothesis, if we assume the orthodox grammar.

It is therefore interesting that CCG makes such fragments as *the doctor/flowers sent for . . .* available in the competence grammar, complete with an interpretation, and comparable in every way to more traditional constituents like the clause and the predicate. To the extent that the empirical evidence—for example, from comparison of the garden path effect in similar minimal pairs of sentences by Trueswell and Tanenhaus and colleagues—suggests that interpretations are available to the processor for such fragments, it follows that the present theory of grammar delivers a simpler account of the processor, without compromising the strict competence hypothesis. Derivations like (56) in chapter 6 show that this claim extends to the SOV case.[12]

It is important to be clear that this problem for traditional right-branching grammars is independent of the particular algorithms discussed in section 9.1.2. It applies to bottom-up and top-down algorithms alike, so long as they adhere to the strict competence hypothesis. Top-down algorithms have the apparent advantage of being syntactically predictive, a fact whose psychological relevance is noted by Kimball (1973) and Frazier and Fodor (1978). However, neither algorithm of itself will allow an interpretation to be accessed for the leftmost substring, in advance of their being combined into a constituent. Therefore, neither algorithm unaided will allow word-by-word incremental semantic filtering as a basis for the oracle within right-branching constructions.

To say this is not of course to deny that incremental interpretation is possible for right-branching grammars if they do *not* adhere to the strict competence hypothesis in this extreme form. In fact, the requisite information is quite easy to compute from the rules of the grammar. It would not be unreasonable to postulate a language-independent mechanism using functional composition to map traditional grammar rules onto new rules defining parser-specific entities like S/NP.

For example, Pulman (1986, 212–213) proposes a bottom-up shift-reduce processor that includes a rule "Clear" that combines subjects like *the flowers* and a transitive verb *sent* (with the "summon" reading) on a stack, thus:[13]

(13)

$$\boxed{\begin{array}{l} VP/PP : \lambda x.summon'x \\ \hline S/VP : \lambda p.p\,flowers' \end{array}} \quad \Longrightarrow \quad \boxed{S/PP : \lambda x.summon'x\,flowers'}$$

The rule Clear corresponds to an operation of semantic composition on categories on the parser's stack, as distinct from a grammatical rule. It therefore violates the strict competence hypothesis. If such violations are permitted, then it is clearly easy for a processor to gain access to interpretations more incrementally than the grammar would otherwise allow.

However, this argument cuts two ways. If such entities can be associated with semantic interpretations, why are they *not* grammaticalized? Under the assumption that grammar is just the reification of conceptual structure, why are these apparently useful concepts getting left out?

Of course, there is a lot that we don't know about the conceptual infrastructure of grammar. We are not yet in a position to say whether or not there is anything odd about those concepts that causes them to be left out. However, given that such conceptual objects seem to be accessible to the parser for resolving nondeterminism, it is interesting to remember at this point that categorial grammars of the kind discussed here already *do* grammaticalize the fragments in question. Since they do so by including composition as a component of competence grammar, they predict that the same operation should be available to the processor, under the strict competence hypothesis, rather than requiring it as an extra stipulation and thereby violating that principle.

There is in fact no sense in which a parser using a right-branching grammar under strict competence can access interpretations for substrings that are not constituents. In the case of (12b), this means that the anomaly of the clausal reading of the substring *the flowers sent for the patient* cannot be detected until after the word *patient*. However, this is rather late in the day. The very next word in the sentence is the disambiguating main verb *arrived*. Since we know that there is a garden path effect in (12a), and we know that in context the grammatical reading can be comprehended, we have reason to believe that the human disambiguation point must be earlier, around the verb or the preposition. If so, then the degree of incremental interpretation permitted under the strict competence hypothesis for standard right-branching grammars for this construction is of insufficiently fine grain.

Stabler (1991), criticizing an earlier version of this proposal (Steedman 1989), has argued that the present claims are in error, and that incremental interpretation of right-branching constituents is in fact possible without violating the strong competence hypothesis in the strict sense used here.

Stabler does not in fact adhere to the strict form of the strong competence hypothesis. It is clear that he is assuming a weaker form of the competence hypothesis, although he gives no explicit definition (see Stabler 1991, 233, n.1). In particular, in his first worked example, (p. 226) he binds a variable *Subj* in the interpretation of the sentence to the interpretation of the actual subject, via Prolog-style partial execution in the rule *11* (p. 208). This is possible only because he is using the grammar as a predictive parser. He uses this information to identify the fact that since the context includes only one predication over this subject, that must be the one that is to come, under a caricature of incremental evaluation similar to that used above.[14]

However, we have seen that this much is merely information that could legitimately have been built into the grammar itself, via type-raising. (In fact, this analogy seems to be effectively embodied in Stabler's second example using an LR parser (Aho and Johnson 1974), although the details here are less clear.) As in the example offered above, Stabler's processor has not actually handled any interpretations that correspond to nonconstituents. It is therefore more important to ask whether it adheres to the strict competence hypothesis in all other respects by entirely avoiding interpretation of nonconstituents of the *the flowers sent* variety, or whether it violates the hypothesis by covertly constructing interpreted objects that are not merely constituents according to the competence grammar, either in the form of dashed categories or in the form of partially instantiated semantic interpretations.

Curiously, since his paper is addressed to a predecessor of the present proposal, and even though he technically allows strict competence to be compromised, all of Stabler's examples take the first tactic. Thus, in his exegesis of the (right-branching) sentence *The joke is funny*, there is no sense in which there ever exists an interpretation of the nonconstituent *the joke is*, or indeed anything comparable to *The flowers sent* (see Stabler 1991, 215, and 232).[15] His parser offers no help with the question raised by (12). It is neither consistent with the strict competence hypothesis nor incrementally interpretative in the sense argued for here.

Shieber and Johnson (1993) have also argued against the same earlier version of the present proposal on a rather different ground. They freely admit (p. 29) that their proposal for incorporating a version of incremental interpretation in a more or less traditional grammar violates of the strict competence hypothesis. (The violation arises when they exploit the fact that the state of their LR parser encodes a shared forest of possible interpretable partial analyses in much the same way as Pulman's (1986) parser discussed above; see pp. 18–22.) However, they claim that within such a not strictly competence-based parser, incremental interpretation is actually simpler than strictly constituent-based interpretation. The reasoning behind this interesting claim is that, once interpretation of nonconstituents is allowed by the addition of extragrammatical apparatus, imposing strict competence on the system requires the reimposition of synchrony, via further additional mechanisms such as a clock or switch.

As in the simpler examples discussed earlier of incrementally interpreting parsers using categories and the stack as interpretable objects, the real force of this argument depends upon the extent to which the apparatus for interpreting LR states as encoding partial analyses can be given some independent motivation. All the earlier questions about why these interpretations are *not* grammaticalized also remain to be answered, especially when it is recalled that other competence phenomena (e.g. coordination, considered in part II) suggest that similar interpretations indeed behave like grammatical entities. Such questions are simply open, and they will remain so until the rival competence theories attain something closer to descriptive adequacy than any of them do today.

The resolution of the apparent paradox of incremental interpretation does not lie in Stabler's or Shieber and Johnson's parsers, but in the observation that strings like *Anna married* and *the flowers sent* are in the fullest sense constituents of competence grammar. We can retain the strict version of the strong competence hypothesis and continue to require the grammar to support incremental interpretation, if we also take on board the combinatory theory of grammar. This theory offers a broader definition of constituency, under which more substrings, and in particular more left prefixes, are associated with interpretations as a matter of grammar. The interpretations of such nonstandard constituents can therefore be used to compare rival analyses arising from nondeterminism on the basis of their fit to the context, without violating the strict competence hypothesis.

9.2 Toward Psychologically Realistic Parsers

How could a reasonably efficient parser of this kind be built? One possibility is a very simple modification of the breadth-first incremental CKY parser sketched in section 9.1.2. The modification is that when a new constituent (i, j) is found, we not only check that it is not already present in the chart before adding it. We also check that it makes sense by evaluating it either with respect to a priori likelihood with respect to the knowledge base, as Winograd (1972) suggests for disambiguating compound NPs like *water meter cover adjustment screw* or (if it is a main-clause prefix) with respect to referential context, as in the flowers/doctor example (12).

We noted in the earlier discussion that we need only consider new arcs ending at j when the categories of the jth word a_j are shifted, and that it is necessary to compute the new entries (i, j) bottom up—that is, by starting with $i = j - 2$ and stepping down to $i = 0$. For each i we ask for all k where $i < k < j$ whether there are entries spanning (i, k) and (k, j) that reduce. If so, then the result is added to the table t as $t(i, j)$ if it survives the matching check. The algorithm can be defined as follows. (Compare Harrison 1978, 433, and example (5) above—the present version differs only in assuming that categories are accompanied by interpretations and that all reductions are considered in the innermost loop.) A, B, C are category-interpretation pairs $\Sigma : \Lambda$ as before:

(14) 1. **for** $j := 1$ **to** n **do**
   begin
   $t(j - 1, j) := \{A | A$ is a lexical category for $a_j\}$
   2. **for** $i := j - 2$ **down to** 0 **do**
   begin
   3. a. $t(i, j) := \{A | $ there exists k, $i < k < j$, such that $B\ C \Rightarrow A$ for some
   $B \in t(i, k), C \in t(k, j)$, and not $present(A, i, j)\}$
   b. $t(i, j) := rank(t(i, j))$
   end
   end

The function *rank* is assumed to order the constituents in $t(i,j)$ according to plausibility, either intrinsically or in terms of the state of the context or database and the Principle of Parsimony (10). For the sake of simplicity I will assume in what follows that the highest-ranked element is assigned a plausibility value of 1 and the rest are assigned a plausibility value of 0, although more realistically a range of values summing to 1 and/or a threshold for entry to the chart could be used.

To make the proposal more concrete, I will again assume a very simplified account of the discourse model related to an extensional version of the Alternative Semantics of Rooth (1985, 1992) used in chapter 5.[16] In particular, I will assume that a context is a database containing modal propositions as individuals, corresponding to the fact that it is possible for a person to send anything for a person, that it is possible for a person to summon a person, that it is possible for anything to arrive, that doctors and patients are persons, and that flowers are not. To further simplify, I will ignore the "send into raptures" sense of *send*. In the null context the discourse model might look something like the following, where the $\Diamond$ prefix means that the event to its right is possible and can be accommodated in the sense defined earlier, and where I use the logic-programming convention that variables are implicitly universally quantified:

(15) $person'x \land person'z \rightarrow \Diamond send'xyz$
   $person'x \land person'y \rightarrow \Diamond summon'xy$
   $\Diamond arrive'x$
   $doctor'x \rightarrow person'x$
   $patient'x \rightarrow person'x$
   $flowers'x \rightarrow \neg person'x$

This database rather crudely represents the fact that propositions about people sending and summoning can be readily accommodated or added to the hearer's representation of the situation, but that in our simplified example no propositions with flowers as the subject of sending or summoning can be accommodated.

As far as the grammar goes, we have the usual problem of deciding whether nouns like *flowers* optionally subcategorize for modifiers like relatives and past participials or not. On the argument given in section 4.3.2 to the effect that anything out of which something can be right node raised must be an argument, examples like the following suggest that such modifiers are arguments:

(16) a. a few *men that I gave and women that I sold* flowers
   b. the *flowers sent for and chocolates given to* the patient

Continuing to simplify, I will represent this by simple lexical ambiguity on the noun *flowers*. For the same reason I will also continue to assume that type-raising applies lexically.

Consider what happens when the sentence *The flowers sent for the patient arrived* is processed in this context. We shift the definite article *the* and the two categories for the noun *flowers*, which can then reduce to yield a subject (among other irrelevant raised categories) meaning something like the following, in which ι is Russell's definite existential quantifier (Russell 1905—see van der Sandt 1988; Beaver 1997):

(17) a. $S/(S\backslash NP) : \lambda p.\iota x.flowers'x \wedge px$

  b. $(S/(S\backslash NP))/(N\backslash N) : \lambda q.\lambda p.\iota x.(flowers'x \wedge qx) \wedge px$

The ι operator in the first category requires the existence of exactly one entity of type *flowers'* The ι operator in the interpretation of the second category requires the existence of exactly one entity of type *flowers'* having one other property q

There are no such entities in the database, but they can be consistently accommodated. Since the first category requires accommodating one proposition and the second requires accommodating two, the first is more plausible. It is therefore ranked 1, and the accommodation is carried out. The second is ranked 0 and not accommodated. Importantly, both categories remain in the table.

Let us represent the accommodation by existentially instantiating the flowers with an arbitrary constant—say, $gensym'_1$—and adding the following fact to the database:

(18) $flowers'gensym'_1$

We next encounter the word *sent*, which has three categories:

(19) a. $((S\backslash NP)/PP)/NP : \lambda x.\lambda y.\lambda z.send'yxz$

  b. $(S\backslash NP)/PP : \lambda x.\lambda y.summon'xy$

  c. $(N\backslash N)/PP : \lambda x.\lambda p.\lambda y.p\ y \wedge send'yxsomeone'$

The raised subject (17a) can compose with the categories (19a,b) to yield the following categories:

(20) a. $S/PP : \lambda y.\iota x.flowers'x \wedge summon'yx$

  b. $(S/PP)/NP : \lambda y.\lambda z.\iota x.flowers'x \wedge send'zyx$

The other subject category, (17b), can compose with the last verbal category, (19c), to yield the following category:

(21) $(S/(S\backslash NP))/PP : \lambda y.\lambda p.\iota x.(flowers'x \wedge send'yxsomeone') \wedge px$

To assess the plausibility of (20a,b), the processor must ask if it is possible for flowers to send things for people or send for people:

(22) a. $\Diamond flowers'x \wedge summon'yx$

    b. $\Diamond flowers'x \wedge send'zyx$

Neither possibility is supported by the database, so both of these categories are associated with a low probability by the ranking function *rank* when entered in the chart.

    The plausibility of category (21) depends on there being just one thing around of type *flowers'* with the property that they were sent. Although there is no corresponding proposition in the database, the knowledge base does at least support the possibility of sending flowers:

(23) $\Diamond flowers'y \wedge send'zyx$

Category (21) therefore ends up as the highest-ranked category for *The flowers sent . . .* , ranked 1 on entry to the chart. Its presuppositions are accommodated by adding the following facts to the database about the already present arbitrary flowers *gensym$_1$*:

(24) $send'z \, gensym'_1 someone'$

    The next word to shift is the preposition *for*, which first reduces with (20b) and (21) by composition. Since flowers cannot send for anything, and can be sent for people, the first is ranked 0 and the second 1 on entry to the chart:

(25) a. $S/NP : \lambda y.\iota x.flowers'x \wedge summon'yx$

    b. $(S/(S\backslash NP))/NP : \lambda y.\lambda p.\iota x.(flowers'x \wedge send'yxsomeone') \wedge px$

Note that this preference for the modified subject reverses that on the subject alone. (Other reductions, which we will come back to later, are possible at this stage.)

    Next we shift *the*, shift *patient*, and reduce to yield a number of categories as in the case of the subject, of which the following (where $NP^\uparrow$ schematizes as usual over various raised categories) carries fewest presuppositions/entailments and is highest ranked:

(26) $NP^\uparrow : \lambda p.\iota x.patient'x \wedge px$

A unique patient must therefore be accommodated using another arbitrary constant:

(27) *patient' gensym'₃*

The raised NP can combine with both categories in (25) for *The flowers sent for* .... Since patients are people and can be summoned and sent things, two categories go in the chart for *The flowers sent for the patient* ...:

(28) a. $S : \iota y.patient'y \land \iota x.flowers'x \land summon'yx$

     b. $S/(S\backslash NP) : \lambda p.\iota y.patient'y \land \iota x.(flowers'x \land send'xysomeone') \land px$

The first of these is again implausible. The second is plausible to the extent that it is possible to send flowers for a patient, and that there is exactly one thing with the property *flowers'* and one with the property *patient'*, and that a proposition subsuming the following one—namely, (24)—is already accommodated:

(29) *send' gensym'₂ gensym'₁ someone'*

The subject in turn can combine with the main verb *arrived* and complete the analysis, since anything can arrive.

This version of the CKY parser is complete, in the sense that it builds all legal constituents, even when they are zero-ranked for likelihood. Other constituents will be built, some of which will be rejected under the matching-entry test as being redundant without any further evaluation and without affecting the rankings already assigned to the equivalent constituents already in the chart. The important thing to note is that the anomaly of the tensed-verb reading is apparent as soon as the ambiguous word *sent* is encountered.

The analysis of the sentence *The doctor sent for the patient arrived* is identical, except that because of the plausibility of doctors sending for people, and the lesser presuppositional demand of the simple NP, the tensed-verb analysis is favored over the modifier analysis until the disambiguation point:

(30) $S/(S\backslash NP) : \lambda p.\iota y.doctor'y \land \iota x.(patient'x \land send'xysomeone') \land px$

     $S : \iota y.doctor'y \land \iota x.patient'x \land \land summon'xy$

Now suppose that a single doctor is already identified in the context.

(31) *doctor' dexter'*

Here the analysis of *The doctor sent for the patient arrived* will proceed exactly as in the null context, except that the unique doctor will no longer need to be accommodated. The analysis will receive a low rank for the same reason.

However, consider the case where there are two known doctors in the context:

(32) *doctor'dexter'*
      doctor'warren'

Even if the entailment of the restrictor (that someone sent one of them for the
patient) is not known and must be accommodated, the simple NP will fail to
refer from the start and the complex NP will be highly ranked, as in the case
of *The flowers sent for the patient arrived.*

We have already noted that the CKY algorithm as described here is complete. This means that it does not of itself predict exactly which sentence-
context pairs will lead to unrecoverable garden paths. Moreover, we have
unrealistically assumed that the ranking function does not need to take into
account the preference values of the inputs to combinations. However, the algorithm shows that alternatives can be ranked consistently with the observed
effects up to the point of disambiguation. This means that less conservative
algorithms such as the beam-searching CCG parser of Niv (1993, 1994), the
best-first chart-parser of Thompson (1990), or a version of CKY in which continuous probabilities are used to calculate exact likelihood values—say, using
methods discussed by Collins (1996, 1997, 1998)—and subjected to a threshold, can be used to make more precise predictions.

9.3 CCG Parsing for Practical Applications

As noted earlier, the CKY algorithm has worst-case time complexity n^3 for
recognition in the context-free case (because it involves three nested loops of
complexity order n), and the n^6 worst-case complexity of recognition for Vijay-
Shanker and Weir's (1990; 1993; 1994) generalization to CCG depends upon
a complex structure-sharing technique for categories. Moreover, polynomial
worst-case complexity for the corresponding parsers depends in both cases
upon similarly subtle techniques for structure sharing among parse trees or
interpretable structures using devices like "shared forests" (Billot and Lang
1989).

However, experiments by Komagata (1997a, 1999) with a CKY parser for
hand-built CCG grammar fragments of English and Japanese for real texts
from a constrained medical domain suggests that average-case parsing complexity for practical CCG-based grammars can in practice be quite reasonable
even in the absence of semantic disambiguation or statistically-based opti-
mization, despite its worst-case exponentiality.[17] To the extent that the psychological processor limits attachment ambiguities by the kind of semantic
strategy outlined here, or by the related probabilistic techniques discussed in

section 9.2, psychologically implausible mechanisms to manage shared forests as a representation of the alternative parsers may also be eliminated.

The modified CKY algorithm is only one among a number of possibilities, including parsers based on more predictive algorithms such top-down and mixed top-down and bottom-up algorithms, such as that of Earley (1970). The important point in terms of psychological realism is that by using CCG as the grammatical module, all such algorithms can be semantically incremental, while remaining entirely neutral with respect to the particular theory of grammar involved and exactly as incremental as the grammar itself allows, in keeping with the strict competence hypothesis.

Nevertheless, for many applications this kind of algorithm will always be vulnerable to well-known limitations on our ability to represent our everyday knowledge about practical domains in ways that will support adequate assessment of plausibility. For many applications such a parser will therefore benefit very little from the pruning step. Moreover, as we saw at the end of chapter 8, this particular algorithm, being bottom-up, inherits the disease of building useless constituents.

Many of the worst effects of the disease can be eliminated by being more careful about which categories for a_j are input to the algorithm in step 1. For example, almost all nouns like *thieves* in English can be either N or NP. However, when preceded by an article, as in *the thieves*, the relevant category is, with overwhelmingly high probability, N rather than NP. This fact provides the basis for a number of low-level, purely stochastic, syntax-independent "part-of-speech-tagging" (POS) methods for disambiguating lexical form-class (Jelinek 1976; Merialdo 1994), based on algorithms that can be automatically trained on text or speech corpora. POS tagging can be used to limit the candidate categories input to the CKY algorithm to the "n-best" or most likely categories, as de Marcken (1990) points out, eliminating much of the disadvantage of bottom-up techniques.

Indeed, it is likely that CCG and other lexicalized grammars, such as TAG, will benefit more from such stochastic filtering. POS tagging is commonly based on around 60 form classes (Francis and Kučera 1964, 23–25), some of which, such as VBZ (verb, 3rd person singular present), are not as informative as they might be. By contrast, CCG and TAG have several distinct categories or elementary trees corresponding to VBZ, distinguishing intransitive and a number of distinct varieties of transitive and ditransitive verbs. This suggests that better POS-tagging algorithms could be developed by using CCG or TAG categories in place of the standard POS categories, a proposal that has been investigated by B. Srinivas and Joshi (1994). Experiments of this kind are reported by B. Srinivas (1997) and Doran and B. Srinivas (to appear), with promising results. One interesting question for this research is whether stochastic methods will be effective in disambiguating type-raising.

Recent work by Collins (1996, 1997, 1998) points to the advantages of an even greater integration of probabilistic information with syntax in parsers for lexicalized context-free grammars, including CCG. Collins (1997, 1998) presents a technique for supervised learning of probabilistic Dependency Grammars, in which the production rules are induced from a tree-bank and probabilities are found for a given rule applying with a given lexical "head" and arguments with other given heads. Some of the distinctive features of the procedure for assigning these probabilities are a method based on maximum likelihood estimation and a "backing off" method for use in the face of sparse data. The probabilities can be used to guide search in any one of a number of standard parsing algorithms, including shift-reduce, beam search, and CKY. This parser was at the time of writing the most accurate wide coverage parser by the standard measures, with precision/recall figures better than 88% on unseen Wall Street Journal text.

Because of its simultaneous clean theoretical separation between competence grammar, parsing algorithm, and probability, and because of its close coupling of these elements in processing, Collins's method is extremely general. More or less any class of lexicalized grammar can be made to yield dependency structures, and so probabilistic parsers can in principle be induced for them too, provided that the tree-bank that is used records the relevant dependencies. Combinatory Categorial Grammar is a particularly interesting case to consider, not only because of the historically close relation between Categorial Grammar and Dependency Grammar, and because the Logical Forms that CCGs build capture the dependencies in question, but also because of the simple way in which they project lexical dependencies, and hence the associated head-dependency probabilities, onto unbounded and fragmentary constructions including coordination. (The advantages of this property for grammar induction have already been mentioned in connection with human language acquisition.)

It is not clear what psychological reality such stochastic methods can lay claim to. It does not seem likely that the semantic methods I have advocated for resolving attachment ambiguities will solve the problem of lexical ambiguity. On the other hand, it does seem possible that human processors could derive plausibility measures directly from properties of the syntax and associative properties of the memory for concepts underlying word meanings, rather than by collecting higher-order statistics over large volumes of data. The rule-based POS taggers of Brill (1992) Voutilainen (1995), Kempe and Karttunen (1996), and Cussens (1997), and related sense-disambiguation work by Resnik (1992) using WordNet (Miller and Fellbaum 1991) are suggestive in this respect. However, to the extent that very transient changes to the sets of referents that are available in the discourse model can affect processing load and garden path effects, as in the experiments discussed earlier, processes of active interpretation, including limited amounts of inference, seem to be the only plausible basis for resolution of structural or attachment ambiguities by the psychological processor.

Chapter 10

The Syntactic Interface

Lofty designs must close in like effects.
Robert Browning, "A Grammarian's Funeral"

This book began by stating some uncontroversial assumptions in the form of the rule-to-rule condition and the competence hypothesis, deducing the even more widely accepted Constituent Condition on rules of competence grammar. The Introduction also endorsed the methodological priority of investigating competence syntax over performance mechanisms. Having noted the difficulties presented by coordination and intonation in relation to the Constituent Condition on Rules, part I of the book went on to advance an alternative combinatory view of competence grammar under which these apparently paradoxical constructions were seen to conform to that condition after all. After putting the theory through its syntactic paces in part II, the progression has been brought full circle in part III by deriving some consequences for the theory of performance under a "strict" version of the competence hypothesis.

10.1 Competence

The competence theory that was developed along the way is conveniently viewed in terms of a third and final version of the by-now familiar Y-diagram in figure 10.1, which combines figures 4.1 and 5.3, again including mnemonic exemplars of the constructs characteristic of each module of the theory. According to this theory, lexical items and derived constituents (including sentences) pair a phonological representation with a syntactic category (identifying type and directionality only) and an interpretation. Chapter 5 showed that the interpretations of the principal constituents of the sentence correspond to the information structural components called theme and rheme. These in turn combine by function application or "β-normalization" to yield fairly standard quantified predicate-argument structures or Logical Forms. Predicate-argument structures preserve fairly traditional relations of dominance and command. In par-

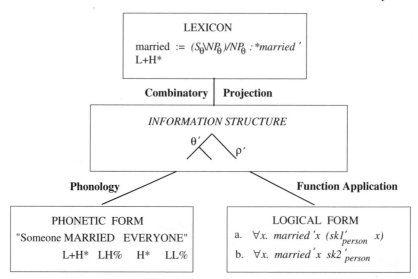

Figure 10.1
Architecture of Combinatory Categorial Grammar III

ticular, they embody the obliqueness hierarchy on grammatical relations over arguments. The order of combination that is defined by the syntactic category need not conform to the obliqueness hierarchy, and in VSO and SVO languages cannot conform to it.

Traditional notions of command and dominance have nothing to do with derivation in this sense. Instead, derivations capture directly the notion of constituency relevant to relativization, coordination, and phrasal intonation, without the invocation of empty syntactic categories or syntactic operations of "movement," "deletion," "copying," or "restructuring," distinct from those implicit in the automatic construction of the appropriate Logical Form. This notion of structure should be identified with Information Structure, rather than traditional Surface Structure. Although it is convenient to represent Information Structures as trees, they do not constitute a level of representation in the theory. In contrast to Logical Form and the associated predicate-argument structural domain of the binding theory, no rule or relation is predicated over such structures.

The responsibility of the combinatory rules is to "project" both components of the lexical categories, synchronously and in lockstep, onto the corresponding constituent components of the derivation.[1] The types of the constituents that they yield are considerably more diverse than those implicated in traditional Surface Structures or GB S-Structures. They provide the input to rules of coordination, parentheticalization, and extraction, all of which are thereby brought under the Constituent Condition on Rules. They also provide the input to purely local phonological processes, such as vowel harmony or *liaison* and the Rhythm Rule (Selkirk 1984), which directly map information-structural constituents onto Phonetic Form proper.

There is no conflict between such a view of surface constituency and more traditional theories of grammar. In categorial terms, such theories can be seen as predominantly concerned with predicate-argument structure and hence with elements of semantic interpretation or Logical Form, rather than syntax proper. To the extent that such theories provide a systematic account of the relation between interpretations in this sense and syntactic categories, they provide what amounts to a theory of the categorial lexicon—a component of the present theory that continues to be lacking in this and preceding discussions of CCG.

By contrast, the normalized Logical Form or quantified predicate-argument structure, which is the exclusive domain of the binding theory, provides the input to such systems as reference and the binding of pronouns. It is presumably at this level that the effects associated with "weak crossover" and "subjacency" make themselves felt. Although we may find it convenient to think about these processes in terms of a further structural level of Logical Form, such a representation is not in principle necessary, for the reasons discussed by Montague (1970), and in fact this level is eschewed in other versions of Categorial Grammar. In chapter 4, I discussed how such systems should capture ambiguities of quantifier scope without movement at LF or the equivalent, drawing on work by VanLehn (1978), Webber (1978, 1983), Reinhart (1991, 1997), Park (1995, 1996), Winter (1997), and Schlenker (to appear).

The question of how well the theory generalizes to more parametrically diverse languages than English and its Germanic relatives, and in particular to languages with freer word order and those that use morphological markers of Information Structure rather than intonational ones, goes beyond the scope of the present book. However, Kang (1988), Segond (1990), Foster (1990) Nishida (1996), Hoffman (1995a,b, 1996, 1998), Bozsahin (1998), Komagata (1997b, 1999), Baldridge (1998, 1999), and Trechsel (to appear) offer CCG analyses for the grammar and Information Structure of Korean, French, Spanish, Old Spanish, Turkish, Japanese, Tagalog and Tzotzil.

10.2 Acquisition

The explanatory adequacy of the theory will also depend on its compatibility with a reasonable account of language acquisition. This question also lies beyond the scope of the present book, and the following remarks are restricted to the briefest of preliminary sketches. (See Briscoe 1997, forthcoming, Osborne and Briscoe (1997), and Watkinson and Manandhar 1999 for specific proposals for acquiring categorial grammars in the face of noise and situational ambiguity, and see Kanazawa 1998 on the computational complexity of the problem.)

The considerations discussed in chapters 1 and 8 suggest that language acquisition mainly reduces to the problem of learning the categorial lexicon and the language-specific instances of the combinatory rule types that are involved. Lexical learning must in the earliest stages depend upon the child's having access to mental representations of the concepts underlying words, in a form more or less equivalent to the lexical Logical Forms assumed here, perhaps along lines suggested in Pinker 1979, Fisher et al. 1994, Steedman 1994, and Siskind 1995, 1996. Under the assumptions inherent in the Principle of Categorial Type Transparency, the semantic type of such concepts defines the syntactic type in every respect except directionality. The Principle of Head Categorial Uniqueness ensures that in most cases the child need have access only to combinatory rules of functional application in order to deduce the latter property, and hence the lexical category or categories of each word. The tendency of languages toward consistency in head-complement orders suggests that this search is constrained accordingly.

As far as the combinatory rules go, it seems likely that the repertoire of semantic combinators is fixed as composition, substitution and (possibly as a lexical rule) type-raising over the categories that are actually encountered in the grammar acquired so far. Once some lexical categories are known, the child is therefore immediately in a position to master constructions like relatives by inducing the particular instances of combinatory rules that the grammar includes—principally those of the composition family— and the categories to which they apply, working on the basis of the lexical categories learned in the manner sketched above and contextually available compound concepts, perhaps along lines sketched in Steedman 1996a. (The fact that lexical learning generalizes in this way is an important reason why natural languages should adhere as closely as possible to the Principle of Head Categorial Uniqueness.) The simplest way to do this would be to include only the most specific instance of a combinatory rule that supports a combination that yields the concept in question. However, such an assumption raises the same questions of inductive generalization and stability in the face of noise and ambiguity that arise in other frameworks.

The most serious problem that this account faces arises from the inclusion of exceptions to the Principle of Head Categorial Uniqueness, such as the subject extraction category stipulated in chapter 4 at example (20) for verbs like *think*. When children who are acquiring English encounter subject extraction, they have three options. They might wrongly assume that the grammar of English includes the rule of crossed composition that was rejected in chapter 4—in which case they will begin to overgenerate wildly. Or they might rightly assume that this counts as a different construction headed by *think*, specified by a separate lexical entry, but wrongly assume that this lexical entry conforms to the Principle of Head Categorial Uniqueness—in which case they will begin to overgenerate sentences like **I think fell the horse*. Or they might correctly further assume that this lexical entry is independent, violating the Uniqueness principle.

One way to ensure that the child makes the right choice, despite the penalty associated with violating this principle, is to stipulate that categories that are not induced via an application-only derivation of the kind described earlier, but (like this one) are first encountered under extraction, are assigned the most conservative category that will allow the sentence—that is, one confined to antecedent government, an assumption analogous to Baker's (1979) proposal for conservative acquisition of dative shift.[2] (Similar remarks may apply to acquisition of the antecedent government–restricted combinatory rules for phenomena like Heavy NP shift, discussed in chapters 4 and 6.) Such a procedure seems to be one that could only be safely applied in the last stages of fine-tuning a stable grammar based on a sizable corpus. Stromswold's (1995) results showing that complement subject extraction is one of the last constructions to be acquired in English (see section 4.2.1) are consistent with this procedure.[3]

10.3 Performance

The architecture schematized in figure 10.1 embodies the strongest possible relation between Surface Structure or derivation, Intonation Structure and Information Structure. The evidence for it is entirely based on linguistic argumentation, and it must in the first place be judged on those grounds. Nevertheless, this property of the theory has significant implications for processing under the strict competence hypothesis. The fact that syntactic constituency subsumes intonational constituency in the sense discussed in chapter 5 implies that modular processors that use both sources of information at once should be easier to devise. Such an architecture may reasonably be expected to simplify the problem of resolving local structural ambiguity in both domains.

However, we have noted that a considerable amount of nondeterminism remains in the grammar, for both spoken and written language. Although this nondeterminism can be kept within polynomial complexity bounds using techniques discussed in chapter 9, the associativity implicit in functional composition means that the average-case complexity potentially remains serious. The properties of the grammar are consistent with the suggestion that the basis for the oracle that renders the process as a whole deterministic is the incremental availability of semantic interpretations (possibly compiled in the form of related head-dependency probabilities of the kind discussed by Collins (1998).)

The generalized notion of constituency that is engendered by the combinatory rules ensures that many leftmost substrings are potentially constituents with interpretations, subject of course to the limitations of the grammar and any further information that may be available from intonation. Such a theory of grammar may therefore have the added advantage of parsimony, in being compatible with such a processor without compromising the strict competence hypothesis.

Indeed, we can stand this argument on its head. If we believe that the parser has to know about interpretations corresponding to strings like *The flowers sent for . . .* , and we identify such interpretations with the notion of abstraction, then advocates of more traditional notions of constituency must ask themselves why their grammar does *not* accord such useful and accessible semantic concepts the status of grammatical constituents.

The claim is strengthened by the observation that the residual nondeterminism in the grammar of intonation, arising in part from the widespread presence of unmarked themes, as discussed in connection with example (55) in chapter 5, is confined precisely to those occasions on which the topic or theme is believed by the speaker to be entirely known to all parties, and to be recoverable by comparing the interpretation of a (usually leftmost) substring with the contextual open proposition or theme. It would be surprising if the mechanism for disambiguating written language were very different from its ancestor in the processor for spoken language.

It is of course unlikely that we will ever know enough about the biological constraints to evaluate the assumptions on which the "strict" version of the competence hypothesis is based with any certainty. In the absence of such certainty, we must beware of falling into the error of evolutionary Panglossism. However, it is appropriate to speculate a little further upon the implications of the Strict Competence Hypothesis for the theory as a whole, for the following reason.

Competence grammar and performance mechanism originally evolved as components of a single biological system. The methodological priority of competence that has been continually endorsed in the present work is no more than a research strategy. Any claim about competence grammar is ultimately a claim about the entire computational package. As soon as our linguistic theories have attained the level of descriptive adequacy, they will have to be judged not merely on their purity and parsimony as theories of competence, but on their explanatory value as part of a psychologically and biologically credible performance system. Chapter 9 noted that all theories will require *something* more, in the form of a language-independent mechanism for resolving local ambiguity, or grammatical nondeterminism, together with a language-independent algorithm and automaton. But if a theory of competence requires much more than that, or if that mechanism in turn implicates a notion of structure that is not covered by the competence grammar, then those assumptions will weigh against it. If there is another descriptively adequate theory that requires fewer such assumptions, perhaps even no further assumptions beyond the mechanism for resolving nondeterminism and the minimal bottom-up algorithm, by virtue of having a different notion of surface syntax, then the scales may tilt in its favor.

None of the current theories of grammar, including the present one, have yet attained the full descriptive adequacy that would allow us to weigh them in the balance in this way. But if it is true that the principal responsibility for local ambiguity resolution lies with word-by-word incremental interpretation (or with correspondingly fine-grain probabilistic evaluation), then any theory that does not make assumptions similar to those of CCG concerning constituency in the competence grammar will, as we saw in chapter 9, have to make some strikingly similar structures available to the processor, complete with interpretations. Such additional assumptions could not by definition be inconsistent with the pure competence theory itself. However, they compromise the Strict Competence Hypothesis. To the extent that a combinatory grammar can achieve the same result without any additional assumptions, and to the extent that it is descriptively correct to include identical structures and interpretations in the competence grammar of coordination and intonation, the combinatory theory may then be preferred as an explanatory account.

Notes

Chapter 1

1. The HOLD-register analysis of *wh*-movement was in part anticipated in earlier work by Thorne, Bratley and Dewar (1968), who called their register *.

2. Wood (1993) provides a useful review of theories by Lambek (1958), Ades and Steedman (1982), Bach (1979), Dowty (1979), Steedman (1987), Oehrle (1988), Hepple (1990), Jacobson (1990, 1992b), Szabolcsi (1989, 1992), and Wood (1988), although my colleagues should not be assumed to endorse all the assumptions of the version that is outlined here. The present proposal is more distantly related to a number of other generalizations of the early categorial systems of Ajdukiewicz, Bach, Bar-Hillel, Dowty, Lambek, Geach, Lewis, Montague, van Benthem, Cresswell, and von Stechow, to many of which the conclusions of this book also apply. In particular, Oehrle (1987), Moortgat (1988a), and Morrill (1994) explicitly relate Lambek-style categorial grammars to prosody.

3. Marr expressed some doubt about whether natural language is in fact a modular system, apparently because he was aware of the way knowledge and inference interact with language understanding. I will argue against this conclusion in chapter 9.

Chapter 2

1. This claim should not be taken as denying that such learning can be usefully thought of in terms of supervised machine learning techniques, or as excluding the possibility that the substrate of such conceptual representations may be associative or probabilistic.

2. The "Standard Theory" presented in Chomsky 1965 did not explicitly recognize any level of Logical Form distinct from Deep Structure. However, had it done so, it would have had to derive it from Deep Structure. The fact that later "Extended," "Revised Extended," and "Principles and Parameters" or "Government-Binding (GB)" versions of Chomsky's theory derived Logical Form from a level called "S-Structure" should not be allowed to confuse the point. S-Structure is not the same as Surface Structure, as will become clear when this level is discussed in more detail below. The rather different view of Logical Form sketched in Chomsky 1971 is discussed in chapter 5.

3. There are a number of well-known exceptions to this generalization, which I will

discuss in chapter 4. The most obvious one in English arises in subject extraction.

4. Certain apparent exceptions to Ross's generalization are discussed in chapter 7.

5. The proposal is also implicit in the approach of Cresswell (1973) and von Stechow (1991) based on "structured propositions."

6. Selkirk's proposal in some respects constitutes a descendant of the proposal in Chomsky 1971 to derive aspects of Logical Form relating to focus from Surface Structure, a level corresponding to what in more modern versions of Transformational Grammar is called Phonetic Form.

7. The indicated dependencies are those between semantically related arguments and predicates, rather than surface dependencies between verbs and NP arguments that would be attributed on a VP analysis of the construction. However, in either case the Dutch dependencies cross.

8. A number of apparent exceptions to Ross's generalization have been noted in the literature, including Zapotec (which is VSO but allows SO and VSO; see Rosenbaum 1977) and German (which is SOV but allows SOV and SO; see van Oirsouw 1987). These are discussed in chapter 7, where I show how they are made possible by the fact that Zapotec (unlike Irish) allows SOV as a main-clause word order, while German and Dutch (unlike Japanese) allow VSO/SVO as main-clause orders. I restate Ross's constraint in terms of overall order properties of languages and constructions rather than any notion of "underlying" word order.

9. Languages that order object before subject are sufficiently rare as to apparently preclude a comparable data set, although any result of this kind would be of immense interest.

10. This Categorial broad church is also closely related to the Dependency Grammar tradition of Mel'čuk and Pertsov (1987), Hudson (1984), and the Prague School (Hajičová and Sgall 1987, 1988), with which it shows some sign of merging (see Pickering and Barry 1993 and Milward 1991, 1994).

11. Wood 1993 has already been mentioned as a helpful guide. Moortgat 1997 and Steedman 1993 offer more partisan reviews. The collections edited by Buszkowski, Marciszewski and van Benthem (1988) and Oehrle, Bach and Wheeler (1988) are important. The reader is warned that because this body of work addresses several distinct and sometimes non-overlapping concerns, there is a variety of notations for categorial grammars.

Chapter 3

1. This chapter and chapter 4 are for the most part a review of earlier work. They can be skimmed or skipped entirely by those already familiar with the approach. For further details see Steedman 1996b.

2. Other superficially similar but different notations are used by some of the other authors referred to here. The present notation has the advantage of maintaining a consistent order of range and domain across the page for leftward and rightward functions. Because of the present concern with semantics, and with comparisons across languages with similar semantic types but different word orders, this consistency is crucial to

readability. It will be apparent in chapter 4, where the full theory is presented, that the notation used here is an abbreviation for a notation in which directionality—that is, relative position—is a property of the argument of a function.

3. This principle and the following Principles of Head Categorial Uniqueness and Categorial Type Transparency replace the Principle of Categorial Government in Steedman 1996b.

4. Interestingly, pure Categorial Grammar is only "weakly" equivalent to Context-Free Phrase Structure Grammar (CFPSG). That is, although we can write a pure categorial grammar to recognize any context-free language, it will not necessarily be possible to write one that will deliver the same trees as a given CFPSG for the same language (see Bar-Hillel, Gaifman and Shamir 1964). For real natural languages, because of the close dependence of syntactic categories on the same semantics as the corresponding CFPSGs, this seems in practice never to be a problem.

5. Some caution must be exercised in invoking feature-matching mechanisms of this kind. In particular, if features are allowed to take unbounded structures as values, then their use can lead to very unconstrained theories indeed (Carpenter 1991). All features used here are simple, in the sense that they do not take unbounded structure as values.

6. However, the theory expressly does not exclude the possibility of a natural language in which the interpretation for the corresponding transitive verb is $\lambda y.\lambda x.marry'xy$, a term in which the λ-binders for the same predicate-argument structure are not eliminable in this way.

7. I do not exclude the possibility of accounting for binding phenomena without such an "intrinsic" use of Logical Form, by using nonconcatenative rules, such as the WRAP rules of Bach (1979, 1980), Dowty (1979), Jacobson (1990), and others. However, such rules appear to complicate the analysis of coordination considerably.

8. The notion "like category" is of course problematic for any theory of syntax, as well-known examples like the following reveal:

(i) Pat is a Republican and proud of it.

I will ignore such problems here, assuming that some finer-grained specification of categories can be applied to the present theory. See Sag et al. 1985, Morrill 1994, and Bayer and Johnson 1995 for discussion of some alternatives.

9. The natural expedient for a categorial approach might therefore seem to be to eschew such syncategorematic rules and drive coordination off the lexical category of the conjunct, following Lambek (1958, 1961), who associated the categorial type in (i) with sentential conjunctions like *and*, where the lexical category itself includes a variable ranging over categories of the same type, written X:

(i) and:= $(X \backslash X)/X$

However, unless further refined, such a category will cause the grammar to overgeneralize, because the constituents such as $[and\ he\ talks]_{S \backslash S}$ that this analysis induces do not behave like other categories with respect to the rules in the rest of the grammar. In particular, the rule of "backward composition" that is central to the analysis of example (40), here given as (iia), interacts with this analysis to wrongly permit (iib).

(ii) a. I gave the teacher an apple and a policeman a flower.

   b. *a man who walks and he talks

Since as we will see the rule involved is a theorem of the Lambek calculus, this observation applies to the entire family of "associative" generalized categorial grammars.

10. The annotation Φ^n on the reduction arrow in the rule is inspired by the combinatory notation of Curry and Feys (1958). Although as usual the semantic details can safely be ignored, the dots schematize over the following family of functionals combining the interpretation of the conjunction b with the two argument interpretations, following Partee and Rooth 1983.

(i) $\Phi^0 bxy \quad \equiv \quad bxy$

   $\Phi^1 bfg \quad \equiv \quad \lambda x.b(fx)(gx)$

   $\Phi^2 bfg \quad \equiv \quad \lambda x.\lambda y.b(fxy)(gxy)$

   $\Phi^3 bfg \quad \equiv \quad \lambda x.\lambda y.\lambda z.b(fxyz)(gxyz)$

   $\Phi^4 bfg \quad \equiv \quad \lambda x.\lambda y.\lambda z.\lambda w.b(fxyzw)(gxyzw)$

They correspond to the different instances of coordination discussed here, and (for English at least) we can assume a bound of $n = 4$, which (as noted earlier) seems to be the highest valency in the English lexicon. The ... convention is therefore merely an expository convenience. Every theory must schematize its constituent coordination rule semantically in the same way.

11. Curry and Feys (1958, 184 fn.) note that Curry called the operation **B** because that letter occurs prominently in the word *substitution*, and because the names **S** and **C** were already in use.

12. The equivalence sign in these definitions is supposed to indicate that the combinators are *primitives*, not that they are defined or interpreted in terms of the abstraction operator λ.

13. We could at some cost to readability write the semantics entirely in combinatory terms, without any use of variables, as Shaumyan (1977) does.

14. There is a lot of semantic detail here that can be skipped. It is fairly obvious that if we have an interpretation for the function *might* (say, as a set of ordered pairs from complement VPs and tensed predicates) and an interpretation for the function *marry* (in the same terms, a set of ordered pairs from NPs like *Manny* to VPs like *marry Manny*), then we know everything necessary to construct a new function from NPs to predicates (e.g. as an ordered set of pairs like *Manny* and *might marry Manny*).

15. The predicate-argument structures as they are given here are simplified and leave out certain details relevant to the implementation of the binding theory and control in the present framework. These further details are made explicit in Steedman 1996b.

16. Though slightly clumsy, the example is parallel to ones that Abbott (1976) shows to be grammatical in English. The related *wh*-extractions like *the policeman to whom I offered and may give a flower*, which (as we will see) hinge on the same generalization of composition, are impeccable.

17. In some early papers the corresponding schema was defined slightly more generally, leading to some overgeneration, which I am grateful to Glyn Morrill for calling to my attention.

18. The same generalization is implicit in the coordination rule (20), whose semantics was defined by Curry's schematic combinator Φ^n. We will see that both families of combinatory rules must be limited to bounded n.

19. T is also the remaining prominent consonant besides B and S in the word *substitution* (see note 11).

20. This remark should not be taken as assuming that the relation between morphological case and grammatical relations like subject is invariably straightforward. Icelandic (Rögnvaldsson 1982; Bresnan and Thráinsson 1990, 361-362) is a frequently-cited example that reveals some complexities that are passed over here.

21. Dowty (1996) has since pointed out that this analysis is incompatible with his (1979) and Bach's (1979) analyses of binding and control, and in fact he now disowns it. However, other analyses of the latter phenomena are discussed below.

22. I omit certain details here, including agreement, which both categories must include. See Steedman 1996b (which unhelpfully uses the $-convention to schematize over the last three categories) for details.

23. Since multiple extractions involve non-string-peripheral arguments, they require a generalization to the composition rules that will be discussed in chapter 4.

24. The suggestion that island phenomena are related to semantic interpretation goes back to Oehrle 1974, Rodman 1976, and Cooper 1982.

25. This property is shared by the GPSG analysis of parasitic gaps in Gazdar et al. 1985.

26. The analysis requires us to assume that even PPs that are apparently not subcategorized for, like the one in *I folded the rug over the painting*, must in some sense be arguments *PP* rather than adjuncts $VP \backslash VP$. Otherwise, the following example would be accepted with an analysis parallel to (55), to mean *I folded the rug over itself*:

(i) * a rug which I will [fold]$_{VP/NP}$ [over]$_{(VP \backslash VP)/NP}$

The unacceptability of this example is discussed further in chapter 4, but the idea that the PP is in some sense an argument is borne out by the fact that such prepositions can strand and therefore must be "composable into," as in the following example:

(ii) the picture which [I will fold the cloth]$_{S/PP}$ [over]$_{PP/NP}$

27. If the rule could apply with X equal to N, native speakers would accept the following with the meaning *a good dog with a dog*:

(i) *[a]$_{NP/N}$ [[good]$_{N/N}$ [with a]$_{(N \backslash N)/N}$]$_{N/N}$ [dog]$_N$

28. Infinitival and gerundival predicate categories are abbreviated as *VP* and *VP*$_{ing}$, and the raised NP object as $NP^\uparrow$, for ease of reading. Again details of the predicate-argument structure are simplified (see Steedman 1996b for a fuller account).

Chapter 4

1. That is not to say that further explanations might not be found—say, in arguments from learnability. But the onus of providing them remains upon us.

2. The Principle of Adjacency defined here is distinct from the similarly named principle used in Dependency Grammar (see Robinson 1970).

3. In terms of standard transformationalist theory, this principle is equivalent to a ban on the use of variables in transformations.

4. This position is closely related to the notion of "directionality of government" in Kayne 1983.

5. Identification of the individual instances that the generalization gives rise to for n up to about 3 is suggested as an exercise. It is easy to see that each combinator X^n makes 2^n syntactic instances available to Universal Grammar. However, the parametric specification of the lexicon of any given language will mean that many of these rules cannot apply in that language. The fact that there appear to be strong learnability-related constraints on possible lexicons for human languages, such as tendencies toward consistent head finality or head initiality, will further restrict the range of rules in any real language.

6. The categories given in (43) of chapter 3 for the relative pronoun is an example of a higher-order functor that induces a word order that would not otherwise be allowed. Dowty (1988) and Steedman (1987) stated the order-preserving property too generally, as Milward (1991, 1994) points out. Milward offers an example that purports to show that rule $<\mathbf{B}$ causes an overgeneration in a fragment of English that includes nonrestrictive relatives, allowing (ib) as well as (ia) with the categories shown.

(i) a.   [John,]$_{NP}$ [who speaks Russian,]$_{NP \backslash NP}$ [reluctantly]$_{(S \backslash NP)/(S \backslash NP)}$ [came]$_{S \backslash NP}$

    b.   *[John]$_{NP}$ [reluctantly,]$_{(S \backslash NP)/(S \backslash NP)}$ [who speaks Russian,]$_{NP \backslash NP}$ [came]$_{S \backslash NP}$

Although the example certainly shows that composition may induce new word orders, the category $NP \backslash NP$ for nonrestrictive relatives is not necessarily correct. In fact, the general immunity of nonrestrictives to constraints on movement makes it likely that they should not be regarded as "in construction" at all, but rather as a variety of parenthetical. The ill-formedness of (ib) can therefore be regarded as proof that the $NP \backslash NP$ category is incorrect, rather than as raising a problem for CCG.

7. See chapter 8 and Vijay-Shanker and Weir (1990, 1994) for discussions of power and complexity of CCG, including a polynomial time worst-case complexity parsing result under the assumptions used here.

8. Under at least some formalizations of the Principles of Consistency and Inheritance, including the one offered in chapter 8, two further non-order-preserving instances of type-raising are potentially allowed:

(i) *The Non-order-preserving type-raising rules*

    a. $X \quad \Rightarrow_{\mathbf{T}} \quad T/(T/X)$ $(>\mathbf{T}_{\times})$

    b. $X \quad \Rightarrow_{\mathbf{T}} \quad T \backslash (T \backslash X)$ $(<\mathbf{T}_{\times})$

If a construction is to be classified as configurational at all, it must entirely exclude such non-order-preserving instances of argument type-raising. We will see in chapter 8 that there is a natural formulation of the Principle of Consistency under which languages must either entirely exclude syntactic non-order-preserving type-raising or must sacrifice configurationality. There is no middle ground. Categories such as relative pronouns, which as we saw in (43) of chapter 3 are related to but distinct from non-order-preserving type-raised categories, are lexically unique words, strikingly prone to case marking. Because of their unique position and intonational markedness, it is assumed that English topicalized arguments are also in effect lexically special items, such as $S_{TOPIC}/(S/X)$, distinguished by intonation or the related comma in written sentences like *This law, the Supreme Court has ruled unconstitutional.* We might plausibly assume that this special category is assigned by a unary rule that only applies to the leftmost item in the sentence, as proposed in Steedman 1987.

9. Whether the specific overgeneralizations identified by Houtman can all be dealt with in this way this way depends on a more formal definition of the constraint than has been given here, and upon some open questions that we will not go into here about his examples, which involve numeric determiners that are known to be special case.

10. Examples like *Dexter, and I think Warren, are geniuses* are better, but only to the extent that *I think* can be read as parenthetical (as agreement reveals).

11. This problem in CCG is more restricted than "Dekker's paradox" concerning the Lambek calculus. Dekker noticed that two legitimate English categories NP/NP and S/S can in the Lambek calculus come to have the same category $(S/(S\backslash NP))/NP$, giving rise to anomalous conjunctions like the following (Dekker 1988, cited in Houtman 1994, 85–89).

(i) *The brother of, and John believes that, Pete slept.

Since CCG lacks the Geach "Division" rule, it does not fall prey to Dekker's overgeneration.

12. This question, including the alternative proposal of Perlmutter (1971), which relates exemption from the Fixed-Subject Condition to the parameter of pro-drop, is discussed at further length in Steedman 1996b.

13. More precisely, the relation that such categories bear to the basic VP/S categories is a first cousin to the Slash Termination Metarule 2 of Gazdar et al. (1985) (see Hukari and Levine 1987; Hepple 1990, 59). The analysis differs from that presented in Steedman 1987; see Steedman 1996b for further discussion of its ancestry.

14. This restriction (which is discussed in more detail in Steedman 1996b) prevents $[the]_{NP/N}$ $[good]_{N/N}$ $[with a toy]_{N\backslash N}$ $[boy]_N$ from meaning *the good boy with a toy.*

15. The feature-value $+SHIFT$ seems to be related to the notion "most oblique." The analysis given here for the restrictions on heavy NP shift differs in minor details from the one given in Steedman 1996b, 68–69.

16. Such rules raise obvious problems for the theory of language acquisition, which are briefly discussed in chapter 10. They are offered as no more than technical solutions.

17. However, if type-raising were lexical, so that *every* were $NP^{\uparrow}/N$, then the restriction would follow without stipulation, since the predicate is not a raisable category.

18. It is assumed here that the level of interpretation in question is neutral with respect to non-argument-structure-dependent aspects of meaning such as quantifier scope, which is discussed in section 4.4.

19. Here, this mechanism is represented by λ-binding of variables. But this mechanism should not be confused with the combinatory rules that establish the long-distance dependency itself. These variables just represent the normal mechanism for binding *all* arguments to predicates.

20. A more complete account of anaphor binding in CCG is offered in Steedman 1996b. The idea that control verbs involve implicit anaphors goes back at least to Helke (1971) and has more recently been proposed by Manzini (1993).

21. Clark's analysis replaces the eccentric proposal to treat auxiliaries as control verbs in Steedman 1996b.

22. The latter is an example of Taraldsen's (1979) anti-c-command condition on parasitic gaps, discussed in Steedman 1996b.

23. For example, in order to obtain the narrow scope object reading for (55b), Hendriks (1993), subjects the category of the transitive verb to "argument lifting" to make it a function over a type-raised object type, and the coordination rule must be correspondingly semantically generalized.

24. Technically, this analysis raises questions which we will pass over here about the status of expressions like $sk'_{sax_1}y$ with respect to the binding theory as it is defined in Steedman 1996b, since they can be bound but do not count as pro-terms for the purposes of c- or f-command.

25. Similar considerations give rise to apparent wide and narrow scope versions of the existential donkey in (56).

26. I am grateful to Gann Bierner for discussions on this problem.

27. The exact facts are hard to pin down in this area, and some judges claim to get the dependent readings. In the terms of the present theory this may mean that they have true quantifier meanings for upward monotone quantifiers. One case where almost everyone seems to get a dependent reading is the following, pointed out to me by Yoad Winter:

(i) A flag was hanging in front of at most two/exactly three/at least four windows.

However, the indefinites that give the appearance of dependency in this way seem to be quite restricted, and may be confined to entities that are inherent duplicates, like flags and books, even when they are definite. So we get

(ii) a. The American flag was hanging in front of at most two windows.
      b. A copy of The Little Red Songbook was seized from at least three bathrooms.
      c. #A woman was waving from at most two/exactly three/at least four windows.

28. The corresponding example for this point in Steedman (1999) is in error.

29. The architecture is therefore close to that implicit in Chomsky (1993, 1995), although the idea is implicit in much earlier systems, including Chomsky's own (1957), Montague Grammar, Woods's (1973) ATN grammars, and earlier versions of the present theory.

Chapter 5

1. This chapter is a completely revised and reworked version of Steedman (1991a).

2. The terms "theme" and "rheme" are taken from Halliday (1967b, 1970), although I follow Lyons (1977) and Bolinger (1989) in rejecting Halliday's requirement that the theme be sentence-initial. I also leave open the possibility that an utterance may involve multiple or "discontinuous" themes and/or rhemes.

3. Wilson and Sperber (1979) and Prince (1986), define the notion here identified as

theme in terms of the related but technically distinct (and as Jackendoff points out less appropriate) notion of "open proposition," or proposition including an unbound free variable.

4.   Oehrle (1987), Moortgat (1988b), Morrill (1994), and Hendriks (1994, 1998) explicitly relate other Lambek-style varieties of categorial grammars to prosody.

5.   Dwight Bolinger and Julia Hirschberg in personal communications have at least half convinced me that there are circumstances under which one or the other is allowed. However, the only claim I make is that if such circumstances exist, they are such as to make *both* more felicitous.

6.   The conspiracy between prosodic phenomena and the notion of constituency that emerges from related grammars including associative operations is noted in Steedman (1985, 540), and by Moortgat (1987, 1988a), and Oehrle (1988). Related points concerning "bracketing paradoxes" in morphology are made by Hoeksema (1984), Hoeksema and Janda (1988), Moortgat (1988a,b), and Morrill (1994). See also other categorial analyses of Wheeler (1981, 1988) and Schmerling (1981).

7.   Steedman (2000) generalizes the system to the remaining pitch accents and boundary tones, and explores further the discourse functions of the tunes considered here.

8.   These were originally written L- and H-, a usage that continues in the ToBI notation (Silverman et al. 1992). (ToBI stands for "Tones and Break Indices".) Here I will follow the notation in Pierrehumbert and Beckman (1988).

9.   Neither Pierrehumbert's theory nor its combinatory expression below should be taken as implying that the null tone corresponds to an absence of pitch. Nor does either version imply that an element bearing the null tone is always realized with the same intonation contour. They merely imply that the intonation is independently specified. It follows that the null tone may carry information about what pitch accents and other tones are downstream of it. As in the case of downstep, it also follows that a processor might make use of this information.

10.   For the moment, the distinction between the intonational phrase proper and what Pierrehumbert and her colleagues call the "intermediate" phrase is ignored. These categories will be seen to differ with respect to boundary tone sequences.

11.   The reason for notating the latter boundary as LL% rather than L again has to do with the distinction between intonational and intermediate phrases, to which I will return.

12.   See Veltman 1984, Heim 1983, Harel 1984, Landman 1986, Groenendijk and Stokhof 1990, Gabbay, Hodkinson and Reynolds 1994, and Steedman 1997 for discussion of various "dynamic" logics that can be used to formalize the notion of updates and side effects.

13.   Discourse models of the kind just sketched can be more or less directly realized using logic programming languages such as Prolog. A model of this kind has been investigated in some detail and implemented computationally by Prevost (1995).

14.   It will be recalled from chapter 3 that $ana'x$ is the equivalent of a PRO controlled subject.

15.   An alternative prosody, in which the contrastive tune is confined to *Anna*, seems

15. An alternative prosody, in which the contrastive tune is confined to *Anna*, seems equally coherent in this context. In Steedman 1991a, I argue that this alternative is informationally distinct and arises from an ambiguity about whether the theme established by the question is *Anna* or *who Anna married*. It too is accepted by the rules below.

16. It is important to know that the term "focus" is used in the literature in several conflicting ways. The present use is common among phonologists, who use the term simply to denote the material marked by the pitch accent(s). Grosz and Sidner (1986), use it to denote something like topic, or theme in present terms. Other authors such as Chomsky (1971), Jackendoff (1972), Gussenhoven (1983), Hajičová and Sgall (1987, 1988), Vallduví (1990), Lambrecht (1994), Erteschik-Shir (1998), and Zubizarreta (1998), in different ways confine its use to the rheme. Still other authors, notably Selkirk (1984), Rooth (1985, 1992), Jacobs (1991), Krifka (1991), É. Kiss (1998), and Rochemont (1998), invoke "two levels" of focus, using the term to cover both comment/rheme *and* phonological focus.

17. The difference between pre- and postnuclear material is underlined by the fact that it is also possible to have an H* pitch accent on *woman* in this example, but not on *musical*.

18. This algorithm is related to one proposed by Dale and Haddock (1991), and forms a central module of the generation system described in Prevost and Steedman (1994).

19. There is a question about how to notate the tune of this example that we will return to below.

20. In this I follow Bird (1991) and Prevost (1995). As noted earlier, there are several other pitch accents in Pierrehumbert's system that are not explicitly covered here. See Steedman (to appear) for discussion.

21. This could be made explicit in the notation by writing the category for the verb with null tone as $(S_\eta \backslash NP_\eta)/NP_\eta : ate'$, with η a variable ranging over θ and ρ.

22. The categories given here constitute a modification to previous versions of the present theory that brings it more closely into line with the proposals in Pierrehumbert and Hirschberg 1990. The idea that boundaries are in categorial terms functors was proposed in Prevost and Steedman 1994; Prevost 1995 and independently by Kirkeby-Garstad and Polgárdi (1994).

23. The three remaining boundary-tones of Pierrehumbert's system, H, HH% and HL%, are omitted because they do not arise in the limited varieties of discourse considered here. They are discussed in Steedman to appear.

24. The present treatment of boundary tones, as exhibited in this derivation, shows how it is possible for a pitch accent and a boundary tone to affect the same word in the string. This detail was left unspecified in earlier work, as Kirkeby-Garstad and Polgárdi (1994) point out in a critique of the earlier papers. The symbol *the'* is no more than a placeholder for a proper semantics of the determiner.

25. In effect, the update action first abstracts over the * constant in the new theme. Higher-order unification provides one mechanism for this task, via the algorithm proposed by Huet (1975), in a manner discussed by Shieber, Pereira and Dalrymple (1996).

Prevost (1995) discusses a related device.

26. Relativization and coordination reveal that the sentences violate island constraints.

27. The prosodic annotation of this example represents a minor departure from Pierrehumbert, whose theory does not permit boundaries without corresponding pitch accents, and who would regard the whole tune as a single H*LL% intonational phrase. The present analysis is quite close to one proposed in a different notation by Bing (1979).

28. A multiple H* pitch accent on the VP is an even more appropriate response and also serves to distinguish these contexts, since it is not appropriate to (69).

29. This freer notion of Surface Structure may also explain some of the examples that Bolinger (1985) has used to argue for an entirely autonomous, lexically oriented account of accent assignment, and that Gussenhoven (1985) has used to argue for a similarly autonomous focus-based account. It may also allow us to eliminate some of the nonsyntactic string-based rules and "performance structures" that Cooper and Paccia-Cooper (1980), Gee and Grosjean (1983), and Croft (1995) have proposed to add to the syntax-driven model.

30. However, it would be a great mistake from a processing point of view—and from the point of view of intelligibility of the present presentation—not to compile out this information, technically redundant though it may be, for it has to be used on a great many occasions.

31. As noted earlier, there is a close resemblance here between Information Structures and the structured-meanings of Cresswell (1973), von Stechow (1991), and Chierchia (1989).

Chapter 6

1. Sections 6.1–6.6 of the present chapter are a complete revision and reworking of part II of Steedman 1985, and together with sections 6.7–6.9 extend the coverage to a considerably larger fragment. The earlier paper used an early version of CCG in which slashes were nondirectional, forward and backward application were called "forward and backward combination," and composition was, following still earlier work with Tony Ades (Ades and Steedman 1982), called "partial combination." This chapter imports the earlier analysis into the more modern framework of this book. In the intervening years the basic analysis of the earlier paper has been criticized and improved upon in a number of different frameworks. The earliest and most influential of these developments was Johnson 1988, chaps. 3 and 5, which led to a number of related proposals within LFG, HPSG, and related unification-based grammar frameworks (see Netter 1988; Hepple 1990; Paritong 1992; Bouma and van Noord 1994; Reape 1994, 1996; Hinrichs and Nakazawa 1994). Many of these proposals have been influenced by Moortgat's similar proposal (discussed in Moortgat 1988a, and developed independently at approximately the same time as the present one), which used functional composition as a lexical, rather than syntactic, operation. Along the way, many of these authors and others such as de Roeck (1984), Janeaway (1991), Houtman (1994), Versmissen (1996), and van Noord and Bouma (1997) have pointed to shortcomings in the original account. I have tried to acknowledge and act upon these

criticisms in the course of the chapter. I am grateful to Gann Bierner, Mimo Caenepeel, Angeliek van Hout, Susanne Kronenberg, Jan van Kuppevelt, Marc Moens, and Annie Zaenen for help with revisions to the grammar and/or informant judgments.

2. Evers (1975, 51, 55) following Bech (1955) states that all but the two most deeply embedded verbs in sentences including tensed auxiliaries and multiple infinitives may occur in the Dutch tensed-first order, requiring forward composition within the verb group, as in (i), potentially inducing crossed dependencies in German:

(i) ...daß man ihn hier wird können lassen liegen bleiben.
     ...that one him here will be-able leave lie   stay
     '...that one will be able to let him stay lying here.'

Certain dialects of German appear to allow *sah füttern helfen* for (6), and some Swiss dialects discussed by Shieber (1985) and Cooper (1988) even appear to allow the full Dutch order, that is, the equivalent of *sah helfen füttern*.

3. There is an increasing processing load that makes such multiple embeddings increasingly unacceptable. By well-known arguments (see Chomsky and Miller 1963), such considerations are irrelevant to questions of grammaticality.

4. See Seuren 1985 for a discussion of certain problems that Dutch clitic pronouns posed for the earlier version of this theory.

5. S_{+SUB} is an abbreviation for $S_{+SUB}^{-CP,+IP}$, a tensed subordinate bare complement clause or IP. *VP* is an abbreviation for the infinitival predicate category $S_{?SUB}^{-CP,-IP}\backslash NP$, unmarked on the feature *SUB*. The categories given here for infinitival complement verbs differ significantly from those in Steedman 1985. The present analysis of bare-infinitival complement-taking verbs as object control verbs follows Johnson 1988, 120.

6. I assume that the awkwardness of passives like *?Dexter was seen eat a frog*, like that of *?Dexter was promised to take a bath*, is semantic in origin, as the increased acceptability of *Dexter was seen eaten by frogs* and *Dexter was promised to be allowed to take a bath* suggests.

7. Koopman and Szabolcsi (1998), referring to Kenesei (1989), discuss data for Hungarian verb raising which appear to suggest that Hungarian has categories corresponding to both (9) and (12).

8. Again, I depart from the earlier analysis and follow Johnson (1988) in assuming an object control verb category for these verbs. VP_{-SUB} is an abbreviation for $S_{-SUB}^{-CP,-IP}\backslash NP$.

9. This is the first of two differently restricted rules of forward crossed composition—see the appendix to this chapter.

10. Increasingly higher-order composition rules are required to combine maximally incremental assembly of a derivation on the basis of the idealized German categories. (Four verbs requires $<B^3$, and so on.) Since there is a small finite bound on $<B^n$, this fact may suggest a reason why in reality German tends to adopt the Dutch tensed-first word order, and hence the Dutch categories, when more than two verbs are implicated in sentences of this kind, as Bech (1955) and Evers (1975) observed. It may also explain the somewhat greater difficulty of processing the "German" order found by Bach,

Brown and Marslen-Wilson (1986). See Joshi 1990 for discussion and an alternative explanation for the result.

11. This change improves upon the earlier analysis. However, there are Germanic languages in which these variants apparently *are* allowed with the corresponding verbs. (An example is the Zürich dialect of Swiss German, which allows the equivalent of (22–24), as well as the order that is allowed in Dutch. See Lötscher 1978, Shieber 1985, Cooper 1988.

12. In Steedman (1985) I reported some doubt among my informants as to whether it is actually ungrammatical. Seuren (1985) includes an extended discussion of these verbs in relation to the theory in Steedman 1985.

13. It seems possible however that there is a purely phonological solution to this problem.

14. The deeper the extracted NP, the more cumbersome the resulting sentence, presumably for pragmatic reasons. Where the semantics permits, as in the ambiguous (i), some informants will only accept the extraction of the higher complement NP:

(i) de jongen die ik het meisje zag kussen
    the boy   that I the girl   saw kiss
    'the boy that I saw kiss the girl/ the boy that I saw the girl kiss'

However, in examples like (35), where semantics will only permit the deeper extraction, they will accept it, so the limitation appears not to lie in the grammar.

15. Under certain circumstances topicalization of objects and the like appears to be allowed in subordinate clauses like (i) (Angeliek van Hout, personal communication):

(i) ... dat zulke lekkere chocola Hendrik altijd in zijn eentje probeert op te eten.
    ... that such delicious chocolate Hendrik always on his own tries up to eat
    '... that Hendrik always tries to eat up such delicious chocolate on his own.'

I assume that examples like these in Dutch are handled by the same mechanism as relativization, discussed below.

16. This analysis is somewhat similar to the adjunction-based analyses proposed in Haegeman 1992, 193 (as opposed to the quite different analysis in Haegeman and van Riemsdijk 1986) and in Rambow 1994a. All of these analyses in turn represent a reversion to the adjunction analysis of Evers (1975).

17. "*" here means "bad under the reading indicated by the subscripts." Such scrambling is allowed under certain conditions in German, a fact that may excuse the use of this sort of stipulative fine-tuning of features to exclude it in Dutch.

18. Of course, the grammar correctly allows two further semantically distinct analyses for the example, which is ambiguous in Dutch. These further readings correspond to the English *the teacher who Jan saw t help Cecilia feed the hippopotamuses* and the semantically anomalous *the teacher who Jan saw Cecilia help the hippopotamuses feed t* (cf. note 14).

19. Maling and Zaenen (1978) note that Icelandic, which is sometimes claimed to be an SVO language, also fails to exhibit the subject/object extraction asymmetry. Elsewhere (Steedman 1996b, 55, example (100)) I show how this fact can be explained in present

terms by assuming (as Mailing and Zaenen do) that Icelandic is a V2 language, and (as I do in section 6.7 for Dutch and German main-clause orders) that V2 order arises from a VSO verb category via leftward-extraction.

20. As before, S abbreviates the category $S^{-CP,+IP}$ of an IP and VP abbreviates $S^{-CP,-IP}\backslash NP$.

21. The present analysis bears some resemblance to Hepple's (1990) account of German main-clause order, in that inverted order is taken as primary in main clauses, and SVX order is assumed to arise from topicalization, in line with the analysis in den Besten 1983. In other respects the analysis differs. A version of the present analysis first appeared as Steedman 1983 and was discussed by Hoeksema (1985), who proposes an alternative analysis (criticized by Hepple) involving multiple lexical entries for the verb.

22. I am grateful to Susanne Kronenberg, Anneke Neijt, and Angeliek van Hout for advice on this corner of the data.

23. Recall that the results of infinitival verbs (etc.) are underspecified with respect to the value of the feature $\pm SUB$. It follows that unification coerces a single lexical category to either value. Thus, this assumption does not entail any expansion to the lexicon. See note 11 for remarks about some Germanic dialects that appear not to draw this distinction.

24. In view of the fact that explicit case and so-called free word order are strongly correlated, we may further conjecture that certain languages with more elaborate case systems, such as Classical Latin and even other dialects of Germanic, may achieve such freedom by exploiting some of the further opportunities for composing cased categories that have been excluded with category-based restrictions on combinatory rules in the grammar of Dutch, as in (54), (60), (61), and (82).

25. Of course, with nonconfigurational languages the whole question of which dependencies are crossed and which uncrossed becomes harder to answer. See note 24.

Chapter 7

1. This chapter is distantly based on some parts of Steedman 1990, which it revises and extends.

2. The adverbial inflection of the verb is required on the first conjunct for clausal coordination, but is not the source of the present anomaly. I am indebted to Nobo Komogata for providing these examples.

3. See Miyagawa 1997 for extended arguments in a different framework that such a base-generative account of scrambling is correct for Japanese, and for semantic arguments for distinguishing extraction from scrambling. See Komagata 1999 for a more extended discussion of CCG and Japanese including OS+OSV coordination, and see Hoffman 1995a,b and Baldridge 1998 for discussion of extended formalisms for unordered categories.

4. See McCloskey 1991. I am grateful to Jim McCloskey for help with these examples.

5. This consequence of the present analysis of the syntactic categories, whatever its

advantages for the theory of coordination, has led Dowty to abandon the idea entirely (David Dowty, personal communication).

6. The following analysis of SVO gapping entirely departs from that in Steedman 1990, in which the right conjunct was assembled by a very restricted form of crossed forward composition.

7. Examples like (28d) are standard in British English, although pseudogapping seems to be less productive in North American dialects (see Levin 1978 for an early discussion).

8. It is an assumption forced by the present theory that strings like *eighty percent* in these examples are complete subjects and that the gaps do *not* include anything corresponding to *of the population*, as the brackets indicate.

9. The analysis presented in this section differs in important respects from that in Steedman 1990, in which a related argument cluster arose from *crossed* composition of the SVO subject and complement.

10. The apparent possibility of examples like the following in dialects which allow pseudogapping (see note 7) suggests that such examples, like certain closely related "comparative subdeletion" examples, are anaphorically mediated, like VP ellipsis:

(i) Warren eats beans, but I doubt whether Dexter does potatoes.

11. To the extent that the NP in question is assumed to be nominative, the composition itself requires an instantiation forbidden by the restriction of type-raising to raising over categories that are permitted by the parametric specification of the lexicon under the Principle of Categorial Type Transparency.

12. The slight awkwardness of such examples is presumably related to that of multiple right node raising, which according to Abbott (1976) lies in the domain of pragmatics rather than syntax (see note 16 in chapter 3).

13. Byron's lines on the syphilitic Lord Elgin and the marbles, which include a gap parallel to (52a), must therefore be explained as having arisen in a poetic idiom in which *What hath wrought the pox?*, and hence OS order, was grammatical:

(i) *Noseless himself, he brings us noseless blocks,*
     To show what time hath wrought, and what, the pox.

14. This observation also holds of the earlier analysis in Steedman 1990, based on crossed composition.

15. I will pass over the question of exactly how the anaphoric operator θ'' works, whether by directly applying higher-order unification to the types and Logical Forms, as in Dalrymple, Shieber and Pereira 1991 and Shieber, Pereira and Dalrymple 1996, or by one of the combinatory abstraction algorithms discussed in chapter 8, or by a more direct Alternative Semantics representation, of the kind discussed by Rooth (1985) and in chapter 5.

16. We could do this explicitly in the grammatical rule. However, this would make the grammar look as if it involved context-sensitive rules, which it does not.

17. This part of the account diverges from Steedman 1990.

18. Since chapter 5 treats discontinuous themes as multiple distinct presuppositions

about the alternative set, there is more to say here about how the corresponding category is generated. One possibility is to generate λ-terms corresponding to the individual presuppositions (in this case corresponding to "wants" and "to win") and to compose them, then generate a syntactic type.

19. In support of this view it is striking that examples parallel to (70) but involving verbs that do not have subject-extracting categories or "exceptional-case-marking" categories seem less good:

(i) #Dexter wonders whether Watford won, and Warren, Ipswich.

This may be because the corresponding contextual open questions are much harder to formulate and accommodate.

20. Steedman 1990 attempts to extend a related analysis to certain cases of "subject gapping" that are found in Germanic languages in sentences like the following (see Höhle 1983; Wunderlich 1988; Heycock 1991; Heycock and Kroch 1993, 1994):

(i) Toen kwam Jan binnen en   dronk bier met ons.
     Then came Jan in   and drank beer with us
     'Then Jan came in and drank beer with us'

A similar extension seems possible in the present framework, but I have not attempted it here.

21. I am grateful to Jason Baldridge for drawing my attention to this consequence of the present analysis, which does not emerge from the earlier analysis in Steedman 1990.

22. Stripping will of course potentially give rise to an extra derivation for right-node-raised sentences, as it will in any theory of grammar that covers the construction at all.

23. See Cormack 1984 and Jacobson 1991 for other categorially based proposals concerning VP ellipsis, and see Romero 1997 for an Alternative Semantics–based account of sluicing.

Chapter 8

1. Here I diverge from the argument on this point in Steedman 1988.

2. See Dowty 1993. However, see Szabolcsi 1989, Cresswell 1990 and Jacobson 1991, 1992a for treatments of such phenomena in variable-free combinatory terms.

3. If we are thinking of the typed calculi, then **I**, **K**, and **S** are schemata over infinite sets of typed combinators.

4. Note that I have not said how the recursive call to *fact* could work. Indeed such recursive definitions are only possible in the untyped calculi. I will return to this point.

5. For expository simplicity I have used the familiar λ-notation to identify the notion of abstraction, rather than Curry and Feys's (1958) "bracket abstraction" notation, which was introduced in order to make it clear that the algorithm constitutes a *definition* of λ-abstraction, rather than invoking it as a primitive.

6. **C** is in fact the combinator that is implicit in one of the Bach/Dowty family of "wrap" operations, which in the present grammar is confined to the lexicon.

7. Smullyan elegantly defines **C** as **BBT(BBT)(BBT)**.

8. See Morrill and Carpenter 1990 for further discussion of the relation between grammar and the λ_I-calculus.

9. Strong generative power is the capacity to generate the trees that a compositional semantics requires, as opposed to the weak generative capacity to generate the set containing all and only the strings of the language. Grammars that generate the same trees for each string of a given language are said to be strongly equivalent, whereas those that assign different trees to the strings are merely weakly equivalent.

10. Interestingly, the parenthesis-free variant of CCG discussed by Friedman, Dai and Wang (1986) and Friedman and Venketasan (1986) is of greater power (see Weir 1988 for discussion).

11. Note also that the category X' in the LIG schemata will not in general be the same as the category X in the corresponding instantiation of the categorial rule. If X is a function category, then X' is its result and the stack ... is its argument(s). In terms of the earlier $ convention, X is of the form X'\$.

12. The above remarks are confined to the intuitive demonstration that any CCG can be translated into a strongly equivalent LIG. It follows that the combinatory categorial languages (CCLs) are a subset of the linear indexed languages (LILs). It does not follow that any LIG can be realized as a CCG. The weak equivalence of CCG and LIG is proved by Vijay-Shanker and Weir (1990, 1994), who show that the set of tree-adjoining languages (TALs) is a subset of the set of CCLs, and that the set of LILs is a subset of that of TALs, from which it follows that the three language classes are identical.

13. The question of the existence of a class of automata that imposes the correct restriction should not be confused with the question of how to naturally constrain the more powerful automaton to capture performance limitations—say via limitations on stack depth, as in much work following Yngve 1960 and Miller and Chomsky 1963, such as Stabler 1994, Gibson 1996, and Lewis 1993.

14. See earlier chapters on the necessary restrictions on these rules.

15. The temptation to write context-sensitive combinatory rules, as in a momentary aberration I proposed elsewhere (Steedman (1987), 413) should also be resisted.

16. This notation is a variant of those proposed by Lyons (1968) and Huck (1985).

17. This device is of course borrowed from Prolog. As in Prolog, different occurrences of the underline symbol represent *distinct* irrelevant variables.

18. Declarativizing positions like this may seem laborious, but we will later be able to borrow the DCG trick of encoding such positions implicitly in difference-lists, so that we will be able to forget about absolute positions entirely.

19. When the rules are further specified in this way, as they must be for real grammars, it is desirable for reasons of efficiency and internal theoretical consistency to further stipulate that L_z be distinct from R_z. This prevents temporary spurious coordination of categories with different directionality.

20. The rules of functional substitution (9) of chapter 4 are also correctly limited to two general and four specific instances by the theory.

21. See below for discussion of how this property interacts with coordination.

22. The categories required for less rigidly configurational languages than English have been investigated by Kang (1988) for Korean, Hoffman (1995a,b) and Bozsahin (1998) for Turkish, Komagata (1999) for Japanese, Baldridge (1999) for Tagalog, and Trechsel (to appear) for Tzotzil. Komagata shows that the underspecification of raised categories can be transmitted under functional composition by similarly underspecified composition rules to capture scrambling in a strictly verb-final language. Baldridge suggests that freely ordering verb categories of the kind proposed by Hoffman should be regarded as schematizing over finitely many directional categories, and that composition and type-raising should be order-preserving.

23. The above argument translates directly into unification-based frameworks such as PATR or Prolog. A small Prolog program is given in Steedman 1991c which can be used to exemplify and check the argument. The program is based on the simple shift-reduce parser/recognizer discussed together with other more practical algorithms in chapter 9 below, and uses difference-list encoding of string position (see Stirling and Shapiro 1986, 239; Pereira and Shieber 1987; Gerdeman and Hinrichs 1990). This program is not proposed as a practical or efficient CCG parser. Although a few English lexical categories and an English sentence are given by way of illustration in Steedman 1991c, the very general combinatory rules that are included there will require further constraints if they are not to overgenerate with larger fragments. (For example, $>\mathbf{B}$ and $>\mathbf{B}_\times$ must be distinguished as outlined above, and the latter must be greatly constrained for English.) One very general constraint, excluding all combinations with or into *NP*, is included in the program, in order to force type-raising and exemplify the way in which further constrained rule-instances may be specified.

The 1991 paper includes a claim that the right conjunct in English gapping under an earlier analysis of the phenomenon than the one presented in chapter 7 has the interesting property of refusing to combine with a "real" SVO verb, because the direction features have the effect of paradoxically requiring that verb to be to the right of the subject and to the left of the object. This claim does not apply to, and is not necessary for, the present analysis.

Chapter 9

1. The division of processing labor between a nondeterministic algorithm and an oracle is not always made explicit, particularly in implementations. However, all processors can be viewed in this way. A more extensive survey of the parsing literature in terms of a similar tripartite architecture can be found in Kay 1980.

2. These remarks should not be taken to imply a stand on either side of the question of whether the appearance of rule learning can or cannot be achieved by probabilistic mechanisms such as parallel distributed processors (Rumelhart, Hinton and McClelland 1986) or neural networks. The fact that many actual rule-like systems such as English past tense morphology include exceptions means that in practice rule-based and probabilistic theories have each come to embody elements of the other (see Prasada and Pinker 1993). To the extent that such hybrid systems embody structure, whether distributed in representation or not, it is likely that these remarks about incremental refinement apply to them as well. In fact, to the extent that connectionists deny the idea

of *any* kind of grammar, let alone a covering grammar, they apply even more strongly.

3. Natural processors might conceivably require grammars to be in some normal form. However, provided that the normal form is a class of grammars of the same automata-theoretic power that the semantics of the language requires (and therefore of the same power as the competence grammar), we would expect that normal form to simply be a characteristic of the grammars we actually observe. In other words, we would view it as a (processing-based) constraint on the form of the competence grammars that actually exist. If on the other hand we are to entertain the possibility that the requirement for a covering grammar might arise from the fact that the mechanisms that have access to the outside world are for some reason of a lesser automata-theoretic power than the competence grammar, then the evolutionary claims become even more far-fetched. It seems inevitable that the mapping between analyses under the two grammars must become more complex. The problem of incremental language learning becomes correspondingly more complex. So of course does the problem mentioned above, of evolving the two systems in lockstep. Indeed, we have to ask ourselves how these two systems, which by assumption have completely different automata-theoretic character, could begin to talk to one another in the first place. We have to ask ourselves whether it would not be simpler for evolution to bring the processor more in line with the requirements of competence grammar—after all, it has already come up with such a mechanism once, in the form of the interpreter for the competence semantics.

4. The Strict Competence Hypothesis is somewhat unhelpfully referred to in Steedman 1989 simply as the "strong competence hypothesis." The version defined there and here is stricter than Bresnan and Kaplan's version.

5. The CKY algorithm requires grammars in Chomsky Normal Form, where all productions are either binary productions with two nonterminals as daughters, or unary productions replacing a nonterminal with a terminal. All the combinatory rules except the unary type-raising rules and the coordination rule are binary. I will defer the question of what to do about these exceptions, merely noting that everything else about CCG is in Chomsky Normal Form.

6. Strictly speaking, even ordinary CFPSG potentially gives rise to multiple equivalent derivations. However, in contrast to those of CCG, all of the derivation trees are isomorphic, and the standard algorithms like the bottom-up algorithms discussed below are guaranteed to find exactly one derivation for each reading.

7. The term is misleading in the sense that *any* theory of grammar that actually covers the range of coordination, intonation, and extraction phenomena addressed by CCG must necessarily include the same ambiguities and encounter the same nondeterminism in parsing them. The ambiguity is there in the language itself.

8. Eisner (1996) has proposed a related technique that annotates constituents in the chart in such a way that multiple copies are never built, avoiding the need for the unification-based matching check. The technique is related to similar proposals for normal form parsing by Hepple and Morrill (1989), Hendriks (1993), König (1994), and Hepple (1999) for the Lambek calculi.

9. This particular algorithm is based on the incremental version 12.4.2 of the CKY algorithm in Harrison 1978, 433. See Briscoe 1984, Pulman 1986, Hausser 1986, Wirén

1992, van der Linden 1993, and Milward 1994, 1995 for alternative approaches to incremental parsing with CG and related grammars.

10. This profusion of ambiguity suggests that there is a pressure to keep words short. Such a pressure presumably reflects the obvious need to keep utterances from taking too long in comparison to the accompanying thought processes.

11. The even earlier fragment *The flowers sent* ... probably does not of itself provide enough information to eliminate the spurious main-clause analysis, because of the potential availability of continuations like ... *the patient into raptures.* This observation is in line with Trueswell, Tanenhaus, and Garnsey's (1994) results from eye-tracking experiments on similar sentences in null contexts, which suggest that reanalysis is triggered at the preposition, rather than at the preceding verb.

12. See Steedman 1985. While I will not attempt to explore this claim fully here, it seems to be supported by experimental observations by Inoue and Fodor (1995), Konieczny et al. (1997), and others, who show that interpretable structure is built in advance of encountering the verb in verb-final constructions in Japanese and German.

13. The notation is adapted. Pulman also proposes an operation corresponding to type-raising as a rule of processing, under the name "Invoke."

14. See Shieber and Johnson 1993 for an extensive critique of this proposal.

15. Stabler's note 3 seems to confirm that he does not see this as the central issue.

16. See Haddock 1987, 1989, Dale and Haddock 1991, Stone and Doran 1997; Stone and Webber 1998 and Stone 1998, 1999 for proposals for efficient constraint-satisfaction-based mechanisms for incremental semantic evaluation of this kind.

17. Komagata's English lexicon contains 1174 words with 272 distinct categories. The Japanese lexicon contains around 200 words. The average number of lexical entries per word averaged over the 3517 words (197 sentences) parsed with the English grammar was 3.8. That for the 431 words (22 sentences) parsed using the Japanese grammar was 4.5. Average case parsing times were better than n^3.

Chapter 10

1. I have borrowed this interpretation of the GB notion of projection from Szabolcsi 1992.

2. The only obvious alternative seems to be for the child to compute the respective effects of the candidates on the existing grammar—say, by computing the number of unattested alternatives to the sentences that the child has actually encountered that is predicted by each. On this measure the most restrictive alternative would be correctly chosen.

3. One would of course predict a quite different course of acquisition for subject extraction in (for example) Italian. According to the account proposed in Steedman 1996b, Italian subject relatives arise from VOS verbs for which the child will have encountered nonextracted sentences. There is therefore a strong prediction that embedded subject relatives should be acquired much earlier in Italian.

References

Aarts, Erik. 1995. *Investigations in Logic, Language, and Computation*. Ph.D. thesis, Universiteit Utrecht.

Abbott, Barbara. 1976. "Right Node Raising as a Test for Constituenthood." *Linguistic Inquiry*, 7, 639–642.

Ades, Anthony, and Mark Steedman. 1982. "On the Order of Words." *Linguistics and Philosophy*, 4, 517–558.

Aho, Alfred, and S .C. Johnson. 1974. "LR parsing." *Computing Surveys*, 6, 99–124.

Ajdukiewicz, Kazimierz. 1935. "Die syntaktische Konnexität." In Storrs McCall, ed., *Polish Logic 1920–1939*, 207–231. Oxford: Oxford University Press. Translated from *Studia Philosophica*, 1, 1–27.

Alshawi, Hiyan, and Richard Crouch. 1992. "Monotonic Semantic Representation." In *Proceedings of the 30th Annual Meeting of the Association for Computational Linguistics*, 32–38. San Francisco, CA: Morgan Kaufmann.

Altmann, Gerry. 1985. *Reference and the Resolution of Local Syntactic Ambiguity*. Ph.D. thesis, University of Edinburgh.

Altmann, Gerry. 1988. "Ambiguity, Parsing Strategies, and Computational Models." *Language and Cognitive Processes*, 3, 73–98.

Altmann, Gerry, and Mark Steedman. 1988. "Interaction with Context During Human Sentence Processing." *Cognition*, 30, 191–238.

Aoun, Joseph, Norbert Hornstein, David Lightfoot, and Amy Weinberg. 1987. "Two Types of Locality." *Linguistic Inquiry*, 18, 537–578.

Asher, Nicolas, and Tim Fernando. 1997. "Labelling Representations for Effective Disambiguation." In *Proceedings of the 2nd International Workshop on Computational Semantics, Tilburg*. Tilburg: Katholieke Universiteit Brabant.

Bach, Emmon. 1976. "An Extension of Classical Transformational Grammar." In *Problems in Linguistic Metatheory: Proceedings of the 1976 Conference at Michigan State University*, 183–224. Lansing: Michigan State University.

Bach, Emmon. 1979. "Control in Montague Grammar." *Linguistic Inquiry*, 10, 513–531.

Bach, Emmon. 1980. "In Defense of Passive." *Linguistics and Philosophy*, 3, 297–341.

Bach, Emmon. 1983. "Generalized Categorial Grammars and the English Auxiliary." In Frank Heny and Barry Richards, eds., *Linguistic Categories: Auxiliaries and Related Puzzles, II*, 101–120. Dordrecht: Reidel.

Bach, Emmon. 1988. "Categorial Grammars as Theories of Language." In Richard T. Oehrle, Emmon Bach, and Deirdre Wheeler, eds., *Categorial Grammars and Natural Language Structures*, 17–34. Dordrecht: Reidel.

Bach, Emmon, Colin Brown, and William Marslen-Wilson. 1986. "Crossed and Nested Dependencies in Dutch and German." *Language and Cognitive Processes*, 1, 249–262.

Bach, Emmon, Eloise Jelinek, Angelika Kratzer, and Barbara Partee, eds. 1995. *Quantification in Natural Languages*. Dordrecht: Kluwer.

Bach, Emmon, and Barbara Partee. 1980. "Anaphora and Semantic Structure." In *Papers from the 10th Regional Meeting of the Chicago Linguistic Society, Parasession on Pronouns and Anaphora*. Chicago, IL: University of Chicago, Chicago Linguistic Society.

Baker, C. L. 1979. "Syntactic Theory and the Projection Problem." *Linguistic Inquiry*, 10, 533–581.

Baker, Mark. 1995. "On the Absence of Certain Quantifiers in Mohawk." In Emmon Bach, Eloise Jelinek, Angelika Kratzer, and Barbara Partee, eds., *Quantification in Natural Languages*, 21–58. Dordrecht: Kluwer.

Baldridge, Jason. 1998. *Local Scrambling and Syntactic Asymmetries*. Master's thesis, University of Pennsylvania.

Baldridge, Jason. 1999. "A Categorial Account of Extraction Asymmetries in Tagalog and Toba Batak." Ms., University of Edinburgh.

Bar-Hillel, Yehoshua. 1953. "A Quasi-Arithmetical Notation for Syntactic Description." *Language*, 29, 47–58.

Bar-Hillel, Yehoshua, Chaim Gaifman, and Eliyahu Shamir. 1964. "On Categorial and Phrase Structure Grammars." In Yehoshua Bar-Hillel, ed., *Language and Information*, 99–115. Reading, MA: Addison-Wesley.

Barendregt, Hendrik. 1981. *The Lambda Calculus*. Amsterdam: North Holland.

Barss, Andrew, and Howard Lasnik. 1986. "A Note on Anaphora and Double Objects." *Linguistic Inquiry*, 17, 347–354.

Bartels, Christine. 1997. *Towards a Compositional Interpretation of English Statement and Question Intonation*. Ph.D. thesis, University of Massachusetts, Amherst.

Barwise, Jon, and Robin Cooper. 1981. "Generalized Quantifiers and Natural Language." *Linguistics and Philosophy*, 4, 159–219.

Barwise, Jon, and John Perry. 1980. "Situations and Attitudes." *Journal of Philosophy*, 78, 668–691.

Bayer, Josef. 1990. *Directionality of Government and Logical Form: a Study of Focusing Particles and* Wh-*Scope*. Universität Konstanz. Habiliationsschrift.

Bayer, Josef. 1996. *Directionality and Logical Form: On the Scope of Focusing Particles and* Wh-in-situ. Dordrecht: Kluwer.

Bayer, Sam, and Mark Johnson. 1995. "Features and Agreement." In *Proceedings of the 33rd Annual Meeting of the Association for Computational Linguistics, June, Cambridge, MA*, 70–76. San Francisco, CA: Morgan Kaufmann.

Beaver, David. 1997. "Presupposition." In Johan van Benthem and Alice ter Meulen, eds., *Handbook of Logic and Language*, 939–1008. Amsterdam: North Holland.

Bech, G. 1955. *Studien über das deutsche Verbum infinitivum, Band I*. Kopenhagen: Munksgaard.

Beckman, Mary. 1996. "The Parsing of Prosody." *Language and Cognitive Processes*, 11, 17–67.

Beckman, Mary, and Janet Pierrehumbert. 1986. "Intonational Structure in Japanese and English." *Phonology Yearbook*, 3, 255–309.

Beghelli, Filippo, and Tim Stowell. 1997. "Distributivity and Negation: The Syntax of *Each* and *Every*." In Anna Szabolcsi, ed., *Ways of Scope-Taking*, 71–107. Dordrecht: Kluwer.

van Benthem, Johan. 1986. *Essays in Logical Semantics*. Dordrecht: Reidel.

van den Berg, Martin. 1996. *The Internal Structure of Discourse*. Ph.D. thesis, Universiteit van Amsterdam.

van Berkum, Jos, Colin Brown, and Peter Hagoort. 1999. "Early referential context effects in sentence processing: Evidence from event-related brain potentials." *Journal of Memory and Language*, 41, 147–182.

Berwick, Robert, and Amy Weinberg. 1984. *The Grammatical Basis of Linguistic Performance*. Cambridge, MA: MIT Press.

den Besten, Hans. 1983. "On the Interaction of Root Transformations and Lexical Deletive Rules." In Werner Abraham, ed., *On the Formal Syntax of the Westgermania*, 47–131. Amsterdam: John Benjamins.

Bever, Thomas. 1970. "The Cognitive Basis for Linguistic Structures." In John Hayes, ed., *Cognition and the Development of Language*, 279–362. New York: Wiley.

Billot, Sylvie, and Bernard Lang. 1989. "The Structure of Shared Forests in Ambiguous Parsing." In *Proceedings of the 27th Annual Meeting of the Association for Computational Linguistics, Vancouver*, 143–151. San Francisco, CA: Morgan Kaufmann.

Bing, Janet. 1979. *Aspects of English Prosody*. Ph.D. thesis, University of Massachusetts at Amherst. Published by Garland, New York, 1985.

Bird, Steven. 1991. "The Intonational Phrase in Sign-Based Grammar." In *Workshop on Declarative Perspectives on the Syntax-Prosody Interface, Utrecht.* Edinburgh: University of Edinburgh.

Bittner, Maria. 1995. "Quantification in Eskimo: A Challenge for Compositional Semantics." In Emmon Bach, Eloise Jelinek, Angelika Kratzer, and Barbara Partee, eds., *Quantification in Natural Languages*, 59–80. Dordrecht: Kluwer.

Bittner, Maria, and Ken Hale. 1995. "Remarks on Definiteness in Warlpiri." In Emmon Bach, Eloise Jelinek, Angelika Kratzer, and Barbara Partee, eds., *Quantification in Natural Languages*, 81–105. Dordrecht: Kluwer.

Bolinger, Dwight. 1985. "Two Views of Accent." *Journal of Linguistics*, 21, 79–124.

Bolinger, Dwight. 1989. *Intonation and Its Uses.* Stanford, CA: Stanford University Press.

Bouma, Gosse. 1985. *Warlbiri Wildness: A Categorial Study of Free Word-Order.* Master's thesis, Rijksuniversiteit Groningen.

Bouma, Gosse. 1987. "A Unification-Based Analysis of Unbounded Dependencies in Categorial Grammar." In *Proceedings of the 6th Amsterdam Colloquium.* Amsterdam: Universiteit van Amsterdam, ILLC.

Bouma, Gosse, and Gertjan van Noord. 1994. "Constraint-Based Categorial Grammar." In *Proceedings of the 32nd Annual Meeting of the Association for Computational Linguistics, Las Cruces, NM.* San Francisco, CA: Morgan Kaufmann.

Bozsahin, Cem. 1998. "Deriving the Predicate-Argument Structure for a Free Word Order Language." In *Proceedings of COLING-ACL '98, Montreal*, 167–173. Cambridge, MA: MIT Press.

Brame, Michael. 1976. *Conjectures and Refutations in Syntax and Semantics.* Amsterdam: North Holland.

Brame, Michael. 1978. *Base Generated Syntax.* Seattle, WA: Noit Amrofer.

Bresnan, Joan. 1972. *Theory of Complementation in English Syntax.* Ph.D. thesis, MIT.

Bresnan, Joan. 1978. "A Realistic Transformational Grammar." In Morris Halle, Joan Bresnan, and George Miller, eds., *Linguistic Structure and Psychological Reality*, 1–59. Cambridge, MA: MIT Press.

Bresnan, Joan, ed. 1982. *The Mental Representation of Grammatical Relations.* Cambridge, MA: MIT Press.

Bresnan, Joan, and Ronald Kaplan. 1982. "Introduction: Grammars as Mental Representations of Language." In Joan Bresnan, ed., *The Mental Representation of Grammatical Relations*, xvii–lii. Cambridge, MA: MIT Press.

Bresnan, Joan, and Höskuldur Thráinsson. 1990. "A Note on Icelandic Coordination." In Joan Maling and Annie Zaenen, eds., *Syntax and Semantics 24: Modern Icelandic Syntax*, 355–365. San Diego, CA: Academic Press.

Bresnan, Joan W., Ronald M. Kaplan, Stanley Peters, and Annie Zaenen. 1982. "Cross-Serial Dependencies in Dutch." *Linguistic Inquiry*, 13, 613–636.

Brill, Eric. 1992. "A Simple Rule-Based Part-of-Speech Tagger." In *Proceedings of the 3rd Conference on Applied Natural Language Processing, Trento*, 152–155. San Francisco, CA: Morgan Kaufmann.

Briscoe, Ted. 1984. *Towards an Understanding of Human Spoken Sentence Comprehension: The Interactive Determinism Hypothesis.* Ph.D. thesis, University of Cambridge.

Briscoe, Ted. 1997. "Learning Stochastic Categorial Grammars." In *Proceedings of the 35th Annual Meeting of the Association for Computational Linguistics, Madrid*, 418–427. San Francisco, CA: Morgan Kaufmann.

Briscoe, Ted. forthcoming. "Language Acquisition: The Bioprogram Hypothesis and the Baldwin Effect." *Language*.

Brody, Michael. 1995. *Lexico-Logical Form: A Radically Minimalist Theory.* Cambridge, MA: MIT Press.

Brown, Gillian. 1983. "Prosodic Structure and the Given/New Distinction." In Anne Cutler, D. Robert Ladd, and Gillian Brown, eds., *Prosody: Models and Measurements*, 67–77. Berlin: Springer-Verlag.

Brown, Roger, and Camille Hanlon. 1970. "Derivational Complexity and Order of Acquisition in Child Speech." In John Hayes, ed., *Cognition and the Development of Language*, 155–207. New York NY: Wiley.

Bruce, Gosta. 1977. *Swedish Word Accents in Sentence Perspective.* Travaux de l'Institut de Linguistique de Lund. Lund: CWK Gleerup/Liber Laromedel.

Bruner, Jerome. 1968. *Processes of Cognitive Growth: Infancy.* Worcester, MA: Clark University Press.

Burge, William H. 1975. *Recursive Programming Techniques.* Reading, MA: Addison-Wesley.

Büring, Daniel. 1995. *The 59th Street Bridge Accent: On the Meaning of Topic and Focus.* Ph.D. thesis, Universität Tübingen.

Büring, Daniel. 1997. "The Great Scope Inversion Conspiracy." *Linguistics and Philosophy*, 20, 175–194.

Buszkowski, Wojciech, Witold Marciszewski, and Johan van Benthem. 1988. *Categorial Grammar.* Amsterdam: John Benjamins.

Carden, Guy. 1973. *English Quantifiers: Logical Structure and Linguistic Variation.* New York: Academic Press.

Carpenter, Bob. 1989. *Phrase Meaning and Categorial Grammar.* Ph.D. thesis, University of Edinburgh.

Carpenter, Bob. 1991. "The Generative Power of Categorial Grammars and Head-Driven Phrase Structure Grammars with Lexical Rules." *Computational Linguistics*, 17, 301–314.

Carpenter, Bob. 1995. "The Turing-Completeness of Multimodal Categorial Grammars." Ms., http://macduff.andrew.cmu.edu/carpenter/research.html.

Carroll, John, Michael Tanenhaus, and Thomas Bever. 1978. "The Perception of Relations." In Willem Levelt and Giovanni Flores d'Arcais, eds., *Studies in the Perception of Language*, 187–218. New York: Wiley.

Chao, Wynn. 1987. *On Ellipsis*. Ph.D. thesis, University of Massachusetts, Amherst.

Charniak, Eugene, Sharon Goldwater, and Mark Johnson. 1998. "Edge-Based Best-First Chart Parsing." In *Proceedings of the 6th Workshop on Very Large Corpora, Montreal, August*, 127–133.

Chierchia, Gennaro. 1988. "Aspects of a Categorial Theory of Binding." In Richard T. Oehrle, Emmon Bach, and Deirdre Wheeler, eds., *Categorial Grammars and Natural Language Structures*, 153–98. Dordrecht: Reidel.

Chierchia, Gennaro. 1989. "Structured Meanings, Thematic Roles, and Control." In Gennaro Chierchia, Barbara Partee, and Raymond Turner, eds., *Properties, Types and Meanings*, 131–166. Dordrecht: Kluwer.

Chierchia, Gennaro. 1995. *Dynamics of Meaning*. Chicago: University of Chicago Press.

Chomsky, Noam. 1957. *Syntactic Structures*. The Hague: Mouton.

Chomsky, Noam. 1965. *Aspects of the Theory of Syntax*. Cambridge, MA: MIT Press.

Chomsky, Noam. 1970. "Remarks on Nominalisation." In R. Jacobs and P. Rosenbaum, eds., *Readings in English Transformational Grammar*, 184–221. Waltham, MA: Ginn.

Chomsky, Noam. 1971. "Deep Structure, Surface Structure, and Semantic Interpretation." In Danny Steinberg and Leon Jakobovits, eds., *Semantics*, 183–216. Cambridge: Cambridge University Press.

Chomsky, Noam. 1975a. *The Logical Structure of Linguistic Theory*. Chicago: University of Chicago Press.

Chomsky, Noam. 1975b. *Reflections on Language*. New York: Pantheon.

Chomsky, Noam. 1981. *Lectures on Government and Binding*. Dordrecht: Foris.

Chomsky, Noam. 1986. *Knowledge of Language*. New York: Praeger.

Chomsky, Noam. 1993. "A Minimalist Program for Linguistic Theory." In Kenneth Hale and Samuel Jay Keyser, eds., *The View from Building 20*, 1–52. Cambridge, MA: MIT Press.

Chomsky, Noam. 1995. *The Minimalist Program*. Cambridge, MA: MIT Press.

Chomsky, Noam, and Howard Lasnik. 1977. "Filters and Control." *Linguistic Inquiry*, 8, 425–504.

Chomsky, Noam, and George A. Miller. 1963. "Introduction to the Formal Analysis of Natural Language." In R. Duncan Luce, Robert Bush, and Eugene Galanter, eds., *Handbook of Mathematical Psychology*, vol. 2, 269–322. New York: Wiley.

Chung, Sandra. 1983. "The ECP and Government in Chamorro." *Natural Language and Linguistic Theory*, 1, 207–244.

Church, Alonzo. 1940. "A Formulation of the Simple Theory of Types." *Journal of Symbolic Logic*, 5, 56–68.

Clark, Robin. 1985. "The Syntactic Nature of Logical Form: Evidence from Toba Batak." *Linguistic Inquiry*, 16, 663–669.

Clark, Robin. 1991. "Towards a Modular Theory of Coreference." In James Huang and Robert May, eds., *Logical Structure and Linguistic Structure: Cross-Linguistic Perspectives*, 49–78. Dordrecht: Kluwer.

Clark, Stephen. 1997. *Binding and Control in Categorial Grammar*. Master's thesis, University of Manchester.

Clifton, Charles, and Fernanda Ferreira. 1989. "Ambiguity in Context." *Language and Cognitive Processes*, 4, 77–103.

Cocke, John, and Jacob T. Schwartz. 1970. *Programming Languages and Their Compilers*. New York: New York University, Courant Institute.

Collins, Michael. 1996. "A New Statistical Parser Based on Bigram Lexical Dependencies." In *Proceedings of the 34th Annual Meeting of the Association for Computational Linguistics, Santa Cruz, CA*, 184–191. San Francisco, CA: Morgan Kaufmann.

Collins, Michael. 1997. "Three Generative Lexicalized Models for Statistical Parsing." In *Proceedings of the 35th Annual Meeting of the Association for Computational Linguistics, Madrid*, 16–23. San Francisco, CA: Morgan Kaufmann.

Collins, Michael. 1998. *Head-Driven Statistical Models for Natural Language Parsing*. Ph.D. thesis, University of Pennsylvania.

Comrie, Bernard. 1981. *Language Universals and Linguistic Typology*. Oxford: Blackwell.

Cooper, Kathrin. 1988. *Word Order in Bare Infinitival Complements in Swiss German*. Master's thesis, University of Edinburgh.

Cooper, Robin. 1979. "The Interpretation of Pronouns." In Frank Heny and Helmut Schnelle, eds., *Syntax and Semantics, Vol. 10: Selections from the 3rd Groningen Round Table*, 61–92. New York: Academic Press.

Cooper, Robin. 1982. "Binding in Wholewheat Syntax." In Pauline Jacobson and Geoffrey K. Pullum, eds., *The Nature of Syntactic Representation*, 59–77. Dordrecht: Reidel.

Cooper, Robin. 1983. *Quantification and Syntactic Theory*. Dordrecht: Reidel.

Cooper, William, and Jeanne Paccia-Cooper. 1980. *Syntax and Speech*. Cambridge, MA: Harvard Univ. Press.

Cormack, Annabel. 1984. "VP Anaphora: Variables and Scope." In Fred Landman and Frank Veltman, eds., *Varieties of Formal Semantics*, 81–102. Dordrecht: Foris.

Cormack, Sophia. 1992. *Focus and Discourse Representation Theory*. Ph.D. thesis, University of Edinburgh.

Crain, Stephen. 1980. *Pragmatic Constraints on Sentence Comprehension*. Ph.D. thesis, University of California, Irvine.

Crain, Stephen, and Mark Steedman. 1985. "On Not Being Led up the Garden Path: the Use of Context by the Psychological Parser." In Lauri Kartunnen David Dowty and Arnold Zwicky, eds., *Natural Language Parsing: Psychological, Computational and Theoretical Perspectives*, 320–358. Cambridge: Cambridge University Press.

Cremers, Crit. 1983. "On the Form and Interpretation of Ellipsis." In Alice ter Meulen, ed., *Studies in Modeltheoretic Semantics*, 145–160. Dordrecht: Foris.

Cresswell, M.J. 1973. *Logics and Languages*. London: Methuen.

Cresswell, M.J. 1985. *Structured Meanings*. Cambridge, MA: MIT Press.

Cresswell, M.J. 1990. *Entities and Indices*. Dordrecht: Kluwer.

Croft, William. 1995. "Intonational Units and Grammatical Units." *Linguistics*, 33, 839–882.

Curry, Haskell B., and Robert Feys. 1958. *Combinatory Logic: Vol. I*. Amsterdam: North Holland.

Cussens, James. 1997. "Part-of-speech tagging using Progol." In Nada Lavrac and Saso Dzeroski, eds., *Inductive Logic Programming: Proceedings of the 7th International Workshop (ILP-97)*, vol. 1297 of *Lecture Notes in Artificial Intelligence*, 93–108. Berlin: Springer.

Dale, Robert, and Nick Haddock. 1991. "Content Determination in the Generation of Referring Expressions." *Computational Intelligence*, 7, 252–265.

Dalrymple, Mary, Stuart Shieber, and Fernando Pereira. 1991. "Ellipsis and Higher-Order Unification." *Linguistics and Philosophy*, 14, 399–452.

Damaso Vieira, Marcia. 1995. "The Expression of Quantificational Notions in Asurini da Trocará: Evidence against the Universality of Determiner Quantification." In Emmon Bach, Eloise Jelinek, Angelika Kratzer, and Barbara Partee, eds., *Quantification in Natural Languages*, 701–720. Dordrecht: Kluwer.

Deacon, Terence. 1988. "Human Brain Evolution I: Evolution of Human Language Circuits." In H. Jerison and I. Jerison, eds., *Intelligence and Evolutionary Biology*. Berlin: Springer-Verlag.

Deacon, Terence. 1997. *The Symbolic Species*. New York: Norton.

Dekker, Paul. 1988. "Flexible Flexibilities." Ms., Universiteit van Amsterdam.

Desclés, Jean-Pierre, Zlatka Guentchéva, and Sebastian Shaumyan. 1986. *Theoretical Aspects of Passivization in the Framework of Applicative Grammar*. Amsterdam: John Benjamins.

Diamond, Adele. 1990. "Developmental Time Course in Human Infant and Baby Monkeys and the Neural Bases of Inhibitory Control in Reaching." In Adele Diamond, ed., *The Development and Neural Bases of Higher Cognitive Functions*, 637–676. New York: New York Academy of Sciences.

van der Does, Jaap. 1992. *Applied Quantifier Logics*. Ph.D. thesis, Universiteit van Amsterdam.

Doran, Christine. 1998. *Incorporating Punctuation into the Sentence Grammar: A Lexicalized Tree-Adjoining Grammar Perspective*. Ph.D. thesis, University of Pennsylvania.

Doran, Christy, and B. Srinivas. to appear. "A Wide Coverage CCG Parser." In Anne Abeille and Owen Rambow, eds., *Proceedings of the 3rd TAG+ workshop, Jussieu, March 1994*. Stanford, CA: CSLI Publications.

Dörre, Jochen. 1997. "Efficient Construction of Underspecified Semantics under Massive Ambiguity." In *Proceedings of the 35th Annual Meeting of the Association for Computational Linguistics and the 8th Conference of the European Association for Computational Linguistics, Madrid*, 386–409. San Francisco, CA: Morgan Kaufmann.

Downing, Bruce. 1970. *Syntactic Structure and Phonological Phrasing in English*. Ph.D. thesis, University of Texas.

Dowty, David. 1979. "Dative Movement and Thomason's Extensions of Montague Grammar." In Steven Davis and Marianne Mithun, eds., *Linguistics, Philosophy, and Montague Grammar*, 153–222. Austin, TX: University of Texas Press.

Dowty, David. 1982. "Grammatical Relations and Montague Grammar." In Pauline Jacobson and Geoffrey K. Pullum, eds., *The Nature of Syntactic Representation*, 79–130. Dordrecht: Reidel.

Dowty, David. 1988. "Type-Raising, Functional Composition, and Nonconstituent Coordination." In Richard T. Oehrle, Emmon Bach, and Deirdre Wheeler, eds., *Categorial Grammars and Natural Language Structures*, 153–198. Dordrecht: Reidel.

Dowty, David. 1993. "'Variable-free' Syntax, Variable-binding Syntax, the Natural Deduction Lambek Calculus, and the Crossover Constraint." In *Proceedings of the Eleventh West Coast Conference on Formal Linguistics, 1992*. Stanford, CA: SLA.

Dowty, David. 1996. "Nonconstituent Coordination, Wrapping, and Multimodal Categorial Grammars: Syntactic Form as Logical Form." In Kees Doets, ed., *Proceedings of the Tenth International Congress of Logic, Methodology, and Philosophy of Science, 1995*. Amsterdam: North Holland.

Dryer, Matthew. 1992. "The Greenbergian Word Order Corrrelations." *Language*, 68, 81–138.

Earley, Jay. 1970. "An Efficient Context-Free Parsing Algorithm." *Communications of the Association for Computing Machinery*, 13, 94–102.

Eisner, Jason. 1996. "Efficient Normal-Form Parsing for Combinatory Categorial Grammar." In *Proceedings of the 34th Annual Meeting of the Association for Computational Linguistics, Santa Cruz, CA.* San Francisco, CA: Morgan Kaufmann.

van Emden, Maarten, and Robert Kowalski. 1976. "The Semantics of Predicate Logic as a Programming Language." *Journal of the Association for Computing Machinery,* 23, 733–742.

Emonds, Joseph. 1976. *A Transformational Approach to English Syntax.* New York: Academic Press.

Emonds, Joseph. 1979. "Appositive Relatives Have No Properties." *Linguistic Inquiry,* 10, 211–243.

Engdahl, Elisabet. 1983. "Parasitic Gaps." *Linguistics and Philosophy,* 6, 5–34.

Engdahl, Elisabet. 1985. "Parasitic Gaps, Resumptive Pronouns and Subject Extractions." *Linguistics,* 23, 3–44.

Erteschik-Shir, Nomi. 1998. "The Syntax-Focus Structure Interface." In Peter Culicover and Louise McNally, eds., *Syntax and Semantics, Vol. 29: The Limits of Syntax,* 212–240. New York: Academic Press.

Espinal, M. Teresa. 1991. "The Representation of Disjunct Constituents." *Language,* 67, 726–762.

Evans, Gareth. 1980. "Pronouns." *Linguistic Inquiry,* 11, 337–362.

Evers, Arnold. 1975. *The Transformational Cycle in Dutch and German.* Ph.D. thesis, University of Utrecht.

Faltz, Leonard. 1995. "Towards a Typology of Natural Logic." In Emmon Bach, Eloise Jelinek, Angelika Kratzer, and Barbara Partee, eds., *Quantification in Natural Languages,* 271–319. Dordrecht: Kluwer.

Fine, Kit. 1985. *Reasoning with Arbitrary Objects.* Oxford: Oxford University Press.

Fisher, Cynthia, Geoffrey Hall, Susan Rakowitz, and Lila Gleitman. 1994. "When It Is Better to Receive Than to Give: Syntactic and Conceptual Constraints on Vocabulary Growth." *Lingua,* 92, 333–375.

Flynn, Michael. 1983. "A Categorial Theory of Structure Building." In Gerald Gazdar, Ewan Klein, and Geoffrey K. Pullum, eds., *Order, Concord, and Constituency,* 139–174. Dordrecht: Foris.

Fodor, Janet Dean. 1978. "Parsing Strategies and Constraints on Transformations." *Linguistic Inquiry,* 9, 427–473.

Fodor, Janet Dean. 1982. "The Mental Representation of Quantifiers." In Stanley Peters and Esa Saarinen, eds., *Processes, Beliefs, and Questions,* 129–164. Dordrecht: Reidel.

Fodor, Janet Dean, and Ivan Sag. 1982. "Referential and Quantificational Indefinites." *Linguistics and Philosophy,* 5, 355–398.

Fodor, Jerry. 1983. *The Modularity of Mind.* Cambridge, MA: MIT Press.

Fodor, Jerry, Thomas Bever, and Merrill Garrett. 1974. *The Psychology of Language.* New York: McGraw-Hill.

Ford, Marilyn, Joan Bresnan, and Ronald M. Kaplan. 1982. "A Competence-Based Theory of Syntactic Closure." In Joan Bresnan, ed., *The Mental Representation of Grammatical Relations*, 727–796. Cambridge, MA: MIT Press.

Fortune, Steven, Daniel Leivant, and Michael O'Donnell. 1983. "The Expressiveness of Simple and Second-Order Type Structures." *Journal of the Association for Computing Machinery*, 30, 151–185.

Foster, John. 1990. *A Theory of Word-Order in Categorial Grammar, with Special Reference to Spanish.* Ph.D. thesis, University of York.

Fox, Danny. 1995. "Economy and Scope." *Natural Language Semantics*, 3, 283–341.

Francis, W. Nelson, and Henry Kučera. 1964. *Manual of Information to Accompany a Standard Corpus of Present-Day Edited American English for Use with Digital Computers.* Providence, RI: Brown University.

Frazier, Lyn. 1978. *On Comprehending Sentences.* Ph.D. thesis, University of Connecticut.

Frazier, Lyn. 1989. "Against Lexical Generation of Syntax." In William Marslen-Wilson, ed., *Lexical Representation and Process*, 505–528. Cambridge, MA: MIT Press.

Frazier, Lyn, and Charles Clifton. 1996. *Construal.* Cambridge, MA: MIT Press.

Frazier, Lyn, and Janet Fodor. 1978. "The Sausage Machine: A New Two-Stage Parsing Model." *Cognition*, 6, 291–325.

Friedman, Joyce, Dawai Dai, and W. Wang. 1986. "The Weak Generative Capacity of Parenthesis-Free Categorial Grammars." In *Proceedings of COLING-86*. San Francisco, CA: Morgan Kaufmann.

Friedman, Joyce, and R. Venketasan. 1986. "Categorial and Non-Categorial Languages." In *Proceedings of the 24th Annual Meeting of the Association for Computational Linguistics, New York*. San Francisco, CA: Morgan Kaufmann.

Furbee, Louanna. 1974. "Identity in Gapping and the Lexical Insertion of Verbs." *Linguistic Inquiry*, 5, 299–304.

Gabbay, Dov, Ian Hodkinson, and Mark Reynolds. 1994. *Temporal Logic: Mathematical Foundations and Computational Aspects*, vol. I. Oxford: Clarendon Press.

Gazdar, Gerald. 1981. "Unbounded Dependencies and Coordinate Structure." *Linguistic Inquiry*, 12, 155–184.

Gazdar, Gerald. 1982. "Phrase Structure Grammar." In Pauline Jacobson and Geoffrey K. Pullum, eds., *On the Nature of Syntactic Representation*, 131–186. Dordrecht: Reidel.

Gazdar, Gerald. 1988. "Applicability of Indexed Grammars to Natural Languages." In Uwe Reyle and Christian Rohrer, eds., *Natural Language Parsing and Linguistic Theories*, 69–94. Dordrecht: Reidel.

Gazdar, Gerald, Ewan Klein, Geoffrey K. Pullum, and Ivan Sag. 1985. *Generalized Phrase Structure Grammar*. Oxford: Blackwell.

Geach, Peter. 1962. *Reference and Generality*. Ithaca, NY: Cornell University Press.

Geach, Peter. 1972. "A Program for Syntax." In Donald Davidson and Gilbert Harman, eds., *Semantics of Natural Language*, 483–497. Dordrecht: Reidel.

Gee, James, and François Grosjean. 1983. "Performance Structures: A Psycholinguistic and Linguistic Appraisal." *Cognitive Psychology*, 15, 411–458.

Gerdeman, Dale, and Erhard Hinrichs. 1990. "Functor-Driven Natural Language Generation with Categorial Unification Grammars." In *Proceedings of COLING-90, Helsinki*, 145–150. San Francisco, CA: Morgan Kaufmann.

Gibson, Edward. 1996. *Memory Limitations and Sentence Processing Breakdown*. Cambridge, MA: MIT Press.

Gleitman, Lila. 1990. "The Structural Sources of Verb Meanings." *Language Acquisition*, 1, 1–55.

Gold, E. M. 1967. "Language Identification in the Limit." *Information and Control*, 16, 447–474.

Goldsmith, John. 1976. *Autosegmental Phonology*. Ph.D. thesis, MIT.

Goodall, Grant. 1987. *Parallel Structures in Syntax*. Cambridge: Cambridge University Press.

Gray, J., and Michael A. Harrison. 1972. "On the Covering and Reduction Problems for Context-Free Phrase Structure Grammars." *Journal of the Association for Computing Machinery*, 19, 385–395.

Greenberg, Joseph. 1963. *Universals of Language*. Cambridge: MIT Press.

Greenfield, Patricia. 1991. "Language, Tools and Brain." *Behavioral and Brain Sciences*, 14, 531–595.

Greenfield, Patricia, Karen Nelson, and Elliot Saltzman. 1972. "The Development of Rule-Bound Strategies for Manipulating Seriated Cups: a Parallel between Action and Grammar." *Cognitive Psychology*, 3, 291–310.

Grimshaw, Jane. 1990. *Argument Structure*. Cambridge, MA: MIT Press.

Groenendijk, Jeroen, and Martin Stokhof. 1990. "Dynamic Predicate Logic." *Linguistics and Philosophy*, 14, 39–100.

Grosz, Barbara, and Candace Sidner. 1986. "Attention, Intention and the Structure of Discourse." *Journal of Computational Linguistics*, 12, 175–204.

Gussenhoven, Carlos. 1983. *On the Grammar and Semantics of Sentence Accent*. Dordrecht: Foris.

Gussenhoven, Carlos. 1985. "Two Views of Accent: A Reply." *Journal of Linguistics*, 21, 125–138.

de Haan, Ger. 1979. *Conditions on Rules*. Dordrecht: Foris.

Haddock, Nicholas. 1987. "Incremental Interpretation and Combinatory Categorial Grammar." In *Proceedings of the 10th International Joint Conference on Artificial Intelligence, Milan*, 661–663. San Francisco, CA: Morgan Kaufmann.

Haddock, Nicholas. 1989. *Incremental Semantics and Interactive Syntactic Processing*. Ph.D. thesis, University of Edinburgh.

Haegeman, Liliane. 1992. *Theory and Description in Generative Syntax*. Cambridge: Cambridge University Press.

Haegeman, Liliane, and Henk van Riemsdijk. 1986. "Verb Projection Raising, Scope, and the Typology of Rules Affecting Verbs." *Linguistic Inquiry*, 17, 417–466.

Hajičová, Eva, Barbara H. Partee, and Petr Sgall. 1998. *Topic-Focus Articulation, Tripartite Structures, and Semantic Content*. Dordrecht: Kluwer.

Hajičová, Eva, and Petr Sgall. 1987. "The Ordering Principle." *Journal of Pragmatics*, 11, 435–454.

Hajičová, Eva, and Petr Sgall. 1988. "Topic and Focus of a Sentence and the Patterning of a Text." In Jänos Petöfi, ed., *Text and Discourse Constitution*, 70–96. Berlin: de Gruyter.

Hale, Kenneth, and Samuel Jay Keyser. 1993. "On Argument Structure and the Lexical Expression of Syntactic Relations." In Kenneth Hale and Samuel Jay Keyser, eds., *The View from Building 20*, 53–109. Cambridge, MA: MIT Press.

Halle, Morris, and Jean-Roger Vergnaud. 1987. *An Essay on Stress*. Cambridge, MA: MIT Press.

Halliday, Michael. 1967a. *Intonation and Grammar in British English*. The Hague: Mouton.

Halliday, Michael. 1967b. "Notes on Transitivity and Theme in English, Part II." *Journal of Linguistics*, 3, 199–244.

Halliday, Michael. 1970. "Language Structure and Language Function." In John Lyons, ed., *New Horizons in Linguistics*, 140–165. Harmondsworth: Penguin.

Hankamer, Jorge. 1971. *Constraints on Deletion in Syntax*. Ph.D. thesis, Yale University.

Hankamer, Jorge, and Ivan Sag. 1976. "Deep and Surface Anaphora." *Linguistic Inquiry*, 7, 391–428.

Harel, David. 1984. "Dynamic Logic." In Dov Gabbay and F. Guenthner, eds., *Handbook of Philosophical Logic*, vol. II, 497–604. Dordrecht: Reidel.

Harrison, Michael. 1978. *Introduction to Formal Language Theory*. Reading MA: Addison-Wesley.

Hausser, Roland. 1984. *Surface Compositional Grammar*. Munich: Wilhelm Fink Verlag.

Hausser, Roland. 1986. *NEWCAT*. Berlin: Springer-Verlag.

Hawkins, John. 1982. "Cross Category Harmony, $\bar{X}$ and the Predictions of Markedness." *Journal of Linguistics*, 18, 1–35.

Hayes, Bruce. 1995. *Metrical Stress Theory*. Chicago: University of Chicago Press.

Hayes, Bruce, and Aditi Lahiri. 1991. "Bengali Intonational Phonology." *Natural Language and Linguistic Theory*, 9, 47–96.

Heim, Irene. 1983. "File Change Semantics and the Familiarity Theory of Definiteness." In Rainer Bäuerle, Christoph Schwarze, and Arnim von Stechow, eds., *Meaning, Use, and Interpretation of Language*, 164–189. Berlin: de Gruyter.

Heim, Irene. 1990. "E-Type Pronouns and Donkey Anaphora." *Linguistics and Philosophy*, 13, 137–177.

Helke, Michael. 1971. *The Grammar of English Reflexives*. Ph.D. thesis, MIT.

Henderson, James. 1992. "A Structural Interpretation of Combinatory Categorial Grammar." Tech. Rep. MS-CIS-92-49, University of Pennsylvania.

Hendriks, H. 1998. "Links without Locations." In F. Hamm and E. Zimmermann, eds., *Linguistische Berichte, Sonderheft 9/1998: SEMANTIK*. Opladen: Westdeutscher Verlag.

Hendriks, Herman. 1993. *Studied Flexibility: Categories and Types in Syntax and Semantics*. Ph.D. thesis, Universiteit van Amsterdam.

Hendriks, Herman. 1994. "The Logic of Tune." In *Proceedings of the 2nd Conference on Logical Aspects and Computational Linguistics, Nancy*, 133–160. Springer-Verlag.

Hendriks, Petra. 1995. *Comparatives and Categorial Grammar*. Ph.D. thesis, Rijksuniversiteit Groningen.

Hepple, Mark. 1990. *The Grammar and Processing of Order and Dependency: A Categorial Approach*. Ph.D. thesis, University of Edinburgh.

Hepple, Mark. 1999. "An Earley-style Predictive Chart Parsing Method for Lambek Grammars." In *Proceedings of the 37th Annual Meeting of the Association for Computational Linguistics, College Park MD*, 465–472. San Francisco, CA: Morgan Kaufmann.

Hepple, Mark, and Glyn Morrill. 1989. "Parsing and Derivational Equivalence." In *Proceedings of the 4th Conference of the European Chapter of the Association for Computational Linguistics, Manchester, April*, 10–18. San Francisco, CA: Morgan Kaufmann.

Heycock, Caroline. 1991. *Layers of Predication: The Non-lexical Syntax of Clauses*. Ph.D. thesis, University of Pennsylvania.

Heycock, Caroline, and Anthony Kroch. 1993. "Verb Movement and the Status of Subjects: Implications for the Theory of Licensing." *Groninger Arbeiten zur Germanistischen Linguistik*, 36, 76–102.

Heycock, Caroline, and Anthony Kroch. 1994. "Verb Movement and Coordination in a Relational Theory of Licensing." *The Linguistic Review*, 11, 257–283.

Hindley, Roger, and Jonathan Seldin. 1986. *Introduction to Combinators and λ-Calculus*. Cambridge: Cambridge University Press.

Hinrichs, Erhard, and Tsuneko Nakazawa. 1994. "Linearizing AUXs in German Verbal Complexes." In John Nerbonne, Klaus Netter, and Carl Pollard, eds., *German in Head-Driven Phrase Structure Grammar*, 11–37. Stanford, CA: CSLI Publications.

Hirst, Daniel. 1993. "Detaching Intonational Phrases from Syntactic Structure." *Linguistic Inquiry*, 24, 781–788.

Hirst, Graeme. 1987. *Semantic Interpretation and the Resolution of Ambiguity*. Cambridge: Cambridge University Press.

Hobbs, Jerry. 1983. "An Improper Treatment of Quantification in Ordinary English." In *Proceedings of the 21st Annual Meeting of the Association for Computational Linguistics*, 57–63. San Francisco, CA: Morgan Kaufmann.

Hobbs, Jerry. 1985. "Ontological Promiscuity." In *Proceedings of the 23rd Annual Meeting of the Association for Computational Linguistics*, 61–69. San Francisco, CA: Morgan Kaufmann.

Hobbs, Jerry, and Stuart Shieber. 1987. "An Algorithm for Generating Quantifier Scopings." *Computational Linguistics*, 13, 47–63.

Hoeksema, Jack. 1984. *Categorial Morphology*. Ph.D. thesis, Rijksuniversiteit Groningen, New York.

Hoeksema, Jack. 1985. "Wazdat?—Contracted Forms and Verb-Second in Dutch." In Jan Faarlund, ed., *Germanic Linguistics*. Bloomington: Indiana University Linguistics Club.

Hoeksema, Jack. 1989. "A Categorial Theory of Reanalysis Phenomena." Ms., University of Pennsylvania.

Hoeksema, Jack. 1991. "Complex Predicates and Liberation in Dutch and English." *Linguistics and Philosophy*, 14, 661–710.

Hoeksema, Jack, and R. Janda. 1988. "Implications of Process Morphology for Categorial Grammar." In Richard T. Oehrle, Emmon Bach, and Deirdre Wheeler, eds., *Categorial Grammars and Natural Language Structures*, 199–248. Dordrecht: Reidel.

Hoeksema, Jack, and Frans Zwarts. 1991. "Some Remarks on Focus Adverbs." *Journal of Semantics*, 8, 51–70.

Hoffman, Beryl. 1993. "The Formal Consequence of Using Variables in CCG Categories." In *Proceedings of the 31st Annual Meeting of the Association for Computational Linguistics, Columbus, OH*, 298–300. San Francisco, CA: Morgan Kaufmann.

Hoffman, Beryl. 1995a. *Computational Analysis of the Syntax and Interpretation of "Free" Word-Order in Turkish*. Ph.D. thesis, University of Pennsylvania. IRCS Report 95-17.

Hoffman, Beryl. 1995b. "Integrating Free Word Order, Syntax, and Information Structure." In *Proceedings of the 7th Conference of the European Chapter of the Association for Computational Linguistics, Dublin*, 245–252. San Francisco, CA: Morgan Kaufmann.

Hoffman, Beryl. 1996. "Translating into Free Word Order Languages." In *Proceedings of the International Conference on Computational Linguistics (COLING-96), Copenhagen*, 556–561. Copenhagen, Denmark: Center for Sprogteknologi.

Hoffman, Beryl. 1998. "Word Order, Information Structure, and Centering in Turkish." In Marilyn Walker, Ellen Prince, and Aravind Joshi, eds., *Centering Theory in Discourse*, 253–271. Oxford: Oxford University Press.

Höhle, Tilman. 1983. "Subjektlücken in Koordinationen." Ms., Universität Tübingen.

Houtman, Joop. 1994. *Coordination and Constituency*. Ph.D. thesis, Rijksuniversiteit Groningen.

Huck, Geoffrey. 1985. *Discontinuity and Word Order in Categorial Grammar*. Ph.D. thesis, University of Chicago.

Hudson, Richard. 1984. *Word Grammar*. Oxford: Blackwell.

Huet, Gérard. 1975. "A Unification Algorithm for Typed λ-calculus." *Theoretical Computer Science*, 1, 27–57.

Huet, Gérard, and Bernard Lang. 1978. "Proving and Applying Program Transformations Expressed with Second-Order Logic." *Acta Informatica*, 11, 31–55.

Hukari, Thomas, and Robert Levine. 1987. "Parasitic Gaps, Slash Termination and the C-Command Condition." *Natural Language and Linguistic Theory*, 5, 197–222.

Huybregts, Riny. 1976. "Overlapping Dependencies in Dutch." *Utrecht Working Papers in Linguistics*, 1, 24–65.

Huybregts, Riny. 1984. "The Weak Inadequacy of Context-free Phrase-structure Grammars." In Ger de Haan, Mieke Trommelen, and Wim Zonneveld, eds., *Van Periferie naar Kern*. Dordrecht: Foris.

Inoue, A., and Janet Dean Fodor. 1995. "Information-paced parsing of Japanese." In R. Masuka and N. Nagai, eds., *Japanese Sentence Processing*. Hillsdale, NJ: Erlbaum.

Jackendoff, Ray. 1971. "Gapping and Related Rules." *Linguistic Inquiry*, 2, 21–35.

Jackendoff, Ray. 1972. *Semantic Interpretation in Generative Grammar*. Cambridge, MA: MIT Press.

Jackendoff, Ray S. 1977. *X̄ syntax: A Study of Phrase Structure*. Cambridge, MA: MIT Press.

Jacobs, Joachim. 1991. "Focus Ambiguities." *Journal of Semantics*, 8, 1–36.

Jacobson, Pauline. 1987. "Phrase Structure, Grammatical Relations and Discontinuous Constituents." In Geoffrey Huck and Almerindo Ojeda, eds., *Syntax and Semantics, Vol. 20: Discontinuous Constituency*, 27–69. Orlando, FL: Academic Press.

Jacobson, Pauline. 1990. "Raising as Function Composition." *Linguistics and Philosophy*, 13, 423–476.

Jacobson, Pauline. 1991. "Bach-Peters Sentences in a Variable-Free Semantics." In *Proceedings of the 8th Amsterdam Colloquium*, 283–302. Universiteit van Amsterdam, ILLC.

Jacobson, Pauline. 1992a. "Flexible Categorial Grammars: Questions and Prospects." In Robert Levine, ed., *Formal Grammar*, 129–167. Oxford: Oxford University Press.

Jacobson, Pauline. 1992b. "The Lexical Entailment Theory of Control and the Tough Construction." In Ivan Sag and Anna Szabolcsi, eds., *Lexical Matters*, 269–300. Stanford, CA: CSLI Publications.

Jacobson, Pauline. 1998. "Where (if Anywhere) is Transderivationality Located?" In Peter Culicover and Louise McNally, eds., *Syntax and Semantics, Vol. 29: The Limits of Syntax*, 303–336. San Diego, CA: Academic Press.

Jacobson, Pauline. 1999. "Towards a Variable-Free Semantics." *Linguistics and Philosophy*, 22, 117–184.

Jaeggli, Osvaldo. 1981. *Topics in Romance Syntax*. Dordrecht: Foris.

Janeaway, Roger. 1991. "Unacceptable Ambiguity in Categorial Grammar." In *Proceedings of the 9th West Coast Conference on Formal Linguistics*, 305–316. Stanford, CA: Stanford Linguistics Association.

Jelinek, Eloise. 1995. "Quantification in Straits Salish." In Emmon Bach, Eloise Jelinek, Angelika Kratzer, and Barbara Partee, eds., *Quantification in Natural Languages*, 487–540. Dordrecht: Kluwer.

Jelinek, Fred. 1976. "Continuous Speech Recognition by Statistical Methods." *Proceedings of the Institute for Electronic and Electrical Engineers*, 64, 532–556.

Johnson, Mark. 1988. *Attribute-Value Logic and the Theory of Grammar*. Stanford, CA: CSLI Publications.

Johnson-Laird, Philip. 1983. *Mental Models*. Cambridge: Cambridge University Press.

Joshi, Aravind. 1990. "Processing Crossed and Nested Dependencies." *Language and Cognitive Processes*, 5, 1–27.

Joshi, Aravind, Leon Levy, and M. Takahashi. 1975. "Tree-adjunct Grammars." *Journal of Computer Systems Science*, 10, 136–163.

Joshi, Aravind, Owen Rambow, and Tilman Becker. to appear. "Complexity of Scrambling—A New Twist to the Competence-Performance Distinction." In Anne Abeille and Owen Rambow, eds., *Proceedings of the 3rd TAG+ workshop, Jussieu, 1994*. Stanford, CA: CSLI Publications.

Joshi, Aravind, and Yves Schabes. 1992. "Tree-Adjoining Grammars and Lexicalized Grammars." In Maurice Nivat and Andreas Podelski, eds., *Definability and Recognizability of Sets of Trees*. Princeton, NJ: Elsevier.

Joshi, Aravind, and K. Vijay-Shanker. 1999. "Compositional Semantics with Lexicalized Tree-Adjoining Grammar (LTAG)." In *Proceedings of the 3rd International Workshop on Computational Semantics, Tilburg, January*, 131–146. Computational Linguistics, Tilburg University.

Joshi, Aravind, K. Vijay-Shanker, and David Weir. 1991. "The Convergence of Mildly Context-Sensitive Formalisms." In Peter Sells, Stuart Shieber, and Tom Wasow, eds., *Processing of Linguistic Structure*, 31–81. Cambridge, MA: MIT Press.

Jowsey, Einar. 1989. *Constraining Montague Grammar for Computational Applications*. Ph.D. thesis, University of Edinburgh.

Kaisse, Ellen. 1985. *Connected Speech: The Interaction of Syntax and Phonology*. Orlando, FL: Academic Press.

Kamp, Hans, and Uwe Reyle. 1993. *From Discourse to Logic*. Dordrecht: Kluwer.

Kanazawa, Makoto. 1998. *Learnable Classes of Categorial Grammars*. Stanford, CA: CSLI/folli.

Kang, Beom-Mo. 1988. *Functional Inheritance, Anaphora and Semantic Interpretation in a Generalised Categorial Grammar*. Ph.D. thesis, Brown University, Providence, RI.

Karlgren, Hans. 1974. *Categorial Grammar Calculus*. No. 2 in Kval publ. Stockholm: Språkförlaget Skriptor AB.

Karttunen, Lauri. 1989. "Radical Lexicalism." In Mark Baltin and Anthony Kroch, eds., *Alternative Conceptions of Phrase Structure*. Chicago: University of Chicago Press.

Karttunen, Lauri, and Stanley Peters. 1979. "Conventional Implicature." In Choon-Kyu Oh and David Dinneen, eds., *Syntax and Semantics 11: Presupposition*, 1–56. New York: Academic Press.

Kay, Martin. 1973. "The MIND System." In Randall Rustin, ed., *Natural Language Processing*, vol. 8 of *Courant Computer Science Symposium*, 155–188. New York: Algorithmics Press.

Kay, Martin. 1980. "Algorithm Schemata and Data Structures in Syntactic Processing." In Barbara Grosz, Karen Sparck-Jones, and Bonnie Lynn Webber, eds., *Readings in Natural Language Processing*, 125–138. San Francisco, CA: Morgan Kaufmann.

Kayne, Richard. 1983. *Connectedness and Binary Branching*. Dordrecht: Foris.

Kayne, Richard. 1998. "Overt vs. Covert Movement." *Syntax*, 1, 1–74.

Keenan, Edward. 1988. "On Semantics and the Binding Theory." In John Hawkins, ed., *Explaining Language Universals*, 105–144. Oxford: Blackwell.

Keenan, Edward, and Leonard Faltz. 1978. "Logical Types for Natural Language." UCLA Working Papers in Linguistics 3. Revised as Keenan and Faltz 1985.

Keenan, Edward, and Leonard Faltz. 1985. *Boolean Semantics for Natural Language*. Dordrecht: Reidel.

Keller, William. 1988. "Nested Cooper Storage." In Uwe Reyle and Christian Rohrer, eds., *Natural Language Parsing and Linguistic Theory*, 432–447. Dordrecht: Reidel.

Kempe, Andre, and Lauri Karttunen. 1996. "Parallel Replacement in Finite State Calculus." In *Proceedings of COLING-96, Copenhagen*. San Francisco, CA: Morgan Kaufmann.

Kempson, Ruth, and Annabel Cormack. 1981. "Ambiguity and Quantification." *Linguistics and Philosophy*, 4, 259–309.

Kenesei, Istvan. 1989. "Logikus-e a magyar szórend?" *Általános Nyelvészeti Tanulmányok*, 17, 105–152.

Kimball, John. 1973. "Seven Principles of Surface Structure Parsing in Natural Language." *Cognition*, 2, 15–47.

Kimball, John. 1975. "Predictive Analysis and Over-the-Top Parsing." In John Kimball, ed., *Syntax and Semantics, Vol. 4*, 155–179. New York: Academic Press.

Kirkeby-Garstad, Trond, and Krisztina Polgárdi. 1994. "Against Prosodic Composition." In Gosse Bouma and Gertjan van Noord, eds., *Computational Linguistics in the Netherlands, IV*, 73–86. Groningen: Rijksuniversiteit Groningen, Vakgroep Alfa-Informatica.

É. Kiss, Katelin. 1998. "Identificational Focus Versus Information Focus." *Language*, 74, 245–273.

Klein, Ewan, and Ivan A. Sag. 1985. "Type-Driven Translation." *Linguistics and Philosophy*, 8, 163–201.

Köhler, Wolfgang. 1925. *The Mentality of Apes*. New York: Harcourt Brace and World.

Komagata, Nobo. 1997a. "Efficient Parsing for CCGs with Generalized Type-Raised Categories." In *Proceedings of the 5th International Workshop on Parsing Technologies, Boston MA*, 135–146. ACL/SIGPARSE.

Komagata, Nobo. 1997b. "Parsing Japanese with Information Structure." Ms., University of Pennsylvania.

Komagata, Nobo. 1999. *Information Structure in Texts: A Computational Analysis of Contextual Appropriateness in English and Japanese*. Ph.D. thesis, University of Pennsylvania.

Konieczny, Lars, Barbara Hemforth, Christoph Scheepers, and Gerhard Strube. 1997. "The Role of Lexical Heads in Parsing: Evidence from German." *Language and Cognitive Processes*, 12, 307–348.

König, Esther. 1994. "A Hypothetical Reasoning Algorithm for Linguistic Analysis." *Journal of Logic and Computation*, 4, 1–19.

Koopman, Hilda, and Anna Szabolcsi. 1998. *Verbal Complexes*. in preparation.

Koster, Jan. 1986. *Domains and Dynasties*. Dordrecht: Foris.

Koutsoudas, Andreas. 1971. "Gapping, Conjunction Reduction, and Coordinate Deletion." *Foundations of Language*, 7, 337–386.

Kratzer, Angelika. 1991. "The Representation of Focus." In Arnim von Stechow and Dieter Wunderlich, eds., *Semantics: An International Handbook of Contemporary Research*, 825–834. Berlin: de Gruyter.

Krifka, Manfred. 1991. "A Compositional Semantics for Multiple Focus Constructions." *Cornell Working Papers in Linguistics*, 10, 127–158.

Kroch, Anthony, and Beatrice Santorini. 1991. "The Derived Constituent Structure of the West Germanic Verb-raising Construction." In Robert Freidin, ed., *Principles and Parameters in Comparative Grammar*, 269–338. Cambridge, MA: MIT Press.

Kuno, Susumu. 1966. "The Augmented Predictive Analyzer for Context-Free Languages: Its Relative Efficiency." *Communications of the Association for Computing Machinery*, 9, 810–823.

Kuno, Susumu. 1973. "Constraints on Internal Clauses and Sentential Subjects." *Linguistic Inquiry*, 4, 363–386.

Kuno, Susumu. 1976. "Gapping: A Functional Analysis." *Linguistic Inquiry*, 7, 300–318.

Ladd, D. Robert. 1980. *The Structure of Intonational Meaning*. Bloomington: Indiana University Press.

Ladd, D. Robert. 1996. *Intonational Phonology*. Cambridge: Cambridge University Press.

de Laguna, Grace. 1927. *Speech: Its Function and Development*. New Haven, CT: Yale University Press.

Lambek, Joachim. 1958. "The Mathematics of Sentence Structure." *American Mathematical Monthly*, 65, 154–170.

Lambek, Joachim. 1961. "On the Calculus of Syntactic Types." In *Structure of Language and Its Mathematical Aspects*, 166–178. Providence, RI: American Mathematical Society.

Lambrecht, Knud. 1994. *Information Structure and Sentence Form: Topic, Focus, and the Mental Representations of Discourse Referents*. Cambridge: Cambridge University Press.

Landman, Fred. 1986. *Towards a Theory of Information*. Dordrecht: Foris.

Langendoen, D. Terence. 1975. "Finite State Processing of Phrase Structure Languages and the Status of Readjustment Rules in Grammar." *Linguistic Inquiry*, 6, 533–554.

Lasnik, Howard, and Joseph Kupin. 1977. "A Restrictive Theory of Transformational Grammar." *Theoretical Linguistics*, 4, 173–196.

Lasnik, Howard, and Mamoru Saito. 1984. "On the Nature of Proper Government." *Linguistic Inquiry*, 15, 235–289.

Lasnik, Howard, and Mamoru Saito. 1992. *Move α*. MIT Press, Cambridge MA.

Lee, Kai Fu. 1989. *Automatic Speech Recognition*. Dordrecht: Kluwer.

Lehmann, Winfred. 1978. *Syntactic Typology: The Phenomenology of Language.* Austin: University of Texas Press.

Levelt, Willem J. M. 1989. *Speaking.* Cambridge, MA: MIT Press.

Levin, Harold. 1982. *Categorial Grammar and the Logical Form of Quantification.* Naples: Bibliopolis.

Levin, Nancy. 1978. "Some Identity-of-Sense Deletions Puzzle Me. Do They You?" In *Papers from the 14th Regional Meeting of the Chicago Linguistic Society,* 229–240. Chicago: University of Chicago, Chicago Linguistic Society.

Levin, Nancy, and Ellen Prince. 1986. "Gapping and Causal Implicature." *Papers in Linguistics,* 19, 351–364.

Lewis, David. 1970. "General Semantics." *Synthèse,* 22, 18–67.

Lewis, David. 1979. "Scorekeeping in a Language Game." *Journal of Philosophical Logic,* 8, 339–359.

Lewis, Richard. 1993. *Architecturally-Based Theory of Human Sentence Comprehension.* Ph.D. thesis, Carnegie Mellon University. Technical Report CMU-CS-93-226.

Liberman, Mark. 1975. *The Intonational System of English.* Ph.D. thesis, MIT. Published by Garland Press, New York, 1979.

Liberman, Mark, and Alan Prince. 1977. "On Stress and Linguistic Rhythm." *Linguistic Inquiry,* 8, 249–336.

Liberman, Mark, and Ivan Sag. 1974. "Prosodic Form and Discourse Function." In *Papers from the 10th Regional Meeting of the Chicago Linguistic Society,* 416–427. Chicago: University of Chicago, Chicago Linguistic Society.

van der Linden, Erik-Jan. 1993. *A Categorial Computational Theory of Idioms.* Ph.D. thesis, Universiteit Utrecht.

Link, Godehard. 1983. "The Logical Analysis of Plurals and Mass Terms." In Rainer Bäuerle, Christoph Schwarze, and Arnim von Stechow, eds., *Meaning, Use, and Interpretation of Language,* 302–323. Berlin: de Gruyter.

Liu, Feng-Hsi. 1990. *Scope and Dependency in English and Chinese.* Ph.D. thesis, University of California, Los Angeles.

Lötscher, Andreas. 1978. "Zur Verbstellung im Zürichdeutschen und in anderen Varianten des Deutschen." *Zeitschrift für Dialektologie und Linguistik,* 45, 1–29.

Lyons, John. 1968. *Introduction to Theoretical Linguistics.* Cambridge: Cambridge University Press.

Lyons, John. 1977. *Semantics, Vol. II.* Cambridge: Cambridge University Press.

Maling, Joan M. 1972. "On Gapping and the Order of Constituents." *Linguistic Inquiry,* 3, 101–108.

Maling, Joan M., and Annie Zaenen. 1978. "Nonuniversality of a Surface Filter." *Linguistic Inquiry,* 9, 475–497.

Mallinson, Graham, and Barry Blake. 1981. *Language Typology*. Amsterdam: North Holland.

Manzini, Maria Rita. 1993. *Locality*. Cambridge, MA: MIT Press.

de Marcken, Carl. 1990. "Parsing the LOB Corpus." In *Proceedings of the 28th Annual Meeting of the Association for Computational Linguistics, Pittsburgh*, 243–251. San Francisco, CA: Morgan Kaufmann.

Marcus, Mitch. 1980. *A Theory of Syntactic Recognition for Natural Language*. Cambridge, MA: MIT Press.

Marr, David. 1977. "Artificial Intelligence: A Personal View." *Artificial Intelligence*, 9, 37–48.

Marslen-Wilson, William, Lorraine K. Tyler, and Mark Seidenberg. 1978. "Sentence Processing and the Clause Boundary." In William J. M. Levelt and Giovanni Flores d'Arcais, eds., *Studies in the Perception of Language*, 219–246. New York: Wiley.

May, Robert. 1985. *Logical Form*. Cambridge, MA: MIT Press.

McCawley, James. 1982. "Parentheticals and Discontinuous Constituent Structure." *Linguistic Inquiry*, 13, 91–106.

McCawley, James. 1989. "Individuation In and Of Syntactic Structures." In Mark Baltin and Anthony Kroch, eds., *Alternative Conceptions of Phrase Structure*, 117–138. Chicago: University of Chicago Press.

McCloskey, James. 1991. "Clause Structure, Ellipsis, and Proper Government in Irish." *Lingua*, 85, 259–302.

Mel'čuk, Igor, and Nicolaj Pertsov. 1987. *Surface Syntax of English*. Amsterdam: John Benjamins.

Merialdo, Bernard. 1994. "Tagging English Text with a Probabilistic Model." *Computational Linguistics*, 20, 155–171.

Merin, Arthur. 1983. "Where It's At (Is What English Intonation is All About)." In *Papers from the 19th Regional Meeting of the Chicago Linguistic Society*. Chicago: University of Chicago, Chicago Linguistic Society.

Miller, Dale. 1991. "A Logic Programming Language with λ-Abstraction, Function Variables, and Simple Unification." *Journal of Theoretical Computer Science*, 1, 497–536.

Miller, Dale. 1995. "λProlog: An Introduction to the Language and Its Logic." http://www.cse.psu.edu/~dale/lProlog/docs.html.

Miller, George. 1967. "Project Grammarama." In G. Miller, ed., *The Psychology of Communication*, 124–181. Harmondsworth: Penguin Books.

Miller, George, and Noam Chomsky. 1963. "Finitary Models of Language Users." In R. Duncan Luce, Robert Bush, and Eugene Galanter, eds., *Handbook of Mathematical Psychology, Vol 2*. New York: Wiley.

Miller, George, and Christiane Fellbaum. 1991. "Semantic Networks of English." *Cognition*, 41, 197–229.

Milward, David. 1991. *Axiomatic Grammar, Non-Constituent Coordination, and Incremental Interpretation*. Ph.D. thesis, University of Cambridge.

Milward, David. 1994. "Dynamic Dependency Grammar." *Linguistics and Philosophy*, 17, 561–605.

Milward, David. 1995. "Incremental Interpretation of Categorial Grammar." In *Proceedings of the Seventh Conference of the European Chapter of the Association for Computational Linguistics. Dublin*, 119–126. San Francisco, CA: Morgan Kaufmann.

Miyagawa, Shigeru. 1997. "Against Optional Scrambling." *Linguistic Inquiry*, 28, 1–25.

Moltmann, Friederike. 1992. *Coordination and Comparatives*. Ph.D. thesis, MIT.

Montague, Richard. 1970. "Universal Grammar." *Theoria*, 36, 373–398. Reprinted in Montague 1974, 222-246.

Montague, Richard. 1973. "The Proper Treatment of Quantification in Ordinary English." In Jaakko Hintikka, J. M. E. Moravcsik, and Patrick Suppes, eds., *Approaches to Natural Language: Proceedings of the 1970 Stanford Workshop on Grammar and Semantics*, 221–242. Dordrecht: Reidel. Reprinted in Montague 1974, 247-279.

Montague, Richard. 1974. *Formal Philosophy: Papers of Richard Montague*. New Haven, CT: Yale University Press. Richmond H. Thomason, ed.

Moortgat, Michael. 1987. "Lambek Categorial Grammar and the Autonomy Thesis." INL Working Paper 87-03, Leiden: Universiteit Leiden.

Moortgat, Michael. 1988a. *Categorial Investigations*. Ph.D. thesis, Universiteit van Amsterdam. Published by Foris, Dordrecht, 1989.

Moortgat, Michael. 1988b. "Mixed Composition and Discontinuous Dependencies." In Richard T. Oehrle, Emmon Bach, and Deirdre Wheeler, eds., *Categorial Grammars and Natural Language Structures*, 319–348. Dordrecht: Reidel.

Moortgat, Michael. 1997. "Categorial Type Logics." In Johan van Benthem and Alice ter Meulen, eds., *Handbook of Logic and Language*, 93–177. Amsterdam: North Holland.

Morel, Marie-Annick. 1995. "Valeur énonciative des variations de hauteur mélodique en français." *French Language Studies*, 5, 189–202.

Morgan, Jerry. 1973. "Sentence Fragments and the Notion 'Sentence'." In B. Kuchru, ed., *Issues in Linguistics: Papers in Honor of Henry and Rene Kahane*. Bloomington: Indiana University Press.

Morrill, Glyn. 1988. *Extraction and Coordination in Phrase Structure Grammar and Categorial Grammar*. Ph.D. thesis, University of Edinburgh.

Morrill, Glyn. 1994. *Type-Logical Grammar*. Dordrecht: Kluwer.

Morrill, Glyn, and Bob Carpenter. 1990. "Compositionality, Implicational Logics, and Theories of Grammar." *Linguistics and Philosophy*, 13, 383–392.

Morrill, Glynn, and Teresa Solias. 1993. "Tuples, Discontinuity, and Gapping." In *Proceedings of 6th Conference of the European Chapter of the Association for Computational Linguistics, Utrecht*, 287–297. San Francisco, CA: Morgan Kaufmann.

Napoli, Donna Jo, and Marina Nespor. 1979. "The Syntax of Word-Initial Consonant Gemination in Italian." *Language*, 55, 812–841.

Neijt, Anneke. 1979. *Gapping*. Dordrecht: Foris.

Nespor, Marina, and Irene Vogel. 1986. *Prosodic Phonology*. Dordrecht: Foris.

Netter, Klaus. 1988. "Non-Local Dependencies and Infinitival Constructions in German." In Uwe Reyle and Christian Rohrer, eds., *Natural Language Parsing and Linguistic Theory*, 356–410. Dordrecht: Reidel.

Nijholt, Anton. 1980. *Context-free Grammars: Covers, Normal Forms, and Parsing*. Berlin: Springer-Verlag.

Nishida, Chiyo. 1996. "Second Position Clitics in Old Spanish and Categorial Grammar." In Aaron Halpern and Arnold Zwicky, eds., *Approaching Second: Second-Position Clitics and Related Phenomena*, 33–373. Stanford, CA: CSLI Publications.

Niv, Michael. 1993. *A Computational Model of Syntactic Processing: Ambiguity Resolution from Interpretation*. Ph.D. thesis, University of Pennsylvania. IRCS Report 93-27.

Niv, Michael. 1994. "A Psycholinguistically Motivated Parser for CCG." In *Proceedings of the 32nd Annual Meeting of the Association for Computational Linguistics. Las Cruces, NM*, 125–132. San Francisco, CA: Morgan Kaufmann.

van Noord, Gertjan, and Gosse Bouma. 1997. "Dutch Verb-Clustering without Verb-Clusters." In Patrick Blackburn and Maarten de Rijke, eds., *Specifying Syntactic Structures*, Studies in Logic, Language and Information, 213–243. Stanford, CA: CSLI Publications/folli.

O'Connor, Joseph, and Gordon Arnold. 1961. *Intonation of Colloquial English*. London: Longman.

Oehrle, Richard. 1994. "Term-Labelled Categorial Type Systems." *Linguistics and Philosophy*, 17, 633–678.

Oehrle, Richard T. 1974. "Remarks on 'the Painting of Rembrandt.'." In *Papers from the 10th Regional Meeting of the Chicago Linguistic Society*. Chicago: University of Chicago, Chicago Linguistic Society.

Oehrle, Richard T. 1987. "Boolean Properties in the Analysis of Gapping." In Geoffrey Huck and Almerindo Ojeda, eds., *Syntax and Semantics, Vol. 20: Discontinuous Constituency*, 201–240. Orlando, FL: Academic Press.

Oehrle, Richard T. 1988. "Multidimensional Compositional Functions as a Basis for Grammatical Analysis." In Richard T. Oehrle, Emmon Bach, and Deirdre Wheeler, eds., *Categorial Grammars and Natural Language Structures*, 349–390. Dordrecht: Reidel.

Oehrle, Richard T., Emmon Bach, and Deirdre Wheeler, eds. 1988. *Categorial Grammars and Natural Language Structures*. Dordrecht: Reidel.

van Oirsouw, Robert. 1987. *The Syntax of Coordination*. London: Croom Helm.

van Oirsouw, Robert R. 1982. "Gazdar on Coordination and Constituents." *Linguistic Inquiry*, 13, 553–556.

Osborne, Miles, and Ted Briscoe. 1997. "Learning Stochastic Categorial Grammars." In *Workshop on Computational Natural Language Learning*, 80–87. New Brunswick, NJ: ACL/EACL. Held in conjunction with the 35th Annual Meeting of the Association for Computational Linguistics and the 8th Conference of the European Association for Computational Linguistics, Madrid.

Pareschi, Remo. 1986. "Combinatory Categorial Grammar, Logic Programming, and the Parsing of Natural Language." DAI Working Paper, University of Edinburgh.

Pareschi, Remo. 1989. *Type-driven Natural Language Analysis*. Ph.D. thesis, University of Edinburgh. Technical Report MS-CIS-89-45, University of Pennsylvania.

Pareschi, Remo, and Mark Steedman. 1987. "A Lazy Way to Chart Parse with Categorial Grammars." In *Proceedings of the 25th Annual Conference of the Association for Computational Linguistics, Stanford*, 81–88. San Francisco, CA: Morgan Kaufmann.

Paritong, Maika. 1992. "Constituent Coordination in HPSG." In Gunther Görz, ed., *KONVENS-92: 1. Konferenz "Verarbeitung Natürlicher Sprache"*, 228–237. Berlin: Springer-Verlag.

Park, Jong. 1995. "Quantifier Scope and Constituency." In *Proceedings of the 33rd Annual Meeting of the Association for Computational Linguistics, Cambridge MA*, 205–212. San Francisco, CA: Morgan Kaufmann.

Park, Jong. 1996. *A Lexical Theory of Quantification in Ambiguous Query Interpretation*. Ph.D. thesis, University of Pennsylvania. Technical Report MS-CIS–96-26/IRCS-96-27.

Partee, Barbara, Alice ter Meulen, and Robert Wall. 1990. *Mathematical Methods in Linguistics*. Dordrecht: Kluwer.

Partee, Barbara, and Mats Rooth. 1983. "Generalised Conjunction and Type Ambiguity." In Rainer Baüerle, Christoph Schwarze, and Arnim von Stechow, eds., *Meaning, Use, and Interpretation of Language*, 361–383. Berlin: de Gruyter.

Pentus, Mati. 1993. "Lambek Grammars are Context-free." In *Proceedings of the IEEE Symposium on Logic in Computer Science, Montreal*, 429–433.

Pereira, Fernando. 1990. "Categorial Semantics and Scoping." *Computational Linguistics*, 16, 1–10.

Pereira, Fernando, and Stuart Shieber. 1987. *Prolog and Natural Language Analysis*. Stanford, CA: CSLI Publications.

Pereira, Fernando, and David Warren. 1980. "Definite Clause Grammars for Language Analysis." *Artificial Intelligence*, 13, 231–278.

Perlmutter, David M. 1971. *Deep and Surface Structure Constraints in Syntax*. New York: Holt, Rinehart and Winston.

Pesetsky, David. 1982. *Paths and Categories*. Ph.D. thesis, MIT.

Pickering, Martin, and Guy Barry. 1993. "Dependency Categorial Grammar and Coordination." *Linguistics*, 31, 855–902.

Pierrehumbert, Janet. 1980. *The Phonology and Phonetics of English Intonation*. Ph.D. thesis, MIT. Distributed by Indiana University Linguistics Club, Bloomington.

Pierrehumbert, Janet. 1993. "Prosody, Intonation, and Speech Technology." In Madeleine Bates and Ralph Weischedel, eds., *Challenges in Natural Language Processing*, 257–280. Cambridge: Cambridge University Press.

Pierrehumbert, Janet, and Mary Beckman. 1988. *Japanese Tone Structure*. Cambridge, MA: MIT Press.

Pierrehumbert, Janet, and Julia Hirschberg. 1990. "The Meaning of Intonational Contours in the Interpretation of Discourse." In Philip Cohen, Jerry Morgan, and Martha Pollack, eds., *Intentions in Communication*, 271–312. Cambridge, MA: MIT Press.

Pinker, Steven. 1979. "Formal Models of Language Learning." *Cognition*, 7, 217–283.

Pinker, Steven. 1994. "How Could a Child Use Verb Syntax to Learn Verb Semantics?" *Lingua*, 92, 377–410.

Poesio, Massimo. 1995. "Disambiguation as (Defeasible) Reasoning about Underspecified Representations." In *Papers from the Tenth Amsterdam Colloquium*. Universiteit van Amsterdam, ILLC.

Pollard, Carl. 1984. *Generalized Phrase Structure Grammars, Head Grammars, and Natural Languages*. Ph.D. thesis, Stanford University.

Pollard, Carl, and Ivan Sag. 1987. *Information-Based Syntax and Semantics, Vol. 1*. Stanford, CA: CSLI Publications.

Pollard, Carl, and Ivan Sag. 1992. "Anaphors in English and the Scope of Binding Theory." *Linguistic Inquiry*, 23, 261–303.

Pollard, Carl, and Ivan Sag. 1994. *Head Driven Phrase Structure Grammar*. Stanford, CA: CSLI Publications.

Potts, Timothy. 1994. *Structures and Categories for the Representation of Meaning*. Cambridge: Cambridge University Press.

Prasada, Sandeep, and Steven Pinker. 1993. "Generalization of Regular and Irregular Morphological Patterns." *Language and Cognitive Processes*, 8, 1–56.

Pratt, Vaughan. 1975. "LINGOL: A Progress Report." In *Proceedings of the 4th International Joint Conference on Artificial Intelligence, Montreal, Quebec*, 422–428. San Francisco, CA: Morgan Kaufmann.

Prevost, Scott. 1995. *A Semantics of Contrast and Information Structure for Specifying Intonation in Spoken Language Generation*. Ph.D. thesis, University of Pennsylvania.

Prevost, Scott, and Mark Steedman. 1994. "Specifying Intonation from Context for Speech Synthesis." *Speech Communication*, 15, 139–153.

Prince, Alan. 1983. "Relating to the Grid." *Linguistic Inquiry*, 14, 19–100.

Prince, Ellen. 1986. "On the Syntactic Marking of Presupposed Open Propositions." In *Papers from the 22nd Regional Meeting of the Chicago Linguistic Society, Parasession on Pragmatics and Grammatical Theory*, 208–222. Chicago: University of Chicago, Chicago Linguistic Society.

Pullum, Geoffrey K. 1987. "Nobody Goes Around at LSA Meetings Offering Odds." *Natural Language and Linguistic Theory*, 5, 303–309.

Pullum, Geoffrey K., and Gerald Gazdar. 1982. "Natural Languages and Context-Free Languages." *Linguistics and Philosophy*, 4, 471–504.

Pullum, Geoffrey K., and Arnold Zwicky. 1988. "The Syntax-Phonology Interface." In Frederick Newmeyer, ed., *Linguistics: The Cambridge Survey, Vol. 1*, 255–280. Cambridge: Cambridge University Press.

Pulman, Steve. 1986. "Grammars, Parsers, and Memory Limitations." *Language and Cognitive Processes*, 1, 197–226.

Rambow, Owen. 1994a. *Formal and Computational Aspects of Natural Language Syntax*. Ph.D. thesis, University of Pennsylvania.

Rambow, Owen. 1994b. "Multiset-Valued Linear Indexed Grammars." In *Proceedings of the 32nd Annual Meeting of the Association for Computational Linguistics, Las Cruces, NM*. San Francisco, CA: Morgan Kaufmann.

Ranta, Arne. 1994. *Type-Theoretical Grammar*. Oxford: Oxford University Press.

Reape, Michael. 1994. "Domain Union and Word Order Variation in German." In John Nerbonne, Klaus Netter, and Carl Pollard, eds., *German in Head-driven Phrase Structure Grammar*, 151–197. Stanford, CA: CSLI Publications.

Reape, Michael. 1996. "Getting Things in Order." In Harry Bunt and Arthur van Horck, eds., *Discontinuous Constituency*, 209–253. The Hague: Mouton de Gruyter.

Reinhart, Tanya. 1991. "Wh-in-situ." In *Proceedings of the 8th Amsterdam Colloquium*. Amsterdam: Universiteit van Amsterdam, ITLI.

Reinhart, Tanya. 1997. "Quantifier Scope: How Labor Is Divided between QR and Choice Functions." *Linguistics and Philosophy*, 20, 4, 335–397.

Resnik, Philip. 1992. "Left-Corner Parsing and Psychological Reality." In *Proceedings of COLING-92, Nantes*, 418–424. San Francisco, CA: Morgan Kaufmann.

Reyle, Uwe. 1992. "On Reasoning with Ambiguities." In *Proceedings of the 7th Conference of the European Chapter of the Association for Computational Linguistics, Dublin*, 1–8.

Rizzi, Luigi. 1982. *Issues in Italian Syntax*. Dordrecht: Foris.

Robinson, Jane J. 1970. "Dependency Structures and Transformational Rules." *Language*, 46, 259–285.

Rochemont, Michael. 1986. *Focus in Generative Grammar*. Amsterdam: John Benjamins.

Rochemont, Michael. 1998. "Phonological Focus and Structural Focus." In Peter Culicover and Louise McNally, eds., *Syntax and Semantics, Vol. 29: The Limits of Syntax*, 337–363. San Diego, CA: Academic Press.

Rochemont, Michael, and Peter Culicover. 1990. *English Focus Constructions and the Theory of Grammar*. Cambridge: Cambridge University Press.

Rodman, Robert. 1976. "Scope Phenomena, 'Movement Transformations,' and Relative Clauses." In Barbara Partee, ed., *Montague Grammar*, 165–177. New York: Academic Press.

de Roeck, Anne. 1984. *Testing Steedman's Categorial Grammar*. Master's thesis, University of Essex, Colchester.

Rögnvaldsson, Eiríkur. 1982. "We Need (Some Kind of a) Rule of Conjunction Reduction." *Linguistic Inquiry*, 13, 557–561.

Romero, Maribel. 1997. "Recoverability Conditions for Sluicing." In Francis Corblin and Danièle Godard, eds., *Empirical Issues in Formal Syntax and Semantics: Selected Papers from the Colloque de Syntaxe et Sémantique de Paris (CSSP95)*. Bern: Peter Lang.

Rooth, Mats. 1985. *Association with Focus*. Ph.D. thesis, University of Massachusetts, Amherst.

Rooth, Mats. 1992. "A Theory of Focus Interpretation." *Natural Language Semantics*, 1, 75–116.

Rosenbaum, Harvey. 1977. "Zapotec Gapping as Counterevidence to Some Universal Proposals." *Linguistic Inquiry*, 8, 379–395.

Rosenbloom, Paul. 1950. *The Elements of Mathematical Logic*. New York: Dover Publications.

Ross, John Robert. 1967. *Constraints on Variables in Syntax*. Ph.D. thesis, MIT. Published as *Infinite Syntax!*, Ablex, Norton, NJ, 1986.

Ross, John Robert. 1970. "Gapping and the Order of Constituents." In Manfred Bierwisch and Karl Heidolph, eds., *Progress in Linguistics*, 249–259. The Hague: Mouton.

Rosser, J. Barkley. 1935. "A Mathematical Logic without Variables." *Annals of Mathematics*, 36, 127–150.

Rosser, J. Barkley. 1942. "New Sets of Postulates for Combinatory Logics." *Journal of Symbolic Logic*, 7, 18–27.

Rumelhart, David, Geoffrey Hinton, and James McClelland. 1986. "A General Framework for Parallel Distributed Processing." In David Rumelhart, James McClelland, and the PDP Research Group, eds., *Parallel Distributed Processing*, Vol. 1, *Foundations*, 45–76. Cambridge, MA: MIT Press.

Russell, Bertrand. 1905. "On Denoting." *Mind*, 14, 479–493.

Sag, Ivan. 1976. *Deletion and Logical Form*. Ph.D. thesis, MIT.

Sag, Ivan, Gerald Gazdar, Thomas Wasow, and Steven Weisler. 1985. "Coordination and How to Distinguish Categories." *Natural Language and Linguistic Theory*, 3, 117–172.

Sag, Ivan, and Jorge Hankamer. 1984. "Towards a Theory of Anaphoric Processing." *Linguistics and Philosophy*, 7, 325–345.

Sag, Ivan, Ron Kaplan, Lauri Karttunen, Martin Kay, Carl Pollard, Stuart Shieber, and Annie Zaenen. 1986. "Unification and Grammatical Theory." In *Proceedings of the 5th West Coast Conference on Formal Linguistics*, 238–254. Stanford University, Stanford Linguistics Association.

Sag, Ivan, and Mark Liberman. 1975. "The Intonational Disambiguation of Indirect Speech Acts." In *Papers from the 11th Regional Meeting of the Chicago Linguistic Society*, 487–497. Chicago: University of Chicago, Chicago Linguistic Society.

van der Sandt, Rob. 1988. *Context and Presupposition*. London: Croom Helm.

Sapir, Edward. 1921. *Language*. New York: Harcourt Brace and Co.

Sauerland, Uli. 1998. *The Meaning of Chains*. Ph.D. thesis, MIT, Cambridge, MA.

Schachter, Paul. 1977. "Constraints on Coordination." *Language*, 53, 86–103.

Schachter, Paul. 1985. "Parts-of-Speech Systems." In Timothy Shopen, ed., *Language Typology and Syntactic Description, Vol. 1: Clause Structure*, 1–61. Cambridge: Cambridge University Press.

Schachter, Paul, and Susan Mordechai. 1983. "A Phrase-Structure Account of 'Nonconstituent' Conjunction." In *Proceedings of the 2nd West Coast Conference on Formal Linguistics*, 260–274. Stanford, CA: Stanford Linguistics Association.

Schlenker, Philippe. to appear. "Skolem Functions and the Scope of Indefinites." In *Proceedings of the 1998 Conference of the North-East Linguistics Society*.

Schmerling, Susan. 1976. *Aspects of English Stress*. Austin, TX: University of Texas Press.

Schmerling, Susan. 1981. "The Proper Treatment of the Relationship between Syntax and Phonology." Paper presented at the 55th annual meeting of the LSA, San Antonio TX.

Schönfinkel, Moses. 1924. "On the Building Blocks of Mathematical Logic." In Jean van Heijenoort, ed., *From Frege to Gödel*, 355–366. Cambridge, MA: Harvard University Press.

Sedivy, Julie, and Michael Spivey-Knowlton. 1993. "The Effect of NP Definiteness on Parsing Attachment Ambiguity." In *NELS 23*. Amherst: University of Massachusetts, GLSA.

Segond, Frédérique. 1990. *Grammaire catégorielle du Français: Etude théorique et implémentation, le système GraCE*. Ph.D. thesis, Ecole des Hautes Etudes en Sciences Sociales.

Selkirk, Elisabeth. 1972. *The Phrase Phonology of English and French*. Ph.D. thesis, MIT. Published by Garland, New York, 1980.

Selkirk, Elisabeth. 1984. *Phonology and Syntax*. Cambridge, MA: MIT Press.

Selkirk, Elisabeth. 1986. "Derived Domains in Sentence Phonology." *Phonology*, 3, 371–405.

Selkirk, Elisabeth. 1990. "On the Nature of Prosodic Constituency." *Papers in Laboratory Phonology*, 1, 179–200.

Selkirk, Elisabeth. 1995. "Sentence Prosody: Intonation, Stress, and Phrasing." In John Goldsmith, ed., *The Handbook of Phonological Theory*, 550–569. Oxford: Blackwell.

Selkirk, Elisabeth, and Tong Shen. 1990. "Prosodic Domains in Shanghai Chinese." In Sharon Inkelas and Draga Zec, eds., *The Phonology-Syntax Connection*, 313–338. Stanford, CA: CSLI Publications.

Seuren, Pieter A. M. 1972. "Predicate Raising and Dative in French and Sundry Languages." Ms., Magdelen College Oxford.

Seuren, Pieter A. M. 1985. *Discourse Semantics*. Oxford: Blackwell.

Shaumyan, Sebastian. 1977. *Applicational Grammar as a Semantic Theory of Natural Language*. Edinburgh: Edinburgh University Press.

Shieber, Stuart. 1985. "Evidence against the Context-Freeness of Natural Language." *Linguistics and Philosophy*, 8, 333–343.

Shieber, Stuart. 1986. *An Introduction to Unification-Based Approaches to Grammar*. Stanford, CA: CSLI Publications.

Shieber, Stuart, and Mark Johnson. 1993. "Variations on Incremental Interpretation." *Journal of Psycholinguistic Research*, 22, 287–318.

Shieber, Stuart, Fernando Pereira, and Mary Dalrymple. 1996. "Interactions of Scope and Ellipsis." *Linguistics and Philosophy*, 19, 527–552.

Silverman, Kim. 1988. "Utterance-Internal Prosodic Boundaries." In *Proceedings of the 2nd Australian International Conference on Speech Science and Technology, Sydney*, 86–91. Canberra: Australian Speech Science and Technology Association.

Silverman, Kim, Mary Beckman, John Pitrelli, Marie Ostendorf, Colin Wightman, Patti Price, Janet Pierrehumbert, and Julia Hirschberg. 1992. "ToBI: A Standard for Labeling English Prosody." In *Proceedings of the International Conference on Spoken Language Processing, Banff, Alberta*, 867–870. Edmonton: University of Alberta.

Siskind, Jeffrey. 1995. "Grounding Language in Perception." *Artificial Intelligence Review*, 8, 371–391.

Siskind, Jeffrey. 1996. "A Computational Study of Cross-Situational Techniques for Learning Word-to-Meaning Mappings." *Cognition*, 61, 39–91.

Smullyan, Raymond. 1985. *To Mock a Mockingbird*. New York: Knopf.

Smullyan, Raymond. 1994. *Diagonalization and Self-Reference*. Oxford: Clarendon Press.

Solias, Teresa. 1992. *Gramáticas Categoriales, Coordinación Generalizada, y Elisión*. Ph.D. thesis, Universitad Autónoma de Madrid.

Solias Aris, Teresa. 1996. *Gramática Categorial: Modelos y aplicaciones*. No. 23 in Lingüística. Madrid: Editorial Sintesis.

Spivey-Knowlton, Michael, John Trueswell, and Michael Tanenhaus. 1993. "Context Effects in Syntactic Ambiguity Resolution: Parsing Reduced Relative Clauses." *Canadian Journal of Psychology*, 47, 276–309.

B. Srinivas. 1997. *Complexity of Lexical Descriptions and Its Relevance to Partial Parsing*. Ph.D. thesis, University of Pennsylvania. IRCS Report 97-10.

B. Srinivas, and Aravind Joshi. 1994. "Disambiguation of Super Parts of Speech (or Supertags): Almost Parsing." In *Proceedings of the International Conference on Computational Linguistics (COLING 94), Kyoto University, Japan, August*. San Francisco, CA: Morgan Kaufmann.

Stabler, Ed. 1991. "Avoid the Pedestrian's Paradox." In Robert Berwick, Steve Abney, and Carol Tenny, eds., *Principle-Based Parsing*, 199–238. Dordrecht: Kluwer.

Stabler, Ed. 1994. "The Finite Connectivity of Linguistic Structure." In Charles Clifton, Lyn Frazier, and Keith Rayner, eds., *Perspectives on Sentence Processing*, 245–266. Hillsdale, NJ: Erlbaum.

Stabler, Ed. 1997. "Computing Quantifier Scope." In Anna Szabolcsi, ed., *Ways of Scope-Taking*, 155–182. Dordrecht: Kluwer.

Stalnaker, Robert. 1974. "Pragmatic Presuppositions." In Milton Munitz and Peter Unger, eds., *Semantics and Philosophy*, 197–214. New York: New York University Press.

von Stechow, Arnim. 1979. "Deutsche Wortstellung und Montague Grammatik." In Jürgen Meisel and Martin Pam, eds., *Linear Order and Generative Theory*, 317–490. Amsterdam: John Benjamins.

von Stechow, Arnim. 1991. "Focusing and Backgrounding Operators." In Werner Abraham, ed., *Discourse Particles: Descriptive and Theoretical Investigations on the Logical, Syntactic and Pragmatic Properties of Discourse Particles in German*, 37–84. Amsterdam: John Benjamins.

Steedman, Mark. 1983. "Categorial Syntax for Subject and Tensed Verb in English and some Related Languages." Ms., University of Warwick.

Steedman, Mark. 1985. "Dependency and Coordination in the Grammar of Dutch and English." *Language*, 61, 523–568.

Steedman, Mark. 1987. "Combinatory Grammars and Parasitic Gaps." *Natural Language and Linguistic Theory*, 5, 403–439.

Steedman, Mark. 1988. "Combinators and Grammars." In Richard T. Oehrle, Emmon Bach, and Deirdre Wheeler, eds., *Categorial Grammars and Natural Language Structures*, 417–442. Dordrecht: Reidel.

Steedman, Mark. 1989. "Grammar, Interpretation and Processing from the Lexicon." In William Marslen-Wilson, ed., *Lexical Representation and Process*, 463–504. Cambridge MA: MIT Press.

Steedman, Mark. 1990. "Gapping as Constituent Coordination." *Linguistics and Philosophy*, 13, 207–263.

Steedman, Mark. 1991a. "Structure and Intonation." *Language*, 67, 262–296.

Steedman, Mark. 1991b. "Surface Structure, Intonation, and 'Focus'." In Ewan Klein and Frank Veltman, eds., *Natural Language and Speech: Proceedings of the Symposium, ESPRIT Conference, Brussels, Nov. 1991*, 21–38. Dordrecht: Kluwer.

Steedman, Mark. 1991c. "Type-Raising and Directionality in Combinatory Grammar." In *Proceedings of the 29th Annual Meeting of the Association for Computational Linguistics, Berkeley CA, July*, 71–78. San Francisco, CA: Morgan Kaufmann.

Steedman, Mark. 1993. "Categorial Grammar." *Lingua*, 90, 221–258.

Steedman, Mark. 1994. "Acquisition of Verb Categories." *Lingua*, 92, 471–480.

Steedman, Mark. 1996a. "The Role of Prosody and Semantics in the Acquisition of Syntax." In James Morgan and Katherine Demuth, eds., *Signal to Syntax*, 331–342. Hillsdale, NJ: Erlbaum.

Steedman, Mark. 1996b. *Surface Structure and Interpretation*. Cambridge, MA: MIT Press.

Steedman, Mark. 1997. "Temporality." In Johan van Benthem and Alice ter Meulen, eds., *Handbook of Logic and Language*, 895–938. Amsterdam: North Holland.

Steedman, Mark. 1999. "Quantifier Scope Alternation in CCG." In *Proceedings of the 37th Annual Meeting of the Association for Computational Linguistics, College Park, MD*, 301–308. San Francisco, CA: Morgan Kaufmann.

Steedman, Mark. 2000. "Information Structure and the Syntax-Phonology Interface." *Linguistic Inquiry*, 34, 649–689.

Steedman, Mark, and Gerry Altmann. 1989. "Ambiguity in Context: A Reply." *Language and Cognitive Processes*, 4, 105–122.

Steele, Susan. 1990. *Agreement and Anti-Agreement*. Dordrecht: Reidel.

Stenlund, Sören. 1972. *Combinators, λ-Terms, and Proof Theory*. Dordrecht: Reidel.

Stillings, Justine. 1975. "The Formulation of Gapping in English as Evidence for Variable Types in Syntactic Transformations." *Linguistic Analysis*, 1, 247–273.

Stirling, Leon, and Ehud Shapiro. 1986. *The Art of Prolog*. Cambridge, MA: MIT Press.

Stone, Matthew. 1998. *Modality in Dialogue: Planning Pragmatics and Computation*. Ph.D. thesis, University of Pennsylvania.

Stone, Matthew. 1999. "Representing Scope in Intuitionistic Deduction." *Theoretical Computer Science*, 129–188.

Stone, Matthew, and Christine Doran. 1997. "Sentence Planning as Description Using Tree Adjoining Grammar." In *Proceedings of the 35th Annual Meeting of the Association for Computational Linguistics and the 8th Conference of the European Association for Computational Linguistics, Madrid*, 198–205. San Francisco, CA: Morgan Kaufmann.

Stone, Matthew, and Bonnie Webber. 1998. "Textual Economy through Close Coupling of Syntax and Semantics." In *Proceedings of INLG-88*, 178–187.

Straub, Kathleen. 1997. *The Production of Prosodic Cues and Their Role in the Comprehension of Syntactically Ambiguous Sentences*. Ph.D. thesis, University of Rochester.

Stromswold, Karin. 1995. "The Acquisition of Subject and Object *Wh*-Questions." *Language Acquisition*, 4, 5–48.

Stump, Gregory. 1978. "Interpretive Gapping in Montague Grammar." In *Papers from the 14th Regional Meeting of the Chicago Linguistic Society*, 472–481. Chicago: University of Chicago, Chicago Linguistic Society.

Swinney, David. 1979. "Lexical Access During Sentence Comprehension: (Re)Considerations of Context Effects." *Journal of Verbal Learning and Behaviour*, 18, 645–659.

Szabolcsi, Anna. 1983. "ECP in Categorial Grammar." Ms., Max Planck Institute, Nijmegen.

Szabolcsi, Anna. 1989. "Bound Variables in Syntax: Are There Any?" In Renate Bartsch, Johan van Benthem, and Peter van Emde Boas, eds., *Semantics and Contextual Expression*, 295–318. Dordrecht: Foris.

Szabolcsi, Anna. 1992. "On Combinatory Grammar and Projection from the Lexicon." In Ivan Sag and Anna Szabolcsi, eds., *Lexical Matters*, 241–268. Stanford, CA: CSLI Publications.

Szabolcsi, Anna, ed. 1997. *Ways of Scope-Taking*. Dordrecht: Kluwer.

Taglicht, Josef. 1998. "Constraints on Intonational Phrasing in English." *Journal of Linguistics*, 34, 181–211.

Tanenhaus, Michael. 1978. *Sentence Context and Sentence Perception*. Ph.D. thesis, Columbia University.

Tanenhaus, Michael, James Leiman, and Mark Seidenberg. 1979. "Evidence for Multiple Stages in the Processing of Ambiguous Words in Syntactic Context." *Journal of Verbal Learning and Behaviour*, 18, 427–441.

Taraldsen, Tarald. 1979. "The Theoretical Interpretation of a Class of Marked Extractions." In Adriana Belletti, Luciana Brandi, and Luigi Rizzi, eds., *Theory of Markedness in Generative Grammar*, 475–516. Pisa: Scuole Normale Superiore.

Terken, Jacques. 1984. "The Distribution of Accents in Instructions as a Function of Discourse Structure." *Language and Speech*, 27, 269–289.

Terken, Jacques, and Julia Hirschberg. 1994. "Deaccentuation of Words Representing 'Given' Information: Effects of Persistence of Grammatical Role and Surface Position." *Language and Speech*, 37, 125–145.

Thompson, Henry. 1990. "Best-first Enumeration of Paths through a Lattice: An Active Chart Parsing Solution." *Computer Speech and Language*, 4, 263–274.

Thorne, James, Paul Bratley, and Hamish Dewar. 1968. "The Syntactic Analysis of English by Machine." In Donald Michie, ed., *Machine Intelligence, Vol. 3*. New York: American Elsevier.

Tomita, Masaru. 1987. "An Efficient Augmented Context-Free Parsing Algorithm." *Computational Linguistics*, 13, 31–46.

Trechsel, Frank. to appear. "A CCG Account of Tzotzil Pied Piping." *Natural Language and Linguistic Theory*.

Truckenbrodt, Hubert. 1995. *Phonological Phrases: Their Relation to Syntax, Focus, and Prominence*. Ph.D. thesis, MIT.

Truckenbrodt, Hubert. 1999. "On the Relation between Syntactic Phrases and Phonological Phrases." *Linguistic Inquiry*, 30, 219–255.

Trueswell, John, Michael Tanenhaus, and Susan Garnsey. 1994. "Semantic Influences on Parsing: Use of Thematic Role Information in Syntactic Ambiguity Resolution." *Journal of Memory and Language*, 33, 285–318.

Trueswell, John, Michael Tanenhaus, and Christopher Kello. 1993. "Verb-Specific Constraints in Sentence Processing: Separating Effects of Lexical Preference from Garden-Paths." *Journal of Experimental Psychology: Learning, Memory and Cognition*, 19, 528–553.

Turner, David A. 1979a. "Another Algorithm for Bracket Abstraction." *Journal of Symbolic Logic*, 44, 267–270.

Turner, David A. 1979b. "A New Implementation Technique for Applicative Languages." *Software—Practice and Experience*, 9, 31–49.

Uszkoreit, Hans. 1986. "Categorial Unification Grammars." In *Proceedings of COLING-86, Bonn*, 187–194. San Francisco, CA: Morgan Kaufmann.

Vallduví, Enric. 1990. *The Information Component*. Ph.D. thesis, University of Pennsylvania.

Vallduví, Enric, and Elisabet Engdahl. 1996. "The Linguistic Realization of Information Packaging." *Linguistics*, 34, 459–519.

VanLehn, Kurt. 1978. *Determining the Scope of English Quantifiers*. Master's thesis, MIT. AI-TR-483, Artificial Intelligence Laboratory, MIT.

Veltman, Frank. 1984. "Data Semantics." In Theo M. V. Janssen Jeroen Groenendijk and Martin Stokhof, eds., *Truth, Interpretation, and Information*, 43–63. Dordrecht: Foris.

Vennemann, Theo. 1973. "Explanation in syntax." In John Kimball, ed., *Syntax and Semantics, Vol. 2*, 1–50. New York: Seminar Press.

Versmissen, Koen. 1996. *Grammatical Composition: Modes, Models, Modalities*. Ph.D. thesis, Universiteit Utrecht.

Vijay-Shanker, K., and David Weir. 1990. "Polynomial Time Parsing of Combinatory Categorial Grammars." In *Proceedings of the 28th Annual Meeting of the Association for Computational Linguistics, Pittsburgh*, 1–8. San Francisco, CA: Morgan Kaufmann.

Vijay-Shanker, K., and David Weir. 1993. "Parsing Some Constrained Grammar Formalisms." *Computational Linguistics*, 19, 591–636.

Vijay-Shanker, K., and David Weir. 1994. "The Equivalence of Four Extensions of Context-Free Grammar." *Mathematical Systems Theory*, 27, 511–546.

Vogel, Irene. 1994. "Phonological Interfaces in Italian." In Michael Mazzola, ed., *Issues and Theory in Romance Linguistics*, 109–126. Washington, DC: Georgetown University Press.

Vogel, Irene, and István Kenesei. 1990. "Syntax and Semantics in Phonology." In Sharon Inkelas and Draga Zec, eds., *The Phonology-Syntax Connection*, 339–364. Stanford, CA: CSLI Publications.

Voutilainen, Atro. 1995. "A Syntax-Based Part-of-Speech Analyser." In *Proceedings of the 7th Conference of the European Chapter of the Association for Computational Linguistics, Dublin*. San Francisco, CA: Morgan Kaufmann.

Wall, Robert E. 1972. *Introduction to Mathematical Linguistics*. Englewood Cliffs, NJ: Prentice-Hall.

Wanner, Eric. 1980. "The ATN and the Sausage Machine: Which One Is Baloney?" *Cognition*, 8, 209–225.

Ward, Gregory, and Julia Hirschberg. 1985. "Implicating Uncertainty: the Pragmatics of Fall-Rise Intonation." *Language*, 61, 747–776.

Watkinson, Stephen, and Suresh Manandhar. 1999. "Unsupervised Lexical Learning with Categorial Grammars." In *Proceedings of the Workshop on Unsupervised Learning in Natural Language Processing, ACL-99, College Park MA*, 59–66. Association for Computational Linguistics.

Webber, Bonnie Lynn. 1978. *A Formal Approach to Discourse Anaphora*. Ph.D. thesis, Harvard University. [Published by Garland, New York, 1979].

Webber, Bonnie Lynn. 1983. "So What Can We Talk about Now?" In Michael Brady and Robert Berwick, eds., *Computational Models of Discourse*, 331–371. Cambridge, MA: MIT Press.

Weir, David. 1988. *Characterizing Mildly Context-sensitive Grammar Formalisms*. Ph.D. thesis, University of Pennsylvania. Technical Report CIS-88-74.

Weir, David, and Aravind Joshi. 1988. "Combinatory Categorial Grammars: Generative Power and Relation to Linear CF Rewriting Systems." In *Proceedings of the 26th Annual Meeting of the Association for Computational Linguistics, Buffalo, NY*, 278–285. San Francisco, CA: Morgan Kaufmann.

Wheeler, Deirdre. 1981. *Aspects of a Categorial Theory of Phonology*. Ph.D. thesis, University of Massachusetts, Amherst.

Wheeler, Deirdre. 1988. "Consequences of Some Categorially Motivated Phonological Assumptions." In Richard T. Oehrle, Emmon Bach, and Deirdre Wheeler, eds., *Categorial Grammars and Natural Language Structures*, 467–488. Dordrecht: Reidel.

Williams, Edwin. 1977. "On Deep and Surface Anaphora." *Linguistic Inquiry*, 8, 692–696.

Williams, Edwin. 1978. "Across-the-Board Rule Application." *Linguistic Inquiry*, 9, 31–43.

Williams, Edwin. 1986. "A Reassignment of the Functions of LF." *Linguistic Inquiry*, 17, 265–299.

Williams, Edwin. 1994. *Thematic Structure in Syntax*. Cambridge, MA: MIT Press.

Willis, Alistair, and Suresh Manandhar. 1999. "Two Accounts of Scope Availability and Semantic Underspecification." In *Proceedings of the 37th Annual Meeting of the Association for Computational Linguistics, College Park MD, June*, 293–300. San Francisco, CA: Morgan Kaufmann.

Wilson, Deirdre, and Dan Sperber. 1979. "Ordered Entailments." In *Syntax and Semantics, Vol. 11: Presupposition*, 299–323. New York: Academic Press.

Winograd, Terry. 1972. *Understanding Natural Language*. Edinburgh: Edinburgh University Press.

Winter, Yoad. 1995. "Syncategorematic Conjunction and Structured Meanings." In *Proceedings of the 5th Annual Conference on Semantics and Linguistic Theory (SALT-5), Austin, TX*. Ithaca, NY: Cornell University.

Winter, Yoad. 1997. "Choice Functions and the Scopal Semantics of Indefinites." *Linguistics and Philosophy*, 20, 399–467.

Winter, Yoad. to appear. "On Some Scopal Asymmetries of Coordination." In *Proceedings of the KNAW Conference on Interface Strategies*. Amsterdam: KNAW.

Wirén, Mats. 1992. *Studies in Incremental Natural Language Analysis*. Ph.D. thesis, Linsköping University. Linsköping University Studies in Science and Technology, 292.

Wittenburg, Kent B. 1986. *Natural Language Parsing with Combinatory Categorial Grammar in a Graph-Unification Based Formalism*. Ph.D. thesis, University of Texas, Austin.

Wood, M. 1988. *A Categorial Syntax for Coordinate Constructions*. Ph.D. thesis, University College, London. Published as Technical Report UMCS-89-2-1, Department of Computer Science, University of Manchester, 1989.

Wood, Mary McGee. 1993. *Categorial Grammar*. London: Routledge.

Woods, William. 1970. "Transition Network Grammars for Natural Language Analysis." *Communications of the Association for Computing Machinery*, 18, 264–274.

Woods, William. 1973. "An Experimental Parsing System for Transition Network Grammars." In Randall Rustin, ed., *Natural Language Processing*, 111–154. New York: Algorithmics Press.

Woods, William. 1975. "What's in a Link: Foundations for Semantic Networks." In Daniel Bobrow and Alan Collins, eds., *Representation and Understanding: Readings in Cognitive Science*, 35–82. New York: Academic Press.

Wunderlich, Dieter. 1988. "Some Problems of Coordination in German." In Uwe Reyle and Christian Rohrer, eds., *Natural Language Parsing and Linguistic Theories*, 289–316. Dordrecht: Reidel.

Yngve, Victor. 1960. "A Model and an Hypothesis for Language Structure." *Proceedings of the American Philosophical Society*, 104, 444–466.

Zaenen, Annie. 1979. "Infinitival Complements in Dutch." In *Papers from the 15th Annual Meeting of the Chicago Linguistic Society*, 378–389. Chicago: University of Chicago, Chicago Linguistic Society.

Zaenen, Annie, and Ronald Kaplan. 1995. "Formal Devices for Linguistic Generalizations: West Germanic Word Order in LFG." In Mary Dalrymple, Ronald Kaplan, John Maxwell, and Annie Zaenen, eds., *Formal Issues in Lexical-Functional Grammar*, 215–239. Stanford, CA: CSLI Publications.

Zec, Draga, and Sharon Inkelas. 1990. "Prosodically Constrained Syntax." In Sharon Inkelas and Draga Zec, eds., *The Phonology-Syntax Connection*, 365–378. Stanford, CA: CSLI Publications.

van der Zee, Nico. 1982. "Samentrekking: Een Kategoriaal Perspektief." *Glot*, 5, 189–217.

Zeevat, Henk. 1988. "Combining Categorial Grammar and Unification." In Uwe Reyle and Christian Rohrer, eds., *Natural Language Parsing and Linguistic Theories*, 202–229. Dordrecht: Reidel.

Zeevat, Henk, Ewan Klein, and Jo Calder. 1987. "An Introduction to Unification Categorial Grammar." In Nicholas Haddock Ewan Klein and Glyn Morrill, eds., *Edinburgh Working Papers in Cognitive Science, Vol. 1: Categorial Grammar, Unification Grammar, and Parsing*, 195–222. Edinburgh: University of Edinburgh, Centre for Cognitive Science.

Zubizarreta, Maria Luisa. 1987. *Levels of Representation*. Dordrecht: Foris.

Zubizarreta, Maria Luisa. 1998. *Prosody, Focus, and Word Order*. Cambridge, MA: MIT Press.

Zwarts, Frans. 1986. *Categoriale Grammatica en Algebraïsche Semantik*. Ph.D. thesis, Rijksuniversiteit Gröningen.

Zwicky, Arnold, and Geoffrey K. Pullum. 1987. *The Syntax-Phonology Interface*. Washington, DC: Linguistics Society of America. Course notes for LI219, LSA Summer Institute, Stanford 1987.

Index

Aarts, 28
Abbott, 266, 277
Accommodation, 77, 100, 247
  of presupposition, 180, 238
  and interactive parsing, 239, 247, 248
  of theme, 190
  of theme alternative set, 107
Ades, 28, 42, 64, 263, 273
Adjacency
Principle of, 54, 148, 187, 218
AGR, 35
Aho, 244
Ajdukiewicz, 28
Alshawi, 83
Alternative Semantics, 99, 247
Alternative set, see Theme/Rheme alternative
  set
Altmann, 238–240
$a^n b^n$, 209
$a^n b^n c^n$, 209
$a^n b^n c^n d^n e^n$, 211
Anomalous subject coordination
  as zeugma/syllepsis, 58
Aoun, 185, 186
Applicative systems, 27, 201–203
arb', 75
Arbitrary object, 74
  and donkey sentence, 75, 270
  and real-world inference, 76
  as Skolem term, 75
  as translation of indefinite, 75, 76
Argument cluster, see Coordination
Arnold, 98
Asher, 83
Asurini, 85
ATN, see Augmented Transition Network
Attachment ambiguity resolution
  context-based, 239, 251
  lexical preference-based, 237
  lookahead-based, 237
  probability-based, 251, 253
  rule-ordering based, 237
  strategy-based, 237
  structure-based, 237

Minimal Attachment, 239
Augmented Transition Network (ATN), 3, 229,
  270
  and bounded/unbounded constructions, 3
  HOLD register, 3
Autosegmental phonology
  nature of tiers in, 90
  and tones, 110

B, see Combinatory rules, composition
Bach, 1, 4, 28, 35, 39, 59, 67, 69, 85, 137, 139,
  263, 264, 275
Background
  defined, 107
Baker, 84, 259
Baldridge, 33, 177, 257, 276, 278, 280
Barendregt, 201, 206
Bar-Hillel, 28, 265
Barry, 47, 264
Barss, 27
Bartels, 98
Barwise, 71, 74, 85
Bayer, 35, 164
Beaver, 248
Bech, 137, 274
Beckman, 95, 97, 113, 271
Beghelli, 80
Bengali, 125
van Benthem, 28, 55, 56, 264
van den Berg, 81
van Berkum, 239, 240
Berwick, 227
den Besten, 276
Bever, 237, 238
Billot, 232, 251
Binding theory
  adjunct-argument asymmetries, 69–70
  in CCG, 64–69, 257
  and Universal Grammar, 26, 27, 37
Bing, 92, 273
Bird, 272
Bittner, 84
Blake, 166, 171
Bluebird, see Combinatory rules, composition

(B)
B^n, *see* Combinatory rules, generalized composition
Bolinger, 270, 273
Bouma, 28, 56, 273
Boundary tone, 96
  category of, 112
  as specifier, 113
Bozsahin, 257, 280
Brame, 15
Bratley, 263
Bresnan, 6, 15, 47, 68, 135, 136, 142, 175, 226, 237, 267
Brill, 254
Briscoe, 258, 281
Brody, 32, 68
Brown C., 240
Brown, C., 137, 239, 275
Brown, G., 107
Brown, R., 11
Bruce, 95
Bruner, 203
Burge, 201
Büring, 99, 108
Buszkowski, 264
Byron, 277

Calder, 28, 47, 214–216
Carden, 73
Carpenter, 28, 213
Carroll, 240
Case
  as type-raising, 45
Categorial Grammar (CG), 28, 31–35
  directionality in, as feature, 213–224
  "Flexible", 28
CCG, *see* Combinatory Categorial Grammar
CCL, *see* Combinatory categorial language
C-command, 127
  defined over Logical Form, 4, 68, 128, 255
  not defined over derivations, 256
Cessens, 254
Chao, 196, 197
Charniak, 241
Chierchia, 76, 202, 273
Choice functions
  vs. Skolem term, 76
Chomsky, xi, 1, 2, 6, 12, 13, 18, 19, 24, 35, 39, 59, 61, 66, 89, 126, 128, 135, 263, 264, 270, 272, 274, 279
Chung, 61
Church, 206
Clark, R., 26
Clark, S., 68, 270
Clifton, 240
Cocke, 230, 232
Collins, 241, 251, 253, 260
Combinator, 27
Combinatory Categorial Grammar (CCG)
  basics of, 31–52
  motivation for, 11–29
  scope and limits of, 53–87

theoretical architecture, 87, 126, 256
  variables in, 211
  weak equivalence to LIG/TAG, 212
Combinatory categorial language (CCL)
  weak equivalence to LIL/TAL, 279
Combinatory Logic, 27, 201–203
  abstraction algorithms, 203–207
  BCSK, 204
  BTS, 206
  SK, 204
  and variable-free calculi, 201
Combinatory rules
  composition (**B**), 40–43, 55–56
  compositional nature of semantics of, 37
  coordination (Φ), 39–40
  "decomposition", 187–198
  dangers of, 197–198
  directionality in, as feature, 213–224
  expressive power, 207–224
  generalized composition (**B**^{n}), 42
  bound on, 210
  generalized coordination (Φ^n)
  bound on, 212
  and language acquisition, 258
  nature of, 201–224
  parametric neutrality of, 187
  substitution (**S**), 49–52, 55–56
  type-raising (**T**), 43–49, 56–58
  as case, 45
  directionality and, 213–224
  order-preserving, 44
  restrictions on, 44, 185, 191, 213–224
  variable in, 44
Competence
  vs. performance, 5–7, 225–227, 255, 261
Competence hypothesis, 6, 255
  strict, 6, 130, 228, 229, 241–245, 255, 261, 281
  and acquisition of language, 62, 228, 259
  and evolution of language, 261
  and parser, 252
  strong, 6, 226, 228
Composition, *see* Combinatory rules, composition (**B**)
Compositional semantics, 1
  assumption of, 7
  and incremental interpretation, 242
  of information-structural constituents, 7
  of tones, 101
Computation, 7, 8, 21, 22, 69, 109, 130, 227, 228, 232, 233, 236, 246, 261, 271
  and alternative sets, 99
  and combinatory representations, 202
  and context, 238
  theory of, 5
  and variable binding, 201
Computational linguistics
  view of Surface Structure, 3, 229
Comrie, 166
Conservativity
  of Generalized Quantifiers, 58
Consistency

Principle of, 54
and decomposition, 191
and ellipsis, 196
explained, 220
Constituent Condition on Rules, 12–14, 225, 255, 257
and processor, 228
Context, 100
Control theory
in CCG, 64–69
Cooper, K., 274, 275
Cooper, R., 71, 73, 75, 76, 83, 85, 267
Cooper, W., 89, 273
Coordination, 7, 8, 16–19
across-the-board condition on, 40
argument cluster, 45–47, 135, 147, 160, 171–198
as gapping in SOV, 172–176
as gapping in SVO, 179–195
as gapping in VSO, 176–179
combinatory rule of (Φ), 39–40
gapping, see Gapping
interaction with intonation, 92, 122–123
"nonconstituent", 7, 46
parallelism condition on, 40, 73, 78, 79
universal word order dependency, 26, 171–198
Cormack, A., 83, 278
Cormack, S., 98
Crain, 238–240
Cremers, 198
Cresswell, 28, 264, 273, 278
Croft, 17, 89, 118, 125, 273
Crossover, 257
Cross-serial dependencies, 25
in Dutch, 7, 133–167
Crouch, 83
Culicover, 98
Curry, 27, 40, 201, 204, 266, 278

Dai, 279
Dale, 272, 282
Dalrymple, 76, 84, 189, 205, 277
Damaso Vieira, 85
Database, 100
Deacon, 203
Deep Structure
in Standard Theory TG, 263
Definite Clause Grammar (DCG), 217
Dekker's paradox, 269
Dependencies
cross-serial, 133–167
and Universal Grammar, 166–167
unbounded
CCG and GPSG/HPSG compared, 33
CCG and TAG compared, 33
Dependency Grammar, 253, 264, 267
probabilistic parsing of, 253
Desclés, 28
Dewar, 263
Diamond, 202
Difference-list

encoding of string position in DCG, 280
Dime-and-parking-meter sentence
and real-world inference, 76
Discontinuity
of gap, 186, 192–193, 195
of theme/rheme, 106, 192
van der Does, 81
$ convention, 42
α/$, 42
α$, 42
α\$, 42
Donkey sentence, 75, 270
Doran, 17, 253, 282
Dörre, 232
Downing, 92
Downstep
of pitch accents, 115
Dowty, 28, 39, 45, 67, 69, 176, 198, 263, 267, 268, 278
Dryer, 167
D-Structure
in GB, 14
Dutch, 8, 133–167, 264
apparent exception to Ross's generalization, 173, 177, 194
argument cluster coordination, 174–176
combinatory rules for, summarized, 167–169
cross-serial dependencies in, 7, 25, 133–167
gapping in, 8
lexicon, summarized, 167–169
main clause, 159–164
gapping as argument cluster coordination, 177–179
as VSX, 159–164
main-clause order, 8
relative clause, 147–149, 155–159
structure of the NP sequence, 146–159
structure of the verb group, 138–146
subject extraction, 158–159
subordinate clause
gapping as argument cluster coordination, 174–176
gapping dependent on word order, 194
verb raising, 8, 133–167

Earley, 232, 252
ECP, see Empty Category Principle
Eisner, 234, 281
Elgin, Lord
Byron on syphilization of, 277
van Emden, 217
Emonds, 15, 17
Empty Category Principle (ECP), 59, 61
End-based phonology, 125
Engdahl, 49, 61, 98
Erteschik-Shir, 272
Espinal, 17
η, see Phonological Categories, pitch accents
η', see Phonological Categories, boundaries
Evans, 75
Event-Related Potential (ERP), 239
Evers, 134, 136, 137, 142, 147, 274, 275

Expressive power
  of natural grammar
    upper bound on, 213
  of theories, 8, 22–27
Extraction, 8
  adjunct-argument asymmetries, 69–70
  left-right asymmetries, 59–64
  of subjects, 59–62
    in Dutch, 158–159
    in English, late acquisition of, 62, 259

Faltz, 28, 58, 73, 84, 167
F-command, see C-command
Fernando, 83
Ferreira, 240
Feys, 40, 204, 266, 278
Fine, 74
Fisher, 12, 258
Flapping, 125
Flynn, 28, 167
Focus
  algorithms for assigning pitch accents, 108,
    272
  vs. background, 106–109
  conflicting definitions of, 272
  and contrast, 108
  defined, 107
Focusing particles
  and intonation, 90, 128
Fodor, J. A., 237, 240
Fodor, J. D., 74, 134, 237, 243, 282
Ford, 237
Fortune, 206
Foster, 257
Fox, 73
Fragments (apparently nonconstituent con-
  structions), 14–22, 26, 28, 29, 109
Francis, 252
Frazier, 237, 239, 240, 243
French, 125, 257
  and ECP, 60
Friedman, 279
Functional projections (GB), 80
Furbee, 194

Gabbay, xiii, 271
Gaifman, 265
Gapping
  as argument cluster coordination, 171–198
  "backward," in SOV, 172–176
  Byronic, 277
  dependent on word order, 171–198
  "forward"
    in SVO, 179–195
    in VSO, 176–179
  right conjunct as argument cluster, 183–187
    in SVO, 8
  SVO gap as theme, 189, 190
  "virtual" left conjunct revealing, 187–193
  multiple/discontinuous, 186, 192–193, 195
  virtual left conjunct in SVO, 187–198
Garden path effect, 237

and construal, 240
and context, 238, 239, 254
and semantics, 238, 240–242, 244
and so-called empty context, 239
and thematic processor, 240
Garnsey, 240, 282
Garrett, 237
Gazdar, xii, 18, 23–25, 35, 39, 48, 61, 207, 212,
  265, 267, 269
GB, see Transformational Grammar
Geach, 28, 73–75
Geach sentence, 73, 74, 77–78
Gee, 89, 273
Generalized   Phrase   Structure   Grammar
  (GPSG), xii, 23, 25, 33, 48, 61, 267
Gerdeman, 214, 280
German, 133–140, 264, 282
Gibson, 241, 279
Gleitman, 12, 258
Gold, 11
Goldsmith, 90, 95, 110
Goldwater, 241
Goodall, 40
Government
  antecedent (GB), 61
GPSG, see Generalized Phrase Structure
  Grammar
Grammar
  as applicative system, 27–29
  covering, 227, 228
  evaluation function, 33
  lexicalized, 32
  mildly context-sensitive, xii, 23, 26, 134, 232
  strong/weak equivalence, 207
  strong/weak generative power, xii, 207
  Universal, xi
Grammars
  leakage in, xii
  strong/weak equivalence, 279
  strong/weak generative power, 279
Gray, 227
Greenberg, 166
Greenfield, 203
Grimshaw, 38
Groenendijk, 75, 271
Grosjean, 89, 273
Grosz, 272
Guentchéva, 28
Gussenhoven, 98, 125, 272, 273

de Haan, 136
Haddock, 272, 282
Haegeman, 147, 165, 275
Hagoort, 239, 240
Hajičová, 128, 264, 272
Hale, 32, 68, 84
Hall, 12, 258
Halle, 90
Halliday, 20, 91, 98, 107, 270
Hankamer, 180, 197
Hanlon, 11
Harel, xiii, 271

Harrison, 227, 230, 246, 281
Hausser, 28, 281
Hawkins, 166
Hayes, 125
Head
defined, 32
Head Categorial Uniqueness
Principle of, 33, 59, 61, 66, 258, 259
and Language Acquisition, 203, 258
Head Grammar (HG), xii
Head-Driven Phrase Structure Grammar
(HPSG), 32, 33, 38, 68, 69, 273
Heavy NP shift, 63, 259
Heim, 76, 271
Helke, 270
Hemforth, 282
Henderson, 57, 58
Hendriks, H., 73, 74, 234, 270, 271, 281
Hendriks, P., 28, 198
Hepple, 8, 28, 56, 61, 67, 69, 198, 234, 263,
269, 273, 276, 281
Heycock, 278
Hindley, 189, 201, 206
Hinrichs, 214, 273, 280
Hippopotamus sentences, 133–144
Hirschberg, 95, 98, 99, 101, 113, 271, 272
Hirst, D., 125
Hirst, G., 238
Hobbs, 73–75, 84
Hodkinson, xiii
Hoeksema, 28, 90, 128, 271, 276
Hoffman, 210, 257, 276, 280
Höhle, 278
Hornstein, 185, 186
Houtman, 28, 57, 58, 198, 269, 273
HPSG, see Head-Driven Phrase Structure
Grammar
Huck, 28, 279
Hudson, 264
Huet, 189, 272
Hukari, 269
Huybregts, 8, 25, 136, 207

Icelandic, 275
IG, see Indexed Grammar
Incremental semantic interpretation
and parsing, 6, 8, 130, 225–254, 260
in SOV, 154, 242, 282
Indexed Grammar (IG), 208
Information Structure, 7, 20, 86, 90, 91, 95, 98
and morphology, 257
focus vs. background, 99, 106–109
and Intonation Structure, 110
as Intonation Structure, 21
multiple/discontinuous theme/rheme, 106
necessity for two orthogonal dimensions, 98
in non-Indo-European languages, 257
and quantifier scope, 79
and spurious ambiguity, 109
as Surface Structure, 7, 109–124, 259
theme vs. rheme, 99–105
and word order, 257

Inheritance
Principle of, 54, 55, 59, 186
explained, 216, 220
Inkelas, 126
Inoue, 282
Intonation Structure, 7, 20–22
and Information Structure, 92
in CCG, 89–130
and parsing, 129–130, 260
and Surface Structure, 7
as Surface Structure, 259
Irish, 26, 177, 264
gapping as argument cluster coordination,
176–177
Italian
and ECP, 60
raddoppiamento syntattico, 125
subject extraction in
and acquisition, 282

Jackendoff, 20, 21, 26, 35, 89, 91, 97, 98, 101,
102, 119, 121, 123, 126, 128, 179, 272
Jacobs, 100, 109, 128, 272
Jacobson, 28, 67, 69, 73, 75, 263, 278
Jaeggli, 60
Janda, 271
Janeaway, 155, 273
Japanese, 26, 177, 251, 257, 264, 280, 282
gapping as argument cluster coordination,
172–174
Jelinek, E., 84, 85
Jelinek, F., 252
Johnson, M., 35, 147, 241, 245, 273, 274, 282
Johnson, S., 244
Johnson-Laird, 100
Joshi, xii, 23, 38, 47, 56, 83, 209, 212, 253, 275
Jowsey, 28

Kaisse, 89, 125
Kanazawa, 258
Kang, 257, 280
Kaplan, 6, 136, 142, 147, 175, 226, 237
Karlgren, 28
Karttunen, 28, 47, 83, 86, 99, 103, 231, 254
Kay, 76, 231, 280
Kayne, 59, 60, 83, 164, 268
Keenan, 15, 26–28, 58, 68, 73, 167, 177
Keller, 73, 75
Kello, 240
Kempe, 254
Kempson, 83
Kenesei, 126, 274
Keyser, 32, 68
Kimball, 237, 243
Kirkeby-Garstad, 272
É. Kiss, 272
Klein, 25, 28, 35, 47, 48, 214–216, 267
Köhler, 203
Komagata, 83, 232, 251, 257, 276, 280, 282
Konieczny, 282
König, 234, 281
Koopman, 274

Korean, 257, 280
Koster, 59, 158, 165
Koutsoudas, 171
Kowalski, 217
Kratzer, 85, 99, 128
Krifka, 100, 109, 128, 272
Kroch, 147, 278
Kučera, 252
Kuno, 64, 180, 181, 189, 227
Kupin, 147

Ladd, 97, 98, 101–103, 109, 112, 118, 119, 125
de Laguna, 202
Lakhota, 85
λ-calculus, 27, 29, 201–203
λ-term
   as information-structural element, 91
Lambek, 28, 263, 265
   calculus, 50, 269
Lambrecht, 272
Landman, 271
Lang, 189, 232, 251
Langendoen, 180
Language acquisition
   and extraction asymmetries, 62, 259
   rules in, 227
   subject extraction in, 62, 259
Language evolution
   and competence hypothesis, 228, 261, 281
   rules in, 228
Lasnik, 4, 27, 61, 68, 128, 135, 147
Leakage in grammars
   proper interpretation of, xii
Lee, 241
Lehmann, 166, 171
Leiman, 240
Leivant, 206
Levelt, 17
Levin, H., 28
Levin, N., 180
Levine, 269
Levy, 23, 47
Lewis, D., 71, 77, 100, 238
Lewis, R., 279
Lexical-Functional Grammar (LFG), 14, 32, 33, 68, 69, 147, 273
Lexical Head Government
   Principle of, 32
Lexicon
   and bounded constructions, 15
   as locus of grammatical information in CG, 31
   Principle of Head Categorial Uniqueness, and evaluation, 33
   semantic nature of restrictions on, 32
   size of, 32
   and grammar evaluation, 33
   theory of, lacking here, 257
LFG, see Lexical-Functional Grammar
Liaison, 125, 257
Liberman, 90, 92, 95, 98, 102, 125
LIG, see Linear Indexed Grammar

Lightfoot, 185, 186
LIL, see Linear indexed language
van der Linden, 28, 282
Linear Indexed Grammar (LIG), 208
   and cross-serial dependencies, 208
   relation to CCG, 209–211
Linear indexed language (LIL)
   weak equivalence to CCL/TAL, 279
Link, 81
Liu, 80
Logical Form
   in CCG, 85–87, 255–261
   in GB (LF), 263
Lötscher, 275
LR parser, 244
Lyons, 270, 279

Maling, 48, 61, 158, 171, 179, 275
Mallinson, 166, 171
Manandhar, 83, 258
Manzini, 270
Marciszewski, 264
de Marcken, 252
Marcus, 231, 236, 237
Marr, 5
Marslen-Wilson, 137, 240, 275
May, 73
McCawley, 17
McCloskey, 276
Mel'čuk, 264
Mental model, 100
Merialdo, 252
Merin, 98
ter Meulen, 71
Miller, D., 217
Miller, G., 12, 254, 274, 279
Milward, 264, 268, 282
Minimal Attachment, 239
Miyagawa, 276
Mockingbird, 206
Modularity, 5, 13, 227, 237, 240, 260, 263
Mohawk, 85
Moltmann, 40
Monostratality
   assumption of, 5, 6, 71, 87
Monotonicity
   in quantifiers, 80
   assumption of, 1, 5–7, 13, 23, 71, 78, 86, 87, 229
Montague, 1, 28, 71, 73, 257
Moortgat, 28, 56, 62, 69, 198, 213, 263, 264, 271, 273
Mordechai, , 46
Morel, 98
Morphology
   bracketing paradoxes in, 271
   and case, 45, 267
   and Information Structure, 257
   rules in language acquisition, 280
Morrill, 28, 56, 69, 198, 234, 263, 271, 281
Movement, 12–14

Nakazawa, 273
Napoli, 125
Navajo, 85
Neijt, 180
Nelson, 203
Nespor, 90, 125
Netter, 147, 273
Neural networks
  and rule-learning, 280
Nijholt, 227
Nishida, 257
Niv, 251
van Noord, 273
Null tone
  effect on categories, 111

O'Connor, 98
O'Donnell, 206
Oehrle, 28, 73, 198, 263, 264, 267, 271
van Oirsouw, 174, 177, 194
Old Spanish, 257
Open proposition
  as information-structural element, 271
Osborne, 258
Ostendorf, 271

Paccia-Cooper, 89, 273
Panglossism
  evolutionary, 261
Parallelism Condition, see Coordination
Parametric licensing
  of type-raised categories, 44, 46, 57, 185, 191
Parametric neutrality of combinatory rules, 187
Parentheticals, 7, 17, 19–22
  interaction with intonation, 92
Pareschi, 187, 188, 231
Paritong, 273
Park, 74, 77, 84, 257
Parsimony
  Principle of, 238
Parsing
  algorithms, 229
  backtracking, 231
  bottom-up algorithms, 230
    CKY, 230
    shift-reduce, 230
  of CCG
    average-case polynomial complexity, 232
    effect of unbounded composition and coor-
      dination rules, 212
    worst-case polynomial complexity, 212
  chart, 231–234
    entries ranked by plausibility, 249, 250
  and spurious ambiguity, 232, 246, 281
  and incremental semantic interpretation, 6, 8,
    130, 225–254, 260
  and intonation, 6, 129–130, 260
  normal-form, 281
  probabilistic, 252, 253
  as compiled incremental semantics, 254, 260
  structure-sharing
    of interpretations, 232, 245, 251, 252

Partee, 4, 18, 68, 71, 73, 85, 128, 266
Partial Combination (composition), 273
Part-of-speech (POS) tagging, 252
  and bottom-up parsing, 252
  and CCG parsing, 252
  and TAG parsing, 252
Pelletier, 76
Pentus, 54
Pereira, 75, 76, 84, 188, 189, 205, 217, 218,
    277, 280
Performance, 8, 225–254, 259–261
Perlmutter, 269
Perry, 74
Pertsov, 264
Pesetsky, 59
Peters, 99, 103, 136, 142, 175
Φ, see Combinatory rules, coordination
Φ^n, see Combinatory rules, generalized coordi-
    nation
Phonetic Form
  in CCG, 86, 127, 257
  in GB, 19, 264
Phonological categories
  boundaries, 112
  and projection of pitch accent, 113
  pitch accents
    downstepped, 115
    η (null tone marker), 272
    η (null tone marker), 111–113
    ρ (rheme-marker), 111–113
    θ (rheme-marker), 111–113
  prosodic phrase
    ϕ (prosodic phrase marker), 112, 113
Pickering, 47, 264
Pierrehumbert, 90, 92, 95–99, 101, 113, 115,
    129, 271, 272
Pinker, 12, 258, 280
Pitch accent, 96
  effect on categories, 110
Pitrelli, 271
Poesio, 83
Polgárdi, 272
Pollard, xii, 32, 38, 47, 68
Potts, 28
Prague School
  on quantifier scope, 128
Prasada, 280
Pratt, 232
Predicate-argument structure, 35–39, 255
Presupposition
  pragmatic, 238
Prevost, 105, 107, 108, 110, 271–273
Price, 271
Prime notation, 217
Prince, A., 125
Prince, E., 180, 270
Projection Principle (GB), 32, 55, 282
Prosodic Constituent Condition (1991)
  eliminated, 110
Pseudogapping
  contrasted with gapping, 179, 277
Pseudosubject category, 58

Pullum, 24, 25, 48, 91, 125, 267
Pulman, 243, 245, 281

Quantification
  scope ambiguities in, 7, 70–85, 257
  directional asymmetries, 82–83, 164–166
  and intonation, 128
Quantifier
  and donkey sentence, 75, 270
  generalized, 71, 74
  conservativity of, 58
  lowering, 73
  monotonicity in, 80
  movement of, 73
  raising, 73
  so-called, as arbitrary object, 78, 80
  synonymy with referring expression, 74, 77
  some, 77
  indefinite, 77
  some, 77
Quantifying In, 73

Raddoppiamento syntattico, 125
Raising
  in CCG, 64–69
Rakowitz, 12, 258
Rambow, 56, 147, 212, 275
Ranta, 28
Reape, 28, 273
Reinhart, 76, 257
Relativization, 181
  interaction with intonation, 123–124
Resnik, 254
Revealing, *see* Combinatory rules, "decomposition"
Reyle, 83
Reynolds, xiii
Rheme, 91
  alternative set, 99, 100, 108
  presupposed by theme, 100
  restricted by rheme, 100
  defined, 99–105
  focus, 107
  multiple/discontinuous, 106, 127
  updater (ρ'), 112, 114
  updates model, 112, 272
Rheme updater
  ρ', 114
ρ, *see* Phonological Categories, pitch accents
ρ', *see* Rheme, updater
Rhythm Rule, 125, 257
van Riemsdijk, 147, 165, 275
Rizzi, 60
Robinson, 267
Rochemont, 98, 128, 272
Rodman, 267
de Roeck, 155, 273
Rögnvaldsson, 267
Romero, 278
Rooth, 73, 90, 99, 103, 128, 189, 247, 266, 272, 277
Rosenbaum, 177, 194, 264

Rosenbloom, 201
Ross, 4, 8, 39, 49, 177, 179
  generalization of, 17, 26, 171, 198, 264
  apparent exceptions, 173, 177, 194
  revised, 195
Rosser, 43, 204
Rule-learning
  and neural networks, 280
  and probabilistic mechanisms, 280
Rules
  combinatory, *see* Combinatory rules
  concatenative, 27
  nonconcatenative, 27, 265
Rule-to-rule relation
  of syntax and semantics, 1, 11–13, 25, 241, 242, 255
Russell, 248

S, *see* Combinatory rules, substitution
Sag, 25, 32, 35, 38, 47, 48, 68, 74, 91, 98, 102, 180, 197, 265, 267
Saito, 4, 68, 128
Saltzman, 203
van der Sandt, 248
Santorini, 147
Sapir, xii
Sauerland, 76
Schabes, 38
Schachter, 39, 46, 197
Scheepers, 282
Schlenker, 76, 257
Schmerling, 98, 119, 271
Schönfinkel, 27, 32, 201
Schwartz, 232
Sedivy, 240
Segond, 28, 257
Seidenberg, 240
Seldin, 189, 201, 206
Selkirk, 20, 21, 90, 92, 94, 95, 98, 116, 124, 125, 257, 272
Semantics
  λ-calculus notation, 29
Sense Unit Condition, 20, 92, 94, 116, 124
Seuren, 136, 144, 152, 274, 275
Sgall, 128, 264, 272
Shamir, 265
Shapiro, 217, 218, 280
Shared forest, *see* Parsing, structure-sharing
Shaumyan, 28, 69
Shen, 125
Shieber, 8, 25, 73, 75, 76, 84, 136, 188, 189, 205, 207, 217, 218, 245, 272, 274, 275, 277, 280, 282
Shillcock, 58
Sidner, 272
Silverman, 96, 115, 271
Siskind, 258
Skolem term, 75
  vs. choice function, 76
  as referent of donkey pronoun, 76
  as translation of indefinite, 76
  and unbound variable constraint, 76

Sluicing, 196
Smullyan, 40, 43, 201, 207, 278
Solias, 198
SOV, 26, 264
  coordination in, 172–176
Spanish, 257
Sperber, 180, 270
Spivey-Knowlton, 240
Spurious ambiguity, 109, 129, 187, 232
  as genuine ambiguity, 232
B. Srinivas, 253
S-Structure
  in GB, 14, 263
Stabler, 80, 244, 245, 279
Stalnaker, 238
Starling, see Combinatory rules, substitution
  (**S**)
von Stechow, 28, 90, 128, 264, 273
Steele, 28
Stenlund, 201
Sterling, 217, 218, 280
Stillings, 180
Stokhof, 75, 271
Stone, 282
Stowell, 80
Straits Salish, 85
Straub, 118
Stripping, 195
Stromswold, 62, 259
Strube, 282
Structured-meanings, 99, 273
Stump, 198
Subjacency, 257
Subject
  anomalous coordination with "pseudosubject", 58
Subject extraction, 59–62
  dependent on word order, 158–159
  in English, late acquisition of, 62, 259
Substitution, see Combinatory rules, substitution (**S**)
Surface Structure, 263
  as Information Structure, 92, 93, 124–130, 255, 259
  as Information/Intonation Structure, 95
  and interpretation, 85–87
  and Intonation Structure, 7, 89, 90, 92
  as Intonation Structure, 22, 124–130, 259
  not a representational level, 3, 85–87, 127, 256
  as PF, 127
  and Phonetic Form, 22
  and S-Structure, 22, 127
SVO, 26, 27
  coordination in, 179–195
Swinney, 240
Syphilization, 277
Szabolcsi, 28, 50, 54, 59, 67, 69, 74, 224, 263, 274, 278, 282

T, see Combinatory rules, type-raising
T (variable in type-raising), 44

Table-driven parsing, see Parsing, chart
TAG, see Tree-Adjoining Grammar
Tagalog, 33, 177, 257, 280
Taglicht, 17
Takahashi, 23
TAL, see Tree-adjoining language
Tanenhaus, 240, 242, 282
Taraldsen, 49, 270
T-diagram, see Y-diagram
Terken, 98
TG, see Transformational Grammar
That-Trace Filter, 61
Theme, 91
  alternative set, 108
  defined, 99–105
  focus, 107
  as gap in SVO, 189, 190
  "isolated", 103
  multiple/discontinuous, 106, 127
  unmarked, 105, 116–119
  vs. background of rheme, 119
    disambiguated by context, 118, 119, 129
    and η', 118
  information-structurally ambiguous, 117, 129
  updater (θ'), 112, 114
  updates model, 112, 272
Theme updater
  θ', 114
θ, see Phonological Categories, pitch accents
θ', see Theme, updater
θ'', 190
Thompson, 251
Thorne, 263
Thráinsson, 267
Thrush, see Combinatory rules, type-raising (**T**)
Tojolabal
  apparent exception to Ross's generalization, 194
  gapping dependent on word order, 195
Tomita, 232
Tones
  boundary, 96
  L,LL%, 95–99, 110–119
  LH%, 95–99, 110–119
  Pierrehumbert notation, 95–99, 110–119
  pitch accent, 96
  H*, 95–99, 110–119
  L+H*, 95–99, 110–119
  ToBI notation, 97, 115, 271
Transderivational constraints, 73, 79
Transformational Grammar (TG)
  Government-Binding (GB) Theory, 14, 32, 33, 66, 68, 69, 127, 263
  Projection Principle, 282
  theoretical architecture, 19, 22
  Minimalism, 68
  Standard Theory, 14, 263
    theoretical architecture, 14
  variables in rules, 268
Trechsel, 257, 280

Tree-Adjoining Grammar (TAG), xii, 23, 32, 33, 147, 212, 252
Lexicalized (LTAG), 38
weak equivalence to CCG, 212
Tree-adjoining language (TAL)
weak equivalence to CCL/LIL, 279
Truckenbrodt, 125
Trueswell, 240, 242, 282
Turkish, 257, 280
Turner, 202, 204, 206
Tyler, 240
Type Transparency
Categorial, Inverse Principle of, 36
Categorial, Principle of, 36, 44, 57, 185, 191, 258
related to X̄ theory, 35, 57
Combinatory, Principle of, 37, 70
explained, 217
Type-Logical Grammar, 213
Type-raising, see Combinatory rules, type-raising (**T**)
Tzotzil, 257, 280

Unbounded dependency
and Principle of Lexical Head Government, 32
Unbound Variable Constraint, 76
Underspecification, 35
Unification
and combinatory rules, 35, 47, 111
higher-order, 188
as abstraction, 189
Update
and boundary tones, 112
Uszkoreit, 28, 47

Vallduví, 98, 272
VanLehn, 74, 76, 257
Variable-free calculi, 201
Veltman, 271
Venkatasan, 279
Vennemann, 166, 167
Verb raising
in Dutch, 8, 133–167
in Hungarian, 274
Verbs
Dutch main clause as VSO, 159–164
English auxiliary as VSO, 183
give-type, 26, 63
heb-type, 174
introduce-type, 27
might-type, 68, 168, 183, 191
persuade-type, 67, 139
prober-type, 144–146, 150, 165
think-type, 59–62, 259
try-type, 66
VSO, 26
zie-type, 138–144, 150
Vergnaud, 90
Versmissen, 198, 273
Vijay-Shanker, xii, 83, 207, 209, 212, 229, 232, 251, 268, 279

Virtual conjunct, see Gapping
Vogel, 90, 125, 126
VOS, 27, 68
Voutilainen, 254
VP ellipsis, 196
contrasted with gapping, 179
VSO, 26, 27, 68, 264
binding in, 37
coordination in, 176–179

Wall, 25, 71, 134
Wang, 279
Wanner, 237, 238
Ward, 98
Warlpiri, 85
Warren, 217
Wasow, 35, 265
Watkinson, 258
Webber, 74–76, 257, 282
Weinberg, 185, 186, 227
Weir, xii, 56, 207, 209, 212, 229, 232, 251, 268, 279
Weisler, 35, 265
Wheeler, 264, 271
Wh-question
related to theme, 91
Wightman, 271
Williams, 38, 40, 48, 83, 180, 197
Willis, 83
Wilson, 180, 270
Winograd, 238, 246
Winter, 73, 76, 257, 270
Wirén, 282
Wittenburg, 28, 47, 85
Wood, 28, 184, 198, 263, 264
Woods, 57, 74, 76, 229, 270
Word order
free, 257
and Information Structure, 257
WordNet, 254
WRAP, see Rules, nonconcatenative
Wunderlich, 278

X̄ theory, 34, 35, 57, 167

Y-diagram, 14, 86, 126, 255
Yngve, 279

Zaenen, 48, 61, 134, 136–138, 142, 144, 147, 158, 175, 275
Zapotec, 8, 264
apparent exception to Ross's generalization, 177, 194
gapping dependent on word order, 195
Zec, 126
van der Zee, 56, 198
Zeevat, 28, 47, 214–216, 223
Zubizarreta, 38, 98, 118, 272
Zwarts, 28, 56, 90, 128
Zwicky, 91, 125